GLOBAL MEDIA GO TO WAR

Role of News and Entertainment Media During the 2003 Iraq War

About the Cover

The cover's background photo, like the Arab region itself, is enigmatic. It is either a sunset over the desert, signaling the end of day and a journey into darkness, or it is a sunrise presaging a new day with new opportunities. Like the merits of the 2003 Iraq War, the reader is left to decide.

Like no other single photograph taken during the 2003 Iraq War, the picture of Marine Corporal Edward Chin draping the American flag over the statue head of Saddam Hussein on April 9, 2003, reverberated throughout the Arab world and cyberspace as a symbol of American arrogance, disrespect, Arab humiliation, and the abusive use of military might. Most Americans, on the other hand, swelled with patriotic pride and thought the picture illustrated a fitting end to the Ba'athists' and Saddam Hussein's viselike grip on tyrannical power.

One picture, two diametrically opposed audience effects. Such is the reality (if not the surreality) of reporting war in the Middle East and the *raison d'etre* of this collection of essays and studies.

RDB

GLOBAL MEDIA GO TO WAR

Role of News and Entertainment Media During the 2003 Iraq War

Edited by Ralph D. Berenger

Preface by Cees J. Hamelink
Foreword by John C. Merrill
Afterword by Kaarle Nordenstreng

MB Marquette Books Spokane, WA

A portion of the proceeds from the sale of this book goes to support the nonprofit Center for Global Media Studies at Washington State University.

Printed in the United States of America

Library of Congress Cataloging-in-Publication Data

Global media go to war : role of news and entertainment media during the 2003 Iraq war / edited by Ralph D. Berenger ; preface by Cees J. Hamelink ; foreword by John C. Merrill ; afterword by Kaarle Nordenstreng.
p. cm.
Includes bibliographical references and index.
ISBN 0-922993-10-6 (pbk. : alk. paper)
1. Iraq War, 2003--Mass media and the war. I. Berenger, Ralph D., 1945-
DS79.76.G58 2004
956.7044'3--dc22

2004008323

MARQUETTE BOOKS
3107 E. 62nd Avenue
Spokane, WA 99223
509-443-7057
books@marquettebooks.org
www.MarquetteBooks.org

To Carol and our children,
who have put up with my dreams for decades,
and to journalists everywhere
who bare their souls in every story

Other Books of Interest From Marquette Books

John C. Merrill, Ralph D. Berenger and Charles J. Merrill, *Media Musings: Interviews with Great Thinkers* (Forthcoming; ISBN 0-922993-15-7).

David Demers (ed.), *Terrorism, Globalization and Mass Communication: Papers Presented at the 2002 Center for Global Media Studies Conference* (2003; ISBN 0-922993-04-1).

Melvin L. DeFleur and Margaret H. DeFleur, *Learning to Hate Americans: How U.S. Media Shape Negative Attitudes Among Teenagers in Twelve Countries* (2003; ISBN 0-922993-05-X).

David Demers (ed.), *Global Media News Reader,* revised edition (2003; ISBN 0-922993-02-5).

Note: A portion of the proceeds from the sale of these books helps support the nonprofit Center for Global Media Studies at Washington State University.

CONTENTS

About the Authors

Abdullah Al-Kindi (Ph.D., University of Reading, U.K.) is an assistant professor of journalism and mass communication at Sultan Qaboos University in Oman. He has presented papers at major international conferences. In 2003 he published two books translated from English into Arabic: *New Media, New Politics*, and *Global Communication*. His research interests are in war reporting, press freedom, and media laws.

Ibrahim Al-Marashi (M.A., Georgetown) is an analyst at the Center for Non-Proliferation Studies in Monterey, California. He holds a master's degree in Arab Studies and is completing a Ph.D. in the Center for Middle Eastern Studies at the University of Oxford. He is a specialist on Iraq's intelligence agencies and Iraqi public diplomacy during the 1990-1991 occupation of Kuwait. Al-Marashi is the author of the *Middle East Review of International Affairs* article, "Iraq's Security and Intelligence Network: A Guide and Analysis," which was plagiarized by the British government in February 2003 as part of its case for going to war in Iraq. This incident briefly catapulted Al-Marashi into the role of international media pundit.

Emmanuel C. Alozie (Ph.D., University of Southern Mississippi) is university professor of media communications at Governors State University, University Park, Illinois. He has taught at Lincoln University, Shaw University, and Edward Waters College and has worked professionally in advertising, public relations and journalism. His research interests are in development communication, international/cultural journalism, advertising, and public relations. An assistant editor with Democratic Communique, Alozie has published conference proceedings, book chapters, and journals. He is co-editor of *Toward the Common Good: Perspectives in International Public Relations* (Allyn and Bacon, 2004).

Muhammad Ayish (Ph.D., University of Minnesota) is acting dean for the College of Communication at the University of Sharjah. He had worked at Yarmouk University in Jordan and in UAE University and Ajman University of Science and Technology. His research interests include Arab world broadcasting, media convergence, political communication, and culture-based communication perspectives. He has published scores of journal articles and book chapters in Arabic and English.

Ralph D. Berenger (D.A., Idaho State University) is assistant professor of journalism at the American University in Cairo where he teaches courses in communication theory, ethics, media management, and international communication. A journalism professional for more than thirty years, he has worked for newspapers such as the *Williston Herald, St. Cloud Daily Times, The St. Paul Pioneer-Press, the Grand Forks Herald*, and *The South Idaho Press.*

Timothy J. Boudreau (Ph.D., Southern Illinois University) is an assistant professor in the Central Michigan University Journalism Department. He has published several scholarly articles dealing with political coverage and newspaper management. Prior to entering academe, he had a ten year career as a reporter, editor, and copy editor in several southern and Midwestern U.S. newspapers.

Lisa Brooten (Ph.D., Ohio University) is an assistant professor at Southern Illinois University Carbondale, Department of Radio-TV. Brooten's research interests include militarization and media, gender, human rights, alternative media, social movements, and globalization. Her regional area of expertise is Southeast Asia, and in particular Burma/Myanmar. Her most recent research examines the ways in which gender, ethnicity, and the global discourse of human rights interact to perpetuate militarized media practices.

Christine Buchinger is a master of arts student in journalism and English at the University of Salzburg, Austria. After completing exchange semesters in Spain and in South Africa (Department of Journalism, University of Stellenbosch), a thesis in international comparative journalism studies is now underway, as are contributions to English-and German-speaking publications in Europe, South Africa, and the United States.

Catherine Cassara (Ph.D., Michigan State University) is an associate professor at Bowling Green State University. Raised in several different countries, she has been an avid consumer of international news for more years than she can count. A former journalist, she teaches reporting, media history, and international press issues, and is the author of book chapters, articles, and conference papers about American coverage of international news and foreign policy.

Dilruba Çatalbaş (Ph.D., Goldsmith's College, University of London) is associate professor of journalism at Galatasaray University in Istanbul. She earned a master of arts degree from Leeds University and a bachelor's degree from the University of Istanbul. She teaches and conducts research on economic, political, international and regulatory dimensions of public communication and journalism. She is currently on leave to Eastern Mediterranean University in North Cyprus.

Jinbong Choi is a doctoral candidate in the Department of Communication Studies at the University of Minnesota and author of four books: *Korean Mass Media and Popular Culture* (2003); *Media Reading by Jinbong Choi* (1998); *Modern Society and Korean Mass Media* (1997); and *Understanding Christian Communication* (1996). He has also published several scholarly articles dealing with international communication, new media and media framing

Stephen D. Cooper (Ph.D., Rutgers) is an assistant professor in the Department of Communication Studies at Marshall University, Huntington, W.Va. He has written about media bias, press coverage of warfare, privacy, computer-mediated communication, and organizational communication. Dr. Cooper thanks Yi-Fan Chen, a graduate student at Marshall University, for research assistance.

Arnold S. de Beer (Ph.D., Potchefstroom, South Africa) is professor emeritus in the Department of Journalism, University of Stellenbosch, South Africa. He serves on the editorial board of *Journalism Studies*; is founder-editor of *Ecquid Novi*, the South African journal for journalism research, and is co-author with John C. Merrill of *Global Journalism* (4th edition, 2004). He has published *inter alia* on news and conflict and the media, and is a member of the appeals committee of the South African Press Ombudsman.

Daniela V. Dimitrova (Ph.D., University of Florida) is assistant professor of journalism and mass communication at Iowa State University. Her research interests focus on new media adoption and political communication, as well as Internet diffusion in post-communist countries. Her research has been published internationally.

Chelsea Ellis is a master of arts student in journalism and mass communication at the University of Florida.

Janet Fine is a contributing editor to the electronic journal, *Transnational Broadcasting Studies* (TBS), *Elan Magazine* in Bombay, India, and *Video Age International Magazine* in New York, specializing in writing on TV and film. In addition, she writes for *Variety* newspaper covering Egypt and also contributes to various journals. She is the author of five books.

George Albert Gladney (Ph.D., University of Illinois) is an associate professor in the Department of Communication and Journalism at the University of Wyoming. He has authored numerous articles in scholarly and professional journals related to journalism and mass communication. His specialty areas include new communication technology and mass media ethics, law, and theory. Earlier in his career Professor Gladney worked as a reporter for the *Los Angeles Times* and *Colorado Spring* Sun and was editor of the *Colorado Springs Gazette* and *Jackson Hole News* in Wyoming.

Naila Hamdy (M.A., American University in Cairo) is a lecturer in journalism at the American University in Cairo while also working as a television journalist for major news networks around the world. Her research interests include effects of the Internet and other new media. She is completing a doctorate at Cairo University and has presented dozens of papers at international conferences. Hamdy is a member of the Broadcast Educators Association (BEA) and is a board member of the Arab-United States Association for Communication Educators (AUSACE). She is a contributing editor to the electronic journal *Transnational Broadcasting Studies* (TBS).

Cees J. Hamelink (Ph.D., University of Amsterdam) is professor of international communication at the University of Amsterdam. He also holds the chair for media, religion, and culture at the Free University of Amsterdam, and teaches media and human rights at the City University of London. Professor Hamelink is editor-in-chief of the *International Journal for Communication Studies: Gazette*. He has written sixteen books on communication, culture, and human rights. His latest book is *Human Rights for Communicators* (Hampton Press, 2004).

Martin Hirst (Ph.D., Queensland University) is a lecturer in journalism and mass communication at Queensland University in Australia and was a journalist for fifteen years before joining the faculties of Charles Stuart University and the University of Western Sydney. He is co-author with Roger Patching of *Journalism Ethics: Arguments & Cafes* (OUP, 2004).

Beverly Horvit (Ph.D., University of Missouri) is an assistant professor of journalism at Texas Christian University where she teaches reporting, editing, public affairs reporting, media writing, and international communication. Before coming to TCU in 2003, she taught at Winthrop University in Rock Hill, S.C., and the University of Texas at Arlington. Her research interests include international news, media and foreign policy, and media ethics.

Thomas J. Johnson (Ph.D., University of Washington) is a full professor in the School of Journalism and Director of Graduate Studies at Southern Illinois

University at Carbondale. His fields of interest are public opinion and political communication research, particularly the role of media in presidential elections. More recently, he has concentrated on how people use the Internet and what effect online media have on them.

Lynda Lee Kaid (Ph.D., Southern Illinois University) is senior associate dean for graduate studies and research and a professor of telecommunication in the College of Journalism and Communications at the University of Florida. She is author or co-author of scores of journal articles, book chapters, and eighteen books, including her latest, *Video style in Presidential Campaigns: Style and Content of Televised Political Advertising* (with Anne Johnston, Praeger/Greenwood, 2001).

Yahya R. Kamalipour (Ph.D., University of Missouri) is professor of mass communication and head of the Department of Communication and Creative Arts, Purdue University Calumet, Hammond, Indiana. He has taught at universities in Ohio, Illinois, Missouri, Indiana, Oxford (England), and Tehran (Iran). He is author or editor of numerous books, including *The Globalization of Corporate Media Hegemony* (2003) and *Global Communication* (Wadsworth, 2002). He is managing editor of *Global Media Journal.*

Barbara K. Kaye (Ph.D., Florida State University) is associate professor in the School of Journalism and Electronic Media at the University of Tennessee-Knoxville. Research interests include media effects and consumer uses of new communication technologies, especially the Internet. Her work has been published in many academic journals. Additionally, she is lead author of *The World Wide Web: A Mass Communication Perspective* (McGraw Hill/Mayfield, 1999, 2001), *Just a Click Away: Advertising on the Internet* (Allyn & Bacon, 2001), and is co-author of *Electronic Media: See It Then, See It Now, See It Later* (Allyn & Bacon, 2004).

Makram Khoury-Machool (Ph.D., School of Oriental and Asian Studies, University of London) specializes in Arab media and culture with special reference on political economy issues. He teaches at the University of Cambridge and is a research fellow at the Truman Institute. He was the first journalist to announce the 1987 Palestinian Intifada. A Reuters Award winner (1990), he was a research fellow at the University of Oxford (1990-1991). In 1996, he was elected as a Young Global Leader of the World Economic Forum, Davos.

Kris Kodrich (Ph.D., Indiana University) is an assistant professor of journalism at Colorado State University. He conducts research on international mass communication and online journalism. He is a former Freedom Forum Asia Fellow, a Fulbright Journalism Fellow (Spain) and a Kiplinger Fellow (Ohio State

University). He is author of *Tradition and Change in the Nicaraguan Press: Newspapers and Journalists in a New Democratic Era* (2002).

Jim A. Kuypers (Ph.D., Louisiana State University) is senior lecturer and director of the Office of Speech at Dartmouth College. He is the author of *Presidential Crisis Rhetoric and the Press in a Post-Cold War World, Press Bias and Politics: How the Media Frame Controversial Issues*, and co-editor of *Twentieth-Century Roots of Rhetorical Studies*. He is a former editor for the *American Communication Journal*. His research interests include political communication, meta-criticism, and the moral/poetic use of language.

Kristen Landreville is a master of arts student at the University of Florida.

Sweety Law (Ph.D., Ohio University) is an associate professor of communication at Texas A&M International University. Her research interests focus on audiences, mass media processes and effects, innovation diffusion, communication campaigns, community development, and intercultural communication. In addition to top papers at ICA, her published work has appeared in *Gazette, Journal of Communication* and *Inter/Sections*. Her most recent work appears in P. Murphy & M. Kraidy (eds.), *Global Media Studies: Ethnographic Perspectives* (Routledge Press, N.Y.).

Laura Lengel (Ph.D., Ohio University) is associate professor in the School of Communication Studies at Bowling Green State University, following seven years at Richmond American International University in London. She began researching international media as a Fulbright Scholar and American Institute of Maghreb Studies Fellow in Tunisia. Her books, *Culture and Technology in the New Europe* (2000), and *Computer Mediated Communication* (with Thurlow & Tomic, 2004), and articles that address political, cultural, and economic influences of media and technology, particularly in the MENA region and Eastern Europe.

Jack Lule (Ph.D., University of Georgia) is the Joseph B. McFadden Professor of Journalism in the Department of Journalism and Communication at Lehigh University, Bethlehem, Pennsylvania. His research interests include cultural and critical studies of news, online journalism, and teaching with technology. He is the author of *Daily News, Eternal Stories: The Mythological Role of Journalism* (Guilford Press, 2001).

Justin D. Martin is a doctoral student at the University of Florida.

John C. Merrill (Ph.D., Iowa) is professor emeritus of journalism and mass communication at the University of Missouri and author of 34 books. His latest, the fourth edition of *Global Journalism*, is co-authored by Arnold deBeer. During the 2003-2004 academic year he was on the faculty of the American University in Cairo where he taught courses in international communication and ethics.

Will Miller (Ed.D., University of Massachusetts) is an unorthodox combination of psychotherapist, ordained minister, and stand-up comedian, and a well-known motivational speaker and television personality in the United States. He is co-author (with Glenn Sparks) of *Refrigerator Rights: Creating Connections & Restoring Relationships*.

Radwa Mobarak (B.A., American University in Cairo) is a master's student at the American University in Cairo where she teaches undergraduate classes in research methodology and continues her research on global communication issues.

James Napoli (M.A., Boston College) did further graduate work in mass communications at the University of Wisconsin-Madison. He currently chairs the Journalism Department at Western Washington University in Bellingham. He has worked extensively in the United States and abroad as a journalist, journalism teacher, administrator, researcher, and media consultant. He spent about ten years at the American University in Cairo.

Kaarle Nordenstreng (Ph.D., University of Helsinki) has been professor of journalism and mass communication at the University of Tampere, Finland, since 1971. Before that he was head of research at the Finnish Broadcasting Company (YLE) and a journalist with Finnish radio (since the age of fifteen in youth programs). His main research areas are international communication, communication theory, and media ethics. He is currently vice president of JourNet, Global Network for Professional Education in Journalism and Media. He has written or edited thirty books and is author of over four hundred scholarly articles or papers.

Stephen Quinn (Ph.D., University of Wollongong, Australia) is an associate professor of journalism at Ball State University. He was director of the Center for Media Training and Research at Zayed University in the United Arab Emirates from January 2002 to June 2003. Prior to joining Zayed he taught journalism in the UK, Australia and New Zealand. Dr. Quinn is the author of *Knowledge Management in the Digital Newsroom* (Focal Press 2002), *Digital Sub-Editing and Design* (Focal Press 2001), *Newsgathering on the Net* (Macmillan 2001, 2nd ed.) and *The Art of Learning* (UNSW Press 1999). He is the only academic on the international advisory counsel for the Newsplex. Between 1975 and 1990, Dr. Quinn worked as a reporter, editor and columnist in Australia, Thailand, the UK and New Zealand.

S. Abdallah Schleifer (M.A., The American University of Beirut) is distinguished lecturer of mass communication, director of the Adham Center for Television Journalism at the American University in Cairo, and publisher/senior editor of the electronic journal *Transnational Broadcasting Studies*. Author of hundreds of academic and general media articles on media in the Middle East, he has been a consultant to CNN International and several Middle East satellite channels. He is executive director of the documentary *Control Room* shot at Al-Jazeera and Centcom HQ during the 2003 Iraq war. Mr. Schleifer served as Cairo bureau chief for NBC News from 1974-1983.

Howard Schneider (B.A., University of Maryland) has been a reporter with *The Washington Post* since 1988, and between 1998 and 2002 was head of *The Post's* Cairo bureau. He has reported extensively on political, religious, and economic affairs throughout the region, with bylines originating from most Arab capitals as well as rural outposts like Khalkhal, in northern Iran, and the Palestinian camps of southern Lebanon. Between 2002 and 2004, on sabbatical from the paper, he served as lecturer in journalism at the American University in Cairo.

Robert Schütze is a Ph.D. scholarship student in the School of Journalism and Communication at the University of Queensland. His doctoral thesis is *Other or Ally? Indonesia in the Australian Press 1945-2004*. He has worked for several news organizations in the Asia-Pacific region and is currently stringing from Brisbane while he finishes his thesis.

Yoichi Clark Shimatsu is former general editor of *The Japan Times Weekly* in Tokyo, a founding faculty member of the Journalism & Media Studies Centre at The University of Hong Kong, and the first English-language journalism professor at the School of Journalism & Communication at Tsinghua University in Beijing. As a writer on military and intelligence issues, he has covered for a number of news publications and television networks the Tokyo subway gassing, the Kashmir conflict and the Afghan war.

Glenn G. Sparks (Ph.D., University of Wisconsin) is professor and assistant department head of the Department of Communication at Purdue University. He is author of *Media Effects: An Overview* (Wadsworth, 2002) and co-author with Will Miller of *Refrigerator Rights: Creating Connections & Restoring Relationships*, which was a finalist in 2003 for the "Books for a Better Life" award by the Multiple Sclerosis Society. His area of expertise is the cognitive and emotional effects of the media. A number of his articles report the results of research on the effects of frightening films and TV programs as well as media violence.

Kaye D. Trammell is a doctoral candidate at the University of Florida. Her research interests revolve around the intersection of computer-mediated communication and political communication. She is a former Navy journalist and currently serves as a public affairs officer in the United States Naval Reserve.

Tim Walters (Ph.D., University of Texas at Austin) is assistant professor of communication and media sciences at Zayed University in the United Arab Emirates. He has taught at several foreign institutions including the Budapest University of Economic Sciences, and has worked professionally in print and publications for more than twenty years.

Herman Wasserman (D.Litt., University of Stellenbosch) is a senior lecturer in the Department of Journalism, University of Stellenbosch. He is deputy editor of *Ecquid Novi*, the journal for journalism research in South Africa. His current research interests include the use of ICTs by civil society organizations and identity construction in the media. He is co-editor (with Sean Jacobs) of *Shifting Selves: Post-apartheid Essays on Mass Media, Culture, and Identity* (2003).

David Weinstock (Ph.D., Michigan State) is an assistant professor of new media technology in the Central Michigan University Journalism Department. In addition, he is a freelance journalist who writes about computer technology and the environment. Prior to his university career, he had a ten-year career as a magazine editor, reporter, and photographer. He has won a number of national writing and photography awards.

Andrew Paul Williams (Ph.D., University of Florida) is assistant professor of journalism and mass communications at Virginia Tech University. His primary research interests are political communication and media studies. Williams is interested in political public relations and how political figures, issues, and events are portrayed in candidate-controlled media and traditional and alternative mass media content.

Margaret (Maggy) Zanger (M.S.L., Yale Law School) is a journalist and academic who witnessed the 2003 Iraq war and its aftermath in the Kurdish area and later in Baghdad where she directed a journalism training program. She has been a lecturer at the American University in Cairo where she taught writing, editing, and publication design, and where she developed a graduate class in media coverage of refugees. Her research interests are on the nexus between conflict, forced migration, and news media.

PREFACE

Reflections on the 2003 Iraq War

Cees J. Hamelink

When the United States and the United Kingdom governments decided to invade Iraq in 2003, they had a serious communications problem. How could a military invasion be justified against a sovereign member state of the United Nations without the consent of the UN Security Council?

The political and moral justification was complicated by the fact that the attack was to be launched against a country where children made up 42% of the population. Many of these children had already been seriously affected by the withholding of five billion dollars in humanitarian supplies during the sanctions against Iraq. It was also widely known that the Iraqi armed forces were enormously weakened after the war against Iran and the Gulf War of 1991.

References to Iraq's refusal to implement UN resolutions or to its poor human rights record would not be very helpful as both the U.S. and the U.K. had never much cared about such issues. The need to control Iraq's energy sources could have been used as a justification, but might not have persuaded political elites and the public at large that murdering Iraqi citizens was justified.

Moreover, the problem was further complicated by the possibility that the invasion would be seen as a crime against humanity. This was a serious possibility as the judges of the International Military Tribunal at Nuremberg (after World War II) had stated that "to initiate a war of aggression" constitutes the supreme international crime. The judges added that there could be no defense for pre-emptive attacks against other countries. Yet the U.S. and U.K. governments wanted to remove Saddam Hussein and needed an invasion that had been on various military and political planning boards for quite some time.

Connecting Iraq with the war on terrorism seemed an attractive strategy. If people could be convinced that the Iraqi president could deploy weapons of mass destruction and possibly make these weapons available to terrorist groups, a military strike against such a ghastly threat could be sold as a legitimate pre-emptive action.

However, UN weapons inspectors had been unable to find the WMDs. And while the U.S. and the U.K. intelligence services might have been uncertain whether Iraq possessed biological and chemical weapons, they were quite certain that Iraq had no nuclear arms program. Actually, the intelligence services were quite unequivocal about the fact that there were no nuclear weapons. It needs to be remembered that only these weapons pose in the real sense a threat of mass destruction. Therefore, Iraq did not pose an imminent threat to the region, let alone to the rest of the world. Even before President Bush, Prime Minister Blair, and Secretary of State Powell publicly used the argument about nuclear weapons, their own sources had already defeated it. Yet the invasion had to take place and had to be sold.

Luckily for the bellicose governments, assistance was coming forward in two forms. First, with the help of bright professional minds such as "perception managers" John W. Rendon[1] and Alastair Campbell,[2] a strategy of propaganda and persuasion was initiated that was bought by a sufficiently large number of gullible news media. Second, in several countries (such as the United Kingdom itself and in some supportive countries like the Netherlands) there was considerable popular protest against the invasion, but, given the ineffectiveness of their democracies, this could be conveniently ignored by the political leadership.

With war propaganda and media complicity in place and a public opinion that was favorably massaged or conveniently ignored, the invasion could begin. Now another communications problem arose: coverage of the war proceedings. This had to be steered in such ways that the media spectacle would present to a global public a war of liberation that was fought swiftly, effectively, and with minimal civilian and coalition casualties.

With some exceptions, the majority of the Western mainstream media was helpful to the invaders. They accepted the censorship of the "embedding" strategy and they gave the war protagonists (Bush, Cheney, Rumsfeld, Powell, Blair, Hoon, and Campbell) ample space to mislead the public.[3] Most of these media acted with little professional inquisitiveness and adopted conveniently the frame of interpretation that was fabricated by spin-doctors. This should surprise no one since it was just a repetition of what happened during the Panama invasion, the Gulf War of 1991, the NATO intervention in Kosovo, and the military operations in Afghanistan.

For the communications student, this raises at least three pressing questions.

Can one so easily refer to "the media" as the preceding text suggests? Of course not. "The media" do not exist. There are big media and small media, media with different ideological positions and political affiliations, and there are mainstream and alternative media. The Iraq invasion news coverage was brought to the public by Western media, but also by Arab media. Little analysis is needed to see that the coverage by the three leading world agencies (AP, Reuters, and AFP)[4] was significantly different from the Inter Press Service newscast. Even superficial observation demonstrates how American broadcasters such as CNN and the Fox network differed from the Al-Jazeera TV station or Abu Dhabi TV.

Even so, the key issue remains: How did opinion-leading news media in the countries that initiated and supported the invasion assist the justification of the attack? This leads to a second question: How can one explain media connivance with partisan propaganda and persuasion? Among the explanatory factors to understand the voluntary "embeddedness" of journalists with the military are the strength of patriotic feelings, the desire to apply crude dichotomies of good versus evil to an increasingly complex world, plain sloppiness, lack of professional skills, and the fact that there is in most societies an elite political consensus that frames contemporary history in accordance with elite interests. Media (and certainly the mainstream international media) are, in many countries, part of that elite and share its consensus.

The third question is: Will media coverage be different during the next international armed conflict? This is a legitimate question since, after the failures of media war coverage in the past, there has been—at least among responsible journalists—a process of critical reflection and firm resolve to do better the next war. However, there is little reason to believe that such intentions will be realized. The institutional context of media coverage with its pressures of political preference, economic interests, and the dictates of time and competition shows no signs of radical change in the years ahead. So, however genuine intentions may be, the next conflict will see that most media again focus more on "shock and awe" than on the murdered victims, and demonstrate more empathy with "Us" than with "Them."

It is also quite probable that in future conflicts the inequality of arms between the propagandists and the journalists will further increase. Whereas many professional journalists have an interest in uncovering the truth, their counterparts in propaganda are not hampered by such moral motives. They can easily resort to lies and deception. In the struggle between truth and lies, the latter are usually the stronger combatants. Also, in the next war's coverage there will inevitably be biased perceptions of reality, partisan preferences, and political and financial obstacles to hamper serious investigative journalism.

If mainly despair is left, why preface this book? A major reason is that without such critical analyses as are presented in this book, the situation might be a lot worse. In times of political insanity, it is necessary and encouraging to find signals of intellectual sanity.

The critical analysis also needs to be made—time and again—in order to alert media audiences to what is being done to their minds. War today is, more than anything else, psychological warfare by governments against their own population. It will be a great day for the democratic ideal when people discover the propaganda and the media distortion and begin to demand that they—to use the words of the judges of the European Court of Human Rights—are informed properly about matters of public interest.

Endnotes

1. Rendon, president of The Rendon Group, a public relations firm that has worked with governments on both sides of the Atlantic, refers to himself as "an information warrior and perception manager." Rendon was credited with shaping the perceptions of Iraq as a threat before the war, and managing the imagery coming out of it during the war. (See Rampton, S., & Stauber, J. *Weapons of Mass Deception: The Uses of Propaganda in Bush's War on Iraq.* New York: Jeremy P. Tarcher/Penguin, 2003.)

2. Until he resigned on February 25, 2004, Campbell was Blair's press secretary. Embattled by the press during the run-up and conduct of the 2003 Iraq war, he was cleared of any wrong doing—particularly the leaking of Dr. David Kelley's name to the press as the source of a BBC report critical of Blair's WMD claims. Dr. Kelley allegedly committed suicide on July 18, 2003, shortly after being grilled by Members of Parliament. The BBC, not Campbell, was strongly criticized for reports by correspondent Andrew Gilligan in the *Report of the Inquiry into the Circumstances Surrounding the Death of Dr David Kelly, C.M.G.* by Lord Hutton. (Available at http://www.the-hutton-inquiry.org.uk/content/report/)

3. Referenced here are U.S. President George W. Bush, U.S. Vice President Richard (Dick) Cheney, U.S. Secretary of Defense Donald Rumsfeld, U.S. Secretary of State Colin Powell, British Prime Minister Tony Blair, UK Secretary of State for Defense Geoffrey W. Hoon, and Blair's Press Secretary, Alistair Campbell.

4. Refers to the Associated Press, headquartered in New York; Reuters, headquartered in London; and Agence France Presse, headquartered in Paris.

FOREWORD

Response to Hamelink

John C. Merrill

Cees Hamelink raises an interesting and important question in the *Preface*: Will the media be different during the next international conflict? He hopes so. Me, too, as do the authors of the stimulating chapters that make up this book.

Hamelink proceeds to provide a cautious answer that goes beyond hope. "Yes, if. " *If* democratic systems begin to offer the opportunity for governments to get the word from the people that they are sick of being lead about by egocentric and plutocratic elites, and *if* the people become more sophisticated about propaganda.

These are big "ifs" and history shows that democracies are largely pseudo in that people never really rule: They are basically followers in various kinds of authoritarian systems. And it seems that media themselves are tied to their respective political systems and have not found a way to provide unbiased and independent coverage of wars. Many "responsible" journalists, as Hamelink points out, may resolve to do better with each war, but will they?

The following pages shed some light on this question. It will take a multitude of "responsible" journalists, not just a few, to bring about real change.

Propaganda persists, as Hamelink says, and I should stress that it comes from all sides, not just from the aggressor who invades a country such as Iraq. Bias leads to propaganda, and all parties are biased. It is true that some biases are more humane and more human than others, but people everywhere fall under the hypnotic spell of the media.

Cees Hamelink clearly shows how wars can start and can be justified by aggressive governments, and how such governments care little about public thinking on the matter. In the United Kingdom and in the Netherlands, for example, there was considerable protest against the Iraq war (he could have mentioned the United States as well), but to no avail.

The Western media did not help calm the war fervor, Hamelink says. They basically accepted the line that Iraq had weapons of mass destruction and went along with the American policy of "embedding" (in-bedding?) journalists with the invading troops. This is true, but it should be noted that the Arab media produced a steady diet of anti-invasion (especially anti-Bush) material and even pulled its own punches in condemning Saddam Hussein and his human rights excesses. Media seem to be warriors for their cause in any war, hot or cold.

Hamelink stresses that critical analyses, such as the reader will find on the following pages, need somehow to reach the people who must be constantly alert about what is being done to their minds. How true. But do the audiences get this propaganda analysis and media criticism, or is it available only to intellectuals and a handful of university students?

Here's the problem: Getting average citizens to know about, even care about, the skewed world the media are foisting upon them. They are so busy being entertained by media that they know little or nothing about their governments and their covert and overt activities. Such a situation, of course, does not bode well for democracy.

It could be that the media—intrinsic institutions of their own cultures—are simply reflecting the biases and values of their people. Perhaps the media will change when the people change. Perhaps it is the people of the various countries who need criticizing; perhaps, as Aristotle pointed out, the individual citizen's values and ethical endeavors must come first. Then, maybe, the leadership will become better. At any rate, it is quite possible that we get the kind of media we deserve.

Hamelink's final sentence is a hopeful clarion call for public enlightenment. He shows, as do a number of the authors of the following chapters, that idealism is not dead and that there are some who believe that knowing about media distortion will end it. A fine hypothesis—one that we need to get busy and try to prove.

INTRODUCTION

Global Media Go to War

Ralph D. Berenger

No other war has been as extensively reported as was the 2003 Iraq War. Through mixtures of new and old media, professional and amateur journalists told the story of Saddam Hussein's Ba'athist regime's fall after nearly a generation of iron-fisted rule. Thanks to the Internet, more "reporters" and "commentators" than ever examined, analyzed, praised, lambasted, speculated about, or criticized every byte of information, every pixel of image, and every thread of uploaded commentary about global media behavior.

The short Iraq war was an artifact of its time. Communication satellites. The twenty-four-hour news cycle. A polarized world still trying to make some sense of the events of September 11, 2001 (and America's rage about it). The near Delphi-like predictions of a "Clash of Civilizations." And, most importantly, transnational media parity for Western and Middle Eastern audiences during an event that affected them both. All was fertile ground for media researchers who looked not only at the messages and messengers, but the effect they had on audiences.

This book was conceived before the first shots echoed across the wind-swept Iraqi desert in March 2003. From its inception only one title summed up what was happening: Global news media were at war not only by reporting an international conflict with global significance, but with themselves in a battle for audience acceptance, with their newsroom cultures that often mediated news from the front lines to fit editorial preconceptions, with general and academic critics on all sides, and with the very people they were trying to cover—at times with lethal consequences.

Covering a war, even a high-tech one, is dangerous duty. Elevated media risks in this war involved a variety of bifurcated side issues such as religious misunderstandings; diverse, disputed, and dysfunctional political ideologies; social, economic, and ethnic inequities; differing cultural norms and values; and a rock-ribbed, regional cynicism that nothing *halal*[1] could possibly come out of the West (thus dooming before they could even begin any liberal democratic changes in post-war Iraq, including a free press and elections).

Also from the inception was the problem of naming this war. Was it, as Arab broadcasters said, "The War on Iraq," "The Aggression on Iraq," "The Anglo-American War on Iraq," "The U.S. Attack on Iraq," or was it "Gulf War II"? For Americans the latter designation, though accurate, is confusing. While Western media were apt to report the conflict as "Gulf War II," that name reflected a particular Western ethnocentrism for Arabs. They still remember the Iran-Iraq War in the 1980s as "Gulf War I," perhaps choosing to forget that both the 1967 and 1973 wars against Israel were also Gulf Wars, in that Persian Gulf nations lined up against Israel with others in the region.

At any rate, since no Arab country openly supported the 2003 war (as they had, however unenthusiastically, the 1991 war), use of the Gulf War designation here seemed inaccurate, and the "U.S./U.K.-Iraq War," appeared unwieldy. A more neutral "2003 Iraq War" emerged as the top contender since it clearly differentiates the previous conflict by year.

Players in this war were more grizzled replicates of the 1991 Iraq War—another George Bush was in office (he had advised his father in 1991). Back were Dick Cheney, Colin Powell, Donald Rumsfeld, and a host of Gulf War policy veterans whose names might never be made public. After a dozen inter-war years, junior officers on both sides during the first war on Iraq were now senior officers in this one.

Of course, Saddam Hussein was back and so was the eloquent Iraqi spokesman, Tariq Aziz, but in a less visible capacity. Early in the war names and faces of the Ba'athist regime leaders would become more familiar to the American and British publics than in the past war, thanks to a Pentagon gimmick: decks of playing cards that entrepreneurs reproduced and quickly sold over the Internet.

The press, too, had stars reprising their roles, some with different networks. Christiane Amanpour was still with CNN doing field reports as an embedded reporter; Robert Fisk for the Independent and John Simpson for the BBC covered the war in-country; John Burns was still with *The New York Times*, reporting from Baghdad; and *The New York Times'* Thomas Friedman was adding his informed commentary from various locations in the Middle East. Peter Arnett, the slightly tarnished media hero of the 1991 Iraq War, proved to be as controversial with NBC, who fired him, as he was with CNN, and all the major American news anchors were still around after the 1991 war. ABC's Peter Jennings, CBS' Dan Rather, and NBC's Tom Brokaw made pilgrimages to Iraq at one time or another. But there were new players in the media as well, many of them from the Middle East.

Even before the first invading/liberating U.S. or U.K. soldier set foot in the Middle East, the Arab press in most of the region's twenty-two countries was brutal and vocal in its assessment of the coming war, as several of the following chapters will attest. The openly hostile Arab media variously framed the seemingly inevitable conflict between the U.S./U.K. coalition and Iraq as a war to avenge the Bush family honor, a ploy by "oil-rich" Bush to control Iraqi petroleum output, an "ignorant" and out-of-control "cowboy" Bush lashing out at terrorist shadows and hurting innocents in the process, and an "evil" if not "satanic" Bush doing the bidding of the Zionists.

The Middle East media were unrelenting in their pre-war, wartime, and post-war criticism of the United States and, in the Iraq context, the Blair government in the United Kingdom. In fact, regular readers of the Arab press are hard-pressed to recall any favorable stories about the United States over the past decade, including perfunctory, carefully parsed, and brief sentiments following 9/11. The general consensus then and sometimes now was that Arabs were incapable of the Twin Towers and Pentagon attacks, and some even suggested that Israel was behind it all. That same level of denial was expressed about Iraq's threat to the region, its WMD capabilities, and, surprisingly, about the ease by which this war would be prosecuted. Many wistfully predicted a protracted war with thousands of allied deaths.

Arab press readers—admittedly less than half of the region's 307 million population—are well attuned to charges that Israel is the source of all malevolence in the Middle East.[2] The United States, since the late 1980s, is supplanting the Jewish state as the most evil of entities because of its wealth, its assumed cultural decadence, its military power and, above all, its perceived blind support of Israel. Those sentiments bubble to the surface in several ensuing chapters.

The West, too, conducted a rigorous propaganda campaign to drum up support for war against Iraq among wobbly-kneed allies. The propaganda machine ground out stories, real and speculative, of Saddam Hussein's intentions in the region, his financial support of suicide bombers' families in Palestine, his continued threats against Iraqi Kurds and Shia'as, his regime's alleged links to al-Qaeda cells and training centers in Iraq, his family's personal extravagance while the average Iraqi suffered through painful international sanctions, and, most importantly, his acquisition of weapons of mass destruction and his willingness to use them against enemies foreign and domestic.

About This Book

From its conception, this book had several operational themes that fashioned themselves into goals. More specifically, the intent was to produce a work that was:

- *Cross-Disciplinary.* This book includes writings from experts in fields other than journalism and mass communication. It was hoped that such contributions would enliven and broaden the debate.

- *Cross-Cultural.* Viewpoints of writers from nearly all continents are represented in this volume, with emphasis on Middle Eastern scholars and journalists who not only examine the war's impact on their region, but on the "Other" as well. Readers will be able to discern the various schemata each writer brings to our understanding of what happened to global media during the conflict.

- *Cross-Generational.* This project, assembled in less than a year, involved studies by undergraduate and graduate students, as well as some of the best-established scholars in the international communication field. Young scholars were selected for their energy and fresh perspectives on media; senior scholars were chosen for their wisdom and experience.

- *Focused on Media Behavior.* The over-riding theme of this work is how media behaved before, during, and after the war. Behavior is critical because in war lives are put at risk, potentially hundreds of thousands of them if Saddam Hussein indeed had a viable weapons of mass destruction program. To get stories inside Iraq, many journalists and TV crews gambled their lives, and some lost.

  It could be argued that at least one person, Dr. David Kelley, Britain's WMD expert, might have been a direct casualty of media war behavior. Dr. Kelley allegedly committed suicide when his personal and professional ethics rubbed against newsroom ethics of the British Broadcasting Corporation, which used him as a source for its stories. At least the Hutton Report strongly suggested that early in 2004.[3]

- *General and Student Reader Appeal.* All of the authors were asked to eschew academese and write their chapters for general audiences. With that in mind, this work could be acceptable as a classroom reader for courses in international relations, political science, sociology and, of course, Middle East and mass communications studies. This edition should also appeal to mass audiences interested in how news media (one of their information connections to the war as it unfolded) behaved during a major international event, and, possibly, how they can become media monitors themselves by using new media.

Overview of the Book

This book contains thirty-four essays, which includes the *Preface*, *Foreword*, *Introduction*, *Afterword*, and thirty chapters. The *Preface* and *Foreword*, written by two world-renowned scholars, involve a dialogue about media, government and war.

Cees J. Hamelink of the University of Amsterdam argues that during the 2003 Iraq War mainstream mass media from coalition countries became tools of "propaganda" for the U.S. and British governments, and that there is little hope that will change in future global conflicts. "If mainly despair is left, why preface this book?" he writes. "A major reason is that without such critical analyses as presented in this book, the situation might be still a lot worse. In times of political insanity, it is necessary and encouraging to find signals of intellectual sanity."

John C. Merrill, professor emeritus at the University of Missouri, agrees with Hamelink that scholars and citizens need to publish "critical analyses," but one of the problems is "getting average citizens to know about, even care about, the skewed world the media are foisting upon them. They are so busy being entertained by media that they know little or nothing about their governments and their covert and overt activities. Such a situation, of course, does not bode well for democracy."

In his Afterword Kaarle Nordenstreng of the University of Tampere in Finland renews a call for international media monitoring, and proposes an international collaborative project of media scholars to collect the burgeoning number of academic studies on media behavior to be issued in an annual report. He urges use of content analysis to identify what is being communicated to whom in what channel.

The book is divided into six major sections: *The Prelude to War*; *The International War of Words*; *The War in the Coalition Press*; *The War in Other Places*; *The War in Cyberspace*; and *The War for Hearts and Minds*.

Part I: The Prelude to War

The first six chapters survey the global media scape before the war, and how news and entertainment media in different parts of the world cultivated their audiences and national policymakers to either support or oppose the war.

James Napoli studied media in two countries opposed to the war, France and Egypt. Jinbong Choi used the diagnostic and heuristic tool of framing to study the meanings of Bush's "axis of evil" pronouncement. Because world audiences receive nearly all their foreign news from international news agencies, Beverly Horvit examines five of them and how they covered the coming war, with some surprising results.

George Gladney deconstructs Marshall McLuhan's "global village" concept and finds it fragmenting into competing ideologies, religious beliefs, and cultures, each currently or potentially supported by media. In a similar vein, Emmanuel C. Alozie's study of print media in different sub-Saharan countries finds a mixture of distrust and disagreement with coalition goals, while Stephen Quinn and Tim Walters relay how Al-Jazeera's impact in the Middle East, even before the latest Gulf war, might be more enduring than Western critics would like.

Part II: The World War of Words

Stuart Hall once wrote that "words have meanings," and this section tries to ascertain the meaning of words used to prepare populations for war.

Yahya R. Kamalipour suggests how words often reported uncritically by journalists create meaning for audiences. Jack Lule extends the concept further when he follows the metaphors used in the 2003 Iraq War. Words played a role in how Turkey's media debated what kind of cooperation, if any, that country should give the United States, one of its most important allies. As the U.S. reaction to Turkey's decision process grew critical, so too did the Turkish press grow critical of providing any help at all to the coalition, Dilruba Çatalbaş discovered.

Ibrahim Al-Marashi, an Iraqi-American doctoral student at Oxford, explains how his academic paper on Iraq's alleged WMD capacity—purloined by the British government—led to a brief (and at times frustrating) career as an international media pundit. Andrew Paul Williams and his colleagues find late-night-TV comedy is serious business when it comes to shaping public opinion.

Part III: The War in the Coalition Press

This section examines how global media from Allied countries behaved.

The Washington Post's Howard Schneider reviews some of the war's biggest press blunders and how the media dealt with them. Martin Hirst and Robert Schütze investigate Rupert Murdoch's flagship paper's (the *Australian*) support of the war; Kris Kodrich and Sweety Law tackle the issue of how "newspapers of record" in England and the United States chose to report the WMD story. Stephen D. Cooper and Jim A. Kuypers compare reporting practices of embedded and non-embedded journalists with unexpected conclusions, and Maggy Zanger reports behind the lines in Iraq on how "journos" scratched for a story that never materialized.

Part IV: The War in Other Places

The section examines how television and print media in countries other than the United States, Great Britain, and Australia covered the war.

While the major media in combatant countries covered the war story, Christine Burchinger, Herman Wasserman, and Arnold de Beer investigated how South African media struggled to make sense of the war and gain a global perspective. Similarly, across the planet, Yoichi Clark Shimatsu followed how the "far-off war" was reported in Hong Kong and in Mainland China.

S. Abdallah Schleifer assessed the job of Middle East broadcasters and, despite some errors of commission and omission, figures the fledgling satellite news operations are on their way to becoming professional, credible news operations in a region unaccustomed to them. Catherine Cassera and Laura Lengel see Al-Jazeera's effect on public diplomacy as similar to CNN's.

Janet Fine looks at media coverage of the war in India, the world's largest democracy, which should have been a huge supporter of the coalition, but wasn't. She offers some suggestions why.

Part V: The War in Cyberspace

Few people routinely used the Internet during the 1991 Gulf War, much less as a network for sharing huge volumes of information. What a change a dozen years makes.

Naila Hamdy and Radwa Mobarak set the tone for this section by providing an overview of the Web during the war, while Daniela Dimitrova, Lynda Lee Kaid, and Andrew Paul Williams find varied news coverage during the first hours of the war. Lisa Brooten explores the phenomenon of *Indymedia.org* and wonders if we are witnessing the future of news interactive—sensational, instantaneous, and opinionated. David Weinstock and Timothy Boudreau offer free advice to news organizations on how to capture and retain young viewers.

Cyberspace is a big, uncharted place several authors found. Barbara K. Kaye and Thomas J. Johnson, for example, look at the do-it-yourself publishing of Weblogs, including the widely followed Baghdad adventures of an Iraqi blogger, "Salam Pax," during the war.

Part VI: The War for Hearts and Minds

A considerable effort is being expended by the U.S. and U.K. governments to win over a skeptical population in the Middle East—reversing years of official Western neglect and indifference which allowed political Islam to take root without critical assessment, which often enacted policies blindly supportive of Israel, which bolstered increasingly repressive regimes that encouraged their media to scapegoat the West and camouflage their own shortcomings, and which influenced some intellectuals whose positions at governmental institutions depend on toeing the party line. This section examines public opinion in the region.

Makram Khoury-Machool shows why the U.K./U.S. coalition met with disbelief and resistance in the Arab media. How did young people view the war? Two chapters concentrate on the effects of media in the United States and in the United Arab Emirates: Glenn Sparks and Will Miller investigate the emotional effects of U.S. children during time of war, while Muhammed Ayish researches students' attitudes at Sharjah University about the 2003 Iraq War.

Finally, Abdullah Al-Kindi looks at the war against media—and the possible effect on journalists' behavior because of it—the war against media's ultimate goal being to control not only what reporters said about the war, but what their viewers, readers, and surfers thought about the conflict.

Endnotes

1. *Halal* is an Arabic word meaning something is accepted by Islam. The opposite is *haram*, which means religiously forbidden.

2. *Arab Human Development Report 2002: Creating Opportunities for Future Generations.* New York: UNDP, pp. 143, 151.

3. Lord Hutton was commissioned by the British government to look into the July 18, 2003 death of Dr. Kelley. The report, issued in February 2004, took the BBC and its reporter Andrew Gilligan to task while clearing the Blair administration of any wrongdoing. It was widely known that Dr. Kelley was the source of anti-administration leaks doubting Iraq's weapons of mass destruction program (See *Report of the Inquiry into the Circumstances Surrounding the Death of Dr. David Kelly C.M.G. by Lord Hutton.* Available at http://www.the-hutton-inquiry.org.uk/content/report)

PART I

THE PRELUDE TO WAR

CHAPTER 1

Hating America: The Press in Egypt and France

James J. Napoli

"Phooey, not another one," I thought, as I considered the umpteenth research proposal on the general topic of the "Arab image" in the American media. Simultaneously inspired and depressed by exposure to heavyweight tracts on how the American media victimize the Arabs, graduate students at the American University in Cairo seemed to queue up to add their two piastres' worth with more research papers or theses on, well, how the American media victimize the Arabs.

It was hard to imagine even then—and this was long before September 11, 2001—that anything fresh could be said on a topic that hadn't already been well and truly flogged by the likes of Edward Said, Jack Shaheen, Noam Chomsky, Alfred Lilienthal, Richard Curtiss and Paul Findley. It wasn't just the repetitiveness of the topic, or even its seeming insubstantiality (Image, shmimage. What about the real world?) or the retreat into comfortable conspiracy theory that it so often implied.

The real problem was that I was annoyed. I was reading every day in the Egyptian and other Arab press, in English, about how America and Americans were arrogant, godless, religion-less, materialistic, rootless, devoid of moral values, obsessed by money, sex-crazed, superficial, imperialistic, cruel, indifferent to their own families, cold, unsympathetic to the sufferings of others, parochial, narcissistic, ignorant of geography, history, and other cultures, blundering, cowardly, satanic, hypocritical, and conspiratorial with Israel and all of the West against Islam and the Arabs.

And this wasn't just the commentary. Some of these assumptions pervaded even routine news coverage, transforming mundane events like the 1994 UN population conference in Cairo into a springboard for paranoid fantasies about U.S. media plots, no doubt inspired by the Jews, to do the dirt on Egypt. But virtually no students saw the American image, which I saw as a stereotype of Americans as idiot savants (clueless, but inexplicably successful) in the Arab press as an issue deserving research attention. Sure I was annoyed.

Now, of course, the issue of the American image abroad is all the rage, at least among Americans. The U.S. news media have been preoccupied since the horrific events of 9/11 (and continuing through the aftermath of the 2003 war in Iraq) with the question, "Why do they hate us?" Scholarly articles and popular books are being published, such as Jedediah Purdy's *Being America: Liberty, Commerce, and Violence in an American World*, that seek to elucidate how the United States, which generally views itself as the beacon of freedom on earth, could somehow be perceived as "the global villain" nearly every place else (Gewen, 2003).

Pollsters are also beavering away to accumulate evidence that public opinion in much of the world is leaning against the United States. In July 2002, when the Independent Task Force sponsored by the Council on Foreign Relations released its report recommending a higher priority for global "public diplomacy," it cited a range of surveys confirming widespread negative attitudes toward the United States around the world. "The findings of a widely publicized Gallup poll on attitudes in nine Islamic countries, a Zogby International ten-nation poll on impressions of America, State Department foreign attitude and media opinion surveys, and views of many informed observers in and out of government are broadly consistent: America does indeed have a serious image problem" (July 2002). This "image problem" was more intense in the Middle East, but also extended among certain groups in Western Europe, Latin America, Asia, and elsewhere, the evidence revealed.

Before the 2003 Iraq war, the Pew Research Center for the People and the Press released a broad summary of public opinion polls in forty-four countries showing that, even though majorities in most non-Muslim countries still rated the United States positively, negative opinions of the United States had widely increased over the previous two years. The press release for the report leads as follows:

> Despite an initial outpouring of public sympathy for America following the September 11, 2001, terrorist attacks, discontent with the United States has grown around the world over the past two years. Images of the United States have been tarnished in all types of nations: among longtime NATO allies, in developing countries, in Eastern Europe and, most dramatically, in Muslim countries (What the World Thinks in 2002, December 4, 2002, p. 1).

The Pew study identified results in France as "notable" because they showed that, despite widespread French criticism of U.S. policies, America's image in France had not grown more negative over the past two years; in fact, it had grown marginally more positive, though remaining among the lowest in Europe (p. 6).

A follow-up survey Pew conducted after the war in twenty countries and the Palestinian Authority showed that favorable attitudes toward the United States had slipped in nearly every country. As might be expected, disregard for the United States grew in most Muslim countries, where people rallied round their co-religionist and, in most cases, fellow Arab Saddam Hussein (pity about the mass murders and torture). But skepticism about U.S. policies and about President Bush had sharply increased even among solid UN and NATO allies Germany and France, whose governments had been involved in a very public rift with the United States over the war. More than 60% of the Germans and French had a positive view of the United States in the earlier poll, but in the follow-up only 45% of the Germans and 43% of the French were well disposed toward the United States (Marquis, 2003, p. A19). *C'est la guerre*!

It is reasonable to assume, as do many other writers and scholars, that anti-Americanism, however defined in a particular country, is influenced by anti-Americanism in that country's press, since, as Richard Lambert recently wrote, "newspapers and magazines tend to reflect and reinforce the views of their readers" (Lambert, 2003, p. 63). "In today's uneasy political climate," he adds, "skewed media representation further shapes and entrenches negative attitudes." Media representation of the United States is not the same everywhere, however, even in those countries where the anti-Americanism strain is strong. "Hating" America means one thing in France and another thing in Egypt. They arrive at the present from different historical contexts, and the distinctive media systems of a European democracy and a Middle Eastern autocracy may reinforce their anti-American sentiments in different ways.

It should be restated at the outset that not everybody hates the United States; the plaintive question "Why do they hate us?" is, at least in part, mere rhetoric. There are substantial percentages of people sympathetic with the United States in most Western countries who also weigh in against U.S. policies. Further, strong majorities in Italy, Australia, Canada, Great Britain, Spain and other countries remain staunch supporters of the United States in, for example, its fight against terrorism. Even in countries where sentiment is deemed unfavorable to the United States, most people said the problem was "mostly Bush," not "America in general" (Marquis). Majorities almost everywhere were positive toward economic and political ideals associated with the United States; that is, free-market capitalism and, most of all, democracy and representative government. Despite the brouhaha between France and the United States over Iraq, former French President Valéry Giscard d'Estaing, who was serving as president of the constitutional Convention on the Future of Europe that year, was flattered, not offended, at being compared to American founding father Thomas Jefferson. Jefferson authored the Declaration of Independence and supported the U.S. Constitutional Congress as U.S. ambassador to France in 1789, and d'Estaing drafted a constitution for a United Europe. He recalled, "I tried to play a little bit the role that Jefferson played, which was to instill leading ideas into the system" (Sciolino, 2003, p. A6).

So, not everybody hates America and not everybody hates it to the same degree, for the same reasons, or in the same way. A brief examination and comparison of "anti-Americanism" in the print media of Egypt and France may provide some insight into the "anti-American" psychology of both countries, as well as into their press systems. It might suggest some policy directions for those in the U.S. government, among others, who would like to cultivate more pro-American attitudes in the foreign media as the reluctant Imperium consolidates its position.

The Egyptian Press: National Context as Default Mode

Many Americans were disturbed by the lack of unalloyed support for America in the Egyptian press—and, in fact, in most of the Arab press—after the events of September 11. Even at its most moderate, the Egyptian press often expressed its sympathy in the most backhanded way: "Oh yes, it was terrible and all that, but really the United States has been asking for this by its unfair policies toward Palestinians and Muslims in general, and maybe it was all arranged by the Jews to make the Arabs look bad."

An anti-American perspective directed much of the commentary from the government press ("The U.S. and terrorists suffuse a foul atmosphere throughout the world," Ahmad Ragab, *Al Akhbar*, September 25, 2001); the "independent" press ("Millions across the world shouted in joy: America was hit!" Nabil Farouq, *Al-Maydan*, September 24, 2001); and the opposition press ("People derived satisfaction from the insult to American pride," Salah A-Din Salim, *Al-Ahrar*, September 25, 2001).

The Middle East Media Research Institute reported in its Special Dispatch Series, No. 281, "Terror in America," October 4, 2001, p. 12: "The Egyptian Government, Opposition, and Independent Press All Celebrate the Terrorist Attacks on the United States." Many Americans were incensed by the general reaction and wrote hundreds of letters to the government English-language *Al-Ahram Weekly* to say so (MEMRI, Special Dispatch Series - No. 306, November 30, 2001, "Americans respond to the Anti-U.S. Egyptian media.")

In fact, however, anti-Americanism, meaning an aggressive bias not only against specific U.S. policies, but against the very idea of America, didn't suddenly erupt on September 11. It suffused reportage and commentary for decades prior to the attack and continued through the 2003 Iraq War and its aftermath. In a range of issues as varied as the widespread practice of female circumcision, the October 1999 crash of EgyptAir flight 990 out of New York, and the trial of civil society activist Saad Eddin Ibrahim, the rhetoric of the press nearly always found its way to a denunciation of the United States and its alleged co-conspirator, Israel.

In recent years, this predisposition has taken an increasingly religious cast, but even that has a long history carried forward from the 1950s by Islamic leaders such as Hassan al-Banna and Sayyid Qutb, who were genuinely appalled by the secular challenge of America. The strength of the religious motive was compounded by the political. One consequence of the 1952 socialist revolution headed by Col. Gamal Abdul Nasser was a state-controlled press mobilized against Western imperialism and Israeli metastasis on Arab land. Though the political and religious influences on the Egyptian press could be at odds on specific issues, they united in trumpeting anti-Americanism which implied, on one hand, a broad distrust of the West and, on the other, a visceral hatred for Israel.

The anti-American rhetoric might have been moderated if the journalists adhered to agreed-upon international professional standards of objectivity, fairness, attribution, and balance. These standards, loose and imperfect though they are, do impose a kind of discipline on journalists who try to comply with them. This has not generally included those working in a state-controlled press. Most Egyptian journalists stick more closely to their religious, political, or personal loyalties than to professional principles, and it shows.

A number of studies, including those by Lamey (1992), Matar (1991) and Hagag (1993), were published after the 1991 Gulf War and criticized the lack of professional standards among Egyptian journalists. Critics honed in on their lack of objectivity, lack of reporting skills, failure to provide adequate background information, and heavy reliance on secondary sources. Others (Mayer and Brooks, 1991) recounted how Saddam Hussein campaigned before the war to win over the Arab press, including Egypt's, with thinly disguised bribes in the form of financing for supportive publications and writers and with new Mercedes-Benzes for select journalists.

With no professional standards to uphold, Egyptian journalists revert to a narrow national context, which provides a tightly focused prism of ideological and religious bias for guidance. Spared the necessity to maintain any distance on events they cover, or to provide for inclusiveness in news and commentary, or even to distinguish between the two, journalists characteristically indulge in the familiar rhetoric of anti-American grievance and defiance.

This doesn't mean that news media in other countries don't also have national contexts that affect coverage. The fact that they do was nowhere more obvious than in the extent of chauvinism in U.S. coverage by American cable news networks (especially, but not only, by Fox News) of the September 11 attacks and subsequent wars in Afghanistan and Iraq. In the end, however, news organizations and journalists that wish to claim professionalism for the sake of their own credibility as a competitive news source are under continuous pressure to provide a measure of balance and fairness. And for the most part, they did and they do.

The experience of the Qatari-based Al-Jazeera television news network is illuminating in this regard. Although it was expected to take a strong pro-Arab position on the news from Afghanistan, Iraq, Israel, and the Palestinian Authority, Al-Jazeera journalists publicly committed themselves to airing every point of view and wound up pleasing neither the Americans nor the Arabs—at least not all of them, all of the time. Its use of multiple sources and its allowing representatives from the United States and even Israel to have their say (even while retaining its orientation to its Arab audience) constitute a revolutionary influence on the tightly controlled Arab news media.

El-Nawawy and Iskandar in their book on Al-Jazeera (2002) call the network's approach on the news "contextual objectivity." The standard is that "the medium should reflect all sides of any story while retaining the values, beliefs, and sentiments of the target audience" (p. 27). Such a standard, if applied in the Egyptian press, would require a significant widening of its comfortable context, which now verges on the solipsistic. It makes hatred of "the Other" too easy.

THE FRENCH PRESS: *L'OBSESSION ANTI-AMÉRICAINE*

As in Egypt, anti-Americanism has a long history in French society and the French press. It dates at least from the late nineteenth century when the power of the new Anglo-Saxons across the Atlantic began to be evident. From writers like Charles Maoris, founder of the royalist *L'Action Françaises*, the stereotype of the United States as the purveyor of ruthless capitalism began to take shape. And to Maoris, too, goes the credit for linking Americans and Jews as a menace to European civilization (Mead, March/April 2003, p. 141), just in time for Vichy.

Anti-Americanism also was a staple of the leftist press after World War II, although its antipathy may have stemmed as much from resentment of the global success of American culture as from U.S. political, economic, and military hegemony (see Revel, 1972, p.139).

After the initial expressions of sympathy for the victims of the September 11 attacks were out of the way, it didn't take long for many French intellectuals to resume their wonted position as critics of the United States. Of special interest was Thierry Masan, whose book *L'Effroyable Imposture* (The Horrifying Fraud) makes the bizarre assertion that American Airlines Flight 77 never existed and that the American military blew up the Pentagon themselves to advance the cause of Big Oil. The book was on the French bestseller list for twelve weeks (Fraser, September 2002, p. 59). Another French intellectual, the philosopher Jean Baudrillard, argued that the horror of dying in the World Trade towers was inseparable from the horror of working in them, suggesting that the victims and West got what they secretly wished for (Menard, September 16, 2002, p. 101). In short, the primary significance of the murder of nearly 3,000 people was its use as a metaphor for self-hating capitalism.

Almost a year after September 11, in late August 2002, the moderate Paris daily *Le Monde* ran a roundup of prominent books published in France about the United States since 9/11. Perhaps the most interesting of the lot was an unsympathetic examination of the prevailing French and European attitudes toward the United States, *L'Obsession Anti-Américaine,* by Jean-Francois Revel. Most famous for his 1972 essay on American cultural and economic vitality, "Without Marx or Jesus," in his latest work Revel examined what he considers Europeans' irrational resentment of the United States.

Others on the list took equally strong positions either defending or attacking the United States and its global role (R.P.D., August 30, 2002, p. viii). *Le Monde* itself, perhaps the most influential newspaper in France, was generally sympathetic with the United States in the months after 9/11. Its director, Jean-Marie Colombani, was even quoted as saying that anti-Americanism had become "irrelevant" because all developed countries now faced a common enemy: terrorism. Nevertheless, by May 2002 the paper was again denouncing Americans as "arrogant, bellicose, and deaf to all criticism" and rejecting a new era of U.S. "messianism" (Blocker, Radio Free Europe/Radio Liberty, May 27, 2002).

But, unlike in the Egyptian press, anti-Americanism is not particularly obtrusive in the French press. France and the United States may differ sharply over Iraq, and, as public opinion polls show, the French public may be increasingly critical of the United States, but the French press seems to remain relatively even-handed toward the world's superpower.

To assess French newspaper attitudes toward the United States this writer conducted a content analysis of *Le Monde*, an elite newspaper whose circulation is heaviest in Paris, and *Ouest-France*, the largest circulation daily in the country, distributed in seventeen editions in Brittany, Normandy, and the Loire country. A sample of newspapers from the last two weeks of August 2002 were examined for articles that were exclusively or primarily about the United States to try to determine an attitude or bias.

In general, any negative comments about the United States in *Le Monde* were embedded in specific assessments of American politics, particularly its foreign policy and wartime behavior in Afghanistan. There were no sweeping denunciations of U.S. "imperialism" or "hegemony" or supposed cultural traits such as violence or racism. Although these and other negative attributes were occasionally mentioned, in none of the articles was there any evidence of broad negative stereotyping of Americans as a people, as distinct from their government. There was plenty of evidence of disagreement with American policies, but none of "hatred" directed either against the American public or the U.S. government.

The positive comments tended to gather around examples of American higher culture, particularly its music, art, film, and literature. Although the French allegedly "hate" American global culture (represented by McDonald's and Disney World), coverage of American culture in its finer manifestations by *Le Monde* was decidedly appreciative.

As one might expect of a provincial daily with less commitment to covering the international or even the national scene, *Ouest-France* was far less occupied by the United States than *Le Monde*. Most of the articles tended to be news stories rather than analyses or opinions. As in *Le Monde*, none of the articles was seemingly designed to promote negative stereotypes of the United States or of Americans. For the most part, negative comments about the United States as a nation were presented as specific responses to the policies or actions of the U.S. leadership, usually by others quoted in the news stories. There was little or no evidence that *Ouest-France* was deliberately cultivating "hatred" of America or Americans. And when it came to American culture, particularly in the form of American film, the United States was treated favorably by the newspaper (Napoli, 2003).

The commentary could, in fact, be quite thoughtful about the quandary facing the rest of the world because of America's preeminent position, as well as the need to avoid badgering and blaming the United States for everything that goes wrong in the world. Karim Dahou ("Developement durable et stabilité internationale," August 28, 2002, p.13) starts out in *Le Monde*, for example, decrying the "various fantasies" ("*diverses fantasmagories*") of Arab and other opinions that try to saddle the United States with responsibility for the 9/11 terrorist attacks. He then argues that Europe, for the sake of international stability, should play a role in America's maturation. Europe, he says, needs to make a greater effort to help the United States appreciate the implications of its own power and the need to avoid unilateral action in the world community.

In short, if the United States and Americans suffer an "image" problem in France, it does not appear to be a function of any reflexive anti-Americanism in the French press. Indeed, a limited study of French television newscasts conducted by American students in France under the tutelage of Robert M. McKenzie showed little daily coverage of news about the United States at all.

At the same time, the students perceived sentiment among the French themselves that Americans are "well-off, spoiled, selfish, bold, aggressive, uncultured, and pushy." America itself, they found, was typically described as a "spoiled materialistic bully" (McKenzie, 1999, p. 125). McKenzie posits that negative images of the United States are not primarily derived from French, but from American, media. In particular, American rock songs, television programs, and movies seem to be the most important envoys of the negative images of violence and greed in America. To those sources must be added other Idols of Invidious American Materialism and Superficiality, such as the Disney theme park outside Paris and the McDonald's restaurants targeted for attack by French anti-globalization activists.

The relative lack of anti-American rhetoric in the French press may, ironically, be a consequence of the Americanization of French journalism. The aggressively ideological, discursive, and literary tradition of the French press has been eroding under the pressure of the more telegraphic style of Anglo-American journalism, particularly as practiced by international news agencies such as the Associated Press and Reuters, since the late nineteenth century. A corollary of the agencies' "breaking news" approach is a set of news writing conventions, including objectivity and balance, that has largely been adopted by contemporary French newspapers. Whereas some politically engaged newspapers of an earlier era might have provided a podium for anti-American tirades, they would be considered journalistically unprofessional by most newspapers today.

Vive la Différence!

Clearly, a comparison of anti-Americanism in the Egyptian and French press argues for the efficacy of professionalized journalism. By "professionalized" is meant the incorporation of standards of objectivity, fairness, balance, attribution, and so forth, recognizable in news provided by major international news agencies which have long propagated them globally. The fact that these standards have never taken firm hold in the Egyptian press may be ascribed, in part, to the retarding effect of state media control.

Generations of journalists have come to positions of leadership in the press with the assumption that national policy, not some abstract professional ethic, should determine how the news should be treated. Further, the anti-American sentiment so strongly expressed in the Egyptian press is also reflective of growing religious fervor which strikes a similar tone of injury and victimization.

In France, which also has a history of anti-Americanism, the press is far less strident and far more "professional." It is, in effect, able to remove itself from the fray and to more effectively objectify the world. Its journalism evolved relatively independent of the government, making it easier for practitioners to identify with the profession as widely practiced elsewhere—and to keep themselves and their views out of their stories. In a freer atmosphere, proponents of anti-Americanism, or any other position, are likely over time to generate their own opposition. And however disagreeable that may be to the journalists, the opposition finds its way into their stories *de rigueur*.

Of course, even a fully professionalized free press is no proof against the tendency to unfairly generalize about other nations and people. As Lambert has pointed out of mutual American-European misunderstandings, the "emphasis on trivia and stereotypes, a feature of reporting on both sides of the Atlantic, reinforces the general sense that the two continents have little in common and are drifting further apart" (p. 72). More contextualized news reports that eschew stereotypes for substance would improve any newspaper. The broader news definitions required, however, are a stronger prospect in an independent than in a state-controlled press.

One other thing: image isn't everything. Criticizing the United States for its policies, including a policy of going to war in Iraq despite the best advice of many U.S. allies, cannot be simply written off as "anti-Americanism." To do so would be to stifle legitimate public debate by employing the old propaganda technique of bundling all political opposition in a dialog-resistant wrapping.

Merely by virtue of being the world's sole superpower, the United States is going to draw much of the world's attention, mistrust, and criticism. That doesn't mean the rest of the world "hates" the United States, or that Americans are justified in posing pathetically as innocent victims of "bad image." Every country has a lot at stake when the United States makes a wager and every country has a right to vigorously express opposition in its press. Sometimes, surely, the United States deserves to be opposed.

References

Americans respond to the anti-U.S. Egyptian media (2001, November 30). Washington, DC: Middle East Media Research Institute. Special Dispatch Series - No. 306. Retrieved online, April 3, 2003, from MEMRI Web site, www.memri.org.

Blocker, J. (2002, May 27). France/U.S.: Bush visit unlikely to lessen French anti-Americanism. Radio Free Europe/Radio Liberty. Retrieved online, July 31, 2002, from Radio Free Europe/Radio Liberty, Inc. Web site, www.rferl.org.

Dahou, K (2002, August 28). *Developpement durable et stabilité internationale. Le Monde*, p. 13 .

El-Nawawy, M. and Iskandar, A. (2002). *Al-Jazeera.* Cambridge, MA: Westview Press.

Fraser, N. (2002, September). *Le divorce. Harper's,* pp. 58-65.

Gewen, B. (2003, March 30). The global villain (Review of *Being America*). *The New York Times Book Review*, p. 7.

Hagag, M. (1991, July-September). The manipulation of Egyptian media in the Gulf crisis. Studies in Mass Communication, *The Arab Institute for Mass Communication Studies, 64,* 108-115.

Lamey, D. (1992). Hot or cool coverage of Iraq. In R.E. Weisenborn (Ed.), *Media in the Midst of War*, pp. 27-31. Cairo: Adham Center Press.

Lambert, R. (2003, March/April). Misunderstanding each other. *Foreign Affairs, 82*(2), 62-74.

Marquis, C. (2003, June 3). World's view of U.S. sours after Iraq war, poll finds. *The New York Times,* p. A19 .

Matar, G. (1991, July-September). The Egyptian media during the Gulf crisis. Studies in Mass Communication, *The Arab Institute for Mass Communication Studies, 46,* 44-57.

Mayer, J. & Brooks, G.(1991, February 15). How Saddam Hussein courted Mid-east press with cars and cash. *The Wall Street Journal*, pp. A1, A6.

McKenzie, R. M. (1999). Images of the U.S. as perceived by U.S. students in France. In Y.R. Kamalipour (Ed.), *Images of the U.S. around the world: A multicultural perspective*, pp. 115-133. Albany: State University of New York Press.

Mead, W.R. (2003, March/April). Why do they hate us? *Foreign Affairs, 82*(2), 139-142.

Menard, L. (2002, September 16). Faith, hope, and clarity. *The New Yorker*, pp. 98-104.

Napoli, J. (2003, February). The anti-American obsession? French press attitudes toward the United States. Paper presented to the 12th annual Intercultural Communication Conference, Coral Gables, Fla.

Public diplomacy: a strategy for reform, independent task force report (2002, July). Washington, DC: Council on Foreign Relations. Retrieved online, July 31, 2002, from Council on Foreign Relations Web site, www.cfr.org.

Purdy, J. (2003). *Being America.* New York: Alfred A. Knopf.

Revel, J-F. (1972). *Without Marx or Jesus.* New York: Dell.

R.P.D. (2002, August 30). *Amérique en débat. Le Monde*, p. viii.

Sciolino, E. (2003, June 15). United Europe's Jefferson? Giscard d'Estaing smiles. *The New York Times,* p. A6.

Terror in America (12): The Egyptian government, opposition, and independent press all celebrate the terrorist attacks on the United States (2001, October 4). Washington, DC: Middle East Media Research Institute. Special Dispatch Series - No. 281. Retrieved online, April 3, 2003, from MEMRI Web site, www.memri.org.

What the World Thinks in 2002 (2002, December 4). Washington, DC: Pew Research Center. Retrieved online, February 3, 2003, from Pew Research Center Web site, www.people-press.org.

CHAPTER 2

Global Village Disconnected?

George Albert Gladney

Global media coverage of the 2003 Iraq War provides an unusual opportunity to examine one of the more provocative concepts given to the world by the late medium theorist Marshall McLuhan. The "oracle of the Electric Age" had famously prognosticated that the new electronic communication technology, particularly television, would transform the world into a "global village."

This chapter examines the nature of global news coverage of the 2003 Iraq War within the context of global village, asking the question: Was the Iraq War a global village event or something quite different? While premature for a final assessment, the evidence seems to suggest that McLuhan's most famous thesis might be seriously, if not fatally, flawed.

"Global Village" Concept

Before examining coverage of the war within the context of global village, it is necessary to understand what "global village" meant to McLuhan, because the concept is much more than just a clever paradox.

McLuhan was a professor of English literature at the University of Toronto, but his interest had been diverted to the study of pop culture and mass communication. In two important early works, *The Gutenberg Galaxy* (1962) and *Understanding Media* (1964), McLuhan explained (although McLuhan never really explained anything, preferring instead to tease his readers with partially completed thoughts, or "probes") some concepts that stimulated the public imagination. Most notable was his perplexing but profound statement, "The medium is the message."

But his metaphor of "global village," further explicated in later works such as *Counterblast* (1969) and the co-authored *War and Peace in the Global Village* (1968) and (posthumously) *The Global Village* (1989), was easier for most people to grasp.

The concept had broad and instant appeal. It made sense to people that transoceanic TV broadcasts made possible by the launch of new telecommunication satellites were ushering in an era in which all humans would be exposed to the same mass-mediated content at the same instant. Time and space—zapped! Humankind was now bound in electric simulation of global consciousness.

In McLuhan's day, transoceanic satellite transmission of TV news coverage of the Kennedy assassination and funeral served as the revelatory demonstration of the global village. Today, the village is best demonstrated by World Cup soccer, with audiences so vast that no one can truly comprehend their size. Nobody really knows, but it is likely that the 2003 Iraq War drew an even larger world audience.

Guided seminally by his tutor and colleague, University of Toronto scholar Harold Innis (1950, 1951), McLuhan became absorbed with the notion that different communication technology (media) have different technological biases; i.e., they exhibit propensities to be used in particular ways with particular effects. Chief among these propensities is to alter social arrangements so as to centralize or decentralize administration of human affairs, or to create "de-tribalizing" or "re-tribalizing" influences on humankind.

The pre-literate or old—primarily oral—tradition (adhesion to the small tribal unit) was characterized by simultaneously shared experience/participation of all members of the tribe, wholeness, homogeneity, intimacy, cultural stability, inclusiveness, empathy, deep integral awareness, and non-linearity of thought and experience. McLuhan thought of this as living in an auditory or "acoustic" environment dominated by the unifying sense of hearing.

The invention of writing (especially the Greek phonetic alphabet) began a radical shift from acoustic space to visual space—transforming spoken words, which exist only in the living present, to visual objects (words on paper). Writing also fostered individualism by enabling individuals to break away from the tribe and it made possible the building of empires; i.e., civil and military rule over vast distances.

Moreover, the printing press accelerated these changes, particularly the rise of individualism (detachment, non-involvement). Print encouraged fragmentation of knowledge and the rise of specialists, and it created uniform and centralizing conditions necessary for political consolidation and the creation of modern nation-states (nationalism).

With the invention of the first electric communication technology—the telegraph—in the 1830s, it appeared that now it might be possible to re-tribalize humankind into, well, a global village. In fact, the medium's inventor, Samuel F.

B. Morse, provided a workable definition when he observed that his invention would make "one neighborhood of the whole country" (Czitrom, 1982, p. 12).

Once people grasped the marvel of the telegraph, there was much utopian rhetoric—talk of how the telegraph would spawn a blissful era of global peace, harmony, unity, communion, understanding, democratization, and egalitarianism. As it turned out, commercial interests rapidly commandeered the technology, and the telegraph business was an oligopoly by the 1870s; as a result, ordinary people were never equipped with sending or receiving sets. Same story with radio, except ordinary people got receiving sets that enabled them to be on the dumb end of a one-way, one-to-many communication dominated by powerful elites.

But, for McLuhan (1968), "the new total field sensibility" of radio provided an important impetus for the global village because it "inspired ... a multiplicity of new images, depriving the country of a simple visual-mindedness" (1968, p. 134). Television merely added pictures to radio, but the critical difference for TV—in terms of the global village—was the launch of telecom satellites and especially multiple satellites in geosynchronous orbit. Suddenly, with TV, the same content could reach all corners of the globe simultaneously, virtually at the speed of light.

For McLuhan, this moment in history was powerfully prophetic because it meant that, once and for all, the broken promise of the telegraph would be fulfilled. With TV, McLuhan thought, all of humankind would be connected as never before. We would all return to the era of the pre-alphabetic tribe, except this time we would gather around the glow and flicker of the cathode-ray tube instead of the aboriginal campfire.

Although McLuhan was writing at a time when the computer was still incipient, he discerned its vast potential as a global extension of our nervous system, observing that the computer "makes natural and necessary a dialogue among cultures which is as intimate as private speech, yet dispensing entirely with speech" (1968, p. 90). Some of his observations seem to eerily presage the Internet and World Wide Web. Like TV, the computer will "[alter] every phase of the American vision and identity," he said (p. 134).

McLuhan's prophecies express optimism and hope, but at the same time he warned that the coming changes caused by the new conditions of the global village would cause turmoil and chaos. He explained that as everyone becomes involved in the affairs of all others (integral inclusiveness) or part of a simultaneous field of human affairs, the self-image of individuals and whole cultures and societies becomes threatened, inviting a mandate for war.

BIFURCATED GLOBAL PERCEPTIONS OF THE IRAQ WAR

Roughly four decades after popularization of the global village concept, the world witnessed the second U.S.-British invasion of Iraq in ten years. Few events have so greatly attracted the world's attention. If the global village concept holds, one would expect that everyone, everywhere would receive essentially the same mass-mediated facts, or portrayal of reality, about the war.

However, this was not the case. To observers of war coverage by both U.S.-British media and media from the Arabic-speaking world, one thing was clear: There was an almost complete disconnect between the two media spheres. As James Poniewozik (2003, April 7, pp. 68-69) points out, it is not unusual "for two camps to see the same war differently," but the Iraq war gave new meaning to "one-sided" coverage for it meant audiences tuned in to preferred versions of reality (p. 68).

Let's now examine how media watchers sized up world media coverage of the war in terms of diversity or sameness of content. Many media watchers during and shortly after the war agreed it was as if the two media spheres were reporting about different wars on different planets.

Poniewozik, a *Time* staff writer, wrote in the magazine's April 7, 2003, issue (p. 68):

> In this war, the mighty but merciful allies target bombs carefully and tend to the enemy's wounded. In that war, the allies blow up women and babies. In this war, Iraq is postponing certain defeat by cheating, killing civilians and using human shields. In that war, a weak nation is steadfastly defending itself using the only effective means available. This war, on American television, is alternately "the war in Iraq" or "Operation Iraqi Freedom." That war, broadcast by the media of the Arab and Muslim worlds, is "the invasion."

Similarly, Delinda C. Hanley wrote in the May 2003 issue of the *Washington Report on Middle East Affairs* (p. 6):

> There are two wars going on in Iraq. One is a gripping made-for-TV show starring brave U.S. and British troops putting their lives on the line to bring freedom to oppressed Iraqis. Little blood is spilled on camera. Soldiers pass food out to starving Iraqi civilians and prisoners. Homesick and on edge, these idealistic servicemen and women remain confident that they will soon win this just war and return to their families.
>
> "Collateral damage," sandstorms, flies, fierce resistance and doubt have not yet worn down [the] gallant troops. This war, featuring their hometown heroes, is the one Americans watch on network and cable TV every night, and read about, complete with moving photos, with their morning coffee.
> The other war is waged by Iraqis desperate to protect their homes and their ancient land against U.S. and British invaders. Bombed buildings, smoke and chaos are the backdrops for this war. Its stars are wounded and screaming Iraqi women and children, captured or terrified Iraqi—and yes, U.S. and British—soldiers. Iraqis' pain is immortalized by the Arab and European press ... ."

Hanley added, "Unlike U.S.-based news stations, Al-Jazeera shows its thirty-five million viewers across the Arab world intensely terrifying scenes of war" (p. 6). Writing in the April 14, 2003 edition of *Newsweek,* Tom Maslund and Christopher Dickey told of an American woman who visited her three-year-old nephew who lives in Lebanon, only to be greeted "with horror." The nephew had "caught a glimpse of footage from Iraq, aired on an Arab TV network, of the headless body of an Iraqi child killed by a Coalition bomb gone astray. 'Don't go back to America,' Khalid urged his favorite aunt. 'They're killing children'" (p. 49). The writers then made the broader point that:

> [T]he war Americans see on their television screens is wholly different from what's shown elsewhere. U.S. programming concentrates on victory. Arab and Muslim TV focuses on victims. Children feature prominently: grisly images of the dead and dying and maimed. Such is the bitterness evoked by this war that even benign acts of charity are tainted. ... While the American public may believe—and share—the administration's hope that this invasion will lead to a more stable and democratic regime, the young and the old, the poor and the rich, the educated and the illiterate of the Muslim world are united in disbelief.

For further evidence of bifurcated news coverage emanating from two distinct media spheres during the Iraq War, consider the following: According to Al-Rashid (2003), much of what was reported from Baghdad by Arab networks, including Al-Jazeera, came from the Iraqi Information Ministry. To wit:

> The result: Even though we were told [by the Ministry] about the drama of (U.S.) jets being shot down over Baghdad, we didn't seem to hear any Arab reporters wondering out loud: "Where are these planes that you are boasting about having shot down?" At the same time, the Western television networks were poking fun at the story and revealed it as an obvious fabrication. (p. 23)

An American living in Canada wrote:

> If [Americans] saw what the Canadian press has been showing—dead and bloodied Iraqi civilians, terrified American POWs, angry European and Arab protesters—they'd likely be appalled. But they don't see much of that stuff. News reports from the States, whether from the rah-rah patriots at Fox News or the seemingly objective staff of *The New York Times*, have been disturbingly partisan in their coverage, protecting Americans from some of the harsher truths about this war. (Considine, 2003, p. 56)

The American Journalism Review observed that with the Iraq war American journalism entered a new era in which:

> it no longer has unquestioned dominance in the global information marketplace.

> During the war in Iraq, television news operations in Arab countries provided viewers throughout the world with an alternative view of the conflict. (Sharkey, 2003a, p. 19)

The magazine quoted Fawaz Gerges, a professor of Middle Eastern studies at Sarah Lawrence College, as saying, "Arabs and Muslims are getting a dramatically different narrative from their American counterparts." The U.S. networks have focused "on the technologically advanced nature of the American military armada. The Arab and Muslim press tend to focus on the destruction and suffering visited on Iraq by this military armada" (p. 19).

According to *U.S. News & World Report,* in Western journalists' dispatches from Iraq "the holy city of Najaf was reported jubilant. It was like the 'liberation of Paris,' an American officer said of the throngs gathered around their liberators" (Ajami, 2003, p. 38). And yet *Time* reported that an overwhelming majority of Arabs it surveyed in Amman and Cairo said that only a fool would believe that the U.S. goal was to liberate Iraqis from tyranny.

Instead, the magazine reported, those Arabs believe that America is "fighting a war of conquest and occupation. For the most part, the war depicted in Arab media is one of subjugation and suffering for Iraqis" (MacLeod, 2003, p. 47). *U.S. News & World Report* added: "A contrived sympathy for the Iraqi people suddenly crowds the airwaves and the printed media of Arab lands" (Ajami, 2003, p. 38).

At one point in the war, Iraqi TV released a videotape showing dead U.S. soldiers in a building. U.S. networks, which had access to the tape through Al-Jazeera, declined to show it, citing issues of "taste and viewers' sensitivities" (Sharkey, 2003a, p. 22). Al-Jazeera defended its broadcast of the tape, saying TV "would be deceiving its audience" if it were to "censor any of the information that actually makes people aware of all aspects" of the conflict (p. 23).

Poniewozik (2003, April 7)) observed that while American TV showed U.S. and British administration and military briefings (talking heads), sound bytes from George W. Bush and Tony Blair, allied advances on the battlefield, interviews with Coalition troops and POWs' families, Al-Jazeera showed some of those things as well, but added blood, mourning, "charred bodies lying beside gutted cars" (p. 69). For Al-Jazeera's viewers:

> cameras linger over dead allied soldiers and bandaged Iraqi children. Mourning families wail, and hospitals choke with bleeding and burned civilians. If the war on American TV has been a splendid fireworks display and tank parade punctuated by press conferences, on Al-Jazeera ... war is hell. (p. 69)

Massing (2003) reported that the U.S. military was unhappy with Al-Jazeera because, unlike U.S. media, it highlighted:

> antiwar demonstrations, the resistance inside Iraq, and angry statements from scholars and clerics. Above all, it was airing footage of civilian casualties. Over and over, it showed hospital wards overflowing with the victims of the fighting: children without limbs, women lying unconscious, men covered with burns. Such images were stoking passions in the Middle East. (p. 37)

Not surprisingly, these anecdotes show that media—whether from the West or from the Middle East—are mindful of political and cultural considerations and play to the emotions and biases of their audience. As Poniewozik (2003, April 7) observed:

> Arab media observers see some slant in the Arab networks' language and image choices, but they also see bias in Western TV, with its reliance on Administration and military talking heads and flag-waving features like MSNBC's pandering 'America's Bravest' wall of G.I. photos. Arab networks play to their audience too, which in their case means skepticism of allied claims, lots of tear jerking, and talking heads who doubt American motives and prowess. (p. 69)

He added that:

> straight news on the Arab networks in many ways [offered] viewers a more complete and inside look at the war than U.S. TV ... . They (were) given greater access by Baghdad, which sees them—as it saw CNN in 1991—as a conduit to the outside world. (p. 69)

These anecdotes suggest two media spheres, each portraying a different reality—one for Arabic-speaking audiences and the other for Western (primarily American-British) audiences. But that is to oversimplify the situation. Even within a country such as the United States, Great Britain, or any one of the Arab-Islamic nations, it is possible for audiences to shop around for media offering particular slants on reality, if not different realities altogether.

Sharkey (2003b) quotes media critic Tom Rosenstiel as saying that the Arabic-language TV networks help U.S. journalists understand the "Rashomon quality of news"—"the phenomenon of different people witnessing the same event and coming away with widely varying interpretations" (p. 26). This phenomenon affected individuals, but also news organizations collectively.

Chasan (2003) asserts that an individual's reaction to visual images of the toppling of the statue of Saddam Hussein in Baghdad's central Fardus Square during the war's third week depended on the individual's allegiance or perspective or bias. For some (i.e., Bush-Blair supporters) it was a moment for jubilation; for others (i.e., people in most Arab capitals) it was an anxious, bitter, humiliating moment.

At the collective level, readers of most large U.S. metropolitan daily newspapers were much more likely to get a positive sense of U.S. military and diplomatic progress than readers of *The New York Times,* whose editorial misgivings (collective) about the conflict were well known. Similarly, TV viewers supporting Bush got upbeat reports of the war's progress on two cable news networks in particular, Fox and MSNBC, both of which used patriotism to lure viewers and enjoyed huge ratings increases during the conflict (Poniewozik, 203, April 14; Sharkey, 2003a). Other U.S. networks "allied themselves with the U.S. forces to some degree," but CBS and ABC executives said "overt displays of patriotism were not appropriate for their newscasts" (Sharkey, 2003a, p. 25).

While most Americans relied on major newspapers and cable networks, satellite dish owners seeking alternative war coverage (such as Arab-Americans, many of whom resented the partiality of U.S. media) were able to watch BBC, Al-Jazeera, and American pacifist stations Free Speech TV and WorldLink TV (Chayet, 2003). If U.S. viewers watched carefully, they could find some Arab perspective on TV. C-SPAN, for example, presented newscasts from stations in the Middle East and Canada. CNN offered a segment called "Arab Voices," a summary of what the Arab media were saying. NBC offered viewers a segment called "Listening Post," which covered international reaction to the war (Sharkey, 2003a).

In Great Britain, according to Abdalla (2003), London's sizable Arab population was in a much better position than Arab-Americans to bypass or counteract what the Saudi government labeled "the allies' propaganda machine" (p. 19). Eighty-seven percent of Arab homes in Britain have access to the Arab satellite and cable networks of Al-Jazeera, Abu Dhabi, and Al-Arabiya Television.

The Arab community in Britain also relies on five London-based, Arab-language daily newspapers. The editor of one of these papers, *Al-Quds al Arabi* (circulation 500,000), is convinced of the importance of newspapers that address the Arab community exclusively. "Arab newspapers are for Arabs, English newspapers are for English people," he said (p. 19). Ajami (2003) asserts that these Arab-language newspapers portrayed the Coalition as "rampaging crusaders bent on dispossessing Iraqis of their oil wealth" (p. 38). Not surprisingly, newspapers in Arab capitals were targeted for the same sort of criticism (Al-Rashid, 2003; Ajami, 2003).

For readers of English dailies in Britain, there was a clear choice of pro-war media and anti-war media. For example, Glover (2003) observed: "After 14 Iraqis had been killed in the first marketplace bomb, the [*Daily*] *Mirror* carried a front-page picture of a laughing George W. Bush with the headline 'He Loves It.' Alone among British newspapers, the *Sun* reported that the unloading of aid from the ship *Sir Galahad* was 'greeted by ecstatic Iraqis.' Readers of these two newspapers are following an entirely different war" (p. 35).

Of course, one must acknowledge that obtaining truth in accounts of war—regardless of the source—is problematic. Much war information is likely to come from government and military sources that, for strategic purposes, systematically distribute disinformation and propaganda. Stephen Franklin (2003), writing in *CJR*, noted that during the Iraq war, Arab television "too often blindly swallowed the words of the Iraqi Information Minister," but he said a broader concern is that the Arab press produces "a make-believe news product put out by intimidated journalists and propagandists stuck on timeworn delusions... It was not made to inform; it was made to fend off information from the outside" (p. 60). Similar charges of propaganda are made against Western governments and media (Miller, 2004).

Global Village Disconnected?

The evidence suggests bifurcated global perceptions of the Iraq war—the existence of dual media spheres that gave people the world over their choice of which reality to have confirmed as they searched for news of the Iraq war. Based on that evidence, it seems reasonable to doubt the continued relevance or application of the global village metaphor—at least for now. Does this mean oracle McLuhan got it wrong?

Looking at the past four decades, one finds evidence both supporting and detracting from McLuhan's prophecy of a global village. As Croteau and Hoynes (2003) point out, implicit in the notion of a global village is the idea that everyone (people in wealthy Western nations and poor, developing nations) can "get a hearing" in the international media (p. 366).

If that's the case, clearly, hordes of humanity are excluded today from the global village and the metaphor fails. To prove that so, Croteau and Hoynes cite the failure in the late 1970s and 1980s of the effort by poorer nations to create a "new world information and communication order," which was promoted by UNESCO (United Nations Educational, Scientific, and Cultural Organization). This movement aimed to alter information production and distribution by curtailing Western domination of the international flow of information (media products) and helping create and support media infrastructure in poorer nations. In short, Third World countries resented media domination (i.e., cultural imperialism) by wealthy Western nations; they wanted to be heard in the international media.

However, Croteau and Hoynes concede that the threat of cultural imperialism by Western media is subsiding as the popularity of U.S. programming in developing nations has declined and large media firms pursue a strategy of localization and tailoring of content to particular countries/cultures.

The global village concept seemed to hold up during the Gulf War of 1991. Back then, as Poniewozik (2003, April 7) points out, "Western, Arab and Muslim audiences used their rooting interests to filter the same source: American TV" (p. 68). But something happened between 1991 and 2003 that changed everything, bifurcating the global village—causing the disconnect between news coverage by Western media and news coverage by Arabic-Islamic media. The difference, explained Nabil El-Sharif, editor of Jordan's *Ad-Dustour* newspaper, is that Arabs saw the 1991 Gulf War through the eyes of CNN, but with the 2003 war, "Now we're seeing the war through Arab eyes" (p. 68).

The Arab-Islamic world also saw the 9/11 destruction of the World Trade Center through Arab eyes, and global coverage of the investigation of that disaster provides the first real compelling evidence of the great disconnect or bifurcation of global media. The evidence came in early 2002 when the Gallup polling organization reported the first-ever opinion poll covering a wide range of Muslim countries. It was based on in-home interviews with ten thousand people in nine countries: Indonesia, Iran, Jordan, Kuwait, Lebanon, Morocco, Pakistan, Saudi Arabia, and Turkey. A key question: "Do you believe news reports that Arabs carried out the September 11 attacks?" The governments of Jordan, Morocco, and Saudi Arabia would not permit that question to be asked.

In the remaining countries, results showed that 18% said Arabs were responsible for the attacks and 61% did not (Whitaker, 2002). What evidence, from what source, led to that belief? The disconnect becomes obvious when one realizes that virtually any American is certain that most (fifteen out of nineteen) of the 9/11 attackers were Saudi (Arab) nationals. What evidence, from what source, led to that belief? We must ask the same question as we examine the disconnect—the break-up of village, the huge split in public perceptions of fact—evidenced by the Iraq war.

World reaction to the U.S. military's capture of Saddam Hussein in December 2003 provides an interesting counterpoint to this disconnect. For one, unlike news of the 9/11 attack, news of the U.S. announcement of Hussein's capture was not reported by some Arab TV stations (Bauder, 2003; "Saddam dominates," 2003). Syria's regime-controlled media, for example, virtually ignored the news (Mixed Reactions, 2003). So much for the global village for those audiences.

Elsewhere in parts of the Middle East, some people simply did not believe the news of Hussein's capture, but the disbelief quickly evaporated (LaBelle, 2003; "Saddam Capture," 2003). That's because news of Hussein's capture was accompanied by the endless replay of powerful video images of a bedraggled, dejected Hussein being checked for lice.

The post-9/11 investigation, on the other hand, had no compelling visuals to persuade or dissuade. As Neil Postman (1985) observed, photographic images present the world as object ("a real slice of space-time") and are therefore essentially irrefutable, whereas language presents the world as idea, inviting propositions, arguments, refutations (pp. 72-77).

In sum, news of Hussein's capture was a discrete event grounded in irrefutable images, while the news of who was responsible for the WTC attack involves assertions, opaque and amorphous, grounded in words. Images of the Hussein capture led to worldwide consensus that, in fact, he had been captured. Lacking pictures for evidence, and relying exclusively on words, the world remains divided about who carried out the WTC attacks. It depends on which proposition (reality) you want to believe and who you want to believe.

As we try to figure if and where McLuhan went wrong, we must consider that in McLuhan's day, transoceanic or global TV transmission was limited largely to content generated by Western nations, especially the United States and Great Britain. Apparently taking Western media domination for granted, McLuhan, it appears, did not foresee the crucial media developments occurring just a few years prior to the Iraq war. He did not foresee the establishment in 1996 of Al-Jazeera, a free and independent (uncensored) TV news operation, based in Qatar and funded by that country's liberal government, that reaches forty-five million people (Sharkey, 2003b) in Arab nations and millions of people outside the Arab sphere. Nor did McLuhan envision the existence today of four other pan-Arab news networks (e.g., Abu Dhabi and Al-Arabiya Television) or two Egyptian satellites to carry them.

In short, McLuhan did not consider that, given time, it might be possible that news of a major world event might be broadcast not just by the Western networks ABC, NBC, CBS, and the BBC, but also by new news operations that are part of the "500-channel" and "1,000-channel" future, or from new global networks emanating from alien cultures.

This chapter has confined its analysis to traditional news media—ignoring the fact that the Internet was used to disseminate a vast array of images and messages related to the Iraq War, which is covered elsewhere in this book. This author argues that the global village concept does not fit the Internet and never will (unless commercial interests succeed in their effort to transform the Net from a many-to-many communication medium to a broadcast-model, one-to-many medium). The Internet had been greeted in its early pioneering days with the old utopian rhetoric, but much of that talk has quieted since the rapid spread of commercial domains beginning in the mid-1990s.

Furthermore, this author argues that if the Internet has a technological bias, it is to counter global homogenization by expanding and accelerating fragmentation and de-tribalizing tendencies in today's global culture. It does that by creating countless virtual (online) communities that have little or no community-to-community interaction. For the most part, online communication is between and among people with like-minded interests and ideas—hardly the sort of medium to foster global understanding, peace, harmony, unity, etc.

In the final analysis, we must not be too harsh or rigid in our assessment of McLuhan's prophecy of global village. Today, in the wake of the 2003 Iraq war, and looking at the whole post-Soviet era—with the United States as the sole and unchallenged superpower—the prophecy seems empty. It is hard to imagine an era of greater global chaos, unrest, and division since World War II. Yet perhaps this is what McLuhan expected, remembering his warning that when self-images (cultural values) are threatened, the result is a mandate for war. Bruce R. Powers, who co-authored *The Global Village,* published almost a decade after McLuhan's death in 1980, wrote in the Preface:

> Electric flow has brought differing societies into abrasive contact on a global level, occasioning frequent worldwide value collisions and cultural irritation of an arcing nature, so that, for instance, when a hostage is taken in Beirut an entire nation on the other side of the world is put at risk. McLuhan said, "In the last half of the 20th century the East will rush Westward and the West will embrace orientalism, all in a desperate attempt to cope with each other, to avoid violence. But the key to peace is to understand both systems." (p. x)

That observation clearly brings to mind the current state of world affairs with respect to the World Trade Center attack and the Iraq war.

When looking at effects of new communication technology, perhaps the longer view is required. After all, even today, TV has barely reached adolescence. McLuhan did not promise that the full effects of global village would transpire overnight. While many experts predict that current tensions between the West and Middle East will take many decades to settle, what will become of the world once those tensions are finally settled?

Maybe we need to let things develop much longer, perhaps over many centuries, before assessing the prophecy of a global village. It took that long for the full effects of writing and the printing press to take hold, and perhaps TV and the Internet will take as long.

References

Abdalla, M. (2003, April 7). Here is the news ... for British Muslims. *Newstatesman*, p. 19.

Ajami, F. (2003, April 14). Through Arab eyes, blindly. *U.S. News & World Report*, p. 38.

Al-Rashid, A.A. (2003, June). The biased truth of Arab media. *World Press Review*, pp. 22-23.

Bauder, D. (2003, December 15). Good news spreads quickly on TV. Associated Press. Retrieved December 15, 2003, from http://www.theledger.com

Chasan, A. (2003, June). No. 2, with a bullet. *World Press Review*, p. 3.

Chayet, S. (2003, June). Eye on the United States: The uneasiness of Arab-Americans. *World Press Review*, pp. 44-45.

Considine, J.D. (2003, April 7). An American in Canada. *Maclean's*, p. 56.

Croteau, D., & Hoynes, W. (2003). *Media/society.* Thousand Oaks, CA: Pine Forge Press.

Czitrom, D.J. (1982). *Media and the American mind: From Morse to McLuhan.* Chapel Hill: University of North Carolina Press.

Franklin, S. (2003, September/October). Fear of waking up. *Columbia Journalism Review*, p. 60.

Glover, S. (2003, April 5). Nobody really knows how the war is going, partly because our governments lie. *The Spectator*, p. 35.

Hanley, D.C. (2003, May). Two wars in Iraq: One for U.S. audiences, the other for the Arabic-speaking world. *The Washington Report on Middle East Affairs*, p. 6.

Innis, H.A. (1950). *Empire and communication*. Oxford: Oxford University Press.

Innis, H.A. (1951. *The bias of communication*. Toronto: University of Toronto Press.

LaBelle, G.G. (2003, December 15). Many Arabs greet news of Saddam's capture with disbelief. Associated Press. Retrieved Dec. 15, 2003, from www.napanews.com

MacLeod, S. (2003, April 21). Arab reaction: Coping with jubilation. *Time*, p. 47.

Maslund, T., & Dickey, C. (2003, April 14). The rage next time. *Newsweek*, p. 49.

Massing, M. (2003, May/June). The bombing of Al-Jazeera. *Columbia Journalism Review*, p. 37.

McLuhan, M. (1962). *The Gutenberg galaxy*. Toronto: University of Toronto Press.

McLuhan, M. (1964). *Understanding media*. New York: McGraw-Hill.

McLuhan, M. (1969). *Counterblast*. New York: Harcourt, Brace & World.

McLuhan, M., & Fiore, Q. (1968). *War and peace in the global village*. New York: Bantam Books.

McLuhan, M, & Powers, B.R. (1989). *The global village*. New York: Oxford University Press.

Miller, D. (Ed.). (2004). *Tell me lies: Propaganda and media distortion in the attack on Iraq*. Herndon, VA: Pluto Press.

Mixed reactions in the Middle East: From skepticism to relief to joy, opinions abound. (2003, December 15). SFGate.com. Retrieved December 15, 2003 from http://sfgate.com

Poniewozik, J. (2003, April 7). What you see vs. what they see. *Time*, pp. 68-69.

Poniewozik, J. (2003, April 14). Whose flag is bigger? *Time*, p. 71.

Postman, N. (1985). *Amusing ourselves to death*. New York: Penguin Books.

Saddam capture reverberates around Arab world. (2003, December 14). BBC News. Retrieved December 15, 2003, from http://news.bbc.co.uk

Saddam dominates world's media. (December 15, 2003). Irelandon-line. Retrieved December 15, 2003, from http://breakingnews.iol.ie

Sharkey, J.E. (2003a, May). The television war. *American Journalism Review*, pp. 18-27.

Sharkey, J.E. (2003b, May). The rise of Arab TV. *American Journalism Review*, pp. 26-27.

Whitaker, B. (2002, March 4). Polls apart. *Guardian Unlimited*. Retrieved May 15, 2003, from www.guardian.co.uk/elsewhere/journalist/story/0,7792,661807,00.html

CHAPTER 3

The Framing of the "Axis of Evil"

Jinbong Choi

Since his inauguration as the 43rd President of the United States, George W. Bush has included the simulative rhetorical phrase "axis of evil" in many of his public speeches. He introduced the phrase in his 2002 State of the Union Address and applied it to three countries: Iran, Iraq, and North Korea. In particular, Mr. Bush used the phrase to help justify the war on Iraq as well as the so-called "war on terror."

After the collapse of the Iraqi government in spring 2003, the other two "axis of evil" countries (Iran and North Korea) have felt threatened by possible preemptive U.S. attacks. Scott Lasensky, a Mideast expert at the New York-based Council on Foreign Relations, termed the fall of the Iraqi government a "wake-up call" to the other two "axis of evil" countries (Ross, April 15, 2002). And it had some effect.

North Korea decided to participate in multilateral discussions with the United States and China concerning its nuclear program. Korea previously had preferred meeting only with the United States, from whom it could have sought concessions. Also, "Iran's former president, long allied with Islamic hardliners against the 'Great Satan' America, is advocating a referendum on renewing ties with the United States" (Ross, 2002).

By framing and naming Iran, Iraq, and North Korea as an "axis of evil," Bush's January 2002 speech functioned to motivate his audience to fear threats against world peace in order to justify expanding the war on terrorism. Through using framing analysis, this study (analysis) will explore what the rhetorical function of the framing and naming of the "axis of evil" is, and to what extent this "axis of evil" framing is reasonable. Specifically, this paper first describes the concept of the terms "evil" and "axis" and then evaluates how Bush uses the naming and framing of "axis of evil."

THE CONCEPT OF FRAMING

Bateson (1972) and Clair (1993) use the "picture example" to explain framing. Photographers must make conscious choices of what to include in a picture. Only a small part of any event or activity is selected as the context of the photograph. The photographer in effect "frames" the photograph and what remains is his or her vision of reality (shaped, of course, by news, values, routines, and organizational constraints).

People who see the finished product might be unaware of the context of the photograph and what was excluded from the photographer's "vision" but will ascribe their own meaning to the picture. The way it is framed offers strong cues that influence their understanding of the photo (especially when people do not have enough information and background about the picture).

Bateson says frames delimit "a class or set of messages (or meaningful actions)" (1972, p.186). "People perceive and evaluate social interactions" in framed messages (Clair, 1993, p.117). In other words, "the frame is involved in the evaluation of the message…as such the frame is metacommunicative" (Bateson, 1972, p.188).

This visual analogy can be extended beyond concrete images to the way a speaker chooses objects to frame in a speech or to weave abstract images into a comprehensible narrative of a speech. Sociologist Erving Goffman (1974) explains that when individuals encounter particular events, they tend to respond through a particular framework, or schemata, of interpretation that is primary to them. "A primary framework is one that is seen as rendering what would otherwise be a meaningless aspect of the scene into something that is meaningful," and that "each primary framework allows its user to locate, perceive, identify, and label a seemingly infinite number of concrete occurrences defined in its terms" (Goffman, 1974, p.21).

Mass communication scholar Robert Entman says to frame is to select some aspects of a perceived reality and make them more salient in a communicating text in such a way as to promote a particular problem definition, causal interpretation, moral evaluation, and/or treatment recommendation for the item described (Entman, 1993, p.52). Entman theorizes that frames are found in four places in the communication process: communicators, the text, receivers, and the culture. Of these, communicators and the text are the most important components for this analysis. In other words, through the use of special and sensational names and frames to describe objects, a communicator (or rhetor) can create fragmentary and distorted images of the objects to provide a communicator's stereotyped images of the objects that guide the audience to a communicator's judgment about the objects.

In addition, Snow & Benford (1992) define a frame as: "an interpretive schemata that simplifies and condenses the 'world out there' by selectively punctuating and encoding objects, situations, events, experiences, and sequences of actions within one's present or past environment" (p. 137). Thus, a frame gives people a standard for how to understand and identify objects. They also argue that frames render objects and occurrences meaningful (Snow, Rochford Jr., Worden, & Benford, 1986). In other words, the concept of framing is developed on "the metaphor of the frame, a structure for containing a representation. As a communication concept, framing is essentially an act of interpretation, a strategy whereby communicators represent ideas and events in an appealing and meaningful way" (Trasciatti, 2003, p. 409).

Kirk Hallahan (1999, p. 224) suggests that people use framing strategies in their speeches to make good public relations. Hallahan argues that framing is essential to public relations. In developing programs or speeches, public relations professionals fundamentally operate as frame strategists, who determine how situations, attributes, choices, actions, issues, and responsibility should be posed to achieve favorable outcomes for clients or audiences. Framing decisions are perhaps the most important strategic choices made in a public relations effort. Out of strategic framing, public relations communicators develop specific themes (i.e., key messages or arguments that might be considered by the public in discussions of topics of mutual concern).

Zhongdang Pan and Gerald M. Kosicki (1993, pp. 59-63) focus on five structural framing devices: syntactical structure, script structure, thematic structure, rhetorical structure, and lexical devices. Two of these—rhetorical structure and lexical devices—are appropriate for this analysis. Pan and Kosicki argue that rhetorical structure refers to particular choices communicators make. This category includes metaphors, catch phrases, depictions, and naming, which can all be used to evoke images and increase the salience or intensity of a particular characteristic. Also, lexical devices refer to word choices or labels (naming) that communicators (speakers) use to frame certain objects (pp. 59-63).

Moreover, Gamson (1989) argues that a frame is the essence of a large unit of public discourse, which is a "package." In terms of his explanation, the package has an internal structure with the frame as a central organizing idea (Gamson & Modigliani, 1989, p. 3). The package works for constructing meaning and incorporating an object or social event into a rhetor's frames (Gamson & Modigliani, 1989). For Gamson, framing is the primary meaning-making activity in public speech (discourse), in which active agents with specific purposes are engaged constantly in a process of providing meaning (Gamson, 1992). Gamson explains that:

> [f]acts have no intrinsic meaning. They take on their meaning by being embedded in a frame or story line that organizes them and gives them coherence, selecting certain ones to emphasize while ignoring others. (1989, p. 157)

As a result, framing and naming are powerful strategies to create special and unique images (negative or positive) of objects for communicators or rhetors. Using a framing strategy, a communicator chooses only one particular image of an object or creates a special image of an object that influences audience understanding of the object. In framing, rhetors adapt different kinds of strategies such as metaphors, catch phrases, keywords, and stereotyped images to evoke special images or particular characteristics of an object.

The Problems of the Concepts of "Axis" and "Evil"

After the September 11 attacks, "evil" has been used by Mr. Bush as a most intensive and prevailing word to describe the targets of his war on terror: non-democratic and dictatorial regimes, terrorists, and organizations allegedly related to the planning and execution of the 9/11 attack. In his 2002 State of the Union Address, Mr. Bush declared the targets of his war on terror as follows: "the United States of America will not permit the world's most dangerous regimes to threaten us with the world's most destructive weapons." Further, he described the world's most dangerous regimes as Iran, Iraq, and North Korea. Yet there are some problems in describing these three countries as "evil."

First, Mr. Bush labeled Iran, Iraq, and North Korea "evil" countries because they have "regimes that sponsor terror from threatening America" (the 2002 State of the Union Address). However, it is hard to find any evidence that Iran and North Korea were linked to the September 11 attack, and the evidence is weak that Iraq was linked to al-Qaeda, who claimed responsibility for 9/11 and other international acts of terrorism. Without inculpatory evidence, Mr. Bush's designation of these countries as "evil" is problematic. Without incontrovertible proof, his idea of "evil" countries comes from his own private schema or deeply held personal beliefs, thereby making his concept of "evil" countries less persuasive for those who do not share his schema.

Second, in his 2002 State of the Union Address, Mr. Bush claimed these three "evil" countries were developing weapons of mass destruction. He named Iran, Iraq, and North Korea as part of an "axis of evil" because they are "arming with missiles and weapons of mass destruction" (the 2002 State of the Union Address). It is irrational to designate a country as an "evil" country just because that country develops WMDs. If that were the case, the United States is an "evil" country—not because its military corporate complex is the most powerful and sophisticated weapons industry in the world, but because it is the only nation ever to have used an atomic bomb (the quintessential WMD) against humans—twice—without distinguishing soldiers from civilians.

Thus, to claim a country is "evil," Mr. Bush needed to prove that Iraq had used WMDs before and would do it again. He pointed to the alleged poison gassing of Kurds in Halabja in 1988 ("Saddam used weapons against his own people") as evidence. If Saddam Hussein had used WMDs on his own people, Bush argued, the Iraqi leader would have no compunction about using them against his neighbors, Israel, or even the United States. But what of the other members of the "axis of evil?" Bush hardly verified that the other "evil" countries have plans to use WMDs, or even that they were developing them.

Even Iraq's "proven" WMD program was in doubt. Although UN inspections (which were suspended in both 1998 and 2003) operated in Iraq to find weapons of mass destruction, the inspection team could not find any, although they did find very small pilot facilities for continuing research. What the U.S. government did have as a common link to the axis were "stories" that Iraq and Iran both had biological and chemical weapons programs and were, like Korea, developing nuclear weapons capabilities. The main fear was that, unlike Iraq and Iran, Korea had developed a missile delivery system it was willing to sell to anyone with hard currency, such as "petro-dollars."

On the other hand, if the threat of WMD proliferation only is considered, India and Pakistan are two of the most dangerous countries in the world because they possess nuclear weapons, WMD programs, and delivery systems capable of reaching each other's capitals. However, Mr. Bush did not put these two countries on his "evil" country list. Both are U.S. allies, albeit shaky ones, and one is the world's largest democracy. Further, in his 2003 State of the Union Address, Mr. Bush insisted that Iran, Iraq, and North Korea are "evil" because they developed biological, chemical, and nuclear weapons. If the development of those weapons was the standard for categorizing the "axis of evil" countries, then "why is it limited to only these three countries when, according to the Department of Defense, the extant and emerging threats to the United States, friends, and allies encompasses twelve nations with nuclear weapons programs, thirteen nations with biological weapons, sixteen nations with chemical weapons, and twenty-eight nations with ballistic missiles?" (Pena, 2002, p. 5).

Third, through using the concept of "evil," Mr. Bush tried to attain the moral high ground that would justify using military action to defeat "evil" countries. In other words, the administration's war on terror was to destroy "evil." "'Evil' is too heavy and radioactive a word; you cannot make a deal with evil, but only kill it" (quoted in Reynolds, January 21, 2003). In short, by using the word "evil," Mr. Bush made it clear that he would not negotiate with "evil" countries. Further, by using the word "evil," Mr. Bush made it easy to see "why the country ([the U.S.]) needs to attack Iraq" (quoted in Reynolds, January 21, 2003). Mr. Bush emphasized that "evil is real, and it must be opposed" (the 2002 State of the Union Address). The ill-defined war on terror then would become a "just war."

Mr. Bush likes to:

> imagine that he can pin down evil in places like Iran, Iraq, and North Korea. He believes that he can contain it there, and destroy it by sending all the weapons at his command hurtling down out of the sky. … In his plan, he will just throw bombs at the problems there in 'evil' land [(countries)], killing as many people as it takes to exorcise the spirit of 'evil.' (*Irregulartimes*, February 22, 2003)

By naming and framing Iran, Iraq, and North Korea as "evil" countries, Mr. Bush used these "evil" countries as targets to justify and continue his war on terrorism. In short, Mr. Bush has failed to describe why and how he chose the term "evil" to designate these three countries instead of other terms, but in advocacy framing, evidence often is not included in the picture one wants to paint.

On the other hand, consider the second concept of an "axis." *The American Heritage Dictionary* defines the term "axis" as meaning partnership or alliance of powers, such as nations, to promote mutual interests and policies. Mr. Bush designated Iran, Iraq, and North Korea as an "axis" because they are "terrorist allies" by saying, "states like these and their terrorist allies constitute an axis of evil" (the 2003 State of the Union Address). However, he has not provided any evidence that those three countries are terrorist allies—he's only offered that possibility in his speech. In short, in spite of the fact that Iran, Iraq, and North Korea have no alliance or conspiracy with one another, Mr. Bush provided a possible military engagement of these countries. For instance, North Korea "remains locked in the grip of an anachronistic communistic dictatorship and, far from colluding with other nations, may instead be the most isolated country in the world" (quoted in Reynolds, January 21, 2003).

Thus, in Mr. Bush's rhetoric, through framing these three "evil" countries as an "axis," the president emphasized that danger is increased significantly and intensively due to an alliance and combination of these "evil" countries although there is no evidence that they are allied as an "axis." Klare (2002) points out that:

> there is absolutely no indication that the three states (Iran, Iraq, and North Korea) in question have conspired together to fight the United States or to cooperate militarily. Indeed, President Bush reportedly was obliged to eliminate language from his speech suggesting such ties because U.S. intelligence agencies were unable to find any proof of a connection.

Although the three "evil" countries should have been treated differently because they have different political and economic situations and different networks of international relations, Mr. Bush categorized them as an "axis," which implied that they posed similar dangers, enhanced by their association. In other words, by framing the three countries as part of an "axis," Mr. Bush tried to raise fears about increased threats to world peace and security to emphasize the necessity of his war on terror without providing any evidence connecting these three countries.

For a sizable population in the world, the word "axis" is evocative of the common threat posed by Nazi Germany, Fascist Italy, and Imperial Japan over half a century ago, a potent historical frame. Even though a White House spokesperson explained that "the President did not mean such a comparison and that the expression was 'more rhetorical than historical'" (Sanger, 2002), Mr. Bush invoked the concept of the "axis powers" of Germany, Italy, and Japan to reflect this negative image to the concept of "axis of evil." Furthermore:

> "simply by uttering the phrase 'axis of evil'—so suggestive of the 'axis powers (Germany, Italy, and Japan)' of World War II—seemed to put the United States on a higher level of war preparation" (Klare, 2002).

In addition, Mr. Bush seemed to have adapted former President Ronald Reagan's "evil empire" rhetoric to rally Americans in a perpetual war against terrorism and the "axis of evil." Just before the end of the Cold War, "Ronald Reagan used the Cold War to lambaste the 'evil empire' of the Soviet Union. Their administrations are strikingly similar not only in their use of adjectives, but also their desires to increase defense spending because of unseen if not illusory enemies" (Turnipseed, 2002).

The Function of the "Axis of Evil" Framing

Through "axis of evil" framing, Mr. Bush warned that Iran, Iraq, and North Korea "constitute[d] an axis of evil, arming to threaten the peace of the world" and that "by seeking weapons of mass destruction, these regimes pose a grave and growing danger." Mr. Bush, again, provided no evidence linking the "axis" to al-Qaeda or Osama Bin Laden. Thus, Mr. Bush's concept of the "axis of evil" was neither persuasive nor logical because he designated Iran, Iraq, and North Korea as an "axis of evil" without evidence. He tried to justify the war on terror and to reduce public opposition to the war by raising the specter of an "axis of evil."

In short, after September 11, President Bush used "evil" as a metaphor to justify his war on terror. To justify his war, Mr. Bush needed an enemy (he used the word *enemy* four times in his 2002 State of the Union Address), one it was necessary to destroy; in creating this enemy, Mr. Bush utilized the *evil* metaphor for three countries: Iran, Iraq, and North Korea. Through framing and naming the three countries as an "axis of evil," Mr. Bush was shaping reality and was persuading a particular perspective on these three countries to his audience.

Furthermore, Mr. Bush's "evil" metaphor became more powerful due to the news media. According to Jeffrey Tulis (1987), because of the news media, Presidential speeches are more frequently available to people today than in any other time in history. Tulis calls this phenomenon the "rhetorical presidency," and argues that media have facilitated the development of the rhetorical presidency "by giving the president the means to communicate directly and instantaneously to a large national audience and by reinforcing ... verbal dramatic performance" (Tulis, 1987, pp. 133-135). Therefore, people's understanding of the political world depends on the president's framing, naming, or description of objects. That is, political issues "are not objective, independent entities, but linguistic constructions" (Bostdorff, 1994, p. 4).

In short, the news media presented Mr. Bush's framing of an "axis of evil" so that audience members would understand that it encompassed three countries: Iran, Iraq, and North Korea. By naming and framing these three countries as the "axis of evil," Mr. Bush not only denounced them, but also announced to the world that he would treat these three countries in a similar fashion. However:

> while Bush could not realistically do this, he found it domestically and internationally desirable to keep using the term, as a way of proving to his country ..., and to the world that the U.S. was now willing to make maximum use of the threat of its power to stamp out terrorism. The unintended consequences have proved considerable" (Saikal, 2003).

Finally, the concept of "axis of evil" was used broadly by President Bush. When Mr. Bush originated the "axis of evil" concept in his State of the Union Address, he seemingly used it only to raise the level of fear over terrorism. Over time, however, he has extended the boundaries of the "axis of evil" concept to other foreign and domestic agendas to achieve his purposes and goals.

Conclusion

In summary, framing analysis was used to study the text of President Bush's 2002 State of the Union Address. In conducting this study, three main questions were asked: for what purpose did Mr. Bush frame Iran, Iraq, and North Korea as an "axis of evil;" what kinds of problems did the concept of "axis of evil" have; and how did the framing of the "axis of evil" work?

After the September 11 attack, President Bush stated clearly in a number of public speeches that "he would love nothing more than to spend the rest of his four-year term ... identifying 'evil-doers' and sending his armies after them with guns blazing and bombs bursting" (*Irregulartimes*, February 22, 2003). The 2002 State of the Union Address is where Mr. Bush stated the goal of his first presidential term.

Through the State of the Union Address, Mr. Bush motivated audiences to fear a threat so that he could gain public support and justify his war on terror.

Because Mr. Bush lacked hard evidence about the "axis of evil" frame, it was ultimately nothing more than an appeal to fear.

References

Bateson, G. (1972). *Steps to an ecology of the mind.* New York: Ballantine.

Bostdorff, D. M. (1994). *The Presidency and the Rhetoric of Foreign Crisis.* Columbia: University of South Carolina Press.

Clair, R. P. (1993, June). The use of framing devices to sequester organizational narratives: Hegemony and harassment. *Communication Monographs*, *60*, June.

Entman, R. (1993). Framing: Toward clarification of a fractured paradigm. *Journal of Communication*, *43*(4).

Gamson, W. A. (1992). *Talking Politics.* New York: Cambridge University Press.

Gamson, W. A. (1989). News as framing: Comments on Graber. *American Behavioral Scientist*, *33*(2), 157-161.Gamson, W. A. & Modigliani, A. (1989). Media Discourse and Public Opinion on Nuclear Power: A Constructionists Approach. *American Journal of Sociology*, *95* (July), 1-37.

Goffman, I. (1974). *Frame analysis: An essay on the organization of experience.* Cambridge: Harvard University Press.

Hallahan, K. (1999). Seven models of framing: Implications for public relations. *Journal of Public Relations Research*, *11*(3).

Irregulartimes (2003, February 22). What is the axis of evil? Retrieved July 18, 2003, from http://irregulartimes.com/axisanagram.html

Klare, M. T. (2002, January 31). Axis of evil crumbles under scrutiny. *Pacific News Service.*

Pan, Z. & Kosicki, G. M. (1993). Framing analysis: An approach to news discourse. *Political Communication*, *10.*

Pena, C. V. (2002). Axis of evil: Threat or chimera? *Mediterranean Quarterly*, *13*(3), Summer.

Reynolds, M. (2003, January 21). Axis of evil rhetoric said to heighten dangers. *Los Angeles Times.*

Ross, S. (2002, April 15). Other axis of evil nations take note of U.S. actions. *Associated Press Worldstream.*

Sager, D. E. (2002, January 31). Bush aides say tough tone put foes on notice. *The New York Times.*

Saikal, A. (2003). Axis of evil is definitely on the turn. In http://www.smh.com.au/articles/2003/01/04/1042520613450.html

Snow, D. A. and Benford, R. (1992). Master Frames and Cycles of Protest." In A. D. Morris & C. M. Mueller (Eds.), *Frontiers in Social Movement Theory* (pp. 133-155). New Haven: Yale University Press.

Snow, D. A., Rochford Jr., E. B., Worden, S. K., & Benford, R. D. (1986). Frame Alignment Processes, Micromobilization, and Movement Participation. *American Sociological Review*, *51*, 464-481.

The American Heritage Dictionary of the English Language (4th ed.). In http://www.dictionary.com/search?q=axis

Trasciatti, M. A. (2003). Framing the Sacco-Vanzetti Executions in the Italian American Press. *Critical Studies in Media Communication*, *20*(4), 407-430.

Tulis, J. K. (1987). *The Rhetorical Presidency.* Princeton: Princeton University Press.

Turnipseed, T. (2002). Bush mimics Regan and the corporate stranglehold on U.S. media tighten. In http://www.counterpunch.org/turnipmimic.html

CHAPTER 4

African Perspectives on Events Before the 2003 Iraq War

Emmanuel C. Alozie

This essay explores how sub-Sahara mass media covered the major events leading to the Anglo-American War—from September 12, 2002, when President Bush launched his campaign to dislodge Saddam Hussein, to March 19, 2003 when he announced the onset of the war. It is often implied that the philosophical, moral, and political perspectives prevailing in that country and region color news media coverage of foreign affairs. As Han Morgenthau (1957) suggests, "All the news that's fit to print," means one thing for *The New York Times*, another for *Pravda,* and yet another for the *Hindustani Times.*

Drawing from literature on international news discourse with emphasis on framing, propaganda, globalization, and social adaptation, this study will employ critical textual analysis to discern how the sub-Sahara African press constructed the events leading to the Anglo-American War. The goal is to determine if there is congruence between the position taken by African news organizations and the consensus among African leaders and the public to seek a peaceful solution.

Two major questions will guide this study: 1) What are the dominant themes and framework in African news discourse? and 2) Did the coverage reinforce the call for a peaceful solution to the crisis?

The analysis will focus on four leading news outlets from three countries: South Africa, Nigeria, and Kenya. South Africa and Nigeria were chosen because they are dominant countries in sub-Sahara Africa, while Kenya was selected because it has suffered from terrorism in recent years and publishes a regional weekly. The three countries also contain significant Muslim and Christian populations, as well as other faiths. It has always been argued that in countries where people profess different faiths (Christianity, Islam, and other traditional beliefs), the mass media play a large role in promoting understanding on national and international issues, especially in cases where there may be religious connotations, such as the 2003 Gulf War.

Review of Literature

Rusciano's (1992) study of media perspectives in editorials in *The New York Times* and *The Times of India* during the 1990-1991 Gulf War supports Morgenthau's assertion that news media coverage of events is colored by national interest and opinion.

The study found that *The New York Times* repeatedly referred to international reactions and determined that world opinion favored the American position on the invasion and the resulting demonization of Saddam Hussein. *The Times of India*, representing a resource-developing nation, offered a greater variety of voices regarding the crisis. The Indian newspaper mentioned other world leaders and Iraqi public opinion in its attempts to define world opinion. Its reactions were then ambivalent regarding the degree of consensus among nations.

Chrisco (1994) conducted an interpretative study to explore the pre-war editorial reactions of six Middle East newspapers during the seven-month Gulf crisis. The study was aimed at better understanding how national newspapers in the conflicted region presented and explained issues surrounding the Gulf crisis in order to discern what stance they took. The newspapers examined included the *Arab News* of Saudi Arabia and the *United Arab Emirate News,* which represented the Gulf Sheikdom. Chrisco found that both papers professed Arab unity, monarchy, and the world community's defense of small Arab nations. (It should be noted the papers in the Gulf States might have taken this stance because they felt Iraq threatened them.)

The *Jordan Times* and *Syria Times* shared the Arab-unity themes and saw Iraq's invasion of Kuwait as an inter-Arab problem. President Saddam Hussein was not demonized, denoting Arabic values of unity and brotherhood. Both papers frequently cited the Israeli territorial aggression and occupation of Arab land. They called for solutions based on economic emancipation of the region, urged Arab unity, and often returned to the issue of Israeli territorial aggression. By linking the Iraq invasion to Arab territories, the Syrian and Jordanian press took a stance on the Gulf crisis based on their internal policies and interests. Despite a frosty relationship between the Iraqi and Syrian leaders, the Syrian newspaper did not demonize Hussein. Syria joined the alliance during the 1991 Gulf War but did not support the 2003 war.

The non-Arab *Kayhan International of Iran* based its approach on Islamic unity and saw Hussein as a victim of U.S. aggression. Iran sought the role of mediator in 1991, despite the bitter eight-year war between the two Gulf states that had ended only a few years earlier. Values centered on Islam, Middle East autonomy, and economic alliances.

On the other hand, the *Jerusalem Post* viewed Israel as the victim of Arabs, as misunderstood by the world community, and as one whose primary overriding values were based on the right of the Jewish state to exist. The newspaper demonized and relied heavily upon the Hussein-as-Hitler theme. Like the Jordan and Syrian press, national interests colored the editorial stance of Iranian and Israeli newspapers.

Chrisco's findings illustrate the complexity of world opinion, while the perspectives held in the conflict zone differed, as Rusciano (1992) found. During the 2002-2003 crisis, the American public was split between those favoring immediate military action and those who supported giving diplomacy and sanctions adequate time to work.

However, some studies have been critical of the U.S. press for failing to reflect the complex perspectives that existed in the United States. That failure in 1990-1991, critics charge, denied the American public balanced information to reach its own decisions on a crisis that led to a war in which thousands of people lost their lives and which caused extensive environmental and property destruction (Lee & Devitt, 1994; Chomsky, 1992).

However, an analysis of the news coverage of the 1990-1991 Gulf crisis in nine prestigious American newspapers differed (Fico, Ku, & Soffin, 1994). Newspapers examined in the study produced a higher number of stories favoring anti-war advocates in their inside pages, while their front pages tended to be more balanced.

Propaganda, Globalization & Social Adaptation: A Nexus

Nohrstedt and Ottosen (2000) contend that international discourse, as in the Gulf crisis, can be studied and understood through an integrative perspective in which propaganda influences on the media are explored in connection to the role of news media for public opinion-building and the globalization of international relations and events.

In most societies, the mass media operate as a public forum where the values and vision of a society are conveyed to its members as civic responsibilities and social realities. To portray and convey these values and realities to a community, the mass media rely on news and related discourses (Park, 1995;

Shoemaker & Reese, 1996). As a product, news discourse allows consumers to receive, consume, perceive, and think about issues and events. News assists the public understanding and establishing an opinion about international and domestic issues and events (Entman, 1991 & 1993; Jensen, 1987; Gamson, Croteau, Hoynes & Sasson, 1992).

Turning to the framing of events leading to the Gulf crisis of 2002-2003, it could be argued that news media frames contributed to the nexus that existed among propaganda, social adaptation, and globalization in its discourse. Propaganda is a "conscious and systematic symbolic activity aimed at creating and reproducing emotional and cognitive support from the target groups for a certain goal" (Nohrstedt & Ottosen, 2000, p. 21). To persuade a community, propaganda uses symbols, emotional appeal, and cognitive content.

Addressing the UN Security Council in February 2003, Secretary of State Colin Powell used these devices when he sought a second resolution to legitimize inevitable military action in Iraq. He produced a vial containing a small amount of white powder as a symbol of biological weapons of mass destruction. His strident pronouncement to the world community urging force, if necessary, to oust the Iraqi Ba'athist regime because it posed a danger to the United States and the world evoked emotion. Playing the taped voices of Iraqi officials allegedly discussing how to hide weapons of mass destruction provided cognitive content.

Mr. Powell's presentation represents a "deliberate and systematic attempt to shape perceptions, manipulate cognitions and behavior to achieve a response that furthers the desired intent of the propagandist" (Jowett & O'Donnell, 1992, p. 4, cited in Nohrstedt & Ottosen, 2000, p. 24). Known as "purpose models of propaganda," developed by Jowett & O'Donnell, the model consists of three elements of implementation. These include:

- Systematic approach with its strict goal orientation—Iraq must be disarmed by any means necessary;
- Exploitation of highly emotional values—protecting the United States and allies from weapons of mass destruction; and
- Frequent and paramount exploitation supplanted with combinations of threat and support as the United States and its allies kept threatening over months.

During the 2002-2003 Gulf crisis, the Bush administration was trying to convince Americans and the international community of its position on Iraq. Those on opposing sides of the issue employed propaganda to achieve their aim, but the degree of their success is difficult to ascertain (Severin & Tankard, 1997).

When relying on news as narrative to deliver information to the public—as in the case of the Anglo-American-Iraq crisis, which involved a global audience—news media organizations provided context and reason. The news media also employed mythical references and metaphors in their text to reciprocate and support each other's arguments and lessons (Nohrstedt & Ottosen, 2000; Bird & Dardenne, 1988; Jensen, 1987; Entman, 1991). It could be argued that the American and sub-Sahara African press similarly used these approaches to support their respective positions on the 2002-2003 Gulf crisis.

Like the earlier 1990-1991Gulf crisis, the extent and manner in which a nation's foreign and security policies are enacted affect an increasingly seamless world. Globalization concerns the ever-increasing complex social connections and interconnections among states worldwide in a manner that makes events, issues, and problems in one part of the world trigger major ramifications for individuals and communities thousand of miles apart (Giddens, 1990, 1991).

Proponents assumed at its inception that globalization would enhance homogeneity, unification, and harmony of states and societies—leading to political and economic order and harmony (Uche, 1997; Nohrstedt & Ottosen, 2000). These premises have not materialized. The world has witnessed growing civilizational, societal, ethnic, regional, and, indeed, individual self-consciousness producing an era of disorder (Robertson, 1992). The divisions that occurred in the former Yugoslavia and disagreements on political and socioeconomic directions taken in the world during the past fifteen years demonstrate the negative impact of globalization (CNN.com, 2001). Globalization enhances the ability of communities in distant places to learn about others through instantaneous delivery of the news, but it has not necessarily promoted understanding and harmony (Robertson, 1992; Nohrstedt & Ottosen, 2000).

The growing expression of differences on a variety of national and international issues raises questions regarding how people learn to adapt to propaganda and the prevailing public opinion of a community in the information age. It also raises questions about the effectiveness of propaganda in both national and global contexts, as exemplified by the failure of globalization to produce the homogeneity, unification, and harmony its proponents promised (Robertson, 1992; Nohrstedt & Ottosen, 2000).

It is essential to observe that there is a mutual dependence, or mutual exploitation, between state and media as a point of departure for analyzing the role of mass media in events leading to the 2002-2003 Gulf crisis. This dependence is a result of the media's reliance on government officials as news sources and newsmakers, and on the ability of the media to build public opinion through edification, conceptualizing, and promoting a view to the public, who rely on them for crystallization and adopting an opinion (Herman & Chomsky, 1988; Nohrstedt & Ottosen, 2000).

Nohrstedt and Ottosen (2000, p. 23) contend that news content helps individuals form an opinion. However, a person may be compelled to change his or her opinion if a large number of community members adopt a contrasting opinion. They describe this form of public opinion evolution as "social adaptation theory of public opinion-building." They argue that news discourse as a vehicle for "propaganda cannot simply be conceived as information injected into the minds of passive receivers. Instead, propaganda messages should be understood as part of the various reality constructions available in the symbolic environment, and thus a condition for the opinion formation carried by members of the target group." The ability of individuals to resist propaganda can be attributed to a number of factors, including active interpretation and production of meaning."

METHOD

This study relies on the electronic versions of *Business Day* of South Africa, *This Dayonline* of Nigeria, *Daily Nation on the Web* and *The East African on the Web* of Kenya. These news outlets were chosen because they are the national leading daily and/or wire service outlet in each country and reach an international audience. Leaders and opinion-makers within and outside their respective countries read them. A computer search strategy was used to identify news, features, editorial, commentaries, and letters concerning the 2002-2003 Gulf crisis.

Qualitative studies, including rhetorical and textual criticisms, are concerned with the explorative description, analysis, interpretation, and evaluation of persuasive techniques in human and mass communications (Brummett, 1994; Mohanty, 2000). The approach examines themes, values, topic categories, images, and texture of the stories to discern its direction. Weston (2003) states that critical textual analysis of newspaper stories is drawn from studies that suggest news conveys social values—that is, news takes on meaning and resonance beyond conveying "facts" about "events." Weston adds that critical textual analysis draws on studies of journalistic practices dealing with selection, exclusion, emphasis, and organization through reporters and editors who mold events or situations into "stories."

Rhetorical and textual criticisms help discern omissions of potentially problematic definitions, explanations, evaluations, and recommendations in news discourse, because omission of these frames is as important as their inclusion in guiding and influencing the public that these persuasive messages reach. When some points of view and arguments are omitted, those views become salient (Gamson & Modiglani, 1989; Gamson, et al., 1992; and others).

Applying critical textual analysis calls for a sequential and multiple reading of the text. The first step entailed a general multiple reading of the text to gain an understanding of the stories, while taking descriptive notes about the content of the articles (Gavrilos, 2002). The online articles were read a second time, along with detailed note-taking to identify certain recurring themes, values, and topic categories. These themes, values, and topic categories were labeled to develop a framework for a third reading: an in-depth interpretation of the articles.

With that in mind, the third reading involved applying critical analysis techniques to gain a deeper understanding of the messages conveyed to discern their implication, connection, stance, and values in relation to the theoretical underpinning and research questions being explored (Gavrilos, 2002).

RESULT AND ANALYSIS

When President Bush launched his propaganda offensive calling for force should the Hussein regime continue flouting UN resolutions requiring disarmament, the world community wavered and advocated a peaceful solution. The world sought a peaceful solution because many argued that a war could produce unintended consequences.

People argued that many questions had not been answered:

- How would a war influence the relationship among nations and peoples of different faiths?
- How would a war affect the ability of the world committee to work in concert in addressing common concerns of the future?
- Would a war exacerbate terrorism, while diminishing international cooperation to fight the scourge?

The results of this textual interpretation of sub-Sahara African mass media coverage of events leading to the 2003 Gulf War demonstrates that these concerns influenced their stand.

The analysis of the African online newspapers produced several themes and frames that largely opposed Bush's administration policies. The anti-war theme and orientations that emerged included:

- Give inspectors more time to do their work. Inspection works.
- Allow diplomatic negotiations to continue in order to resolve the crisis peacefully.
- The United Nations remains relevant.
- A war will scuttle international diplomacy.
- The United States lacks understanding of the world.
- The Americans have not proven their case.
- The United States is arrogant and wants to dictate to the world.
- The United States and her Western allies want to impose their ideologies and will in order to dominate the world.
- The United States is suffering diplomatic isolation.
- The West has double standards.
- Africans have a mission to stop war-mongering through active political initiatives.
- A war would create political instability within and outside Africa.
- Muslims within Africa would regard a war as a religious war.
- A war would have adverse economic consequences for Africa and the

developing world.
- Africa would be neglected.

On the other hand, there were themes and frames that advocated use of military force to disarm Iraq. The themes and orientations were:

- Iraq must be forced to comply in an effort to avoid proliferation of weapons of mass destruction.
- Africans should cooperate in order to avoid offending the United States and her Western allies.
- Saddam is a bad apple.
- The world must build and maintain a sense of cooperation and coalition.

Exploration of these themes and orientations indicates that the stand the African mass media took can be classified within several frameworks and propositions: diplomacy and negotiations; inspections work; economic, socio-cultural, and religious; colonial heritage and dependence; and rising independence. Africa's triple heritage of rich indigenous inheritance, Islamic culture, and the impact of Western imperialism have helped to shape contemporary Africa (Mazuri, 1986) and influence these propositions. These frames will be explored in detail.

Diplomacy and Negotiations

To avoid the sufferings associated with war, sub-Sahara African media regarded diplomatic negotiations as a vehicle for resolving crisis peacefully (Stremlau, 2003 January 14; *Business Day*, 2002, October 23). The region's media gave extensive coverage to diplomatic activities within and outside the UN (Hartley, 2003). The diplomatic, or lack of diplomatic, activities by African countries received critical attention from the *Daily Nation* (2003, January 14). When most African countries failed to declare their position on the crisis, the *Daily Nation* (2003, February 18) questioned their silence and urged them to stop hiding behind the African Union's call that "there should be a second UN resolution before military action," (p. 1 of online printout) which the paper considered a weak position on the imminent war.

On the other hand, Wanyeki (2003) described former South African President Nelson Mandela's pronouncement that "world peace could only be achieved if all nations, including the most powerful, adhered to its founding principles" and heeded calls for diplomatic resolution as a moral stand (*Business Day*, 2002, December 18, p. 1 of online printout). Wanyeki (2003) implied that Mr. Mandela came to rescue African leaders, indicating that the continent's stance for diplomatic negotiations must be allowed to take its course at a time when they were cowing to express their position.

As the United States and its allies sought a second resolution authorization, the sub-Sahara African media commended Angola, Cameroon, and the Guineas, as well as the African members of the UN Security Council, for their steadfast and courageous decision not to reverse their stance, despite intensive American lobbying and bullying to vote in favor of the resolution authorizing force (Kelly, 2003).

Sub-Sahara African media regarded the U.S. failure to gain the support of Turkey, the European Union, France, China, Germany, and the Organization of Islamic Council as diplomatic isolation. Power (2002, September 10) asked whether the world was drifting away from the United States. Describing the imminent war against Iraq as "unjustified," Ochomo (2003, p. 1 of online printout) called the decision of these and other nations and organizations which refused to support the war or offer assistance "commendable." He reminded the United States and its allies that they "must remember that the Gulf War circumstances where America had many allies no longer" holds and warned "war against Iraq will not be a 'walk over'" (p. 1 of online printout).

Weapons Inspections Work

In a UN address in September 2002, Mr. Bush stated that if Iraq did not comply with the "just demands of peace and security" to disarm "action will be taken" (CNN.com/U.S., 2002, September 12, p. 1 of online printout); the United States would act with or without UN sanction. He added that his administration was prepared to take military action to disarm Hussein of his weapons of mass destruction, calling the UN efforts to disarm Iraq and Iraqi compliance "a decade of deception and defiance" (CNN.com/U.S., 2002, September 12, p. 1 of online printout).

The world perceived Mr. Bush's push for military action and willingness to act unilaterally as the reckless, dangerous, and obnoxious act of a superpower requiring immediate attention and amicable resolution. Mr. Bush's drive generated a flurry of activities on weapons inspections at the United Nations and in world capitals. The Security Council met and passed UNSCR 1441; Iraq agreed to comply, enhanced her cooperation with inspectors, and offered a new report about its weapons program as UNSCR 1441 demanded. The UN inspectors continued their inspections and offered periodic reports to the council. Despite these positive movements, the United States, Britain, and Spain insisted weapons inspections were not working and demanded a second resolution permitting the use of force.

Like most people and leaders in other parts of the world, African leaders and people shared the opinion that inspections were working and inspectors should be given time to work. The sub-Sahara African press agreed and adopted a similar tone, arguing that inspections remained the only viable means of resolving the crisis to avoid bloodshed. They called on Iraq to offer full cooperation to UN inspectors, pointing out that inspectors needed time to ascertain the status of Iraq's weapons programs. The following headlines reflect how the African press framed the issue of weapons inspections:

- UN sees progress in talks with Iraq (*Business Day*, 2002, October 1)
- Iraq accepts new round of inspections; party expected in Baghdad in two weeks (*Business Day*, 2002, October 2)
- UN inspectors get ready to begin search; strategy involves paying unexpected visits (*Business Day*, 2002, November 27)
- UN arms inspectors ready to evaluate Iraq (*Business Day*, 2002, November 18)
- Inspectors check an idle Iraqi airfield (*Business Day*, 2002, December 2)
- Arms inspectors spring a surprise (*Business Day*, 2002, December 3)
- Iraq document tells of secret nuclear efforts (*Business Day*, 2002, December 12a)
- U.S. team to speed through Iraq's weapons declaration (*Business Day*, 2002, December 12b)
- UN weapons inspections continue amid a rapid U.S.-led military buildup (*Business Day*, 2003 January 9)
- Iraq signs declaration to cooperate with UN (*Business Day*, 2003 January 21)
- Inspectors find banned weapons in Iraq (*ThisDayonline*, 2003 February 14)
- Iraq has no weapon of mass destruction—UN inspectors (*ThisDayonline*, 2003 February 15)

- Iraq cranks up its concessions to UN (*Business Day*, 2003 February 19)
- UN inspectors submit report, find nothing on Iraq (*ThisDayonline*, 2003 February 28).

Despite their resistance to military action, the sub-Sahara African press believed Iraq's enhanced cooperation with UN inspectors, agreement to provide access to presidential sites, and the destruction of proscribed long-range missiles must be credited to the passage of Resolution 1441 and the Anglo-American military build up in Iraq (*Business Day*, 2003 January 9). With a headline that read, "Iraq's capitulation a victory for Bush," the *Daily Nation* (Giraudo, 2002, September 20) stated that Mr. Bush had scored a diplomatic win for the UN and restored the credibility of the world body (p. 1 of online printout).

However, when the United States and United Kingdom disagreed with the positive assessment of Iraq's cooperation, bombed Iraqi facilities, and continued to threaten unilateral military intervention (*ThisDayonline*, 2003 February 11; *Business Day*, 2003 February 19), the sub-Saharan African press described the position and action as ironical, ominous, irrational, defiant, and akin to playing double standards (Ochieng, 2003 March 9). The United States and its allies were accused of trampling on international conventions and failing, as usual, to meet their obligation to international agreements by acting as rogue nations, threatening the stability of the world (Mnyanda, 2002). Critics contended an attack without UN sanction would jeopardize the institution and destabilize Africa and the Middle East (Mathiu, 2003).

Economic Consequence

The economic impact of an attack gained a great deal of attention in the African press. The accounts and commentaries dealt with the short- and long-term economic impact on Africa and on a global scale. In the short run, the sub-Sahara African media contended that Africa would suffer immensely. Calling the prospect of a U.S. attack on Iraq the hottest international issue, the *Daily Nation* (2003, February 20, p. of online printout) stated, "we cannot look at the likelihood of such a war without considering how it will impact our own economic, security and geopolitical interests."

In the short run, the sub-Sahara African press contended the prospects of an Anglo-American-Iraq war contributed to higher prices in transportation services, as well as petroleum-produced products. For example, in January of 2003 rising oil prices were blamed on alleged U.S. stockpiling in preparation for war (*Daily Nation*, 2003 January 9). The prospect of a war was blamed for the immediate decline in tourism (Bindra, 2003). Other short-term economic problems associated with the war included declining local and international stock prices, declining foreign investments and borrowing from foreign financial institutions (*ThisDayonline*, 2003 January 29a), and a growing number of weakened African and international currencies (*ThisDayonline*, 2003 January 29b). The sub-Sahara African media also argued that the war would have an adverse effect on the global economy by worsening the sluggish conditions the world economy has suffered in recent years (*ThisDayonline*, 2003 January 29a & b; Stremlau, 2003 March 4; Daily Nation, 2003 February 20).

In the long term, Africa contended that if Iraq was attacked and the war then dragged on, the United States, Europe, and other donor groups and organizations would neglect Africa (*East African on the Web*, 2003, p. 3 of online printout). One official underscored the impact of the crisis on Africa when he stated, "as it is now, the Iraqi issue is eclipsing other world needs to focus on such issues as the fight against AIDS, pervasive hunger in Africa."

When Mr. Bush canceled a proposed visit to Africa, the *Daily Nation* (2002, December 26) reported that the fears of Africans had been realized. The paper cited *The Washington Post*, which condemned the cancellation and argued that, "Africa is taking a back seat in policymaking." The story stated that the cancellation of the visit would deter the World Bank and International Monetary Fund from releasing about $200 million in suspended aid that Kenya would have received if the president had visited after Kenya's successful election and peaceful transition of power in 2002.

Press accounts stated that the African Union's stance against war created a rift between the continent and the United States and its allies, and that rift may lead to economic reprisals against those nations that opposed the United States. However, the sub-Sahara African press also noted that the United States was paying more attention to oil-producing countries in order to cultivate them as an alternative source of energy, rather than the Middle East (Kelley, 2002, September 16).

Discussion and Conclusion

The sub-Sahara African media—as forums for discourse where information and commentaries are presented and shared to influence the course of events, policies, national and international leaders, and the public—urged the Bush administration to be patient, to not attack Iraq, and to allow diplomacy to take its course. As they advised Mr. Bush to show restraint, they called on African leaders and institutions to resist the drive to use force.

The sub-Sahara media contended that if the Americans and the British carried out the attack on Iraq without UN support, hostility and animosity toward the United States would increase in the Middle East, Africa, and worldwide (Akinterinwa, 2003). The attack would inflame religious intolerance (*ThisDayonline*, 2003 January 31) and swell terrorist attacks and violence worldwide (*ThisDayonline*, 2003 February 12; *Daily Nation*, 2002, October 16; *Business Day*, 2002, November 19). They also contended it would lead to weapons proliferation (*ThisDayonline*, 2003 January 10), destabilize the world economy (Akinterinwa, 2003; Osambi, 2003) and eclipse the focus on Africa's crippling problems of AIDS, debt burden, and famine (*East African on the Web*, 2003 March 24). This fear of diminished attention was realized when Mr. Bush canceled a proposed visit to Africa (*Daily Nation*, 2002, September 26). (Six months later, Mr. Bush embarked on a five-day, five-nation visit of Africa.)

The sub-Sahara African media argued that the ongoing crisis, preparation for, and imminent war created a rift among nations and disrupted the diplomatic process. Despite their overwhelming support for a peaceful resolution of the crisis, the growing pluralism in sub-Sahara Africa is demonstrated through the diversity of opinion contained in articles supporting the United States' use of force. Such articles contend that the United States must be supported for its efforts to remove a dictator—a subject most Africans continue to suffer (*Business Day*,

2003 February 12). Supporters of the Bush administration policy railed against African leaders who opposed the United States' use of force, thus offending the United States and risking their national welfare (Hartley, 2002, November 6).

Judging from the overall coverage of the events leading to the 2003 Gulf War, this study suggests that sub-Sahara Africa opposed unilateral use of force because it would create political, social, economic, and religious upheaval in the region (Chaudhary, 2001). This finding supports the concept that media coverage of issues is colored by the prevailing conditions in a country. Whether they took this position to support the policies of the government, as suggested by Herman & Chomsky (1988), remains a subject for another study to explore. Research suggests that the South African and Kenyan media tend to drive and influence policies, instead of being driven and influenced by government policies.

References

Akinterinwa, B. (2003). Iraq: Old Europe versus new American. *ThisDayonline*, February 17. [Online]. Available at http://www.*ThisDayonline*.com/archive Retrieved June 12, 2003.

Bindra, S. (2003). War with Iraq: Some facts you may not know. *Sunday Nation on the Web,* February 16. [Online]. Available at http://www.nationaudio.com/News/DailyNation Retrieved June 27, 2003.

Bird, E. & R. Dardenne (1988). Myth, chronicle, and story: Exploring the narrative qualities of news. In J. Carey (ed.), *Media, myth, and narratives: Television and the press,* pp. 67-86. Newbury Park: Sage Publications.

Brummett, B. (1994). *Rhetoric in popular culture.* New York: St. Martin's Press.

Business Day (2002, October 1). UN sees progress in talks with Iraq, [Online]. Available at http://www.bday.co.za/bday/content Retrieved May 29, 2003.

Business Day (2002, December 12a). Iraq document tells of secret nuclear efforts [Online]. Available at http://www.bday.co.za/bday/content Retrieved May 29, 2003.

Business Day (2002, December 12b). U.S. team to speed through Iraq's weapon declaration, [Online]. Available at http://www.bday.co.za/bday/content Retrieved May 29, 2003.

Business Day (2002, December 18). Mandela criticizes the United States for its arrogant approach to Iraq [Online]. Available at http://www.bday.co.za/bday/content Retrieved May 29, 2003.

Business Day (2002, December 2). Inspectors check idle Iraqi air field [Online]. Available at http://www.bday.co.za/bday/content Retrieved May 29, 2003.

Business Day (2002, December 3) Arms inspectors spring a surprise [Online]. Available at http://www.bday.co.za/bday/content Retrieved May 29, 2003.

Business Day (2002, November 18). UN arms inspectors ready to re-evaluate Iraq [Online]. Available at http://www.bday.co.za/bday/content Retrieved 29, 2003.

Business Day (2002, November 19). Walking the diplomatic tightrope [Online]. Available at http://www.bday.co.za/bday/content Retrieved May 29, 2003.

Business Day (2002, November 27). UN inspectors get ready to begin search; strategy involves paying unexpected visit [Online]. Available at http://www.bday.co.za/bday/content Retrieved 29, 2003.

Business Day (2002, October 2). Iraq accepts new round of inspection; party expected in Baghdad in two weeks [Online]. Available at http://www.bday.co.za/bday/content Retrieved 29, 2003.

Business Day (2002, October 23). UN council resumes talks about Iraq-U.S. war [Online]. Available at http://www.bday.co.za/bday/content Retrieved May 29, 2003).

Business Day (2003, February 12). No need for SA to suffer from Iraq [Online]. Available at http://www.bday.co.za/bday/content Retrieved May 29, 2003.

Business Day (2003, February 19). Iraq cranks up its concession to UN [Online]. Available at http://www.bday.co.za/bday/content Retrieved 29, 2003.

Business Day (2003, January 21). Iraq signs declaration to co-operate with UN [Online]. Available at http://www.bday.co.za/bday/content Retrieved May 29, 2003.

Business Day (2003, January 9). UN weapons inspections continue amid a rapid U.S.-led military buildup [Online]. Available at http://www.bday.co.za/bday/content Retrieved May 29, 2003.

Butler, R. (2002, September 13). Just how dangerous is Iraq's rogue leader? *Business Day* [Online]. Available at http://www.bday.co.za/bday/content Retrieved May 29, 2003.

Chaudhary, A. (2001). International news selection: A comparative analysis of negative news in *The Washington Post* and *The Daily Times* of Nigeria. *The Howard Journal of Communication 12,* 241-254.

Chomsky, N. (1992). The media and the war: What war? In H. Mowlana & G. Gerbner (ed.). *Triumph of the Image, the Media's War in the he Persian Gulf: A Global Perspective*, pp. 51-63. Boulder, Colorado, Westview Press.

Chrisco, C.. (1994). *Pre-war and war reactions to the Persian Gulf: A study of editorials in the conflict zone.* Ph.D. Dissertation. University of Southern Mississippi, Hattiesburg, Miss.

CNN.com (2001, January 25). Social forum seeks alternative agenda [Online] Available at http://www.cnn.com/2001/world Retrieved January 25, 2001.

CNN.com./U.S. (2002, September 12). White House spells out case against Iraq [Online]. Available at http://www.cnn.com/2002/US/09/12/iraq.report Retrieved May 5, 2003.

Daily Nation on the Web (2002, December 26). Bush calls off historic visit to Kenya in January [Online]. Available at http://www.nationaudio.com/News/DailyNation Retrieved June 27, 2003.

Daily Nation on the Web (2002, October 16). What lessons from Bali? [Online]. Available at http://www.nationaudio.com/News/DailyNation Retrieved June 27, 2003.

Daily Nation on the Web (2003, February 18). Stand up on Iraq [Online]. Available at http://www.nationaudio.com/News/DailyNation Retrieved June 27, 2003.

Daily Nation on the Web (2003, February 20). Declare real stand on war [Online]. Available at http://www.nationaudio.com/News/DailyNation. Retrieved June 26, 2003.

Daily Nation on the Web (2003, January 14). War: Why is Africa so quiet? [Online]. Available at http://www.nationaudio.com/News/DailyNation Retrieved June 27, 2003.

Daily Nation on the Web (2003, January 9). Fare rise fears as fuel prices up [Online]. Available at http://www.nationaudio.com/News/DailyNation Retrieved June 27,

2003.

Entman, R. (1991). Framing U.S. coverage of international news: Contrasts in narratives of the KAL and Iran Air incidents. *Journal of Communication 41*, 6-27.

Entman, R. (1993). Framing: Toward clarification of a fractured paradigm. *Journal of Communication 43* (4), 51-58.

Fico, F., L. Ku & S. Soffin (1994). Fairness, balance of news coverage of U.S. in Gulf War. *Newspaper Research Journal 15* (1), 30-41.

Gamson, W. & A. Modiglani (1989). Media discourse and public opinion on nuclear power: A constructionist approach. *American Journal of Sociology 95*(1), 1-37.

Gamson, W., D. Croteau, W. Hoynes & T. Sasson (1992). Media images and the social construction of reality. *Annual Review of Sociology 18,* 373-393.

Gavrilos, D. (2002). Arab Americans in a nation's imagined community: How news constructed Arab American reaction to the Gulf War. *Journal of Communication Inquiry 26*(4), 426-445.

Gidden, A. (1991). *Modernity and self-identity. Self and society in the late modern age.* Stanford, CA: Stanford University Press.

Giddens, A. (1990). *The Consequences of Modernity.* Stanford, CA: Stanford University Press.

Giraudo, P. (2002). Iraq's capitulation a victory for Bush, *Daily Nation on the Web* September 26. [Online]. Available at http://www.nationaudio.com/News/ DailyNation Retrieved June 27, 2003.

Hartley, W. (2002, November 6). Opposition urges Mbeki not to heed invitation to Baghdad. *Business Day*. [Online]. Available at http://www.bday.co.za/ bday/content Retrieved May 29, 2003).

Hartley, W. (2003, February 12). SA disarmament team is set for Iraq peace mission. *Business Day*. [Online]. Available at http://www.bday.co.za/bday/content Retrieved May 29, 2003.

Hawk, B. (1992). Introduction. In B. Hawk (ed.), *Metaphors of African Coverage, Africa's Media Image.* West Port, CO: Praeger, pp. 1-7.

Herman, E. & N. Chomsky (1988). *Manufacturing consent: The political economy of the mass media*. New York: Pantheon Books.

Jensen, K. (1987). News is ideology: Economic statistics and political ritual in television news. *Journal of Communication 37*, 8-26.

Jowett, G. & V. O'Donnell (1992). *Propaganda and persuasion.* London: Sage

Kelley, K. (2002, September 16). U.S. moves to protect interest in African oil. *The East African on the Web*. [Online]. Available at http://www.nationaudio.com/News/ EastAfrican. Retrieved June 27, 2003.

Kelley, K. (2003, March 3). U.S. bullying African states to support war. *The East African on the Web*. [Online]. Available at http://www.nationaudio.com/News/EastAfrican Retrieved June 23, 2003.

Lee, M. & T. Devit (1991, Winter). Gulf war coverage: Censorship begins at home. *Newspaper Research Journal,* pp.14-22.

Mathiu, M. (2003). Regular cull of the "barbarians." *Sunday Nation on the Web.* Available at http://www.nationaudio.com/News/DailyNation Retrieved June 27, 2003.

Mazrui, A (1986). Preface. In A. Mazrui & T. Levine (eds). *The Africans: A reader,* pp. xv-xviii. Westport, CT: Praeger.

Mnyanda, L (2002). Mandela criticizes the United States for it arrogant approach to Iraq. *Business Day*, December 18. [Online]. Available at http://www.bday.co.za/bday/content Retrieved May 29, 2003.

Mohanty, D. (2000, October). Framing of *New York Times* coverage of the Elian story and general immigration stories. Paper presented at Global Fusion 2000, Communication and Culture—Bridging Borders, St. Louis, MO.

Morgenthau, H. (1957). *Politics among nations.* New York: Knopf Press, pp. 201-22.

Nohrstedt, S. & R. Ottosen (2000). Studying the media Gulf war. In A Nohrstedt & R. Ottosen (eds.), *Journalism and the New World Order: Gulf war, national news discourse and Globalization I,* pp. 11-34. Goteborg University: NORDICOM

Ochieng (2003). Three cheers to managers of new Hitler. *Sunday Nation on the Web,* March 9. [Online]. Available at http://www.nationaudio.com/News/DailyNation Retrieved June 27, 2003.

Ochomo (2003). War against Iraq unjustified. *Saturday Nation on the Web,* February15. [Online]. Available at http://www.nationaudio.com/News/DailyNation. Retrieved June 27, 2003.

Osamgbi, P. (2003). Why the Gulf war is unnecessary. *ThisDayonline*, March 1. [Online]. Available at http://www.*ThisDayonline*.com/archive Retrieved June 11, 2003.

Power, J. (2002, September 10). Is the world drifting away from U.S. *Daily Nation on the Web*. [Online]. Available at http://www.nationaudio.com/News/DailyNation. Retrieved June 27, 2003.

Robertson, R. (1992). *Globalization: Social theory and global culture.* Thousand Oaks, CA: Sage.

Rusicano, F. (1993). Media perspectives on world opinion during the Kuwaiti crisis. In *The media and the Persian Gulf War,* pp. 71-89. Westport, Connecticut: Praeger.

Severin, W. & J. Tankard (1997). *Communication theories: Origins, methods, and uses of in the mass media* (4th edn.), White Plains, NY: Longman.

Shoemaker, P. & S. Reese (1996). *Mediating the message.* New York: Longman

Stremlau, J. (2003, January 14). UN can be used to influence U.S. policy. *Business Day*, [Online]. Available at http://www.bday.co.za/bday/content. Retrieved May 29, 2003).

Stremlau, J. (2003, March 4) SA help to keep the dogs of war on a leash. *Business Day*. [Online]. Available at http://www.bday.co.za/bday/content. Retrieved May 5, 2003.

The East African on the Web (2003, March 24). War: U.S. warming to 'willing' East African states, [Online]. Available at http://www.nationaudio.com/News/EastAfrican Retrieved June 27, 2003.

ThisDayonline (2003, January 29a). War fears keep bourses under pressure. [Online]. Available at http://www.ThisDayonline.com/archive. Retrieved June 12, 2003.

ThisDayonline (2003, January 29b). Dollar hits fresh lows as Iraq fears dominate [Online]. Available at http://www.ThisDayonline.com/archive. Retrieved June 12, 2003

ThisDayonline (2003, February 12). Iraq: Bin Ladin wants Muslims to fight U.S. [Online]. Available at http://www.ThisDayonline.com/archive. Retrieved June 12, 2003.

ThisDayonline (2003, February 14). Inspectors find banned weapons in Iraq, [Online]. Available at http://www.*ThisDayonline*.com/archive Retrieved June 12, 2003

ThisDayonline (2003, February15). Iraq has no weapons of mass destruction: UN inspectors." [Online]. Available at http://www.ThisDayonline.com/archive Retrieved June 12, 2003.

ThisDayonline (2003, February 28). UN inspectors submit report, finds nothing on Iraq; Annan pleads for more time. [Online]. Available at http://www.ThisDayonline.com/archive. Retrieved June 12, 2003.

ThisDayonline (2003, February11). Bush to UN Inspectors: Iraqís compliance too late; Pope send peace message [Online]. Available at http://www.ThisDayonline.com/archive. Retrieved June 12, 2003.

ThisDayonline (2003, January 10). Arab countries urged to seek nuclear arsenal [Online]. Available at http://www.ThisDayonline.com/archive. Retrieved June 12, 2003

ThisDayonline (2003, January 31). Mandela accuses U.S. of planning holocaust [Online]. Available at http://www.ThisDayonline.com/archive. Retrieved June 12, 2003

Uche, L. (1997, September). The economic and emancipative potentials of the information superhighway regime for Africa south of the Sahara. Paper presented at the Regional Workshop on Media Ownership and Control in West Africa, Yaounde, Cameroon.

Wanyeki, M. (2003, March 10). Bush is fighting for oil? So should we! *The East African on the Web*, March 10. [Online]. Available at http://www.nationaudio. com/News/EastAfrican. Retrieved June 23, 2003.

Weston, M. (2003). Post 9/11 Arab American coverage avoids stereotypes. *News Research Journal 24* (1), 92-113.

CHAPTER 5

Al-Jazeera: A Broadcaster Creating Ripples in a Stagnant Pool

Stephen Quinn and Tim Walters

"Al-Jazeera is a drop of fresh water that was dropped into a pool of stale water that stood still for decades," said Jihad Ali Ballout, who was responsible for media relations at the Qatar-based channel a few days before the war broke out. "Al-Jazeera has created ripples that refreshed the water. The more the water moves the fresher it gets, until such a time that we have really fresh water for the audience to take from" (Ballout, 2003).

In the Arab world of state-controlled and stale media, Al-Jazeera has indeed caused ripples. The staff of the satellite-delivered television channel see those ripples as creating a "revolution" in the Arab world. Ballout, in particular, views Al-Jazeera as a major force in developing freedom of expression and liberalizing the marketplace of ideas in the Arab world.

Traveling this pathway has not been easy—politics, laws, and customs in the Middle East sometimes make covering stories difficult. A raft of privacy laws, plus custom and respect for authority, make covering certain subjects either uncomfortable or off limits. Timeliness is sometimes a problem as well. Mohammed Jasim Al-Ali, the channel's director-general, has noted that a host of agreements between Arab television stations obliged them not to broadcast any report before transmission by official news agencies. Practically speaking, this has meant waiting several hours before broadcasting a report.

"Arab information mentality must change and develop, and not remain as it was many years ago," Al-Ali said (Al-Farah, 2003). Al-Ali and his staff want Arab audiences to return to trusting the Arab media, especially the news. "You should bring them the truth, not false information, or they won't watch. We treat them as an intelligent audience, rather than the conventional idea that they'll take whatever you give them" (quoted in Schleifer, 2000).

Al-Ali has said the broadcaster was a demonstration of faith in the message of freedom. "When the channel became operational, everyone wanted to silence this free voice," he told *Al-Dustur*, Jordan's leading establishment daily (Al-Farah, 2003). The Middle East media have a reputation for being censored and controlled. "All media business in the Middle East is controlled by the government. The leaders of Qatar wanted to change that; they wanted to have a satellite channel with the aim of no longer hiding any information," Al-Ali said (Schleifer, 2000).

AL-JAZEERA: EQUAL OPPORTUNITY OFFENDER

Al-Jazeera is becoming an equal opportunity offender, irritating almost every government in the region and many outside the Gulf. At one time or another, governments from Algeria to Yemen have lodged complaints against the station. Tunisia, Morocco, and Libya have all recalled their ambassadors from Doha in protest of Al-Jazeera coverage, reinstating them once their point was made.

Dr. Faisal Al-Qassem, who presents the high-rated but controversial "The Opposite Direction," said Egyptian police once dragged Qassem's brother—a pop star—out of his home in his pajamas and bundled him on a plane to Jordan as a warning to Qassem. "In Algiers," Qassem said, "they cut off the electricity supply so that people could not watch the program because we were talking about the military generals and how they are wasting the money of Algerians" (quoted in Whitaker, 2003, p. 1).

Egypt's state-owned media ran a campaign against Al-Jazeera's programs, describing the station as a "sinister salad of sex, religion and politics" topped with "sensationalist seasoning." Yasir Arafat was reportedly incensed by Al-Jazeera's frequent interviews with the Hamas spiritual leader, Sheikh Ahmed Yassin. The network upset Palestinian authorities with a preview of a March 2001 documentary that explored the role of Palestinian guerrillas in the 1975-1990 civil war in Lebanon. Jordan temporarily closed Al-Jazeera's bureau in the capital, Amman, after a guest on a debate program criticized the government.

Sheikh Hamad bin Khalifa Al-Thani, chairman of the board of Al-Jazeera, recalls that when Al-Jazeera covered events in Iraq, it was accused of being a channel financed by Iraq or Saddam Hussein.

"When we reported on the Israeli elections and when we ran interviews with Ehud Barak and Shimon Peres, Al-Jazeera was immediately accused of being financed by the Mossad. When we reported on events or issues within the United States from our office in Washington we were accused of being financed by the CIA" (quoted in Sullivan, 2001).

According to the channel, some Arab viewers have even accused it of promoting U.S. propaganda when it puts U.S. officials or statements on air. Al-Jazeera broadcasts all White House, Pentagon, and State Department press briefings from Washington (Campagna, 2001).

Broadcasts of videotapes featuring Osama Bin Laden have generated the most fame and notoriety for the channel. Al-Jazeera's long 1998 interview with Bin Laden, which it rebroadcast with English subtitles not long after the September 11, 2001, attacks, brought the channel praise and condemnation in almost equal measure.

A month later, *The New York Daily News* editorialized that Al-Jazeera was "one of the most potent weapons in the Islamic Axis arsenal." The newspaper then opined, almost hysterically: "It is an Arab propaganda outfit controlled by the medieval government of Qatar that masquerades as a real media company. For years, it has inflamed the Arab world against the United States and its allies." The paper concluded that dealing with the station was "a job for the military." "Shutting it down should be an immediate priority because, left alone, it has the power to poison the air more efficiently and lethally than anthrax ever could" (*New York Daily News*, 2001).

During a meeting in Muscat in October 2002, the ministers of information in all six Gulf Co-operation Council states recommended that Al-Jazeera be banned in their countries because the station's news and programs "offend the whole Gulf region" (*The Gulf News*, 2002, p. 1). The United Arab Emirates and the Sultanate of Oman subsequently decided to allow the channel to stay.

Saudi Arabia forbids Al-Jazeera staff from entering its territory, and in 2003 extended the ban to special events such as the hajj, the annual pilgrimage to Mecca. Al-Ali was philosophical about these bans, suggesting that satellite technology allowed them a virtual form of entry. "True," he said, "we do not exist in Bahrain, but we do cover events there. The same can also be said about Kuwait and other places, regardless of whether we have a presence there or not. We have been covering events without any problem. No one can say that they can boycott Al-Jazeera, because that is very difficult" (Al-Farah, 2003).

Others inside the station agreed with this assessment. "Some of Al-Jazeera's coverage of events ran against the grain of several Arab states to say the least, and the reverberations of which we can still feel, with the refusal to let us work in several states. We only have two bureaus, one in the UAE and one in Oman. While Saudi Arabia, Kuwait and Bahrain have a problem with the way we do our business. So yes, it has caused us some problems, but it goes with the territory. I think if everyone was happy with us, we won't be doing our job" (Ballout, 2003).

Since 2001 various Western government leaders have asked Qatar's emir, Sheikh Hamad bin Khalifa Al-Thani, to restrain the station. The U.S. embassy in Qatar filed a formal diplomatic complaint with local authorities regarding Al-Jazeera's coverage. Bush administration officials made it clear that they were upset by what they viewed as Al-Jazeera's "unbalanced and anti-American" coverage. And in the aftermath of September 11, many Washington officials refused to appear on the channel despite numerous requests from Al-Jazeera's Washington bureau (Sullivan, 2000).

Defenders of Al-Jazeera

But Al-Jazeera has its defenders too. Organizations like the Committee to Protect Journalists (CPJ) and Journalists sans Frontieres have complained about the aggressive statements coming out of the United States. "Arab government attempts to influence Al-Jazeera have garnered widespread attention over the years. We are disheartened to see U.S. officials adopting similar tactics," said CPJ executive director Ann Cooper (quoted in Sullivan, 2000). Former CNN correspondent Peter Arnett rhetorically asked: "What about the U.S. right-wing press that's been [bashing] Arabs? Do they rein them in? Do they rein in Fox TV? Are we going to order our own media to rein in its coverage? It's getting out of hand."

Aside from the press freedom implications, CPJ Middle East coordinator Joel Campagna noted, U.S. calls for Qatar to censor Al-Jazeera may have backfired by generating criticism from the Arab world at a time when the United States needed the support of people in the region. "I think this elevates Al-Jazeera into an even more powerful organization than it is," agreed Arnett. "Simply, it's a news source that's threatening the U.S. They don't have any guns. They haven't been traced to Bin Laden" (quoted in Campagna, 2001).

Some critics of Al-Jazeera have maintained that the station is willing to criticize Arab government in the region, but will not challenge Qatar's rulers. *New York Times* columnist Thomas Friedman argues that Al-Jazeera sometimes "goes easy" on the Doha government. "To be sure, Al-Jazeera goes easier on Qatar than it does on Saudi Arabia, but it has actually aired charges of torture in Qatar" (Friedman, 2001).

The CPJ argues that the station has generally been well regarded for its editorial independence, despite being funded by the emir of Qatar until November 2001. "Nevertheless, it has been taken to task for usually avoiding tough scrutiny of Qatari affairs and any strong criticism of the ruling Al-Thani family" (Campagna, 2001). Qatari families sometimes wonder the same thing.

More seasoned thinkers believe that muzzling Al-Jazeera would be a case of shooting the messenger. Yosri Fouda, head of Al-Jazeera's London bureau, asked rhetorically: "If Bin Laden is going to send a tape, who will he send it to? To CNN, who he probably considers a representative of 'the enemy'? No. To an Arab government channel? No, because there's just as much animosity there." Al-Jazeera was relaying valuable information that the West did not have, Fouda said, and it would continue doing so "for as long as everything is verified and as long as time and space are given for different viewpoints" (Sullivan, 2000).

Arab journalists see U.S. policy as hypocritical for pressuring Al-Jazeera to modify its coverage, given the American view of itself as a symbol of freedom and democracy. Daoud Kuttab, director of the Institute of Modern Media at Al-Qud University on the West Bank and an observer of Arab regional media, believes Al-Jazeera's work has been professional and balanced:

> As to the Americans, they are completely wrong and apply a double standard. I can see why they are angry but it is not because Al-Jazeera is not fair. On the contrary, I think they wish for Al-Jazeera to be biased to the U.S. (quoted in Campagna, 2001).

Al-Jazeera's creators appreciated early on the power of media technologies, particularly satellites and more recently the Internet to enter Arabian homes and tell compelling stories:

> You could once control the information before there was Internet, before there was satellite. People got much of their information from government sources. When satellite channels started, it was no longer possible to hide the sources of information from the viewing audience. This is the atmosphere in which Al-Jazeera started (quoted in Schleifer, 2000).

Many countries have managed to block the BBC terrestrial services, but they cannot block satellite channels or the Internet, Al-Ali said. "If something is on a Western channel, it has a limited effect. But Al-Jazeera affects a much larger audience, because it's in Arabic" (quoted in Schleifer, 2000).

Breaking Down Communication Barriers

The barriers that prevented dissemination of information to Arab citizens have been torn down because of developments in information technology and telecommunications worldwide, Al-Ali said. "The Arab information ministries can no longer control information. No one can control information." In the 21st century, the news business has changed but the news mentality in many Arab states has not. "And, if there has been a change, it is very modest and has not caught up with the rapid change in the technology and information sectors worldwide" (quoted in Al-Farah, 2003).

Others who work at the station agree with this assessment, notes Jihad Ali

Ballout, and "Al-Jazeera has managed to push a crack in the dogma of media in the Arab world. I think we have the lead and people now are following. Al-Jazeera has blasted the censors. The rest are stepping, a step at a time, towards perhaps how media should be practiced professionally, with lesser censorship, lesser control, lesser influence of whatever powers that be" (Al Farah, 2003).

On his part, Ballout is happy to see that Arab media have moved towards the type of service that the Arab public deserves.

"For decades," he said, "the Arab public has been treated by the media as simply a pot where news is chosen, disinfected, doctored and thrown in." And the public had to accept it. The difference today is that the public can now see news "as raw, as it is."

> We are proud to say, that this is what Al-Jazeera has started. Someone has said that Al-Jazeera has started a revolution in media, and I think this statement is born out because so many media are trying to base their ethos along the lines that Al-Jazeera has come out openly with. (Ballout, 2003)

Al-Jazeera has made television news both interesting and topical in the Arab world, through a combination of professionalism and controversy. Before Al-Jazeera went on the air in November 1996, Arab stations ignored news, concentrating on entertainment. That has changed. And more changes are afoot. Viewers were turned off because the media gave the official side. Al-Jazeera was different because it stuck to "the viewers' side, which is the most important" (Al-Farah, 2003).

PROGRAMMING ON AL-JAZEERA

Al-Jazeera gives more than the official view, deliberately offering opinions from different viewpoints. This policy is reflected in the station's motto, emblazoned in Arabic on its publicity brochure: "*al-ra'i ... wal-ra'i al-akhr*." In English it means "opinion ... and the other opinion." This is reflected in the titles of its talk programs—"The Opposite Direction," "More Than One Opinion" and "No Frontiers"—which screen about 9:30 p.m. most evenings.

Its news programs offer breadth and depth of content, with bulletins at the top of the hour plus a full hour at dawn, early morning, midday and late evening. The channel boasts two flagship investigative programs that screen after the evening talk shows about 10 p.m. All station timings are based on Saudi Arabian time, which is three hours ahead of GMT.

From Ballout's perspective, the origins of this varied programming are simple:

> To gel all this together, to come up with a good product. You need a constant

> measure of freedom, for your journalists to express themselves through. And here we have the acid test. Al-Jazeera has taken the element of freedom and transparency to extremes perhaps, some people say . We believe we can still go further than that. It's just a matter of if the others can create for themselves a playing field the boundaries of which are wide enough for them to express themselves satisfactorily, to be happy with themselves in the first place as journalists and then to satisfy the audience that [we] have spoiled for all intents and purposes by getting them used to news that has been unedited, uncensored and to a very considerable extent balanced.

If that news is imperfect, that is just because of the way people are, he said. After all:

> a journalist is a human being at the end of the day. He's got his loves, his likes, his hates. So perhaps it is very difficult for a journalist, like any other person, to be fair, because fairness is a matter of the heart and the spirit. I would not claim that any of my colleagues have attained a spiritual clarity. (Ballout, 2003)

What should happen, he thinks, is that a journalist can create a level playing field by being balanced. "If a journalist can manage to do that ... he would be going a long way towards doing his job," Ballout said. This search for balance is the way in which Al-Jazeera sees itself as revolutionary.

Some commentators think that station may have gone too far, complaining the station deliberately courts controversy. Some believe that the "raw, as it is" method of presenting leads to the "if it bleeds, it leads" mentality of local U.S. news. Others believe that Al-Jazeera's choice of content reflects the Arab perspective on world events, telling the truth through Arabic eyes. That means the war in Iraq was presented through the eyes of average Iraqis, not through the eyes of coalition soldiers. This is very much a different perspective.

Dr. Lena Jayyusi (2003), a Palestinian media commentator, applauds Al-Jazeera's news for its depth, breadth and analysis:

> I was in Paris when the war against Iraq started. I had access to CNN and BBC there around the clock. But, despite the pleas and warnings of friends and relatives about flying back to the Gulf, and questions about whether I was worried or fearful about doing so whilst the war was taking place, I could not wait to get back, just so I could follow the war through the coverage of Al-Jazeera. Literally. I knew I would not get one-sided propaganda on this issue, and I would get to see really what was going on at ground zero. This has indeed been the case, at a time when networks like the BBC and CNN sanitize the images and reports they air. This reaction is pretty well general in the Arab world.

AL-JAZEERA AND FREEDOM OF EXPRESSION

Dr. Badran Badran (2003), another Palestinian media commentator who is an avid Al-Juazeiro viewer, believes the station leads in the area of freedom of expression:

> Arabs appreciate a station that covers all major events very well and is not afraid to tell the truth. I appreciate the station's coverage of inter-and intra-Arab issues in a transparent and open manner. I also admire the station's echoing of Arab voices against what they perceive to be an ineffective and dysfunctional Arab body politic.

Dr. Badran said he appreciated Al-Jazeera's commitment to be balanced and objective. "[But] I do not appreciate the lack of intellectualism in some of its talk shows which smell of political agitation without a real agenda" (Badran, 2003). Ballout counters that this lack of an agenda has its own value:

> I think that our *raison d'etre* is the other opinion. I believe without freedom of expression, a human being is missing. Without a human being able to express himself, in a responsible way, without being told 'this is a taboo, don't touch' in other words you are telling him not to think. Ultimately people will become stale. If they can't express why should they think. Or they would think and bottle it up until such a day that they would explode. It's not only that we believe in freedom of expression, we practice it.

Beyond attracting an audience, Ballout believes that freedom of expression ultimately will profoundly impact the entire Arab world:

> I was discussing the issue of freedom of expression and democracy with a senior colleague the other day. My colleague said that Al-Jazeera will have another role, and that's leading with freedom of expression towards democratizing the community and Arab society. This idea made sense to me. I have reached the stage where I have started thinking [that] freedom of expression and democracy are one in the same, and there is hardly any difference. Because to be able to practice democracy you have to have freedom of expression, and to have freedom of expression you have to have democracy. So perhaps there is a fine line that separates freedom of expression and democracy. So in essence, for you Americans, we are practicing democracy in Qatar.

This wasn't always the case in Qatar. In 1995 Sheik Hamad, then crown prince of Qatar, overthrew his father on holiday in Europe in a bloodless coup. Analysts say the crown prince was impatient with his father's reluctance to release funds for investment. The new emir and his foreign minister, Sheikh Hamad bin Jassim bin Jabr Al-Thani, promptly announced a new order and set out to challenge Saudi primacy in the Gulf region. They hoped that Al-Jazeera would demonstrate the country's independence and give the small kingdom a voice in the world (Curtiss, 1998). Sheik Hamad founded Al-Jazeera by decree in February 1996 and it started broadcasting on November 1 that year. Initial funding of about $140 million was provided on the understanding that the station would be self-sustaining within five years of debut. The station operated for six hours a day initially, quickly moved to 12, and on New Years Day 1999 it began broadcasting around the clock (Zednik, 2002).

The emir, Sheik Hamad, abolished the position of minister of information in 1998. Sheikh Hamad bin Thamer Al-Thani is chairman of the Al-Jazeera board and a member of the royal family. He noted that the ministry of information in Arab countries controls the news media, observing that the West has advanced media and no information ministries.

AL-JAZEERA'S AUDIENCE

Audience data are not easily available in the Arab world, but the generally agreed figure before the 2003 Gulf War was that at least 35 million households watch Al-Jazeera regularly—a huge audience, given the large number of people in extended Middle East households.

Most households receive it via satellite. Dishes are almost ubiquitous in the Arab world—tens of millions of Arab families own them—and dishes cost less than $100. "They are as common in Cairo slums as they are in Dubai mansions. Al-Jazeera beams its signal free of charge to most countries." Outside the Arab world, in countries like the United Kingdom and United States, Al-Jazeera is usually offered as part of a subscription package (Ajami, 2001).

Managing director Al-Ali attributes the station's success to three factors. "First is the financial means, which, if available, would ensure the technical resources, which are equally important. Second is the existence of a specialized, good working team, which is under constant training. Third and most important is the availability of a margin of freedom" (Al-Farah, 2003). Al-Jazeera has earned a reputation that inspires love and hate in almost equal measures (Whitaker, 2003, p. 1). Until Al-Jazeera arrived, Arab viewers rarely recognized newscasters, though the people who introduced variety programs were well known. Al-Ali noted that in the past few years, presenters and newscasters have become famous—"like film stars"—because of their exposure on the channel.

AL-JAZEERA: THE ORGANIZATION

For a station with such a large reach and loud voice, Al-Jazeera is located in a small building with a tiny newsroom and—by Western standards—a minuscule staff. The palm trees, satellite dishes, and transmission masts outside dwarf the headquarters building in Qatar's capital, Doha. Egyptian president

Hosni Mubarak, touring the building in 2000, is said to have exclaimed: "This matchbox? All this noise is coming out of this matchbox?" (quoted in Friedman, 2001; Zednick, 2002).

The main newsroom, with about seventy workstations, measures 45 feet (14 meters) in each direction. Al-Jazeera has 755 employees worldwide compared with CNN's 4,000. Only seventy-five journalists work in the Doha newsroom, said Ballout, who is one of three people authorized to give media interviews (Ballout, 2003).

The others are managing director Al-Ali and chairman Sheik Hamad. Reporter Rick Zednik, who spent twelve days in Qatar in late 2001, described the journalists in the newsroom as a loose, sociable bunch, representing almost all twenty-two members of the Arab League. "Moroccan producers, Syrian talk show hosts, Iraqi translators, Algerian fixers, Sudanese librarians, Palestinian secretaries, and Qatari executives all speak together in Arabic" (Zednik, 2002). No one nationality dominates, though almost all are Muslims. The newsroom is a secular place, but a tiny mosque sits behind the main building.

Journalists are united through their language and religion, though not necessarily their politics. Al-Ali believes this gives his station an edge over rivals in the region. "In Iraq we know the language," Ali-Ali has said. "We know the mentality. It's very easy for us to find out things and move around there" (quoted in Whitaker, 2003, p.1). The journalists come from many different backgrounds, Al-Ali said. "There are communists, secularists and Islamicists. But they produce professional work in the end" (Al-Farah, 2003).

Dima Khatib has worked as a reporter and producer for Al-Jazeera since 1997. A Syrian, she initially worked for Swiss Radio International in Berne. On the evening we interviewed her, it was her day off and she had already spent seven hours at the station, and was about to return to translate Spanish prime minister Jose Maria Aznar's broadcast from the Azores. Khatib speaks seven languages fluently and loves working at the channel. When she started it "felt like home" because it gave her a chance to "put all her experiences together" in an Arab context. "There is no typical day in my life, actually. This would be the hardest question for me to answer."

Working for Al-Jazeera gave her huge opportunities for travel, and to show the world that many of their perceptions of Arab women were stereotypes (Khatib, 2003).

Al-Ali maintains that his journalists' style is more similar to the BBC than CNN: "We are closer to the ideas and the rhythm of the reports of the BBC." Chief editor Ibrahim Helal said Al-Jazeera was set up about the same time that the Orbit-funded BBC Arabic TV service was closed down. Al-Jazeera brought seventeen former BBC staff to Doha to help build the channel.

"We built Al-Jazeera up on the Western experience we had," said Helal, who moved from London to Qatar. "From Day One most of our editorial staff were from this BBC environment: assignment editors, interview producers, news-gathering editors, even picture editors ... even after five years if we're in doubt in a certain situation, we convene and ask ourselves, if we were in London now what would we do?" (Sullivan, 2001). Al-Jazeera's staff are Arabs but most have had experience working with Western media—"they're ex-BBC, ex-U.S. media, but all are Arabs."

Reporters gained the professional experience from the BBC, but their background as Arabs meant they adapted this experience to the Arab world. "We know the mentality of the Arabs—but we also want the expatriate Arab audience, who are used to Western media." Al-Jazeera had worked hard to create a "culture of television journalism" in the newsroom, Helal said (quoted in Schleifer, 2000).

In an interview with Transnational Broadcasting Studies Journal, Al-Ali pointed out that chairman Sheikh Hamad had worked as a journalist for fourteen years and "thinks like a journalist" implying that he appreciated freedom of expression. "He's got good experience in the media. He's a graduate in communications from Qatar University ... [and he] thinks as a journalist, and that helps us a lot. He knows what we want exactly" (Schleifer, 2000). *Asia Times* magazine, based in Hong Kong, said Qatari officials likened their relationship with the channel to what the British Broadcasting Corporation enjoyed with the British government, but added a codicil: "It is a well-known fact that Qatari foreign minister Sheikh Hamad bin Jassim bin Jabr Al-Thani owns 35% of the channel and is a cousin of the Qatari emir" (Janardhan, 2002).

Al-Jazeera is not a member of the Arab States Broadcasting Union (ASBU). The channel initially applied for membership, but the union rejected it, claiming that Al-Jazeera failed to respect the union's code of honor, which includes not broadcasting material critical of any Arab head of state. Al-Ali admitted the channel tried to join in the beginning. "We would be an addition to them as much as they could be a support to us. We are not losing anything by not being part, though; there's no advantage for us" (quoted in Schleifer, 2000). By 2003, the channel was seeing its non-membership as a badge of honor, an indication that it was not part of the broadcasting establishment.

Al-Jazeera's chairman, Sheik Hamad, has maintained that the channel is going in the same direction as the state of Qatar. He cited elections for a chamber of commerce, plans for Parliamentary elections, and municipal elections with women's participation as candidates and voters as recent examples of modernization. Qatar was the first Gulf nation to hold elections for municipal positions. "I think this direction corresponds with the direction of the media, be it Al-Jazeera or lifting censorship on local Qatari newspapers. The two go together in this stage, and I think the direction of Al-Jazeera is a natural one that corresponds with the strategy Qatar is taking," Sheikh Hamad said (Sullivan, 2001).

AL-JAZEERA COPYCATS

With the onset of conflict in Iraq, it appears that several other broadcasters are looking at recreating the Al-Jazeera formula. Late in 2002 the U.S. Congress approved $30 million for creation of the Middle East Television Network (METN). The Arabic channel is said to be the brainchild of Kenneth Tomlinson, president of the United States Broadcasting Board of Governors in charge of radio and television broadcasts targeting foreign audiences. Tomlinson said a U.S. state-run television broadcast via satellite was "an important step towards reaching the people in the Arab world with accurate news and the message of freedom and democracy" (Tomlinson, 2003).

Abu Dhabi Television, the flagship of Emirates Media Incorporated, has an extensive news operation that gained much attention from Arab viewers because of its coverage of the Intifada violence from September 2001. It set up a bureau in a prime location in central Baghdad several months before the war started. The station also distributed $8 million worth of backpack video equipment with satellite uplinks to people on the ground in Iraq. Many of these people were not trained as reporters but they have managed to get some impressive footage. These strategic moves have meant the channel has been able to provide superior coverage of the war in the capital, especially after Iraq evicted CNN's four journalists soon after war started.

Late in 2002, the Saudi-owned Middle East Broadcasting Center (MBC), with headquarters in Dubai in the United Arab Emirates, announced the formation of Al-Arabiya, a twenty-four hour news channel. It launched on February 20, 2003, broadcasting for twelve hours a day, and sees Al-Jazeera as its main competition. Salah Negm, head of news at MBC, said journalists with TV experience at an international level were rare in the Arab world. "The industry is not yet mature and the training in most of the mass communication schools is not up to the required standards," he said. Negm worked for Al-Jazeera from July 1996 until September 2001. The $300 million investment in Al-Arabia is said to come from private Saudi, Kuwaiti, and Lebanese businessmen, but the Saudi government, through parent company MBC, will be able to exercise influence (Khalaf, 2003).

In Beirut, the Lebanese Broadcasting Corporation (LBC) and the London-based newspaper Al-Hayat will spend $12 million a year in a joint venture in which the newspaper's sixty-nine correspondents supply news for LBC International's three, half-hour bulletins each day. Jihad Khazen, Al-Hayat's founding editor-in-chief, and LBCI's managing editor Salameh Nemett said if the venture succeeded another twenty-four hour news channel could emerge. Saudi money is also partly behind this partnership (Khalaf, 2003).

For his part, Ballout is not worried. "If imitation is any indication of respect, then Al-Jazeera is doing well. This little bit of competition is always healthy."

THE ECONOMICS OF AL-JAZEERA

One key issue in the drive for editorial independence will be revenue streams for all stations. Despite the fact that Al-Jazeera has the most popular news and is the second most-watched pan-Arab station, it generated only about $66 million in advertising revenue in 2002. By contrast, the Lebanese Broadcasting Company (LBC)—the region's most-watched network—attracted about $93 million. MBC generated about $300 million, and LBCSAT generated about $66 million (Pan Arab Research Center, 2003).

Most Arab stations earn about 90% of their revenue from advertising. But commercials account for only 40% of Al-Jazeera's revenues. The rest comes from renting equipment, cable subscription fees, and selling programs and videotapes. Three-minute sections of Bin Laden footage have reportedly fetched as much as $250,000 apiece. As of early 2002 the station operated without government subsidies, Al-Ali said (Zednik, 2002).

Yet this is not the same as paying for itself. Seven years after launching and sixteen months after it was cut loose from the emir's financial umbilical cord—and despite a huge audience of at least thirty-five million households—Al-Jazeera was not making money as of early 2003. "We have not yet reached the profit-making phase," said Al-Ali in January 2003. "In fact, we are still trying to break even by covering our expenses from our work as much as possible and by diversifying the sources of income" (Al-Farah, 2003). The sale of footage from the Afghan conflict to other television channels has boosted revenue, as should footage from the Iraqi war.

Meanwhile, some major advertisers operate an undeclared boycott, Al-Ali admitted. "Advertising in the Middle East is not based on the commercial, it is based on the political," he said, though he declined to give more details. Others blame Saudi influence and moves by the Gulf Co-operation Council against the channel (Whitaker, 2003, p. 2).

In another, earlier interview, Al-Ali said the channel needed to change the mentality of the businessman in the region. "Usually when you have a large audience, all the advertising companies come to you. Here, all the advertising businesses are impacted by political considerations; they think about the political side rather than business side. I think this will change, just like the freedom of the press has changed on the editorial side" (quoted in Schleifer, 2000).

Regional and multinational companies tend to avoid ruffling the feathers of host governments, so they also have not bought advertising. Al-Ali admitted that Saudi Arabian companies had tried to influence Al-Jazeera's coverage by cutting advertising budgets for the station or threatening to do so. The tactic had no effect, he said. "We would lose our credibility with the audience." PepsiCo and General Electric canceled advertising campaigns worth a combined $3 million in 2001, Al-Ali said (Zednik, 2002). Some marketing people have suggested taking advantage of the Al-Jazeera brand, probably one of the most valuable in the Middle East. A tobacco company wanted to use the channel to sell Al-Jazeera cigarettes but that idea was dropped. Branded sunglasses might be a safer option, marketing staff suggested (Whitaker, 2003, p. 2).

Al-Jazeera still has big plans, despite cash shortfalls. On March 16, 2003, it announced that an English-language Web site would be launched that month, just more than two years after launch of *aljazeera.net*. The new site debuted ten days later, presumably hastened by the need to cover the Iraq war (see http://english.aljazeera.net/), and immediately became a target for hackers, which shut the site down almost as soon as it opened.

Al-Jazeera also said it would be broadcasting in English early in 2004. It remains to be seen whether the latter occurs, because other broadcast plans announced years earlier have failed to materialize. Late in 2001, Al-Ali announced plans to launch new Arabic-language networks, including a business news channel in cooperation with CNBC and a documentary channel along the lines of National Geographic or Discovery.

In January 2003 Al-Ali repeated the plan to establish an Arabic-language documentary channel by the end of that year, along with opening bureaus in Jakarta and Kuala Lumpur (Al-Farah, 2003), respectively the capitals of Indonesia and Malaysia. Indonesia has the world's largest Muslim population. The channel has signed an agreement with the BBC to set up a training center, because Al-Ali appreciates the importance of training. To stay at the top, he said, "we have to keep up with the latest in the technological and technical fields and raise the efficiency of the technicians and employees."

Conclusion

Despite the number of pretenders Al-Jazeera intends to stay at the top. It has the advantage of a good reputation among Arab viewers, the benefit of being the first twenty-four hour news and talk station in the Arab world, and dedicated and well-trained staff.

The major issue will be its ability to pay for itself and to keep key people. Despite having a smaller staff budget compared with CNN and BBC World, broadcasting remains an expensive business. Small staff numbers mean that reporters work long hours, and it may prove difficult to retain staff over the long term if they are tired, and if richer channels come by with checkbooks open.

Regardless of whether reviewers have been negative or positive, it is safe to say Al-Jazeera has attracted great attention, putting tiny Qatar with its population of perhaps 600,000 on the world map. And, while some critics object to the "how" and the "what" that the stations put on air, those who work at Al-Jazeera believe in their mission.

"The journalist always makes a difference. From a basic reporter up to the editor-in-chief, everyone makes a difference. We feel that we are making a difference, especially in view of how the traditional Arab media has been for the past four or five decades," said Ballout. Al-Jazeera and its staff, he believes, are a breath of fresh air. They are happy to be creating ripples in the stagnant pond of Arabic broadcasting.

REFERENCES

Ajami, Fouad. (2001, November 18). What the Muslim world is watching. *New York Times Magazine.*

Al-Farah, Mohammed Khayr. (2003, February 1). Al-Jazeera TV head views factors behind channel's success. Al-Dustur, Amman. Translated from Arabic.

Anonymous. (2002, June 11). Interview with authors in Doha, Qatar.

Badran, B. (2003, March 26). Interview with authors in Dubai.

Ballout, J.A. (2003, March 16). Interview with authors in Doha, Qatar.

Campagna, J. (2001). Between two worlds: Qatar's Al-Jazeera satellite channel faces conflicting expectations. *Committee to Protect Journalists*, October 2001. http://www.cpj.org/Briefings/2001/aljazeera_oct01/aljazeera_oct01.html

Curtiss, R. (1998). Being there: Spring 1998 in the Persian/Arabian Gulf. *The Washington Post*, Report on Middle East Affairs, May-June 1998. http://www.washington-report.org/backissues/0598/9805017.html

Friedman, T. (2001, February 27). Glasnost in the Gulf. *The New York Times.*

Gulf News. (2002, October 10). Call to ban Al-Jazeera in Gulf states, p1.

Janardhan, N. (2002, August 15). Al-Jazeera: Qatar's secret weapon? *Asia Times online*, Hong Kong, http://www.atimes.com/atimes/Middle_East/DH15Ak01.html

Jayyusi, L. (2003, March 30). Email interview with authors.

Khalaf, R. (2003, February 2). Arab TV gears up for fight on home front. *Financial Times*, London.

Khatib, D. (2003, March 16). Interview with authors in Doha, Qatar.

New York Daily News. (2001, October 14). Editorial: Al-Jazeera unmasked: An Arab propaganda machine in the guise of real journalism.

Pan Arab Research Center. (2003). Dubai. http://www.arabiandemographics.com

Schleifer, A. (2000, Fall/Winter). A dialogue with Mohammed Jasim Al-Ali, managing director, Al-Jazeera. *Transnational Broadcasting Studies Journal, 5*, Fall/winter 2000. http://www.tbsjournal.com/Archives/Fall00/al-Ali.htm

Sullivan, S. (2001, Fall). Transcript of interview with Sheikh Hamad bin Thamer Al-Thani, chairman of the board of Al-Jazeera. *Transnational Broadcasting Studies Journal, 7*, Fall/Winter2001. Retrieved from http://www.tbsjournal.com/Archives/Fall01/Jazeera_chairman.html

Tomlinson, K. (2003, March 29). Personal conversation with authors in Abu Dhabi.

Whitaker, B. (2003, February 7). Al-Jazeera: Battle station. *The Guardian* media section, pp.1-2.

Zednik, R. (2002). Inside Al-Jazeera. *Columbia Journalism Review*, February 2002. http://www.cjr.org/year/02/2/zednik.asp

CHAPTER 6

Global News Agencies and the Pre-War Debate: A Content Analysis

Beverly Horvit

In his January 2002 State of the Union address, President George W. Bush described an "axis of evil" that he said included Iraq, Iran, and North Korea.

Although the United States had persuaded thirty countries to support its efforts to oust Iraqi leader Saddam Hussein by the invasion of Iraq on March 20, 2003, many influential nations, including Russia, China and France—all permanent members of the UN Security Council—remained steadfastly opposed to U.S.-led military attack. Each of those countries is also home to a global news agency—agencies that sometimes are accused of either being biased toward their home countries or as being propaganda tools for those same countries. Similarly, the United States is home to the world's dominant news agency, The Associated Press (Hachten & Scotten, 2002, p. 33).

Forty years ago, Bernard C. Cohen (1963, p. 13) noted, "The world looks different to different people, depending not only on their personal interests, but also on the map that is drawn for them by the writers, editors, and publishers of the papers they read." More than 80% of the material in newspapers and other media worldwide emanates from global news agencies based in four of the world's major capitals—all of them in the West (Hachten, 1993, p. 165).

How might the world look different depending upon where one gets his or her news? Are different news sources allowed to dominate the debate? Is U.S. policy portrayed more negatively or positively, depending upon where a particular news service is based?

This study compares coverage of the pre-war debate in five news agencies—The Associated Press, Agence France Presse, Xinhua, ITAR-TASS, and the Inter Press Service—to determine how, if at all, the coverage varied by the type news agency in terms of sourcing and the tone of coverage.

THE NEWS AGENCIES

News is transmitted around the globe largely through the efforts of major "world agencies," such as The Associated Press, Agence France Presse, and ITAR-TASS (Hachten & Scotten, p. 33). The AP, a U.S.-based nonprofit cooperative, supplies a high percentage of the international news in most U.S. daily newspapers (Hertog, 2000, p. 616) and is the "dominant institution in the world news system" (Hachten & Scotten, p. 33). For its part, Agence France Presse is subsidized by the French government (Hachten, p. 33) and "has not been able to shrug off allegations that it is linked to French government interests" (Alleyne, 1995, p. 80).

Like the United States and France, Russia and China also have major news agencies based in their countries. ITAR-TASS (the Information Telegraph Agency of Russia) has traditionally been considered among the Big Five news agencies, but it has not been viewed as a serious rival to the Western agencies because of its history of direct control by the Soviet government. In 1970, Schwartz wrote bluntly:

> TASS and other communist news agencies are servants of the governments which own and control them. These state-operated agencies are propaganda instruments, and the news they disseminate publicly reflects the policy objectives of their masters (p. 743).

Of course, the Soviet Union no longer exists and TASS can no longer be considered a communist news agency. In addition, the introduction of *perestroika* in the late 1980s "meant a new role for TASS, more approaching that of the Western agencies" (Alleyne & Wagner, 1993, p. 41). Like ITAR-TASS, Xinhua was established as a state-controlled official spokesman for its communist government. Even in the 1990s, its Hong Kong branch was used for diplomatic functions (Chu, 1999), and Xinhua correspondents enjoyed diplomatic immunity (Chaudhary & Cooper-Chen, 1995, p. 307).

In addition to Xinhua and TASS, another news agency likely to provide a different perspective on world events than that provided by the Western news agencies is the Inter Press Service (IPS). To compensate for the Western agencies' near monopoly on the flow of news, IPS was created to provide coverage of the developing world. IPS is now "the largest international agency specializing in Third World News" (Giffard & Rivenburgh, 2000, p. 12). Altschull (1995) reports that by the 1980s, IPS had become the sixth-largest world news agency (p. 312). According to the Inter Press Service Web site, "IPS focuses its news coverage on the events and global processes affecting the economic, social and political development of peoples and nations" (IPS, 2003).

Hachten and Scotten (2002) argue that Western news media have more freedom and independence to report world news and, thus, have more credibility "than media of other nations" (p. 32). But other scholars are skeptical about the Western agencies' ability to provide objective, independent reports. Indeed, part of the 1970s and 1980s debate over the flow of news stemmed from developing countries' belief that the big news agencies were not reporting objectively, but instead were reinforcing negative stereotypes and reporting more about the interests of wealthy countries than developing ones (Altschull, 1995, p. 307). And, Richstad (1981) notes, "Imbalance in the flow of news, for example, is viewed as a serious problem to the United States understanding of the world, particularly of the non-Western world (p. 248)."

Overall, then, various scholars have argued that news agencies—whether Western or non-Western—represent the interests and ideologies of the countries in which they are based. Is this true for perhaps the most significant of news stories: an international debate on whether the 2003 Gulf War was justified?

Media and Foreign Policy

Where foreign policy is concerned, one would expect state-owned and/or state-controlled agencies, such as Xinhua and ITAR-TASS, to promote their governments' views. Could that promotion also occur in the Western press? Scholars assert that it sometimes does. If so, the news agencies would be prone to quote sources from the news organization's home country.

Hertog (2000) identified three major influences on American media coverage of foreign policy: administration press management (the administration's ability to shape how news is presented), press professionalism, and public patriotism. Press professionalism refers to the Western journalistic tradition of objectivity and reporting "both" sides of an issue, and public patriotism refers to the press and public's tendency to rally around the flag during emergencies like war. Berenger and Hulsman (2001) discovered a similar rallying effect when Egyptian papers—even "opposition papers"—felt their regime was "threatened" by political dissidence, much less a war.

Bennett's "indexing" hypothesis (1990) suggests that U.S. journalists choose news sources that mirror the range of mainstream views expressed during a national debate on a topic. So, when would U.S. journalists be most likely to turn to international news sources? When opposing views are difficult to find in the United States (Althaus et al., 1996, p. 13). Of course, opposing views on the imminent war with Iraq were easy to find in both the United States and elsewhere. Thus, to what degree do news agencies from around the world choose to report those opposing views?

Drawing on the arguments above, this study will test four hypotheses:

H1: *The news agencies' sourcing practices will reflect the agencies' national origin by quoting a higher percentage of sources from their home countries.*

H2: *The news agencies' sourcing practices will reflect the Western vs. non-Western background of the agencies.*

H3: *The tone of the non-Western news agencies' coverage will reflect the foreign policy of the country (or countries) each agency serves.*

H4: *Despite the journalistic code of objectivity, Agence France Presse's coverage will be more negative toward the United States than will be the coverage of the AP.*

Methodology

A random sample of twenty articles was selected from each of the five wire services—The Associated Press, Agence France Presse, Xinhua, TASS and Inter Press Service—for a total of one hundred articles.

The stories were selected from the Lexis-Nexis database using "Iraq" and the "United States" as key words, the individual news agency as the source, and between January 29 and February 11, 2003, as the date—the two weeks following President Bush's State of the Union address.

Only stories longer than 150 words that focused on the U.S.-Iraq conflict were included. Using those search terms, The Associated Press transmitted about 660 original articles for the two-week period, Agence France Presse transmitted about 830; Xinhua, 410; TASS, seventy; and IPS, twenty.

Each paragraph of the one hundred selected stories—1,306 paragraphs in all—was then analyzed for the nationality of the sources cited. Each paragraph also was analyzed for the valence of the content—positive, negative, or neutral—toward U.S. policy on Iraq.

The author and a team of eight undergraduate coders conducted three pretests using nine randomly selected stories from AP, AFP, and Xinhua that did not duplicate stories chosen for the actual study. On the third pretest, the level of agreement was 81% for the valence coding and 91% for the source coding.

TABLE 6.1 THE NEWS AGENCIES' USE OF SOURCES

News Agency	Mean percentage of source type per story by news agency							
	American	United Nations	Chinese	French	Iraqi	Russian	Other Western	Other non-Western
AFP (N=20)	32.9	5.7	0	1.3	9.4	0.3	21.2	29.2
AP (N= 18[1])	38.2	4.3	0.3	9.9	6.4	0.7	27.6	12.5
IPS (N=20)	37.3	7.5	0.2	4.5	1.0	1.4	4.0	44.1
ITAR-TASS (N= 18[1])	8.5	0	3.3	0	5.6	43.7*	16.7	22.2
Xinhua (N= 18[1])	34.5	0	5.6	3.3	6.7	2.2	15.3	32.4

[1] Some stories had no sources, so they were treated as missing values. * $p < .0001$

Although all team members helped catalog the stories and record the sources, only the author and two other team members did the valence coding. On the third pretest, those three coders had agreed with the majority on the valence issues between 81% and 92% of the time.

FINDINGS

H1: *The news agencies' sourcing practices will reflect the agencies' national origin by quoting a higher percentage of sources from their home countries.*

Only partial support was found for the first hypothesis.

For four of the five news agencies, sources from the United States were by far the most likely to be quoted (see Table 6.1). Such a trend in coverage is not surprising given that the United States is the world's lone superpower and the decision to go to war against Iraq rested in Washington.

The exception was ITAR-TASS, whose sourcing reflected its national origins. Nearly 44% of the sources cited by ITAR-TASS were Russian, compared with less than 1% for the AP and Agence France Presse, and 2% for Xinhua.

Although 38% of the sources cited by The Associated Press were from the United States—the highest percentage of U.S. news sources used by any news agency—its use of U.S. sources was not significantly different, statistically speaking, from the percentage of U.S. sources used by the other news agencies.

Similarly, although Xinhua used a higher percentage of Chinese sources

TABLE 6.2 EAST VS. WEST NEW AGENCY SOURCING

New Agencies	Mean percentage of Western vs. non-Western sources per story by news agency	
	Western sources	**Non-Western sources**
Western agencies	65.0	30.0
Agence France Presse (N=20)1	55.4	38.9
Associated Press[1] (N= 18)	75.7	20.0
Non-Western agencies	41.5	55.8
Inter Press Service[1] (N=20)	45.8	46.8
ITAR-TASS (N= 18)	25.2*	74.8*
Xinhua (N= 18)	53.1	46.9

[1]The percentages do not total 100 because the percentage of U.N. sources is not shown. *Significant difference from the other four agencies at p=.05, F=3.88, DF=4, n=93.

than any other news agency, the differences were not significant. Interestingly, Agence France Presse used a smaller percentage of French sources than all other agencies besides ITAR-TASS, which might be explained because its Nicosia, Cyprus, bureau covers the Middle East.

H2: *The news agencies' sourcing practices will reflect the Western vs. non-Western background of the agencies.*

Overall, the second hypothesis was supported.

As a group, the non-Western news agencies were more likely to use non-Western sources than were the Western news agencies. Nearly 56% of the sources cited by the non-Western agencies were non-Western, compared with 30% in the Western agencies (see Table 6.2). By the same token, 65% of the AP and AFP's sources were Western, compared with nearly 42% of the sources cited by the non-Western agencies.

However, when examining each news agency's sourcing practices individually, the hypothesis was not supported for Xinhua. More than 53% of the Chinese news agency's sources were from the West. As for the Inter Press Service, the difference between the use of Western vs. non-Western sources was minimal. Interestingly, the most significant differences in coverage appeared between The Associated Press and ITAR-TASS. Nearly 76% of The Associated Press' sources were Western, compared with about a fourth of the sources used by ITAR-TASS. In a mirror image, nearly 75% of ITAR-TASS' sources were non-Western, compared with only 20% of the AP's sources. (UN sources make up the differences.)

> **H3:** *The tone of the non-Western news agencies' coverage will reflect the foreign policy of the country (or countries) each agency serves.*

The data generally support the third hypothesis.

As expected, the articles written by the Inter Press Service and ITAR-TASS presented much more negative information toward the United States than positive and presented significantly more negative coverage than did the two Western agencies. On average, nearly 47% of the paragraphs in the Inter Press Service stories were negative toward U.S. policy, compared with 13% positive. Similarly, 54% of the ITAR-TASS paragraphs were negative on average, compared with 19% positive.

For the Western news agencies, nearly 35% of the information was positive, compared with 34% negative—what one would expect, given the Western concept of objectivity. Xinhua, on the other hand, reported more positively on U.S. policy than even the Western news agencies. Xinhua also presented less negative information about the United States—as a percentage of each story—than did any other news agency. Indeed, Xinhua presented more than twice as much positive information about the United States as negative (41% to nearly 19%).

For the Chinese news agency, H3 was not supported, even though the Chinese government did not support the U.S. decision to go to war.

> **H4:** *Despite the journalistic code of objectivity, Agence France Presse's coverage will be more negative toward the United States than will be the coverage of the AP.*

Although a higher percentage of information in Agence France Presse's report was negative than in the AP's report (36% compared with 32%), the difference was not statistically significant, and the hypothesis was not supported.

Discussion

This study confirms what researchers have come to expect from Western news agencies, but it also raises both theoretical and methodological issues that might be investigated further, particularly the role of the Xinhua.

The Western news agencies examined in this study performed as expected. Yes, they quoted Western sources more than non-Western sources, but neither The Associated Press or Agence France Presse blatantly advanced the viewpoints of their different governments.

Although the methodology may have been too simplistic to capture the nuances of international reporting and the amount of credibility conveyed upon a source, the AP and AFP did a remarkable job of balancing negative and positive information about U.S. policy. There were no statistically significant differences in the numbers of positive vs. negative paragraphs, which seems to indicate the agencies' paramount goal was objective reporting, getting both sides of a story.

But did the Western agencies really get both sides of the story? No. The U.S.-led war was a war against the government of Iraq, and yet Iraqi sources were difficult to find in this sample. Only 7% of the attributed paragraphs in the Western agencies' stories were attributed to Iraqis, compared with more than 30% attributed to Americans. Even so, the Western agencies were more likely to quote Iraqis than were the non-Western agencies. Even if journalists judged statements from Iraqi government officials as lacking credibility, surely the views of ordinary Iraqi citizens were relevant. It might be, of course, that those average Iraqi views were too difficult to get while Saddam Hussein's authoritarian regime was still in power.

Just as Western news agencies reported the U.S.-Iraq story as expected, so did two of the three non-Western news agencies, ITAR-TASS and IPS. Despite assumptions that ITAR-TASS has become more independent from its government since the collapse of the USSR, this study found the agency had not changed that much from the Cold War and still tended to disseminate propaganda rather than news. Although the major world news from January 31 to February 11, 2003 was the proposed U.S. action against Iraq, ITAR-TASS was more interested in reporting what the Russian government had to say than what was being said by U.S. officials who were making the final decisions about going to war.

Similarly, while the Western news agencies balanced positive vs. negative information toward the United States, ITAR-TASS' coverage leaned toward strongly negative. This study cannot answer why. Further study is needed to investigate these findings that contrast with ITAR-TASS' self-proclaimed mission to deliver balanced news to residents of Eastern Europe.

Inter Press Service's coverage was even more negative toward U.S. policies than ITAR-TASS' coverage. The key differences, though, were in its sourcing practices. IPS quoted Americans to the same degree as the other agencies, except ITAR-TASS. However, staying true to its mission of reporting on the developing world and those nations' concerns, IPS used the highest percentage of non-Western sources (not including Russian sources). If agencies such as IPS were created to give the developing world a voice, that need became more apparent in this study. In the Western news agencies' stories, about 30% of the cited information came from non-Western sources, compared with nearly 56% non-Western sourcing by the other agencies. This disparity is even more striking given that the war would take place in the non-Western world.

The biggest surprise in this study is the performance of Xinhua. Unlike the other two non-Western agencies, Xinhua did not perform as expected. Its coverage toward the U.S. policy on Iraq was the most positive of any news agency, and it did not use Chinese sources significantly more than the other agencies did. Just as critics have accused the West of stereotyping the developing world, the Xinhua exception in this study shows the danger in stereotyping news agencies. The stereotypes might not hold true when put to systematic analysis.

Was Xinhua "objective" in its reporting? Not if one uses a simple measure of objectivity, such as balancing positive vs. negative information—"both sides" of a story. However, neither did the state-controlled Chinese news agency use its English-language stories to spread China's point of view. On the other hand, the Chinese government might have orchestrated Xinhua's coverage to further its national directions. *The Baltimore Sun* noted that China's primary concern related to Iraq was to try to maintain a peaceful international environment:

> Relations with the United States have become an integral part of that calculation. The United States is a key trading partner, major source of investment, and now a convenient ally in efforts against terrorism. As a result, China has opposed aggressive actions against Iraq and North Korea, while trying not to directly oppose the United States (Epstein, 2003, p. 11A).

More research is needed to determine whether Xinhua's English-language coverage was premeditated, so to speak. This study cannot answer that question.

Implications for Further Research

Although this study finds that the non-Western news agencies did not transmit as much information to support U.S. policy as did the Western news agencies, this study cannot answer the question why, or determine what impact such reporting might have had on world opinion. More research is needed on the credibility of the news organizations in their home countries, and on the news organizations' reach via the other media in their countries.

In addition, what is true for a news agency based in a particular country surely is not true for all media in a country, particularly a democracy. Patterson and Donsbach (1996) note that many newspapers in Europe are associated with particular political parties or ideologies (p. 455). "Journalists are not nonpartisan actors; they are simply more or less partisan, depending on the country and arena in which they work (Patterson & Donsbach, p. 465)."

While a content analysis can systematically examine coverage and pinpoint differences, the content itself does not answer the question why. Why do some news agencies gravitate to some sources rather than others? Why do some news agencies seem to meticulously balance positive and negative information while others have a different mode of operation? How do journalists working for world news agencies see themselves and their roles? Do their perceptions match reality?

Finally, how the content is interpreted obviously depends on who's doing the coding. How does one's perception of whether a paragraph provides information to support or oppose U.S. policy depend on whether one is a U.S. citizen, a French citizen, or an Iraqi? How much does the coding depend on what a particular paragraph states vs. what the coder believes to be the context implicit in the information presented? Whether coders of different nationalities would obtain the same results is worth investigating.

Despite the limitations of the study, this research indicates that four of the news agencies studied are not overly nationalistic, and that the Associated Press and Agence France Presse did a remarkable job—for better or worse—of balancing positive and negative information. This study also points out the danger of stereotyping all non-Western agencies as nonobjective and biased toward the West. ITAR-TASS' coverage during this two-week period only confirmed its nationalistic, nonobjective image, but Xinhua's coverage was more positive toward the United States, used more Western sources, and used fewer Chinese sources than one would have predicted. The next question is why.

REFERENCES

Alleyne, M.D. & Wagner, J. (1993). Stability and change at the "Big Five" news agencies. *Journalism Quarterly, 70*(1), 40-50.

Alleyne, M. (1995). *International power and international communication.* New York: St. Martin's Press.

Althaus, S.L., Edy, J.A., Entman R.M., & Phalen, P. (1996). Revising the indexing hypothesis: officials, media, and the Libya crisis. *Political Communication, 13,* 407-421.

Altschull, J.H. (1995). *Agents of power: The media and public policy.* White Plains, NY: Longman.

Bennett, W.L. (1990). Toward a theory of press-state relations. *Journal of Communication, 40*(2), 103-125.

Berenger, R.D. & Hulsman, C. (2001, April 20) The rallying effect of the Egyptian media in the case of Saad Eddin Ibrahim: A preliminary executive summary of the Arabic Press. Paper presented at the Western Social Science Association Conference, Reno, NV, April 18-21.

Chaudhary, A.G. & Cooper-Chen, A. (1995). Asia and the Pacific. In J.C. Merrill (Ed.). *Global journalism: Survey of international communication.* (3rd. Ed.). White Plains, NY: Longman, pp. 269-328.

Chu, Y. (1999). Overt and covert functions of the Hong Kong branch of the Xinhua News Agency, 1947-1984. *Historian, 62*(1), 31-47.

Cohen, B.C. (1963). *The press and foreign policy.* New Jersey: Princeton University Press.

Epstein, G.A. (2003, March 11). China keeping its focus inward on Korea, Iraq; taking a cautious stance, Beijing aims to preserve stability at home, abroad. *The Baltimore Sun*, p. 11A.

Giffard, C.A. & Rivenburgh, N.K. (2000). News agencies, national images, and global media events. *Journalism & Mass Communication Quarterly, 77*(1), 8-21.

Hachten, W.A. & Scotten, J.F. (2002). *The world news prism: global media in an era of terrorism.* (6th Ed.) Ames, IA: Iowa State Press.

Hertog, J.K. (2000). Elite press coverage of the 1986 U.S.-Libya conflict: a case study of tactical and strategic critique. *Journalism & Mass Communication Quarterly, 77*(3), 612-627.

Inter Press Service. (2003). About us. Retrieved April 1, 2003, from http://ips.org/.

Patterson, T.E. & Donsbach, W. (1996). News decisions: journalists as partisan actors. *Political Communication, 12,* 455-468.

Richstad, J. (1981). Transnational news agencies: issues and policies. In J. Richstad & M.A. Anderson (Eds.) *Crisis in international news: policies and prospects.* New York: Columbia University Press, pp. 241-267.

Schwartz, H. (1970). Covering the foreign news. *Foreign Affairs,* 48(4), 741-758.

Part II

THE WORLD WAR OF WORDS

CHAPTER 7

Language, Media and War: Manipulating Public Perceptions

Yahya R. Kamalipour

In the dawn of the third millennium, we are witnessing an unprecedented period in history in which a technological revolution and multiplicity of communication channels impact human life, thought, and consciousness. The Age of Information is here and so is the Age of Manipulation. We are immersed in a sea of information yet unable to distinguish between reality and unreality.

As Mar Slouka (1995, pp. 1-2) puts it: "Increasingly removed from personal experience and over dependent on the representations of reality that come to us through television and the print media, we seem more and more willing to put our trust in intermediaries who 're-present' the world to us." This situation is intensified during conflicts and wars in which highly charged terms such as "fundamentalism," "terrorism," "jihad," and "evil" are used to influence public opinion in favor of a particular government agenda.

While language shapes our reality, war shatters our reality. "The language of war is created long before the first plane takes off; long before the first missile is fired; long before the first soldier sets foot on foreign soil. It is created by a consciousness, whether individual or collective, that chooses war as the most effective response to threat. This choice, in turn, shapes the consciousness of a nation" (World Watch, 2003, p. 1).

Propaganda and Media

One of the early masters of propaganda, Joseph Goebbels, said: "We do not talk to say something, but to obtain a certain effect." In other words, the main goal of propaganda is to achieve a specific result (e.g., altering public opinion), usually through military or economic actions, such as imposing an embargo on a certain nation.

Perhaps Harold Lasswell's definition of the goal of propaganda is still accurate: "To maximize the power at home by subordinating groups and individuals, while reducing the material cost of power." Similarly, explains Jacques Ellul, "In war, propaganda is an attempt to win victory with a minimum of physical expenses. Before the war, propaganda is a substitute for physical violence; during the war, it is a supplement to it" (Ellul, 1965, p. x).

In contemporary societies, particularly in the technologically advanced nations, mass media have without doubt become the conveyors of propaganda. To reach the masses, either nationally or internationally, propagandists have no other choice than to utilize the existing channels of mass and global communication. Of course, for propaganda purposes, a centralized system of communication is much more efficient and effective than a decentralized system. In 1965, Ellul wrote:

> To make the organization of propaganda possible, the media must be concentrated, the number of news agencies reduced, the press brought under single control, and radio and film monopolies established. The effect will be still greater if the various media are concentrated in the same hands (p. 102).

Interestingly, in 2003 a handful of transnational conglomerates own and control most of the channels of communication in the United States, and indeed, throughout the world. According to an American newspaper columnist, William Safire (2003),

> The sleeper issue is media giantism. People are beginning to grasp and resent the attempt by the Federal Communications Commission to allow the Four Horsemen of Big Media—Viacom (CBS, UPN), Disney (ABC), Murdoch's News Corporation (Fox) and G.E. (NBC)—to gobble up every independent station in sight.

The Language of War

Words are symbolic representations of human thoughts, actions, and feelings. Their shared meanings, among members of a particular group, form language. Language, to use a dictionary definition, is "the expression and communication of emotions or ideas between human beings by means of speech and hearing." Psychologically, words are as powerful as icons, signs, and flags.

Hence, to reduce their emotional impact, especially in war, army generals and the Pentagon's communication planners devise words and phrases that are often unknown to the general public and are, therefore, devoid of any emotions.

> Language, like terrorism, targets civilians and generates fear in order to effect political change. When our political leaders and our media outlets use terms like Anthrax, terrorist threat, madmen, and biological weapons, a specific type of fearfulness emerges, both intentionally and unintentionally. We are all targets for this type of language, and we are all affected by it as well. (Collins & Glover, 2002, p. 2)

To manipulate public opinion, communication and war strategists of a given nation concoct numerous words and phrases to justify any political conflict or military action against another nation. The language of war is intended to soften the tragic realities of human blood and gore through highly sophisticated manipulation techniques involving the creation of words, phrases, euphemisms, and images that are intended to sanitize and, in the process, desensitize human feelings toward mass killings and destruction. In order to achieve their goals, government and military leaders, aided by the mass media professionals, displace reality with fiction, fact with symbolism, and truth with propaganda. Indeed, truth is always the first casualty of war.

The process is that government and military officials unveil their concocted terms in their pronouncements prior to war; mass media reporters incorporate them into their daily reports; and, through repetition, the mass audiences (public) add them to their conversations, often without knowing their true meanings. In other words, military jargon, hyped by the mass media, becomes public jargon. Consider the following military jargon, from the two Persian Gulf wars and the War on Terrorism, which have become common public expressions:

Collateral Damage: Civilians killed or injured.
Friendly Fire: Soldiers killed or injured by their own coalition partner troops.
Shock and Awe: Scaring the wits out of the Iraqi regime and people to affect surrender to the Anglo-American forces.
Pre-Emptive Strike: Attacking a nation or group, unilaterally, based on assumptions of a threat.
Just War: Justifying an attack based on such assumptions.
Coalition of the Willing: The thirty countries out of the nearly two hundred nations *that are assisting or supporting the American-led attack against Iraq.*
Embedded Reporters: Journalists who are willingly cooperating and are literally accompanying the military forces
The Mother of All Bombs: A 20-ton weapon of mass destruction.
The Mother of All Battles: An unprecedented military operation or war.
Operation Iraqi Freedom: Getting rid of the Ba'ath regime and replacing it with a regime which would ensure the interests of the invading forces, multinational

corporations, and oil companies.

Operation Desert Storm: Invading and partitioning Iraq without removing the •dictator, Saddam Hussein, or his regime.

Theater of Operation: Battleground or war front.

Turkey Run: Randomly killing a massive number of people.

Carpet Bombing: Indiscriminate bombing of selected locations.

Body Bags: Killed soldiers.

Bunker Buster: Bombs dropped on safety shelters.

Daisy Cutter: A bomb capable of penetrating and destroying caves and their occupants.

Sorties: Bombing missions on various targets.

Peacemakers: Soldiers and even bombs.

Attacking Positions: Attacking soldiers or people.

Attacking Targets: Attacking buildings, military installations, or other infra-structures.

Decapitation: Killing and destroying any opposition.

Terrorist: Any individual, group, or nation that one may dislike.

The Patriot: A missile.

Patriotic: Describing an individual who unconditionally supports the government and its military actions even if they are contrary to the spirit of the nation's Constitution, international rules, human rights, UN mission, and world public opinion.

The language of war reaches beyond our common history. Countless war-like conflicts pursued by the British, French, Spanish, Portuguese, Italian, Russian, Germanic, and U.S. powers against Afghanistan, India, Africa, Hawaii, Cuba, China, Indonesia, New Zealand, the island of Grenada, and almost everywhere else were called "expeditions," "skirmishes," "campaigns," "invasions," "mutinies," "conflicts, "occupations," and "militia/vigilante actions." Such terms of art for acts of war were a kind of coded justification (Adamson, 2003, p.1).

In other words, when a nation prepares for war, the language its leaders use not only has been predetermined, but also is aimed at justifying a nation's action (war) and achieving a predetermined objective (victory).

The United States and the Middle East

The United States is militarily and economically the most powerful nation in the history of the world. Hence, as a lone superpower, its activities and foreign policies affect the lives of people throughout the world.

Rhetorical pronouncements and sophisticated propaganda packages, even if paved with good intentions, are not sufficient in themselves to produce the desired results of less terrorism or a more peaceful world. Furthermore, the history of U.S. involvement in the affairs of other nations does not, unfortunately, lend itself to optimism. America's well-documented track record is perhaps one of the reasons that people of the world perceive the United States in a negative light (this negative view, by the way, is not confined only to the Islamic or Middle Eastern countries).

Mass media's stereotypical representations of ethnic groups form public perceptions. Perceptions become realities and these realities (often actually fictional) influence the ways in which people act or react toward one another. Although there is no justification for any terrorist act by anyone anywhere, portraying an entire nation, religion, and culture as terrorists is clearly unjust, illogical, undemocratic, and counterproductive. Unfortunately, terrorism (carried out by various groups and states) has existed throughout human history and has never been confined to a particular region, religion, nation, or culture. It has become a global phenomenon that all of humanity must collectively reckon with and resolve.

In the aftermath of 9/11, the U.S. government arrested and jailed, in most cases without charge, over a thousand individuals, virtually all either Arab or Muslim (Collins & Glover, 2002, p. 6). Nearly three years later, hundreds of these prisoners were still confined at the Guantanamo Bay Naval Station in Cuba without any specific legal reasons or charges. The attacks of September 11,

> ... did not "change everything," but accelerated the continuity of events, providing extraordinary pretext for destroying social democracy. The undermining of the Bill of Rights in the United States and the further dismantling of trial by jury in Britain and a plethora of related civil liberties are part of the reduction of democracy to electoral ritual: that is, competition between indistinguishable parties for the management of a singly-ideology state. (Pilger, 2003, pp. 1-2)

Unfortunately, there are individuals, groups, politicians, and governments who tend to justify practically any action, including terrorizing or dehumanizing a particular ethnic or religious group in the name of national security, as war on terrorism, freedom, or other concocted reasons. This can be done verbally, as with Jerry Falwell's and Pat Robertson's derogatory comments about Islam; violently, as with the terrorists' bombings in Bali, Kenya, Saudi Arabia, and elsewhere; psychologically, as with discriminatory detentions and fingerprinting of members of certain ethnic groups; and finally, military, as with massive military assault. Of course, occupying Iraq has given the U.S. control over substantial oil resources in the Middle East and increased its global power but, at the same time, U.S. aggression has tarnished its global image. Tyrannical rulers, such as Saddam Hussein and his ilk, must be removed, but not through destroying the infrastructure of a nation and certainly not at the cost of sacrificing innocent civilian lives.

MEDIA AND PERCEPTION

The late Canadian media guru, Marshall McLuhan, predicted in the 1960s that future wars will not be fought with conventional weapons on the battlegrounds, but rather with images portrayed by the mass media. Today, "the war of images" is in full swing, and image-makers are busily packaging and selling everything from soap, toys, and breakfast cereals to presidential candidates, nations, religions, and ideas.

The words and pictures conveyed to us by the mass (global) media form our perceptions of the world beyond our immediate environment. In other words, "While we do not always realize it, language acts as a determinate factor in the formation of our perceptions of the world" (Collins & Glover, p. 4).

Wars produce casualties, and in the contemporary war of images, words, and military aggression, the Middle East and everything associated with it suffers, physically and psychologically, from a relentless attack by U.S. and British politicians and the mass media.

One of the ironies of the information age is that it has become increasingly difficult to distinguish between reality and unreality. More information, distributed at the speed of light, does not necessarily lead to a more informed or engaged public. Furthermore, the packaging of information—aided by digital technology and sophisticated propaganda techniques used by media experts—creates an environment in which an average individual becomes confused, often unable to sift through a sea of news and information. Consider the following:

> As everyone knows, unreality increases with speed. Walking across a landscape at six miles an hour, we experience the particular reality of place: its smells, sounds, colors, textures, and so on. Driving at seventy miles an hour, the experience is very different. The car isolates us, distances us; the world beyond the windshield—whether desert mesa or rolling farmland—seems vaguely unreal. At supersonic speed, the divorce is complete. A landscape at 30,000 feet is an abstraction, as unlike real life as a painting (Slouka, p. 3).

WAR AND PEACE

Throughout history, war-makers have created new words and phrases to sanitize the gruesome realities of war and, in the process, neutralize or deflect public sentiments in favor of their actions. "Blitz" was used in World War II, "friendly fire" in the Vietnam War, "the mother of all battles," in the 1991 Gulf War, and "shock and awe" in the 2003 Gulf War . Unfortunately, numerous tyrants, through propaganda, have turned "civilized" citizens into "murderers." Such villainous figures riddle human history. Hitler in Germany, Milosevic in

Yugoslavia, Pinochet in Chile, Pol Pot in Cambodia, and Saddam Hussein in Iraq are just few cases in point.

In the early part of the 21st century, McLuhan's global village is in turmoil, and the prevailing attitudes are "us against them" and "them against us." The post-Cold War and September 11 eras attest to a total breakdown in communication, trust, civility, international law, human rights, freedom, and a lack of progress in terms of humanity and global progress toward achieving a relative state of harmony in the world.

The September 11 terrorist attacks on the World Trade Center and the Pentagon will forever be etched into the memories of the people who personally experienced the events or viewed the images of these unimaginable tragedies on television screens throughout the world. These tragic events, along with the less televised, disastrous wars on Iraq and Afghanistan, have made it quite apparent that we, as human beings, have made no progress toward elevating humanity to its potential level of civility. Rather, we have marched backward into the savageries of the Stone Age and succumbed to a vicious circle of violence that continues to plague our lives, curtail our freedoms, alter our way of life, damage our relationships, and distort our perceptions of one another. We are caught up in a complex web of destruction of our own making.

According to John Pilger (2003), in George Orwell's prophetic novel, *1984*:

> ... three slogans dominate society: War is Peace, Freedom is Slavery and Ignorance is Strength. Today's slogan, 'war on terrorism,' also reverses meaning. The war *is* terrorism. The most potent weapon in this 'war' is pseudo-information, different only in form from that Orwell described, consigning to oblivion unacceptable truths and historical sense. Dissent is permissible within 'consensual' boundaries, reinforcing the illusion that information and speech are 'free' (p. 1).

In this so-called "Information Age" or "Communication Age," ironically, the missing components are reliable information and meaningful communication. Perhaps the terms "Disinformation Age" or "Babble Age" would more accurately describe this gloomy period in history. Today, more than ever before, we need to devise mechanisms for making sound decisions for resolving domestic, regional, and global conflicts through dialogue rather than imposing a particular agenda, plan, or perspective on the entire world through military force, bribes, arm-twisting, and sophisticated propaganda techniques.

The world cannot afford to continue living one-fifth rich, two-fifths in abject poverty, and another two-fifths struggling for mere survival. As Huxley has said, "Civilization is a race between education and catastrophe." Furthermore, nothing can justify the killing of innocent people, regardless of their race, creed, location, or religion.

Robin Theurkauf, a lecturer in international law at Yale University, who lost her husband in the attack on the Twin Towers in New York City, wrote: "Terrorist impulses ferment in poverty, oppression and ignorance. The elimination of these conditions and the active promotion of a universal respect for human rights must become a priority" (quoted in Pilger, p. 1).

Furthermore, to envision and plan for a better future, we must replace the language of "hate" with "love" and the language of "war" with "peace." There is always hope for a better tomorrow and a relatively peaceful and harmonious world. As the American Indian Chief Seattle once said, "Man did not weave the web of life, he is merely a strand in it. Whatever he does to the web, he does to himself."

References

Adamson, R. L. (2003, March 7). Adamson: The language of war. *Indian Country,* Retrieved July 21, 2003, from http://www.IndianCounty.com.

Collins, J. & Glover, R. (2002). *Collateral damage: A user's guide to America's new war.* New York: New York University Press.

Ellul, J. (1965). *Propaganda: The formation of men's attitudes.* New York: Vintage Books.

Pilger, J. (2003). *The new rulers of the world.* London, England: Verso.

Safire, W. (2003, July 24). "Bush's Four Horsemen," *The New York Times,* op/ed pages.

Slouka, M. (1995). *War of the worlds: Cyberspace and the high-tech assault on reality.* New York: Basic Books.

World Watch. (2003). The language of war. Retrieved July 15, 2003, from http://www.omegastar.org/worldwatch/America/Language_of_War.html

CHAPTER 8

Metaphors of War: News Reporting and the 2003 Iraq War

Jack Lule

In the first months of 2003, the Bush Administration attempted to build national and international support for war against Iraq. Through speeches, press conferences, committee reports, UN sessions, televised addresses, and other venues, the president and his spokespersons proffered rationales for war.

Saddam Hussein, the president said, had weapons of mass destruction and was a threat to U.S. security and world peace. Saddam was linked to terrorism, particularly the activities of al-Qaeda. Saddam was a despotic ruler over the people of Iraq. Saddam was an impediment to peace in the Middle East ("In the President's Words," 2003; "Excerpts from Bush's News Conference," 2003; "Bush's Speech on Iraq," 2003; "Bush's Speech on the Start of War," 2003).

Others were unconvinced. Members of the UN Security Council, including France, Russia, and Germany, argued for a process of inspection and eventual destruction of Iraqi weapons; they refused to pass a war resolution. In March 2003, millions of people held peace rallies in cities around the world. The Bush administration, allied with leaders of Britain and Spain, pressed forward. On March 19, 2003 U.S. jets bombed Baghdad and war began.

How did U.S. news media report events in the crucial weeks before war?

It is almost commonplace that the determination to go to war is perhaps the most critical decision a nation can make. The news media should play a vital role in the decision-making process. As a nation prepares for war, the news media should offer sites in which rationales for war are identified and verified, official claims are solicited and evaluated, alternate views are sought and assessed, costs—both human and material—are weighed, legalities are established, possible outcomes and aftermaths are considered, and wide-ranging debates are given voice. The consequences of war seem to require no less from the news (Galtung, 1986; Galtung & Vincent, 1992; Mathews, 1957; Roach, 1993).

Metaphor and the News

Metaphor provides one means of analyzing such news coverage.

As Sontag (1978, 1989), Lakoff & Johnson (1980), and numerous others (Burke, 1945, 1950; Deetz, 1984; Ortony, 1993; Ricoeur, 1978, 1981) have made clear, metaphor is integral to human understanding—an inescapable aspect of human thought. Indeed, metaphor may be the only way for humans to comprehend profound and complex issues, such as life, death, sickness, health, war, and peace. Metaphor thus has offered an important tool to probe subtleties of news reporting on complex subjects such as social movements (Neveu, 2002), the information highway (Berdayes & Berdayes, 1998), AIDS (Sontag, 1989), conflict in Kosovo (Kennedy, 2000; Paris, 2002), cloning (Hellsten, 2000; Nerlich, Clarke & Dingwall, 2000), and international affairs (Kitis & Milapides, 1997).

Metaphor may prove particularly useful for study of news coverage of the prelude to the 2003 conflict in Iraq. At the end of 1990, Lakoff (1991) published an "open letter to the Internet" arguing that the political and media discourse surrounding justification for the eventual 1991 war against Iraq "was a panorama of metaphor." Iraq was often reduced through *State is a Person* metonymy to the figure of Saddam Hussein, Lakoff said. Saddam Hussein himself was depicted metaphorically. Saddam, it was said, had invaded Kuwait. In more lurid speech, Saddam had raped Kuwait. Saddam was a threat to his neighbors and the world.

The United States, in contrast, was cast metaphorically as hero and savior. By liberating Kuwait, the United States, thus personified, repulsed the villain, saved the victim, and took the lead role in *the fairy tale of the just war* (Greenberg & Gantz, 1993; Kellner, 1992; MacArthur, 1992; Mowlana, Gerbner & Schiller, 1992).

The day before the 2003 war began, Lakoff (2003) issued another critique over the Internet, this time of the metaphor system "being used to justify Gulf War II." He stated that many previous "metaphorical ideas are back, but within a very different and more dangerous context." He found that *State is a Person* allowed continued demonization of Saddam Hussein and hostility to states such as France that were not "loyal friends." He found the "rescue scenario" in which American forces rescue the Iraqi people and Iraq's neighbors. He concluded that metaphor once again had driven U.S. foreign policy.

RESEARCH QUESTIONS

Can Lakoff's critique be extended to news? Have metaphors shaped news reporting of the buildup to the second Gulf war? Here, then, are the research questions that guide this paper:

1. What metaphors, if any, can be identified in U.S. news language concerning the rationale for war with Iraq in 2003?
2. If metaphors did indeed inform news reporting in the weeks before the conflict, what were possible interpretations and implications of those metaphors?
3. If metaphor is an inescapable aspect of human thought, what are the implications of metaphor for news language of war?

METHOD

Methodology for study of metaphoric language has been set forth in work by Lakoff & Johnson (1980), Ricoeur (1978; 1981), Deetz (1984), van Dijk (1988), Cameron & Low (1999), and others.

Metaphors are considered on two levels. The semantic level considers the lexical choice (choice of word, such as "the showdown") and the propositions proffered by the choice. This can be particularly important for study of news. "Lexical choice," van Dijk writes (1988, p. 177) "is an eminent aspect of news discourse in which hidden opinions or ideologies may surface." Analysis also considers the syntactic level, the relationship of word choices within a single text and within a series of texts. Common and recurring metaphors are noted, organized, and clustered. The relationship of the metaphors to other narrative elements is made clear and, finally, the role of metaphor in the text is suggested and explored.

For this analysis of metaphor in news reporting of the prelude to war with Iraq, NBC Nightly News was selected for study. At the time of this research, NBC Nightly News was the most watched U.S. evening news show, averaging close to 12 million viewers nightly, according to Nielsen Media Research. The time period selected was February 5, 2003, the day of Secretary of State Colin Powell's report to the UN Security Council, laying out the Bush administration's rationale for war with Iraq to March 19, 2003, the day bombs first fell on Baghdad. In that time period, reporting focused on a number of topics: inspectors were trying to ascertain if Iraq possessed "weapons of mass destruction," as charged by the Bush administration; the United States and Britain pressed for a UN Security Council resolution for war with Iraq; other members of the Security Council, particularly

France, Germany and Russia, were attempting to provide more time for inspections; the United States and Britain continued the build-up of forces in the Persian Gulf; President Bush and his administration attempted to build support for the war among the American people.

Broadcasts were studied nightly and transcripts were obtained for each newscast. A total of 404 reports were aired over the six-week period. Of that total, 171 stories—42%—focused on some aspect of the possible conflict with Iraq, a significant percentage that reflected the importance of the subject. These were the stories analyzed each evening and through subsequent transcripts.

RESULTS

Within individual news stories on NBC each night, metaphoric language was used as anchors and reporters strove to make sense of events for viewers. Each report, of course, might have drawn upon a huge trove of figurative language. The analysis revealed, however, a surprisingly limited cluster of metaphors in reporting the prelude to war with Iraq. Four metaphors in particular dominated reporting, connecting coverage night after night: the Timetable; the Games of Saddam; the Patience of the White House, and Making the Case/Selling the Plan.

Four Metaphors

In the reporting of NBC Nightly News, the administration had a timetable it was trying to follow, a timetable with a final and inevitable destination: war. The timetable, however, was threatened by the games of Saddam who adroitly played hide and seek with weapons, and bluffed and gambled his way through weeks of negotiations. The White House was losing patience with the process, the United Nations and eventually, its allies. Subsequently, the administration was forced to make its case, sell its plan to the American people, the UN Security Council, and the world community. In the midst of making the case, the administration led the United States into war.

This was the metaphoric system that connected NBC news reports on Iraq in the weeks preceding the war. NBC Nightly News was particularly interested in dramatizing and personalizing the process by which the nation eventually, seemingly inevitably, entered into conflict. The network showed much less interest in exploring calls for peaceful alternatives or evaluating the progress of inspections. It also devoted little time or language to verifying claims, assessing evidence, establishing legalities, or weighing outcomes and aftermaths.

Was Saddam Hussein a threat to the United States? Did Iraq have weapons of mass destruction? Was Saddam Hussein linked to al-Qaeda and Osama Bin Laden? Was Iraq an impediment to Middle East peace? These questions went unasked by the broadcast. Instead, as the following will show, the evening broadcast was most interested in the unfolding of the timetable, the machinations of Saddam, the frustration of the White House, and the administration's failure or success at making the case to go to war.

The Timetable

NBC Nightly News referred often to a timetable for war that was controlling the situation between the United States and Iraq. The language of time pervaded broadcasts. Some of this language came directly from the Bush administration, whose officials spoke often of deadlines and of Saddam running out of time. Newscasts adopted and extended such language. For example, on February 17, 2003, after world-wide protests against military action, a report stated, "the U.S. reassesses its timetable for war." The following day, the newscast said, "the timetable for war has been slowed by the epic diplomatic struggle between the United States and others on the UN Security Council."

Other metaphors of time supported the notion that the nation was on a timetable for war. On February 15, a report said, "some military experts believe the use of force in Iraq is now just a matter of time." The following day, a story said, "Military action is likely weeks away." On February 18: "The idea of war and the casualties it will surely bring, perhaps days away." Iraq and Saddam Hussein were said to be running out of time. "Even as President Bush warns Iraq it's running out of time to disarm .... ," said a report on February 22. The following day: "After weeks of saying that time is running out for Iraq to disarm, President Bush now says it's time for the world to act."

The metaphor could be seen in numerous other reports. "So the clock does seem to be ticking faster on two fronts tonight," said a February 26 story. On March 4: "Target Iraq. The shifting timetable. Will the U.S. skip the UN and attack Saddam within days?" In that same broadcast, a story asked: "So what is the timeline for war?" On March 5: "It has been an up and down day for the Bush administration as the countdown to war now appears to be in its final stages." And on March 6: "On the brink of war, President Bush calls a rare prime time news conference. Will he reveal a new timetable?" On March 11: "Pentagon officials say the current UN debate has pushed the military's timetable for war back by only a matter of days, not weeks."

The notion of the timetable and deadline went unquestioned. Anchors and reporters did not pursue the rationale behind a timetable or deadline for war. Why set a deadline? What was its purpose? Why name a particular date? Why not wait, as other nations urged? Rather, the timetable and deadline proved to be convenient devices for network coverage, providing a sense of urgency and drama that spanned the weeks.

The Games of Saddam

In the portrayals offered by NBC Nightly News, the timetable for war was threatened by the games of Saddam. The metaphor actually combines two tropes. The game metaphor was applied to Iraqi actions during weapons inspections. Saddam was the metonymic replacement of ruler for state of which Lakoff (1991; 2003) has written. (Metonymy is understood here as a figure of speech in which a word or phrase is substituted for another with which it is closely associated.)

Although metaphors of war and sports often overlap, with military action taking on the language of sports and sports adopting the language of war, games in the sense employed by NBC Nightly News refer more to children's diversions or card games than to sports. With the games of Saddam, Saddam Hussein was said to be playing hide and seek with weapons of mass destruction during inspections. He was bluffing the United States and the United Nations, as if in a poker game, gambling with his future and the future of his people.

For example, on February 9 a story stated that "President Bush kept up the pressure on Iraq today, accusing Saddam Hussein of playing a game of hide and seek with weapons of mass destruction." The words hide and seek came from the reporter rather than the president. March 21 saw the same words: "U.S. military intelligence sources say the Iraqis have played a game of hide and seek, firing mobile launchers in southern Iraq even as American forces invade." Reports of March 1 and 2 referred to Saddam's "game of deception."

Other reports cast Saddam's actions as card games. For example, on February 24, anchor Tom Brokaw said, "Tonight the great debate about Iraq resembles a three-handed game of showdown poker with Saddam now sitting at the table playing his cards out in the open." On March 10 Brokaw continued the metaphor: "We've gone from showdown poker to fifty-two pickup, the kid's game in which all the cards are on the floor and all the players are turning them over, trying to find a winning hand." On March 6 a story said, "Secretary of State Colin Powell made a very strong case for war, saying Saddam Hussein has thrown away his last chance."

The games of Saddam metaphor personalizes, dramatizes, and perhaps trivializes, the weeks of negotiation that preceded the war with Iraq. The metaphor continues the theme of the showdown, the finale of a card game, with Saddam Hussein at the table against President Bush, the United States, and the world. The metaphor also offers a sinister depiction of the Iraqi leader. It portrays Saddam Hussein as a ruler willing to treat war as a game, play with the future of his country and the region, and gamble with the lives of his people.

The Patience of the White House

Another important metaphor on NBC Nightly News represented the weeks before war as a time that tested the patience of the White House. The metaphor suggested that the White House was losing patience with the negotiation process, the United Nations, and its allies. This metaphor again combines two tropes. The White House is another metonymy; it replaces President Bush and his administration with the building itself. The metaphor then personalizes the metonymy by attributing patience to the building or administration.

Early in the period studied, on February 7 a report said, "President Bush, impatient with the United Nations, said today it better make up its mind soon about whether to side with the United States." Throughout the month, the metaphor continued to be used. The lead report on March 9 stated: "For weeks now, the White House has said it wanted to give diplomacy a chance. Well, now it appears that the White House's patience is running out."

Other reports drew upon similar language. On February 9, the newscast stated, "Mr. Bush also said the United Nations must soon decide whether it's going to be relevant." The introduction to the broadcast of February 13: "Countdown Iraq. The eve of the weapons inspectors' report, President Bush tells the UN to show some backbone." Another report, on February 19, began: "Countdown Iraq. The U.S. will bring a new war resolution to a vote of the UN. President Bush calls it the last chance." That report included a brief quotation from President Bush: "At some point in time, obviously, this must come to an end. Yeah, it's sooner rather than later, I think is the best way to describe it." On March 6, the newscast reported, "Privately, White House sources say the president has voiced his frustration with the diplomatic stalemate at the UN."

The metaphor of the patience of the White House surely personalizes the prelude to war, but also casts the Bush administration in an authoritative, almost paternal, role in relation to Iraq, the UN and its allies. Parents, for example, lose patience with the games played by children. The metaphor also trivializes the possibility of conflict. Losing patience hardly seems justification for war.

Making the Case/Selling the Plan

The final dominant metaphor in NBC Nightly News coverage of the prelude to war with Iraq depicted the Bush administration making the case for war or, in another variation, selling the plan. A case can mean providing facts or evidence in support of a claim for law or a product. In this metaphor, the administration and its spokespersons were portrayed either as prosecutors presenting a case against a defendant or as salespeople trying to sell a product: war.

This metaphor was apparent in reporting on Secretary of State Colin Powell's February 5 presentation to the United Nations. That night, NBC Nightly News said Powell "spelled out with visual aids and a prosecutor's rhetoric the administration's case against Saddam Hussein." Another report—an interview with a former weapons inspector—said, "His case was devastating." And later: "I think that the case that [sic] was made and was compelling" and "Almost all, Republicans and Democrats, praising the strength of Powell's case." That same day, the report said of the president and secretary of state: "The two men tried to build a case of Iraq's deception and denial." The case metaphor was used often throughout the time period studied. On March 5 the newscast began: "Countdown Iraq. The secretary of state makes the strongest case yet for war." The report said of Powell that "today, he marshaled the administration's case against Saddam."

The case metaphor was used for other stories, such as reports on allegations of ties between Saddam Hussein and al-Qaeda: On February 6 a story reported allegations and asked: "How strong is that case?" The story continued, "In making his case, Powell claimed the ties between Osama Bin Laden and Saddam Hussein go back nearly ten years and the threat continues today." On February 8 a story summarized the reactions of the German ambassador to Secretary of Defense Rumsfeld, "You have to make the case." On February 9 weekend anchor John Seigenthaler asked: "And does this make it more difficult for the United States to make its case for the use of force?"

The Bush administration was not the only entity portrayed using the metaphor. On February 14 Iraq too was reported to be "making its case to a global audience." The following day, massive peace protests were framed with the same metaphor: "Washington has failed miserably to convince most of Europe about the need for force when it comes to Saddam Hussein," and so, "On this one day, so many people in so many different parts of the world making their case for peaceful solution to Iraq." And, "To them, the president's case against Saddam Hussein remains unconvincing." Reacting to the protests, on February 18 the United States and U.K. "are now on the defensive, trying to make their case for war against overwhelmingly negative world opinion."

Making the case eventually also became selling the case. The lexical change was significant. The administration figures were no longer prosecutors marshaling facts and pressing a case against defendants, but salespeople "pitching" an idea, selling a product or plan. On February 6 the newscast described Bush and Powell: "First team. The president and Colin Powell, side by side, selling the case on Iraq." On February 14 a report said, "Attempting to sell the war at home, Mr. Bush argued again today that any battle against terror must include Iraq." The February 12 newscast said, "While Bush administration officials are convinced this latest Bin Laden tape is proof of Iraq's ties to terrorists, it's a hard sell to the rest of the world." On February 26 the newscast began: "Target: Iraq. President Bush talks about Iraq after a war, part of the administration's final campaign to sell the plan." The next day the broadcast reported, "The administration's stepped-up efforts to sell the war extended to Capitol Hill today." But the next day the broadcast said, "It's not an easy sell."

Making the case and selling the plan borrow language from law, business, and marketing to proffer portrayals of the weeks before war. Making the case proposes an interesting metaphor: Is the United States the prosecutor? Saddam Hussein the defendant? And who is the jury? The American people? The world? Selling the plan provides a more invidious perspective. No longer a time for the presentation of facts in a legal case, the weeks before war became a time for the huckster or the salesperson making a pitch or hawking a product. And what is the product? "President Bush is selling the war."

DISCUSSION: METAPHORS CAN KILL

This chapter is not about war, nor the moral or political rightness or wrongness of U.S. war with Iraq. The subject is news language: the uses and implications of war and its metaphors in the news, the use of metaphor in the configuration of war, and, more specifically, the use of metaphors in reporting the prelude to war with Iraq in 2003. As a nation makes the decision to go to war, the news media should play a number of crucial roles. The news media can evaluate the rationale for war. They can verify claims. They can seek alternate views. They can weigh human and material costs. They can assess outcomes. And they can give voice to wide-ranging debates.

The results of this study, while narrow in scope, suggest that the news media, at least the top-rated U.S. evening newscast, failed to provide a site in which the decision to go to war was assessed, evaluated, and debated. In February and early March 2003, war was not inevitable. American allies worked furiously to forestall war. The UN Security Council refused to back conflict. The UN Secretary General and the Pope both urged restraint. Millions protested for peace in the United States and around the world. And yet, through metaphor, through the language of its newscasts, NBC Nightly News portrayed the United States on a seemingly inevitable path to war.

Rather than investigate, analyze, or debate the rationale for war, the broadcast instead offered, through metaphor, a dramatization of war unfolding. Accepting that the nation was on a timetable, dismissing inspections as the games of Saddam, giving voice to the frustration of the White House as it lost patience with the process, the broadcast then simply reported how the administration might make its case and sell its plan.

This research adds support to those who have already charged the news media with failing in its duty to provide debate, history, context, and reporting on the decision to go to war with Iraq (Solomon & Erlich, 2003). Kamiya (2003), for example, has decried "the vulgar flag-waving bombast of the mass media" and "the pro-war chest-beating or too-little, too-late reservations of the nation's leading newspapers." Writing of *Washington Post* coverage, Greider (2003) noted omissions and commissions with stark similarities to NBC Nightly News coverage. He wrote, "Instead of examining the factual basis for targeting Iraq, *The Post* largely framed the story line as a Washington drama of inside baseball." *The*

Post, Greider charged, "sold this war" (p. 22). Metaphor provides a means to understand how the prelude to war was framed and portrayed by news media that anticipated rather than debated the prospect of war.

"Metaphors can kill," said Lakoff (1991; 2003) in the introductions to essays on metaphor and the Gulf Wars of 1991 and 2003. And Sontag (1990, p. 102), writing on illness and metaphor, said: "The metaphors and myths, I was convinced, kill." For Lakoff, metaphors used by the first and second Bush administrations led to unjust, unjustified wars that resulted in the killings of thousands. For Sontag, metaphors used for cancer and AIDS led people to reject treatments, follow useless remedies, and resulted in the killings of thousands. In these perspectives, metaphors indeed can kill.

Yet metaphor is a routine and unalterable aspect of human understanding. This chapter has not then critiqued NBC Nightly News or other news outlets for employing metaphor in reporting the prelude to war with Iraq. It might as well critique the newscast for using words. But this chapter has critiqued and pointed out grim implications of particular metaphors used by the newscast. It critiqued the use of metaphors that accepted as inevitable a timetable for war. It critiqued the use of metaphors that personalized complex issues into the games of Saddam and the fraying patience of the White House. It critiqued the use of metaphors that directed primary attention to how the administration was selling the war.

The metaphors used by NBC Nightly News displaced other possible tropes that might have better profited a nation considering war. For example, the metaphor of a claim might have been a fruitful term to employ. Through this metaphor, the Bush administration could have been understood as making particular claims about the regime of Saddam Hussein. Newscasts could have asked what evidence was introduced in support of those claims. Could the claims be verified? How did Saddam Hussein respond to those claims? How did other nations view the claims? The metaphor of the claim, as opposed to, for example, the games of Saddam, would have suggested more questioning and reporting by the news media.

Another possible metaphor might have been a debate. The Bush administration could have been seen as engaging in a debate with Iraq, the United Nations, or its allies. What were administration arguments in support of war? What were counter-arguments? Who made the counter-arguments and to what effect? Many other metaphors might have been employed.

Perhaps metaphors of negotiation, of process, of decision-making, and of deliberation could have offered other directions. The purpose would have been to self-consciously employ language that invited debate, encouraged the investigation of claims, invited the assessment of outcomes, and ultimately strived to fulfill the crucial role of the press for a nation considering war.

REFERENCES

Berdayes, L. & Berdayes, V. (1998). The information highway in contemporary magazine narrative. *Journal of Communication, 48,* 109-24.

Burke, K. (1945). *A grammar of motives.* New York: Prentice-Hall.

Burke, K. (1950). *A rhetoric of motives.* New York: Prentice-Hall.

Bush's speech on Iraq: 'Saddam Hussein and his sons must leave.' (2003, March 18). *The New York Times,* p. A-14.

Bush's speech on the start of war. (2003, March 20). *The New York Times,* p. A-20.

Cameron, L. & Low, G. (Eds.). (1999). *Researching and applying metaphor.* Cambridge, England: Cambridge University Press.

Deetz, S. (1984). Metaphor analysis. In W. Gudykunst & Y. Kim (Eds.), *Methods for intercultural communication research* (pp. 215-28). Beverly Hills, CA: Sage.

Excerpts from Bush's news conference on Iraq and likelihood of war. (2003, March 7). *The New York Times,* p. A-12.

Galtung, J. (1986). On the role of the media for world-wide security and peace. In T. Varis (Ed.), *Peace and communication* (pp. 249-66). San Jose, Costa Rica: Editorial. Universidad para la Paz.

Galtung, J. & Vincent, R. (1992). *Global glasnost: Toward a new world information and communication order?* Cresskill, NJ: Hampton Press.

Greider, W. (2003, March 24). Washington Post warriors. *The Nation*, pp. 6-7, 22.

Greenberg, B. & Gantz, W. (Eds.). (1993). *Desert Storm and the mass media.* Cresskill, NJ: Hampton Press.

Hellsten, I. (2000). Dolly: Scientific breakthrough or Frankenstein's monster? Journalistic and scientific metaphors of cloning. *Metaphor and Symbol, 15*(4), 213-21.

In the president's words. (2003, February 27). *The New York Times,* p. A-10.

Kamiya, G. (2003). Sleepwalking toward Baghdad. Salon. [Online]. Available: http://www.salon.con/opinion/feature/2003/03/10/hourglass/print.html

Kellner, D. (1992). *The Persian Gulf TV war.* Boulder, CO: Westview Press.

Kennedy, V. (2000). Intended tropes and unintended metatropes in reporting on the war in Kosovo. *Metaphor and Symbol, 15*(4), 253-65.

Kitis, E. & Milapides, M. (1997). Read it and believe it: How metaphor constructs ideology in news discourse. A case study. *Journal of Pragmatics, 28,* 557-90.

Lakoff, G. (1991). Metaphor and war: The metaphor system used to justify war in the Gulf. [Online]. Retrieved January 23, 2004, from: http://lists.village.virginia.edu/sixties/HTML_docs/ Texts/Scholarly/Lakoff_Gulf_ Metaphor_1.html

Lakoff, G. (2003). Metaphor and war, again. [Online]. Retrieved January 23, 2004, from: http://www.alternet.org/story.html?StoryID=15414

Lakoff, G. & Johnson, M. (1980). *Metaphors we live by.* Chicago: University of Chicago Press.

MacArthur, J. (1992). *Second front: Censorship and propaganda in the Gulf War.* New York: Hill and Wang.

Mathews, J. (1957). *Reporting the wars.* Minneapolis: University of Minnesota Press.

Mowlana, H., Gerbner, G. & Schiller, H. (1992). *Triumph of the image: The media's war in the Persian Gulf: A global perspective.* Boulder, CO: 1992.

Nerlich, B., Clarke, D. & Dingwall, R. (2000). Clones and crops: The use of stock characters and word play in two debates about bioengineering. *Metaphor and Symbol, 15*(4), 223-39.

Neveu, E. (2002). The local press and farmers' protests in Britanny: proximity and distance in the local newspaper coverage of a social movement. *Journalism Studies, 3*(2), 289-300.

Ortony, A. (Ed.). (1993). *Metaphor and thought* (2nd ed.). New York: Cambridge University Press.

Paris, R. (2002). Kosovo and the metaphor war. *Political Science Quarterly, 117*(3), 423-50.

Ricoeur, P. (1978). *The rule of metaphor* (Trans., R. Czerny). London: Routledge and Kegan Paul.

Ricoeur, P. (1981). Metaphor and the central problem of hermeneutics. In J. Thompson (Ed.), Paul Ricoeur: *Hermeneutics and the human sciences* (pp. 165-81). Cambridge, England: Cambridge University Press.

Roach, C. (Ed.). *Communication and culture in war and peace.* Newbury Park, CA: Sage.

Solomon, N. & Erlich, R. (2003). *Target Iraq: What the news media didn't tell you.* New York: Context.

Sontag, S. (1978). *Illness as metaphor.* New York: Farrar, Straus and Giroux.

Sontag, S. (1989). *AIDS and its metaphors.* New York: Farrar, Straus and Giroux.

Sontag, S. (1990). *Illness as metaphor AND AIDS and its metaphors.* New York: Doubleday.

Van Dijk, T. (1988). *News as discourse.* Hillsdale, NJ: Lawrence Erlbaum.

CHAPTER 9

An Insider's Assessment of Media Punditry and "Operation Iraqi Freedom"

Ibrahim Al-Marashi

When high-intensity combat in Operation "Iraqi Freedom" came to a close in May 2003 the United States declared victory in achieving its objectives. But it failed to predict the wide-scale looting that would erupt after the war, as well as the sustained animosity and low-intensity warfare directed against American forces that killed over five hundred U.S. soldiers by the war's first anniversary.

Given the rapid pace of this campaign, most media analyses focused on the course of the war, with little academic assessment of the war and its aftermath on Iraq. Part of the inaccurate assessments of the situation in Iraq from the U.S. side could be blamed on the structure and nature of the American media's coverage of the build-up and course of the war.

This chapter is based on my experience as an "overnight media pundit" in these very media circles. The experience gave me an insider's perspective on how media operated during this conflict and areas where it needed reform.

As an insider in these media circuits, I noticed during this war that media pundits only confused the coverage of the war rather than complimented it, converging misinformation and entertainment in one package.

Misinformation and Media Punditry

In the U.S. media, "overnight experts" dominated the airwaves and the discourse on Iraq. As someone who has devoted my life to the study of Iraq since the beginning of my academic career in 1991, nothing irritated me more than seeing people on the airwaves who marketed themselves as "Iraq experts." In fact, prior to the buildup to the war there were few academics who were devoted to the study of Iraq. Those few prominent Iraq scholars were not featured prominently in the media talk-interview circuit, perhaps out of their own volition, or they were never contacted.

In American media circles, former military generals dominated media outlets, demonstrating how the U.S. media were obsessed with how Iraq was being destroyed, while little attention was focused on how it would be rebuilt. Many of these military experts could tell American audiences the weapons used to destroy Baghdad, but few, if any, could explain the cultural nuances of the Iraqi citizenry, and how the country would react to the presence of U.S. troops on its soil.

For example, one of the media pundits was General Wayne Downing, a retired 1991 Gulf War general and special operations expert. He was one of the prominent TV generals who explained U.S. military plans in detail, but who could say little about the country that was being bombed. In an interview with Fox News on September 29, 2002, Downing was asked how he predicted the Iraqi military would perform in a war with the United States:

> Even the Republican Guards, their elite units, are ones that we have a very, very good possibility that they will fold early in a conflict against a backdrop of overwhelming American force.

While Downing predicted that the Republican Guard deployed on the outskirts of the capital would not serve as an enthusiastic fighting force, nor put up much resistance to an American attack, the Guard demonstrated a sustained will to engage U.S. and U.K. forces during the conflict.

After the Iraqi Shi'a and Kurds revolted against the regime in the aftermath of the 1991 Gulf War, the weakened Republican Guard rallied behind Saddam Hussein and brutally suppressed the insurrection. This uprising took on an ethnic and sectarian nature, and it appeared as if the predominantly Arab Sunni Republican Guards were defending their privileged status in the Iraqi state. In their perception, this privileged status would not be guaranteed in a post-Saddam Iraq, and thus could explain their motivation in defending a regime where they were the elite stratum in Iraq's society, as well as the premier fighting unit. However, Downing's analysis focused on the military capabilities of the Guard, without taking these Iraqi cultural or historical nuances into account.

In another interview on November 29, 2002, on MSNBC's Hardball, the general was asked about how post-war order and security in Iraq would be restored. He responded:

> We have some very, very highly trained people, most of them in our reserve component, our civil affairs units who are experts at going in, restoring government services, restoring power, sewage, water, these types of things, and knowing how the military works, they've got detailed plans on how they'll do that. How long it's going to go, it's going to depend on the situation and how it evolves.

However, the military seemed to have no plan whatsoever to restore order or rehabilitate the nation's infrastructure once Saddam's regime collapsed. As a military expert, Downing had the knowledge to testify about the destruction of Iraq, but had little authority to inform the public as to how Iraq would be rebuilt.

As a result, the dearth of public knowledge on Iraq and the emergence of these "overnight experts" led to many false predictions of how the war would evolve, as well as how the Iraqis would react to the American and British presence once Saddam was removed. The neglected study of the internal dynamics of Iraq's domestic politics and security apparatus led to many failed forecasts when U.S. and U.K. forces went to war against those institutions of the Iraqi state. The American media, as well as its policy-making "think tanks," provided many failed assessments of how the war would be fought.

Generally, these institutions predicted that the Shi'a of southern Iraq would revolt against their Sunni, Tikriti masters, leaving the "decapitation"of the regime in Baghdad the toughest battle. On the contrary, the Shi'a did not rise against the Ba'th, the most pitched battles were in the south, and Baghdad fell relatively easily.

It was predicted that Saddam's elite Special Republican Guard and myriad security organizations would fight to the very end to defend the capital; however, the para-military organizations such as the Fedayeen Saddam, which did not have formal military training, posed the most serious challenge to coalition forces. Saddam's feared weapons of mass destruction were not deployed against military forces as they approached Baghdad; in fact, a year after the war they have yet to be uncovered, and in January 2004 even official Washington questioned whether Iraq had WMDs.

Finally, it was mistakenly predicted that Iraq's oil wells would be set ablaze in large numbers, as were the Kuwaiti fields in 1991.

The late Edward Said (1998) articulated another flaw in the American media in an article on the 1991 Gulf War. He criticized the media for failing to feature Arab commentators who were neither pro-American, nor pro-Saddam. He argued that if the media were to do so, it would have been perhaps too confusing for the audiences. Yet his comments after the 1991 war touch on the problem that the media failed to remedy after more than a decade.

As a whole, media pundits mistakenly classified the Iraqis into two camps: pro-Saddam or anti-Saddam and, thus, once the Saddam government was vanquished, the anti-Saddam tendencies in Iraq would rally behind the United States. However, Arab or Iraqi commentators who were neither pro-Saddam, nor pro-American, were rarely seen among these media circles. It could have been those commentators who would have warned that there are Iraqi's who are neither pro-Saddam, nor pro-American, and while many Iraqis would be happy to see Saddam leave, they would not welcome an American occupation.

Once the high-intensity war was over, it was believed that American forces would be greeted as liberators and Iraqi exiles would be enthusiastically received. Richard Perle, chairman of the Pentagon's Defense Policy Board, and a fellow at the conservative think tank, The American Enterprise Institute, argued on the media circuit that the Iraqi people would rejoice at Saddam's downfall and that the Iraqis would welcome the American liberators with open arms. In an October 6, 2002, interview on NBC's Meet the Press, Perle stated:

> Well, I think he will certainly discover, and I think he actually already knows, that very few Iraqis are loyal to Saddam Hussein, which is hardly surprising, given the brutality of his rule over a long period of time. So whether it's an assassination or whether he goes the way of Ceausescu in Romania, where the moment he was seriously challenged, his own people brought him down, I don't know. But there will be very few Iraqis prepared to fight for Saddam Hussein

His last sentence was brought into question by the fact that there was a stiff resistance to the coalition assault in first week of the war, and there had been a sustained series of attacks against coalition forces since the official cessation of hostilities. Perle's assessments failed to take into account the almost immediate animosity directed towards the United States once Saddam was removed, and what the Iraqis envisioned for their future state.

Kenneth Pollack, a former CIA analyst during the Clinton administration and CNN analyst, was one of the more prominent "talking heads" during this conflict. He is a Brookings Institute senior fellow and author of *The Threatening Storm: The Case for Invading Iraq*, published in 2002. While Pollack provided expert analysis on Iraq during the conflict, he did make mistakes as well. In an interview on CNN's Capital Gang on November 23, 2002, Pollack was asked about the possibility of chemical weapons being used in the war. He replied, "I think there's no question he will at some point in time. The key issue is when. Does he use them right at the outset, or does he try to wait?"

I had hoped to do my part in changing these aforementioned flaws once I entered the arena of media punditry, however I made failed assessments about Iraq's WMD program, similar to Pollack's comments in the preceding interview.

What allowed me to enter the media circles was not that I had devoted my life to the academic study of Iraq's culture and history, nor my publications on this subject. My "claim to fame" emerged when an U.K. intelligence dossier on Iraq's intelligence agencies presented by Colin Powell to the UN Security Council in February 2003 was in fact plagiarized from a historical, academic article I had written on Iraq's intelligence agencies (See Al-Marashi, 2002).

As I was inundated by media requests, I thought that this plagiarism incident gave me a chance, as an Iraqi-American, to enter the mainstream media circuits. First, it allowed me a chance to dispel the images of those Iraqi exiles with heavy accents begging the United States to liberate their country. Second, it allowed me to present my insight into the Iraqi conflict, giving both an Iraqi and American perspective, something that was glaringly absent from the media.

However, my hopes were quickly dashed as I conducted my first barrage of media interviews. I assumed that if my research was valuable enough to have been presented as an U.K. intelligence source, then surely my analysis on the situation with Iraq would be sought after by the media. On the contrary, in most instances the interviews were forums to "sling mud" at the British government, focusing on the scandal rather the upcoming war itself.

Since the story of my plagiarized article emerged on February 7, 2003, I had conducted over two hundred interviews with the media within a ninety-day span Only 10% of those interviews asked for my analysis on the war with Iraq, without commenting on my plagiarism incident. During those interviews, I noticed another structural flaw in the media, which was articulated by Edward Said in an article on the 1991 Gulf War. I noticed that most media channels would give me or any other pundit no more than two to three minutes to speak. Said (1998) said:

> Once in the fifteen seconds I was given, when I began to elucidate an argument about the relationship between Iraqi aggression and American imperialism, I was cut off abruptly: "Yes, yes, we know all that."

The media's addiction to neat, concise sound bytes, and its reliance on splash rather than substance, forced me to gloss over the complexities of not just the upcoming war, but more importantly, its aftermath. In most interviews, I had two minutes to comment, and then a commercial or the next speaker would cut me off. Iraq is not a country one can summarize a minute before the commercial break and the time constraints caused me to neglect many minute details of Iraq's politics and internal dynamics. Under the pressure of bright lights and commercial breaks, concise sound bytes did not allow me to convey certain information correctly.

Iraq's Weapons of Mass Destruction

Most media pundits also overstated the case of Iraq's possession of weapons of mass destruction. William Kristol, co-author of *The War on Iraq: Saddam's Tyranny and America's Mission* (2003), and also the chairman and co-director of the Project for the New American Century, stated that the Iraqi leader would never peacefully dismantle his weapons program. In an interview with Ted Koppel on ABC's Nightline on March 5, 2003,Kristol said:

> Well, look, I think when we go into Iraq and after we remove Saddam, we'll have to stay there for a while. We'll have to remove the weapons of mass destruction. But I think we owe it to the people of Iraq to help them reconstitute their society and to help them establish a decent and, I really hope, democratic government there. That would be a great, it would be great to help the people of Iraq liberate themselves, for one thing, they've suffered under such a cruel and brutal dictator. And it would be a great thing for the Middle East to have a functioning democratic country right in the middle of that region.

However, his justification of an American presence for the sake of the removal of those weapons of mass destruction has proved unfounded, and the debt to the Iraqi people to establish a democracy has not been forthcoming.

David Kay, the chief UN nuclear weapons inspector after the 1991Gulf War, and senior fellow at the Potomac Institute for Policy Studies, also argued that the nature of Saddam's regime would indicate that Iraq would never give up its pursuit of weapons of mass destruction.

When interviewed on CNBC News January 29, 2003,about the risks of going to war with Iraq, he said:

> I think the—Iraq actually, as a result of military action in the United States, there is at least the distinct and I think a high probability that the results are going to be extremely favorable for the Middle East and for the region.

Granted that Kay has the authority and expertise to speak about Iraq's WMD program, his predictions that the war would be favorable for the region may have been overly optimistic. In the immediate aftermath of the war, tensions escalated between the United States, on one hand, and Iran and Syria on the other; there were terrorist attacks in places ranging from Morocco to Saudi Arabia; and the post-war chaos in Iraq may have given al-Qaeda agents a new base from which to continue their campaign against the United States.

I would also fall into the category of misrepresenting Iraq's WMD threat during my media interviews. For example, on numerous occasions I was asked if Iraq possessed WMD capabilities. In one instance I had ten seconds left in an interview to answer one question, "Does Iraq have a weapons of mass destruction capability?" This question was not a "yes" or "no" answer. In my opinion, Iraq had a WMD capability in the past and probably retained the infrastructure to reconstitute that capability. Even so, if Iraq had these weapons, they posed a threat to Iraq's people in the past and invading Iranian soldiers during the Iran-Iraq War. These weapons hardly posed a threat to world security as had been portrayed by other media pundits. However, in this instance I did not have time to give a nuanced answer like this. In this interview, I answered "yes."

THE WAR ON TERROR

The war against Iraq was justified in many media outlets as a continuation of America's "War on Terror." On the Fox News Network, after the commercial break, the words "Operation Iraq Freedom" would dissolve into "The War on Terror" whereupon the news program would begin. Linking the war against al-Qaeda and the Iraq war in certain media outlets blurred the nature of both conflicts.

Some of the media pundits had studied Iraq for a while, perhaps for too long. Many of those pundits who argued the most vehemently for the overthrow of Saddam Hussein originally argued in the 1980s that the dictator was America's staunchest regional ally to contain Iran's Islamic revolution.

For example Laurie Mylroie (2001) was one of those "experts" who argued that it was in America's interests to cultivate ties with Iraq during the Iran-Iraq War. After the 1991 invasion of Kuwait, she rehabilitated herself and was one of the first authors to contribute to the demonization campaign against Saddam. She considers herself an Iraq scholar and was the author of *A Study of Revenge: The War Against America, Saddam Hussein, and the World Trade Center Attacks* (2001), which linked Iraq to both World Trade Center attacks in 1993 and 2001.

She vehemently argued that Iraq and Osama Bin Laden worked together. Osama Bin Laden provided the "martyrs" while the Iraqi intelligence services trained al-Qaeda. In her media appearances, she argued the necessity of striking Saddam before he and Osama could hatch another terrorist attack. In an interview on the Fox News Network, she claimed that UN inspections were ineffective in that they were failing to protect U.S. security:

> I, for one, like the vice president, did not want to go to the Security Council for precisely these reasons, partly because UNMOVIC is not UNSCOM. UNMOVIC is very weak. It's broken down. And another thing is, for the defense of the United States, we shouldn't be having to go and ask Russia and France, Oh, please, pretty please, can we defend ourselves? (Fox News, Fox On The Record with Geta Van Susteren, December 9, 2002).

As the interview continued, she reiterated her case for Iraqi responsibility for the 1993 and 2001 World Trade Center bombings: "The other alternative is to go back to terrorism, 9/11, the 1993 bombing of the World Trade Center, and show that Iraq has been involved in these attacks on the United States." While there was little concrete evidence behind this theory, she may have accidentally predicted the cooperation that apparently has emerged between Saddam loyalists and al-Qaeda elements, the caveat being that this cooperation emerged in the aftermath of the latest war.

James Woolsey, CIA director under President Clinton, stated that Saddam had ties to al-Qaeda and supported Laurie Mylroie's theories of an Iraq/al-Qaeda link. In an interview on the same Fox News program, he was asked in February 2003 about the possibility of Saddam attacking the United States during the buildup to the war. He said:

> I think what he's likely to do is provide something like, you know, anthrax or something like that to terrorist groups, al-Qaeda or some other. He and these terrorist groups are sort of like Mafia families, particularly the ones that are religiously based, in part, like al-Qaeda. They hate each other and they kill each other and they criticize each other, but they're willing to work together on this and that because they hate us more. (Fox News, Fox on the Record With Greta Susteren, February 26, 2003).

Additionally, Frank Gaffney, president and CEO of the Center for Security Policy, argued that Saddam's Iraq had a record of supporting terrorism, including the 1993 World Trade Center bombing. An interview with Katrina Vanden Heuvel on CNN's Talkback Live on January 6, 2003,transpired as follows:

> GAFFNEY: Yeah. Well, I think the main point that needs to be borne in mind here is we're dealing with a country in Saddam Hussein that has been bent on revenge ever since 1991. And I simply disagree that there's no evidence of involvement between Saddam and acts of terror in this country. There is considerable evidence of it. The case needs to be prosecuted.
>
> VANDEN HEUVEL: Frank, I mean, he may be a brutal dictator...
>
> GAFFNEY: Excuse me just a second, Katrina. The case needs to be properly prosecuted and it hasn't been to my satisfaction to this point. But the larger message is unmistakable. Saddam Hussein's influence is real and is growing in this region, if we allow him to gain access to weapons of mass destruction beyond those he already has. The nuclear weapons in particular. That influence will metastasize even further and be vastly more destabilizing than the act we need to take, which is to liberate the Iraqi people.

In another interview (with Paul Begala on CNN Crossfire on October 7, 2002) Richard Perle also reiterated the claim of a Saddam-9/11 link:

BEGALA: Why are you pushing this line if our intelligence officers say it is not so?

PERLE: They're wrong.

BEGALA: Can you give us some reasons without breaching classified data? President Kennedy showed us the pictures of the missiles in Cuba. Have you got some proof?

PERLE: We don't have pictures. We have intelligence reports that I believe are reliable. I think there are other indications of other meetings with other members of al-Qaeda including hijackers and intelligence officials from Iraq. The Iraqis—a fellow by the name of al Amni (ph). I think the evidence is compelling. If others think it isn't, there is just a difference of opinion between us.

In the exchange with Begala, Perle stated that U.S. intelligence officers are mistaken for not emphasizing this link, but then contradicts himself by stating that the evidence for such a link is based on U.S. intelligence reports. While there was barely any evidence that Saddam had cooperated with al-Qaeda in the past, it seems that in the post-war anarchy ensuing in Iraq, al-Qaeda elements may have penetrated the country and in fact be cooperating with Saddam loyalists, providing a magnet for fighters to enter Iraq and target American soldiers. Thus "Operation Iraqi Freedom" only intensified the War on Terror, which none of the aforementioned media pundits predicted.

The Language of the Media and its Pundits

I could not help but notice how the war was not portrayed in the media as a war against Iraq or the Iraqi people, but as a war against Saddam Hussein, his two sons, and the Fedayeen (depicted as a group of unprofessional bandits and mercenaries in the service of the dictator as opposed to the professional, technologically-advanced American and British armed forces). The war was almost portrayed as the forces of "good" battling against Saddam's minions of "evil."

The villianization of Saddam and his family emerged into an elaborate soap opera of family intrigue with stories of the abuses of Uday Hussein, Saddam's eldest son, featured prominently in men's entertainment magazines, such as *Maxim* and *Esquire*. On the other hand, I would argue during media interviews that Uday received undue attention as opposed to Abid Hamid Mahmoud, the Iraqi presidential secretary who was responsible for Saddam's security apparatus as well as his personal protection. However Mahmoud, perhaps the second most powerful man in Saddam's regime, with the title of presidential secretary and his long Arabic name did not have as sinister a tone as "Uday, the son of Saddam," and I was never asked to elaborate further on his role.

Saddam, Uday, and the Fedayeen emerged as the array of icons and symbols throughout the media. Just as in any film, villains and heroes emerged throughout the conflict. Ali Hassan Al-Majid, Saddam Hussein's cousin, was usually referred to with the euphemistic title of "Chemical Ali," an odious nickname to acknowledge his use of chemical weapons to eliminate large segments of Iraq's Kurdish population. However, Chemical Ali was soon overshadowed by "Comical Ali," Mohammad Al-Sahhaf, the Iraqi Minister of Information, whose exaggerated claims of Iraqi battlefield successes unintentionally won him international recognition and celebrity.

Along with the sinister list of regime cronies, there were other characters such as Dr. Huda 'Ammash known as "Mrs. Anthrax" or "Chemical Sally" and Dr. Rihab Taha, known as "Dr. Germ." Only among U.S. and U.K. media circles, did I notice the pundits' use of nicknames to describe the members of Saddam regime. Even I discovered that is was useful at times to utilize these titles during media interviews because it made the interviews livelier. Thus, I, too, fell into the trap of not only informing the audience, but entertaining them as well.

During the course of the war, the U.S. Defense Intelligence Agency produced its first "Iraqi Most Wanted" playing cards, printing and cutting out two hundred decks by hand. They were initially created for use by U.S. soldiers in Iraq to identify and capture high-ranking Ba'athists. Various companies such as Great USA Flags started to market these cards over the Internet, selling over a million Most Wanted decks at $5.95 apiece. The emergence of these cards not only was a profitable venture, but it added an element of entertainment to the media's coverage of Iraq. The capture of the former Iraqi Ba'athists became a game, enhancing the entertainment nature of this conflict. The cards of Iraqi officials, many of them war criminals, could be collected as if they were baseball cards. Figures such as Abid Hamid Mahmoud were no longer the Iraq's "presidential secretary" but rather the "Ace of Diamonds."

On the CNN program American Morning on June 23, 2003, former general-turned-pundit David Grange was asked about the ongoing hunt for members of Saddam's ousted regime. He responded:

> Well ... we can talk about ... Task Force 20. [I]t's a special operations force made up of several services that all bring different capabilities to this task force. It could even have coalition members from British forces as an example. Its primary missions are to go after the card deck of fifty-five, the top people, to kill or grab these enemy leaders, hostage rescue, and also sensitive or highly sensitive possible WMD sites.

Thus, the hunt for some of the members of the most odious regime in the history of the Middle East was reduced to a game of playing cards.

The military conflict that began between Coalition forces and Iraq on March

20, 2003, has been referred to as "Operation Iraqi Freedom" by the U.S. side, while the Arabic satellite station Al-Jazeera, as did many other Arab circles, labeled it as "al-Harb al-Khalijiyya al-Thalitha," or "The Third Gulf War." Such titles are key to understanding how media outlets perceive the conflict. The U.S. media would call military actions against Iraq "Operation Desert Storm," "Operation Desert Fox," and "Operation Iraqi Freedom." It was as if the use of the term "operation" sanitized the attacks being carried out against Iraq. The Al-Jazeera term, "The Third Gulf War," made more sense, as for the region it was in fact the third Gulf War. Once, when I tried to employ this more politically correct term for the conflict in a media interview, I was corrected by the news anchor, who said, "You mean Operation Iraqi Freedom."

Comparing U.S. and U.K. Media

After the British government had copied my article on Iraq's intelligence agencies, I often traveled to the United Kingdom to participate in interviews during the war. My experience in the U.K. media circuit gave me valuable insight into how American media coverage could be improved. Granted, some could argue that the U.K. media also served as a vehicle to glorify the British campaign in Iraq, but it also featured outside commentators who gave a more balanced commentary of the war. For example, on Sky News, a London-based Iraqi dissident expressed his eagerness to see Saddam Hussein removed, yet was deeply disturbed by the devastation of his native country. He argued:

> You cannot put in place a democratic government. That's an oxymoron. A democracy has to be built up gradually according to the culture of a place.

This is a stark contrast to the American media that rarely gave a voice to Iraqis. Iraqi officials such as Mohammed Saeed Al-Sahhaf gave the official Iraqi perspective, but numerous Iraqi community leaders in the West were rarely featured in these media circles. In the few instances they were featured, they had heavy accents and were apparently chosen because they supported the war.

Conclusion

The purpose of this chapter is not to criticize the inability of the media pundits to predict how the war in Iraq would unfold, as doing so would be difficult for the most dedicated analysts who study the region. Rather, this chapter demonstrates how those pundits with a political agenda, such as the neo-conservatives, advanced their views while at the same time they were played off as "experts" on Iraq or the region. Their analyses—broadcast through various media outlets—misled viewers on the nature of Iraq's WMD program and its role in the War on Terror.

The media's failure to understand Iraq's history and politics led to many miscalculations of how "Operation Iraqi Freedom" would evolve, and how the Iraqi people would react to an American occupation. Additional miscalculations could have disastrous results. If I had been given the chance, as an historian of Iraq, I could have used the media to warn that the United States should heed the lesson of the Great Iraqi Revolution of 1920, which united the disparate communities of the Shi'as, Sunnis, and Kurds in the newly created mandate of Iraq in their common animosity to British forces based in Iraq.

All the ingredients are present for a second Great Iraqi Revolution. The Iraqi nation was created from the ravages of the First World War, a nationwide revolt in the 1920s, and the uncertainties of World War II. It underwent revolutions in 1958, 1963, and 1968; dealt with an almost continuous Kurdish rebellion; a mass uprising in March of 1991; and three disastrous wars with foreign powers. Neither Iraq, nor the Americans stationed there, need a second Great Revolution.

References

ABC News, Nightline, (2003, March 5).

Al-Marashi, I. (2002). Iraq's security and intelligence network: A guide and analysis. *Middle East Review of International Affairs, 6*:3

CNBC News, The News with Brian Williams. (2003, January 29).

CNN, CNN American Morning. (2003, June 23). Transcript # 062302CN.V74

CNN, CNN Capital Gang. (2002, November 23), Transcript # 112301cn.V40.

CNN, CNN Crossfire. (2002, October 7). Transcript # 100700CN.V20

CNN, CNN Talkback Live. (2003, January 6). Transcript # 010600CN.V14

Fox News Network, Fox News Sunday. (2002, September 29). Transcript # 092902cb.250.

Fox News Network, Fox On The Record With Greta Van Susteren. (2002, December 9). Transcript # 120902cb.260.

Fox News Network, Fox On The Record With Greta Van Susteren. (2003, February 26). Transcript # 022602cb.260.

Kristol, W. & Kaplan, L.F. (2003) *The war over Iraq: Saddam's tyranny and America's mission.* San Francisco: Encounter Books.

Mylroie, L. (2001) *A study of revenge: The war against America, Saddam Hussein and the World Trade Center attacks.* New York: Harper Collins.

MSNBC, Hardball. (2002, November 8). Transcript: # 110800cb.461

NBC News, Meet the Press. (2002, October 6).

Pollack, K. (2002) *The threatening storm: The case for invading Iraq.* New York: Random House.

Said, E.W. (1998) Thoughts on a war: Ignorant armies clash by night. In Bennis, P. (Ed.) *Beyond the storm: A Gulf crisis reader.* Northampton, MA: Interlink Publishing Group.

CHAPTER 10

The 2003 War in Iraq and Perspectives on Turkish Media

Dilruba Çatalbaş

The 2003 war in Iraq proved to be as controversial in Turkey as it was in the West. A long-time political and military ally and supporter of U.S. international policies, Turkey found itself torn between its loyalties and conflicting interests.

Although the neo-Islamist AKP (Justice and Development Party) government declared its support for U.S. policy, opinion polls showed a strong majority of people were against the war and any kind of Turkish military involvement in it. The Army chose not to declare any opinion, at least until the end of the crucial vote in the Parliament. President Ahmet Necdet Sezer, a staunch defender of secularism, and the head of the Turkish National Assembly, Bülent Arinç, a respected Islamist, questioned the legitimacy of the military action on Iraq in the absence of a UN resolution, demonstrating the eclectic and ideologically diffused nature of the anti-war front.

There were also considerable differences of opinion among journalists, who split into two major groups independent of the ideological leanings of their members. The first group of journalists and commentators opposed the war because they found it illegal and unfair, and they objected to Turkey's participation in it. In opposition to that group there was a crowded field of pragmatists, who said that the war was unfortunate but Turkey must go along with the United States in order to turn it into her advantage (Atabeyoglu, 2003). Those who supported the United States and argued for the inevitability of war often hold leftist, Islamist, and Kurdish *entel*s, a kind of derogatory expression in Turkish for bogus intellectuals responsible for the anti-war sentiment in Turkey.

Disagreement among journalists tended to be even sharper in relation to Turkey's role in the war and its stance against the United States. Some high-profile liberal journalists and commentators in the mainstream media argued that Turkey could not afford to offend the United States. It was impossible for Turkey, they argued, to say no to the United States because of its difficult economic condition, its astronomical foreign debt, and its need for U.S. support in major political matters like Cyprus and the EU membership. Cooperating with the United States was not a matter of choice, they insisted, but necessity.

Moreover, these pragmatists hoped that by helping the United States, Turkey could have a say in the Anglo-American-made new order in the Middle East and strengthen its military presence in northern Iraq to keep better track of Turkish Kurdish guerrillas, prevent the establishment of an independent Kurdish state, and become the protector of the Turkoman population living in the Kirkuk and Mosul regions of Iraq. Therefore, they were deeply disappointed by the Parliamentary vote on March 1, 2003, that rejected deployment of U.S. troops on Turkish soil.

These journalists and commentators were quick to announce the end of the "fifty-year-old strategic partnership" between Turkey and the United States, and predicted that the Americans would politically and economically punish Turkey. Months later most of them were still speculating on what went wrong in the voting and in U.S.-Turkey relations. Therefore, remarks similar to those expressed by Paul Wolfowitz, U.S. Deputy Secretary of Defense, which called on Turkey to apologize, were headline news in both print and electronic media. Wolfowitz later claimed he asked not for an apology, but an admission by Turkey that "she was in the wrong" in her position. His words caused resentment among Turkish people and provoked protests from AKP government and the Army.

The media interest in disseminating disapproving comments like Wolfowitz's indicated the perseverance of the major editorial concern of war coverage in Turkey: U.S.-Turkey relations. However, there seemed to be a growing discrepancy between the ways these comments and criticisms originating from American sources were presented by some liberal journalists and commentators, and the ways in which they were understood and interpreted by a significant portion of people in the street.

A large number of Turks seemed truly annoyed and frustrated by what they perceived and what was reflected by the media as a colonialistic and retaliatory attitude by the Bush administration against Turkey. Thus, any negative word or incident that had a bearing on Turkish-American relations, like the arrest of

Turkish special forces in northern Iraq by the American Army on July 4, 2003, aggravated the irritation and created popular pressures on the AKP government. This last incident also provoked widespread protests even from the most enthusiastic supporters of the United States in Turkish media. Interestingly, the papers that initially published most openly pro-U.S. headlines, turned out to be the fiercest U.S. critics in this incident.

This chapter investigates the major fault lines between the journalism community and U.S.-Turkey relations over the war in Iraq. It attempts to reveal the inconsistencies and contradictions inherent in pro-U.S. views and comments advanced by liberal journalists and commentators in relation to Turkish Parliament's decision on deployment of American troops in Turkey. In doing so, it hopes to explain why efforts of these journalists largely failed, as the Bush administration's "pre-emptive war doctrine" did, to win the hearts and minds of the majority of people in Turkey.

Hard Choices for Turkey: Being Dragged into War or Not?

The neo-Islamist AKP, which emerged from the general elections on November 3, 2002, as the largest party in the Parliament, winning 363 of 550 seats, soon felt the immense weight of the country's internal and external problems. Repairing and reconstructing the enfeebled and crisis-prone economy, carrying out negotiations with the International Monetary Fund, finding a permanent solution to the Cyprus problem, and accomplishing Turkey's forty-year-old goal of full European Union membership were only a few of them.

The AKP government pledged to speed up Turkey's drive to join the EU, re-examine the IMF plans for the Turkish economy, and negotiate UN Secretary General Kofi Annan's plan for a solution to divided Cyprus. However, before making progress on the Cyprus problem, the AKP government came under intense pressure from the Bush administration to make yet another tough decision, this time on neighboring Iraq. The previous government had made it clear that Turkey would not back a military attack on Iraq because it could lead to its partition, bringing out further problems for Turkey and the region. There was also a belief in Ankara that, thanks to UN sanctions and no-fly zones, Saddam would be unable "to mount the level of threat that Washington attributes to him" (Park, 2002).

However, when faced with the inevitability of the war, the AKP government decided to support the United States, despite the popular resistance from its own constituency. But this time the government seemed determined to limit the possible damages the war might cause Turkey. The 1991 Gulf War had extensively damaged the Turkish economy and undermined border security by allowing PKK (Kurdistan Worker's Party) guerrillas to operate in Kurdish-controlled northern Iraq. Turkey had lost some 30,000 of its people and several billions of dollars in its struggle with Kurdish separatists since the 1991 Gulf War.

The AKP government and the U.S. administration negotiated agreements on military, political, and economic consequences of the war. As a result, on February 5, 2003, Turkish Parliament accepted a proposal to allow American technicians and soldiers to stay in Turkey for three months to renovate military bases and harbors. In the meantime, the slow progress in the negotiations was being interpreted in the American media as Turkey's attempted to extort more U.S. financial aid. Turkish media published those reports and caricatures from Western, and particularly American papers, that framed Turkey as a cunning belly dancer or a mercenary. These images enraged not only ordinary Turks, but also members of parliament, which intensified the popular pressures on the government to reject any U.S. deal.

On March 1, 2003, in an extremely charged climate, Parliament rejected by a narrow margin the government resolution authorizing deployment of U.S. combat troops that would have opened a northern front against Iraq. The main opposition party, CHP (Republican People's Party), voted unanimously against it. However, what was more damaging for the AKP leadership was the large number of dissident MPs who defected from the party line.

A second motion to grant the U.S. permission to use Turkish airspace and allow the Turkish army to send personnel into northern Iraq passed on March 20, 2003, the day the allies attacked Iraq. But following the second parliamentary vote, it seemed Turkish and American sides could not reach a prompt agreement on overflight rights. Media speculated the delay was caused by disagreement over northern Iraq. The American and Iraqi Kurdish military and political spokesmen were sending open messages that they would not accept Turkish troops entering northern Iraq. On the other hand, Turkey had declared it would not accept a *fait accompli* of an independent Kurdish state, and said it would intervene if Kurdish peshmerga groups entered Mosul and Kirkuk, threatening the local Turkoman population.

The fact that Turkish parliament did not provide the level of cooperation wanted by the Bush administration led to a gloomy prospect for the future of American-Turkish relations. While some influential commentators claimed U.S.-Turkey relations were on the verge of collapse, others asserted that the relationship was stronger and deeper-rooted than the pessimists assumed. The Bush administration's later allocation of $1 billion in aid to Turkey and an unexpected visit to Ankara by Defense Secretary Colin Powell were seen as indications of improved relations. But even after the war, the estrangement between the United States and Turkey remained a popular topic of discussion in both Turkey and the United States. Turkish newspapers continued to quote from critical pieces on the shaky relationship published in respected American papers like *The Wall Street Journal, The Washington Post* and *The New York Times.*

THE WAR IN IRAQ AND GLOOMY PROSPECTS FOR U.S.-TURKEY RELATIONS

The rift the Iraq war caused in journalism circles was also evident within the same newspaper and television stations. While one columnist favored the U.S. attack, another, writing on the same page, was against it. There were also notable differences between the tone of headlines and the views and analyses expressed in opinion columns. The newspaper and television stations that belonged to the same media group also displayed bifurcated editorial stances.

However, on the whole, liberal mainstream media envisioned a swift victory for the United States (Çatalbaş, 2003). The flicking pictures from cameras of embedded reporters showing the U.S. Army rolling unopposed through the desert reinforced this prediction. That kind of footage and information were also in accordance with the framework in which the war had been presented to the public: the invincible superpower sweeping across Iraq in a matter of days. In the first days of the war, *Hürriye*t, the largest selling daily of Dogan Media Group, the biggest media group in Turkey, went on with a headline, "Full Speed to Baghdad!"

Military experts, international relations and foreign policy analysts, ex-diplomats and politicians dominated much of the TV coverage, not unlike what was happening on Fox or CNN in the United States. The dominance of these so-called authoritative sources left little room for the views of the person in the street. Although media knew that Turkish public opinion was decisively against the war, there were hardly any *vox populi*. Another group largely ignored by the Turkish media was the anti-war movement and peace activists. Their activities, whether at home or abroad, were covered almost entirely as street protests with no background information about who these people were and what they wanted.

Although the focus was overwhelmingly on "what is happening today," there was also extensive analysis in the media on the background and probable consequences of the war. It was frequently speculated that the war was part of a larger American strategy not just for the region, but for the entire world. The real motives behind the war, many commentators agreed, were to secure the control of oil reserves, to defeat the competition from the EU, and to strengthen the security of Israel. Some commentators insisted that this war should be understood as an attempt to change the maps in the old Ottoman hinterland.

In addition to the continuous news reports of what was going on in the front during the war, media coverage centered mostly on what was relevant to Turkey. A more global perspective regarding the unfolding of the events and debates in other countries was largely missing. This evidently ethnocentric media approach focused on U.S.-Turkey relations. Another significant aspect of the Turkish treatment of the war in Iraq was the emphasis placed on its impact on the already feeble economy and on the role of Turkey in the post-Saddam order.

Views on U.S.-Turkey relations seemed to be grouped into three major arguments (Ekrem, 2003):

1. Complete harmony with the USA's global policies;
2. Turkey could support the war in return for concessions beneficial to her national interests;
3. Whatever the costs, Turkey should follow an independent and consistent policy as desired by the majority of her citizens.

In the run-up to the war, most of the commentaries seemed to adopt the first and second arguments. "The dominant press outlets pressed for involvement, stressing the state's 'interest' and the necessity of acting alongside the 'superpowers'" (Belge, 2003). They said Turkey could not refuse to help the United States because she needed American support to overcome the economic crisis and manage its foreign debts. Some insisted that Turkey still should have participated in the war, even if its economy was in a slump because of its strategic partnership with the United States. These commentators believed the Iraq war should be seen as overthrowing a brutal dictator, just like Serbian leader Slobadan Milosevic. They urged that Turkey's geo-strategic position was an important determinant of the war (Güven, 2003).

These writers and journalists also claimed that foreign policy should be run in the direction of national interests and in the framework of international power relations. Co-operating with the United States in Iraq, they argued, would give Turkey a say in the new order of northern Iraq and the Middle East. Turkish military would also be able to control the distribution of arms to the Kurdish rebels in order to prevent them from being turned against Turkey in the future. Meanwhile, Turkish firms and businessmen could share in the rebuilding of Iraq after the war. Some influential columnists especially emphasized the opportunity this war could provide for Turkey to again become a "great country," reminiscent of rhetoric from the late President Özal.

Rejection of the government motion on March 1, 2003, was a major blow for the pro-U.S. journalists and commentators. Some well-known television journalists voiced concerns that the disagreement between the United States and Turkey was taking the relationship to a dangerous level. They claimed Americans felt deceived and would take out their anger on Turkey. The United States, they feared, would blame Turkey for U.S. war casualties because Turkey had withheld its military support.

These views echoed on CNN TURK in the words of some American commentators such as Henry Barkey, Morton Abromowitz, and Helena Finn. Largely negative observations by American commentators and the apologetic responses of some Turkish journalists and commentators further divided the journalism community in Turkey. Anti-war camps accused some pragmatists of war-mongering, such as Ertugrul Özkök, the editor in chief of Hüriyet and one of the top executives of the Dogan Media Group. Those in the camp of pragmatists, on the other hand, accused writers, commentators, and everyone else on the anti-war front of ignorance, naivety, demagogy, and even disloyalty.

The pragmatists had a very long list of those culpable for the refusal of the government proposal: the president, the head of the Parliament, the Army, the chief of staff, the dissident AKP MPs, the opposition party CHP, the National Security Council, peace protesters, leftists, Islamists, and Kurds. Ordinary people were also guilty of being so naive that they were fooled by them.

Most of the journalists and observers who favored the government's proposal complained that the National Security Council, which "declared opinion on almost all matters," had failed to support the government. In their view, Hilmi Özkök, the chief of staff, was also too late to declare the Army's support for the motion. But these commentators seemed to forget that the influence of the National Security Council and the Army over politics has long been identified as one of the major obstacles for true democracy in Turkey. As it turned out, this time, the problem was their lack of influence.

While President Ahmet Necdet Sezer and the head of the Parliament, Bülent Arinç, were criticized for misinterpreting international legality, AKP leaders were accused of failing to persuade the Turkish people and their own MPs. Critics said Abdullah Gül and his successor, Tayyip Erdogan, had not exhibited sufficient decisiveness. They should have explained to the people why Turkey should support the war. People still might have objected to Turkish involvement in the war, but they would have understood it, critics claimed.

Mainstream media commentators also argued that the AKP leadership had made a mistake by not forcing their MPs to vote as a bloc. However, the same kind of dissent in Britain against Tony Blair had been represented as the power of democracy. They argued that the rejection of the motion was not the result of intra-party democracy, but of the ineptness of the AKP government.

Another group the pragmatists often targeted was anti-war protestors. Particularly singled out were extreme left and Kurdish political groups, human rights and other civil society organizations, and workers' unions. One influential newspaper editor, who asked that the identity of the dissident AKP MPs be revealed, later claimed that most of them were from southeastern provinces, where the majority of the population is of Kurdish ethnic origin (Özkök, 2003, March 19).

He also wrote that "the (negative) attitude taken against the government policy by the Turkish media ha(d) great importance for the future of Turkish-American relations" (Özkök, 2003, March 22). He opined that this attitude also demonstrated that the claim that "94% of the Turkish people were against the war" was a fiction. Whether the media represent 100% of the people in Turkey is highly contentious. But these views provided evidence for the AKP government's complaint that the Turkish press supported the U.S. policy against Turkey, rather than supporting Turkish policy against the United States.

The journalists who wanted Turkey to take an active role in Iraq offered a number of speculations on the consequences of the Parliament's decision. Some claimed that the result delighted Saddam and Iraqi Kurdish groups. They speculated that a Kurdish federal state would soon be established while Turkomans would be left at the mercy of the Kurdish peshmergas who would capture Kirkuk and Mosul. Turkey would be left out of the new order in the Middle East and would have to be content with being a modest Middle Eastern state instead of being a "great" country. Moreover, Turkish soldiers in Northern Iraq would come under threat and Turkey would have to reconsider its policy towards the establishment of an independent Kurdish state.

As Turkish refusal did not find any visible EU support, there was also a great danger of facing isolation in the international arena. Some liberal journalists argued that without American aid, Turkey could have yet another economic crisis and be worse off than Argentina, causing a problem for the political regime. These kinds of comments met with widespread condemnation as some feared this could be interpreted as calls for the Army to seize power and mend relations with the United States—relations that Islamists in power had allegedly turned into a mess.

In sum, the main pro-U.S. journalists claimed that those who had opposed deployment of the American troops in Turkey had put the country in peril. They claimed the anti-war front had failed to understand that it was the rejection, not the approval, of the motion that would lead to Turkey into war. The disputes in northern Iraq in July 2003 between Turkish special forces and the U.S. military were used to argue how right they were in their anticipation. But this time they had no qualms about who was straining the relations: the Americans were seeking revenge.

Even though journalists and television commentators were divided about the war and its implications for Turkey-U.S. relations, they seemed equally disillusioned with the government. AKP government had to face serious condemnation from many different quarters for failing to manage the Iraq crisis. Of course, what these parties expected from this crisis management was completely different. "Supporters of military involvement in Iraq were obviously angered by the parliamentary vote, but those against were hardly enthused, because the vote was more of the effect of a series of mistakes and misunderstandings than of a principled action against war and invasion."(Belge, 2003, May 21). Nevertheless, many commentators on the anti-war front still thought Turkey's position was better than active military involvement.

CONCLUSION: RETURN FROM 'REALPOLITIK' TO REAL POPULISM

Turkish media, like the politicians, needed to find ways of resolving the tension created by the conflicts between emotional, religious, humanitarian, and ideological concerns of their constituencies and audiences and the country's perceived political and economic interests. The country was deeply divided. Many well-known journalists and television commentators sneered at public sentiment, which was decidedly against the war and supported not the Saddam regime, but Iraqi civilians, most of them fellow Muslims. The pundits did not take into account widespread public opinion that the strategic interests of Turkey might not conform to American plans in the Middle East and particularly in northern Iraq.

What these journalists and commentators argued was that the war was inevitable and there was nothing Turkey could do about that fact. But they failed to provide sufficient justification for an attack on Iraq by Anglo-American forces. It might be naive to expect commentators to achieve something even President Bush and Prime Minister Tony Blair seemed unable to do: make war credible, if not just. Blair was roundly criticized by members of his Labor Party for leading his country into a "phony war." Therefore, pro-U.S. commentaries advanced by some influential, liberal writers and broadcasters in Turkey were largely inefficient, sometimes even counterproductive, in terms of winning the public consent for the war. This was hardly surprising, considering the growing disconnect between the attitudes of large segments of the population and the Turkish core media as evidenced by AKP's victory in the last election, despite the negative coverage that it received in the liberal mainstream media.

It is remarkable that the emerging differences of interests between the United States and Turkey in northern Iraq, and a few unwelcome incidents involving each side's military forces, made the liberal Turkish press return to populism. Some journalists were as critical of the United States at the end of 2003 as they were supportive at the beginning of the year. It would be unfair to say the Iraq war led to deep-seated anti-Americanism in Turkish society. Although a large majority of the people in Turkey still make a distinction between the U.S. and Bush administration policies, they find it hard to reconcile what they perceive and what media represents as a bully for an ally.

References

Atabeyoglu, S. Accessed July 2003 at http://www.dorduncukuvvetmedya.com/article.php?sid=1858

Belge, M. (2003, May 21) The Turkish refusal, Open Democracy, Retrieved from http://www.opendemocracy.net/ debates/article-2-95-1231.jsp

Çatalbaş, D. (2003, Spring-Summer). Divided and confused: The reporting of the first two weeks of the war in Iraq on Turkish television channels. *Transnational Broadcasting Studies Journal, 10*, Accessed at http://www.tbsjournal.com/catalbas%20turjey.html

Ekrem, S. (2003, July) Turkiye'de Irak Savasi'nin Okunusu, Retrieved from http://www.patikalar.net./selim6.htm

Güven, E. (2003, March 2). Radikal.

Özkök,E. (2003, March 19). Hurriyet.
Özkök, E. (2003, March 22). Hurriyet.
Park, B. (October 2002) "Bridgehead or bridge?" *World Today, 58,* 10.

CHAPTER 11

Late-Night Talk Shows and War: Entertaining and Informing through Humor

Andrew Paul Williams, Justin D. Martin, Kaye D. Trammell, Kristen Landreville and Chelsea Ellis

Late-night talk shows are increasingly popular and reach a broad audience. They provide researchers with ample information about not only popular culture, but also politics and international affairs. Forty-five of the one hundred highest-rated television shows in history are comedies, making humor the most popular TV category (Zillman & Bryant, 1991). In the case of late-night comedy talk shows, millions of U.S. viewers tune in on any given night for both entertainment and information. During the first week of Operation Iraqi Freedom, over seven million adults ages 18-49 watched The Tonight Show with Jay Leno and Late Night with Conan O'Brien (Nielsen, 2003).

The popularity of these talk shows, along with their informative and political natures, renders them important areas of analysis. Indeed, according to the Pew Research Center for People and the Press, 79% of adults thirty and younger claim they regularly or sometimes obtain information about political candidates and elections from nontraditional media sources, like comedy programs and MTV.

Former President Bill Clinton revived his sputtering political campaign in

1992 by playing the saxophone on the Arsenio Hall Show and later gave the first presidential candidate interview on MTV. Politicians like John McCain, Joseph Lieberman, and George W. Bush appeared on late-night talk shows in recent years to attract young voters who tune in. Mainstream media even seriously critiqued their "performances" on those shows. And in August 2003 action actor Arnold Schwarzenegger announced his candidacy for California governor on The Tonight Show with Jay Leno (*St. Petersburg Times'* Wires, 2003). Schwarzenegger easily won the California Recall Election in October 2003.

This study content-analyzed late-night political humor to evaluate the amount of humor, the nature of the humor, the focus of the humor, and the categories of humor dealing with the 2003 war with Iraq. This study explored the relationship between entertainment and humor and the nature of the delivery thereof by late-night comedians.

The research assessed the total amount of war-related humor during the first month. The humor was also evaluated according to the nature of the humor and categorized as positive, negative, neutral, or mixed. In addition, the humor was classified according to its focus on individuals or issues/events and categorized according to function.

METHOD

The late-night talk show sample consisted of the five highest rated national broadcasts: The Late Show with David Letterman, The Daily Show with Jon Stewart, The Late Late Show with Craig Kilborn, The Tonight Show with Jay Leno and Late Night with Conan O'Brien.

The opening monologue vignettes were the units of analysis, and these humorous segments were studied using quantitative content analysis. Researchers defined a vignette as a war-related joke or series of jokes on a similar topic. Shows were coded during the first four weeks of the war—between March 19 and April 18, 2003. The total number of vignettes identified as dealing with the war on these dates was 261, and these vignettes were examined by five trained coders. Intercoder reliability was assessed at +.86 using Holsti's formula (North et al., 1963).

Each vignette was coded in order to establish the broad nature of the humor, and to establish which category best described the position taken about the U.S. war in Iraq: positive, negative, or neutral. Humor defined as positive was clearly supportive of the U.S. military action and was typically exemplified by the use of comedy that made fun of Saddam Hussein or of anti-war protesters. Humor defined as negative was clearly against the U.S. invasion of Iraq and often made President Bush and his administration the brunt of jokes characterizing them as overly dogmatic. Humor defined as neutral was not clearly supportive or unsupportive of the U.S. war against Iraq and often made fun of both American and Iraqi cultures without vilifying them.

These categories provided insight as to the nature of each vignette—ranging from supportive to subversive—and to each comedian's ideology—inclined toward a hawk (pro-war) viewpoint, inclined toward a dove (anti-war) viewpoint, or inclined toward a sparrow (somewhat in the middle) viewpoint.

Coders also evaluated whether each vignette focused more on individuals or on issues/events. After making this distinction, coders selected from a predetermined list in order to establish who or what was the brunt of the joke. Additionally, coders evaluated the vignettes to determine which of the four following comic categories best defined the use of humor:

1. *Escapist*—This type of comedy is often absurd and silly and was selected for vignettes in which the humor was unrealistic and can be used as a coping mechanism to get the audience's mind off the reality of the war. This category links closely with Freud's relief theory and is humor that is absurd and pointless, except to create laughter;

2. *Informative*—This type of comedy provides real information about actual events and was selected for vignettes in which the humor was realistic and recapped actual events and added humor to the news events or persons. This category exemplified vignettes where the comedians used real or altered news segments and where humor was inserted by adding technical distortions or by the talk-show host's physical reactions and comments about the news;

3. *Meaningful*—This type of comedy focuses on the deeper meaning and understanding of what is actually occurring and is often reflexive, thoughtful and analytical, not just informative. Meaningful vignettes were ones in which the comedian actually paused to examine the real-life events in terms of the broader effects of the war on humanity, or the world in general;

4. *Dramatic*—This type of comedy focuses on dramatic elements of real-life events, emphasizing actors or occurrences, as if what is happening in the war was plot or character-driven, similar to a play or a movie. This category is based largely on Burke's dramatistic theory, in which people are portrayed as heroes, villains, or fools; the emphasis is on the story line and the players, not actual information, escapism, or meaning.

RESULTS

Amount of Humor

There was a dramatic difference in the amount of war-related humor among the late-night shows. Almost half (123 or 47%) of all of the 261 vignettes

TABLE 11.1 NATURE OF HUMOR DURING THE WAR

Network Late Night Show	Percent Positive	Percent Negative	Percent Neutral
The Late Show with David Letterman	8	4	88
The Daily Show with Jon Stewart	17	27	57
The Late Late Show with Craig Kilborn	42	7	52
The Tonight Show with Jay Leno	40	8	53
Late Night with Conan O'Brien	42	2	57
Total (N=261)	35	8	57

occurring during this time were on The Tonight Show with Jay Leno. The Late Night with Conan O'Brien show contained fifty-two (20%), and the remainder were about equally spread among the other three programs: The Late Show with David Letterman (twenty-six or 10%), The Daily Show with Jon Stewart (twenty-nine or 11%), and The Late Late Show with Craig Kilborn (thirty-one or 12%).

While talk show hosts supported the American war effort and addressed the topic regularly, they differed somewhat in amount of coverage, with NBC programs providing most of the late-night television humor about the war. The Tonight Show with Jay Leno, for example, offered longer opening monologues and more war-related jokes within brief vignettes. The other NBC late-night talk show, Late Night with Conan O'Brien, ranked second in war-related humor, but contained lengthier vignettes.

CBS competitor The Late Show with David Letterman joked much less about the war and covered the conflict less than any of the five shows compared in this study. The Late Late Show with Craig Kilborn, another CBS enterprise, also covered the war infrequently. Finally, The Daily Show with Jon Stewart contained the fewest vignettes in this study. However, this may have been due to the program's format. The Daily Show's opening monologue was much longer than any of the other four shows and individual vignettes also devoted more time to specific topics.

Nature of the Humor

The nature of humor in each show is shown in Table 11.1. While most of the talk-show commentary was neutral (57%), roughly one in three vignettes (35%) were positive, and very few were negative (8%). In all, the five talk show hosts were supportive of the war effort, portraying it in a positive way.

Vignettes subversive to the war were infrequent. Similarly, the host's ideology was predominantly a combination of a hawk (pro-war) and sparrow (somewhat in the middle) stance, whereas dove (anti-war) sentiments were

Table 11.2 Vignette Focus

Network late-night show	Percent about Individuals	Percent about Issues/Events
The Late Show with David Letterman	60	40
The Daily Show with Jon Stewart	43	57
The Late Late Show with Craig Kilborn	63	37
The Tonight Show with Jay Leno	50	50
Late Night with Conan O'Brien	74	26
Total (N = 261)	56	44

minimal. One reason for this finding may be network writers' attempt to reflect national public opinion, but avoid zealotry. In recent years, there has been an obvious resurgence in patriotism in the United States, and media and political personalities expressing critical, alternate views have been labeled unpatriotic and have faced negative repercussions. Such examples include the backlash against outspoken Dixie Chick Natalie Maines, and the firing of controversial comedian-turned-pundit Bill Maher, former host of Politically Incorrect.

Additionally, Vietnam veteran and double amputee, U.S. Senator Max Cleland was labeled unpatriotic after expressing opposition to military action in Iraq. The current political mix of intolerance and patriotism might explain our findings of mostly neutral and positive war-related humor and emphasis thereof in late-night talk shows.

Focus of the Humor

Collectively, jokes and vignettes that focused on individuals and issues/events provided their audiences with insights about the day-to-day realities during the war through humor. Looking back, we can see that the focus of the comedy used in these monologues informed us of the cultural climate, but it also reveals the fine line comedians walked as they approached their subject.

Overall, talk-show hosts focused on individuals 56% of the time and 44% of vignettes emphasized issues/events, as indicated in Table 11.2. While the majority of vignettes focused on an individual rather than issues/events, both categories provided much comic material. Late-night hosts frequently made fun of Hollywood celebrities, "The Axis of Weasels" (e.g. France and Germany), and journalists. Some issues emphasized were war strategy, anti-war protests, and rebuilding Iraq (e.g., exporting oil and importing Starbucks). These broad categories provided the late-night talk show hosts with many memorable comic opportunities to lambaste specific individuals and to critique the issues/events during this military conflict.

TABLE 11.3 CATEGORIES OF HUMOR DURING THE WAR

Late-night television	Percent Escapist	Percent Informative	Percent Meaningful	Percent Dramatic
The Late Show with David Letterman	60	28	12	0
The Daily Show with Jon Stewart	30	30	37	3
The Late Late Show with Craig Kilborn	52	45	0	3
The Tonight Show with Jay Leno	38	56	5	1
Late Night with Conan O'Brien	47	30	21	3
Total (N = 261)	42	44	12	2

Leno often ridiculed both individuals and collective groups. For example, he opened his monologue one evening with a jab at both the UN and its former weapons inspector by saying, "At this year's White House Easter Egg Hunt, Hans Blix was the only person who didn't find an egg."

After Saddam Hussein's statue fell in Baghdad, Conan O'Brien showed footage of an Iraqi citizen sitting on Hussein's face, then the comedian displayed a large statue of himself to his audience and suggested it as a possible replacement.

Jon Stewart took a swing at Vice President Dick Cheney's former employer Halliburton in reference to its attempt to acquire Iraqi oil contracts during the conflict by saying, "The exciting financial opportunities of this catastrophe don't have to wait for the war to end."

Craig Kilborn sounded off on U.S. military action by analogizing that when President Bush threw Frisbees to his dog on the White House lawn "the Frisbee missed the dog and hit an innocent civilian."

With Saddam's fate uncertain, David Letterman said: "The big debate right now is if Saddam is alive or dead. He's dead, then he's alive, then dead, then alive. It's just confusing. Today they showed videotape and Saddam was speaking at his own funeral."

Categories of Humor

Similar to the focus of the humor, our analysis of humor categories showed an almost even split between two main categories of humor emphasized in the vignettes: escapist and informative (only a small percentage were characterized as meaningful or dramatic).

Collectively, 42% of war-related vignettes were escapist, 44% were informative, 12% were meaningful and 2% were dramatic. Table 11.3 provides a detailed breakdown of these four categories per show.

During Operation Iraqi Freedom, late-night comedians joked a great deal about the conflict. Unlike the tragedy of 9/11, the anticipated war provided talk show hosts with appropriate material. A patriotic public granted comedians considerable latitude for addressing a serious topic.

Conclusion

This study strongly indicates that writers and late-night talk show hosts carefully weighed their audience's need for facts and for levity during a time of uncertainty. This finding also suggests that since these popular shows exposed viewers equally to factual information embellished by humor and purely escapist humor, the public was gaining knowledge about the war through what has been considered by many to be strictly entertainment.

As with any research, there were limitations. This study only focused on a month of content and examined only the opening monologues. A quantitative content analysis, we did not measure for effects and can only draw conclusions based on observations of the shows.

Despite limitations, this study explored an increasingly interesting area of research. Through their viewers and substantive content, late-night television shows and humor have the potential to entertain and inform the public about issues of great importance. With political and government leaders increasingly turning to these shows to boost their popularity among potential constituencies, and with significant issues/events being discussed in this alternative media format, it is logical to assume that an increasing number of people will turn to these shows for information as well as, or in lieu of, traditional news broadcasts.

These late-night shows particularly appeal to young audiences and future studies should assess the impact of these shows on public perception. Longitudinal studies evaluating these shows and their content, from the opening monologue through the entire show, would be useful in understanding the type and amount of informative and entertaining material presented. These programs entertain and inform, through humor, large young audiences throughout the world. Understanding more about the nature of the comedy and its effects merits the attention of researchers interested mass communication effects as well as American popular culture.

References

Nielsen, A.C. (2003). Nielsen television ratings from 3/17/03 to 3/21/03, retrieved from Garrison Clark Enterprises URL: http://www.garrisonclark.com/late-night-ratings.htm

North, R.C., Holsti, O.R., Zaninovich, M.G, & Zinnes, D.A. (1963). *Content Analysis: A handbook with applications for the study of international crisis.* Evanston, IL: Northwestern University Press.

Pew Research Center for The People and The Press (2001). Audiences fragmented & skeptical: The tough job of communicating with voters. Retrieved August 7, 2003, from www.people-press.org <http://www.people-press.org>.

St. Petersburg Times' Wires, (2003, August 7). Signs on to play GOP hero in recall. *St. Petersburg Times.*

Zillmann, D., & Bryant, J. (1991). Responding to comedy: the sense and nonsense in humor. In J. Bryant & D. Zillmann (Eds.), *Responding to the Screen: Reception and reaction processes* (pp. 261-279). Hillsdale, NJ: Erlbaum.

Part III

THE WAR IN THE COALITION PRESS

CHAPTER 12

The Press Made Mistakes Covering the 2003 Iraq War, But It Also Corrected Them

Howard Schneider

Reporting in Iraq was never easy, and the difficulties began well before the first interview. Acquiring a visa and entering the country was, under the old regime, an exercise in the crudest sort of manipulation. The long train of bribery started at the Iraq Embassy in Amman, included health and customs workers at the border ($50 to avoid an AIDS test; $20 to have your satellite phone made "legal"), and did not cease until a wiry accountant named Jameel certified that you had paid all of the hundreds of dollars in fees and charges the Iraqi government required of foreign journalists.

Jameel always pocketed an extra $20 or so as he exchanged pleasantries and stamped receipts. The people around him at the Ministry of Information were more voracious, and enjoyed a steady flow of money, booze, electronic equipment (a group of reporters once pooled their cash and smuggled in a fax machine in return for visas), and clothes.

For the privilege of having your work watched and frequently obstructed, the ministry's corps of "minders" wanted $50 a day in tips—small wonder given their devalued official salaries of around $2 a month. One official whose finger was on the switch to admit journalists maintained his family in designer clothes culled from Amman's toniest boutiques. Reporters would tote along a fresh load each time they made the twelve-hour road trek from Amman, and sometimes be asked to take back items for exchange if the color did not suit, or if gifts for his wife and daughter did not fit.

Big deal, one might say. Isn't the Middle East rife with such corruption? Doesn't it thrive on bribes (*bakeesh*) and personal favors (*wasta*)?

Perhaps. But Iraq under Saddam Hussein was of an altogether different magnitude. Countries like Syria and Egypt, for example, keep their most important officials—those that run the defense and intelligence agencies, for instance—as far out of public view and as far away from the foreign press as the regime in Baghdad. But you don't have to corrupt yourself to enter or work in either place. Journalists can fly into Jordan or Lebanon with no prior notice, buy a visa at the airport, and start reporting.

Iraq was a truly dismal beat to work, a place where foreign reporters were tolerated as a source of payola even as they were watched by an array of informants—from the hotel clerks to the drivers to who knows who else—lest anyone should try to develop independent sources. Virtually the only stories that could be told were the ones that the Iraqi government allowed, and even then information was scarce.

To go beyond the lines risked, at a minimum, blacklisting—a threat that any foreign correspondent had to take seriously for fear that, when a big story broke, their paper would be excluded. Even seemingly small slights could earn temporary banishment. You didn't have to hunt down torture victims or write about the opposition, for example, but simply run a picture of a palace that ministry officials didn't like or employ an "offensive" metaphor. A *Los Angeles Times* correspondent was once punished with a twenty-four-hour wait at the Jordanian border because officials were upset that he had compared the minarets at the new Mother of All Battles Mosque with the shape of a Scud missile.

Once inside the country, the government would offer a set parade of officials whose interviews predictably ranged from rants at the United States to tangled analyses of Iraq as the world's last defense against American hegemony. Field trips always had a propaganda edge—to the hospital, for example, where doctors would discuss the deprivations of sanctions (once, literally, standing in front of a state-of-the-art MRI machine), but hesitate when asked if the Ministry of Health was setting the correct priorities in ordering supplies. They might complain about their lack of access to scholarly journals (blamed on the United States), but demur when asked if that could not be fixed with access to the Internet (forbidden by their own government).

In a place like Basra, top generals and doctors might be assembled to discuss the elevated levels of cancer that depleted uranium (DU) rounds from the 1991 Gulf War allegedly caused among the people of that southern city.

What were cancer rates before the war?

No one could answer that.

How was the effect of DU isolated from the chemical soup already present in Basra from the oil and other industries?

No one could answer that either, leaving reporters in a quandary: Do you ignore the story altogether—hardly fair, in a way, to the Iraqi side—or report on a study that is so obviously incomplete?

It is important to keep this reporting environment in mind when evaluating coverage of the war, because it got even worse during the conflict. Correspondents in Baghdad said that as hostilities neared the usual staff of the information ministry was replaced with new "minders" who clearly came from the intelligence services. Their attitude was more brusque and their demeanor unnerving enough that it convinced some correspondents to pull out.

Those who stayed, and the news organizations that supported them, showed a commitment to the story that should be weighed in any critique. There was little hope that correspondents like Anthony Shadid of *The Washington Post*, or *The New York Times'* John Burns, would get an exclusive interview with Saddam Hussein, or otherwise come up with a "scoop" that on its own would justify the personal risk and the tens of thousands of dollars in expenses required for them to stay in Baghdad for the duration of the war.

While there may be suspicion that news organizations consider war profitable, it is quite the opposite for newspapers: ad revenue doesn't go up when a war starts, but the flood of bills from hotels, satellite phone companies, local drivers, translators, and other items can be budget-busting. Newspaper "space banks"—the amount of newsprint set aside by management—are typically depleted by events like this as column inches are added to do the story justice.

Just like air time for a television network, paper is the print journalist's basic resource. But unlike television, newspapers can expand the resource to fit the news—an expensive decision, given the cost of newsprint, and the other expenses needed to accommodate the information.

Thankfully, however, there are still publishers and editors at U.S. papers like *The Post* and *The Times* and some others who feel that cost control can't wholly dictate their mission. The fact that these and other organizations kept journalists in the hyper-controlled atmosphere of Baghdad—tolerating restricted movement and the fantasy land diatribes of Information Minister Mohammed Saeed Al-Sahhaf—proves an important point about management of the U.S. print media: they want to keep all sides in play.

I emphasize the print media here because, unlike CNN or Al-Jazeera or the other broadcast outlets that maintained Baghdad operations through the war, pictures are not the purpose. For television, "being there" is an end in itself: any network that did not have a camera panning the Baghdad skyline at the start of the bombing would quickly lose viewers to those who did.

What of the print corps? Would *The Washington Post* or *The New York Times* have lost circulation if Shadid and Burns had pulled out? Doubtful.

In addition to those in Baghdad, each paper had a small armada of other correspondents engaged in coverage. *The Times* had at least eighteen other bylined reporters writing from different Middle East venues in the first few days of the war, from Turkey to Qatar to a few "embedded" with the troops. This was in addition to the many other reporters engaged from newsrooms in Washington and New York, at military bases and hometowns in the United States, and in other world capitals where the story unfolded.

Was all this necessary? What would have been lost?

Here is what:

> In Baghdad's largest slum, Yasser Abdel-Hassan broods over the life that he wants, then faces the life that he has.
>
> His dream, an obsessive and almost blinding desire, is to become an engineer, like his father. But already eighteen, he has yet to master a computer. He studies until 11 p.m., but his school in Saddam City promises only dead ends, with broken windows, battered desks, five hundred students and ten computers, still in boxes. His father earns $35 a month, barely enough for food and clothing.
>
> That was before the war.
>
> Now Abdel-Hassan stands listlessly on a street corner with his friends, spending an idle moment in a city on hiatus. School is canceled, with no plans for its resumption. His home is crammed with the stuff of a long, unpredictable siege: a metal vat filled with water, cylinders of kerosene and bags of flour piled against a wall of peeling paint, patched with uneven cement.

That was Shadid reporting in *The Washington Post* on March 29, 2003, one in a series of dispatches that took readers consistently into the homes and neighborhoods and hospitals of Baghdad while the war was underway—work for which he was awarded the Pulitzer Prize.

Two days later, in a dispatch that counter-balances any claim with which the U.S. media tried to soften the edges of this conflict, Shadid wrote:

> On a cold, concrete slab, a mosque caretaker washed the body of fourteen-year-old Arkan Daif for the last time.
>
> With a cotton swab dipped in water, he ran his hand across Daif's olive corpse, dead for three hours, but still glowing with life. He blotted the rose-red shrapnel wounds on the soft skin of Daif's right arm and right ankle with the poise of practice. Then he scrubbed his face scabbed with blood, left by a cavity torn in the back of Daif's skull.
>
> The men in the Imam Ali mosque stood somberly waiting to bury a boy who, in the words of his father, was "like a flower." Haider Kathim, the caretaker, asked: "What's the sin of the children? What have they done?"

For any who think the U.S. print press is easy on the government, undertaking a "smear campaign" against Arabs or Muslims, or blinded by prejudice, work like this stands as a counterpoint for anyone willing to read it. These reporters hung on, at no small personal risk, to maintain witness at a critical moment, out of duty, perhaps out of empathy, surely out of a desire to further accountability.

There were misfires, of course, and no doubt broad objections will be raised about the work done in Iraq—arguments that objectivity is impossible; that all "truth" is relative; that human eyes and ears are not only fallible in the moment but biased at birth, the cognitive equivalent of original sin. Granted and beside the point. It is a given that no individual can escape their own perceptions or be fully aware of the elements in their own psychology that might push them in one direction or another, make them listen harder at one juncture and ignore another, elevate a certain point and overlook a different one.

But the subjectivity inherent in life is different from the sort of crude bias media critics presuppose to be at work among journalists, particularly, these days, journalists from the United States. It is a far different thing to say that a person's values or history affect what they consider important, than it is to say that, as a result, they intentionally seek to manipulate their copy in order to promote those values or validate that history.

No doubt there are journalists at work who do just that. Among the Western print media, I believe that they are few. Indeed, one of the more central discussions in U.S. print newsrooms over the last fifteen years has been over how to diversify hiring policies. This is out of recognition that different people from different backgrounds will bring a different understanding of the world into play, and that this is a healthy thing for a newspaper, not a source of inaccuracy. Media critics tend to miss this important distinction. It is one thing to concede the limits of perception. It is another to say that journalists don't honestly report what they see and hear because they don't like it.

The broader "truth" which journalists allegedly miss, in other words, is different from the "facts" that—at least in my experience—most working reporters try to respect and communicate. They are, in large part, happy to leave that former commodity with theologians, politicians, academics, and anyone else presumptuous enough to try to define it.

So the argument will inevitably ensue: how does this square with what we read from Iraq?

Was the quick (and inaccurate) reporting of the surrender of Iraq's 51st Division not connected to a submerged hope among the Western press for a quick allied victory, or perhaps to a working assumption that a quick capitulation was possible? There was equally quick and inaccurate reporting on the death of "Chemical Ali" in a bombing attack fairly early in the war. The man known as Chemical Ali (Ali Hassan Al-Majid) was believed killed in a missile attack in April but was arrested August 21 where he had been in hiding for most of the post-war period. Had the international media fallen prey to an assumption (propaganda) of omnipotent military might that could target individuals at will, or was it merely a lapse in military intelligence? Was the dramatic rendering of Private Jessica Lynch's rescue unconnected to the hunt for a home team hero?

Before answering, examine some converse examples. Was the initial reporting about the sack of the Baghdad Museum of Civilization downplayed or softened in any way to avoid embarrassing the United States? No. Were the clashes with Fedayeen fighters around Nasariyah, in retrospect, inflated in a way that made the United States look vulnerable, when they in fact proved to be militarily insignificant? Yes. If the sandstorms that bogged the troops for two days could, with apparent sincerity, be reported from the Iraqi perspective as a sign of God's favor—a story that coursed through the Western press—why weren't the preponderance of clear days from then on discussed as proof that God's favor had changed?

The prism of the moment perhaps invariably distorts and exaggerates each day's events. The point for a journalist and, I would argue, anyone examining journalistic behavior from a realistic perspective is this: you use reasonable precautions, reasonable sources, reasonable common sense, a reasonable sense of balance, and a reasonable amount of time, and go with the story regardless of who looks good or bad as a result. This is the first rough draft of history, not the pondering of academe.

What matters is not whether there were embarrassing moments for the press in Iraq. These were inevitable. What matters is what happened on day two. Did the media police itself well? When inaccuracies came to light, were they reported? Is the composite, over time, in reasonable focus?

Reporting events like the war in Iraq involve a kind of rolling refinement, with the successes, limits, and miscues of one-day feeding the next day's agenda.

The process worked for all the stories mentioned above, and others as well.

The surrender of Iraq's 51st Division was widely reported on March 22, and interpreted, particularly in mid-size papers like the *St. Petersburg Times* ("Iraqis Quick to Wave White Flag," the headline read) as a sign of early Iraqi collapse. Within two days, however, papers like *The New York Times* and *The Washington Post* were fixing the record, explaining that the "commander" who surrendered was a lower level officer angling for better treatment. *The Post* went a step further on March 28, reporting that elements of the 51st had grouped around Nasariyah and were involved in the fighting there.

Likewise, the first reports of Private Jessica Lynch's early April rescue from an Iraqi hospital were breathless in their description of Special Operations Forces "swooping down" and storming her hospital room under fire. The drama continued unfolding on the second and third days, with accounts of her "multiple gunshot wounds," and "bloody firefight" in which she held off Iraqi forces until she ran out of bullets.

Exaggerated? Yes, it turns out. Proof that the U.S. press is on the government's leash?

Along with running one of the more dramatic accounts of the original Lynch story, here is what *The Post* reported from Nasariyah two weeks later, when the Iraqi resistance had left town and journalists could interview freely:

"Accounts of the U.S. military's dramatic rescue of Pfc. Jessica Lynch from Saddam Hospital here two weeks ago read like the stuff of a Hollywood script," Keith Richburg wrote. "For Iraqi doctors working in the hospital that night, it was exactly that—Hollywood dazzle, with little need for real action." Many papers followed the emerging, and more accurate, story of Lynch's rescue. In the case of *The Post*, the paper's ombudsman, Michael Getler, even dissected the coverage, concluding "what really happened is still not clear. In the sweep of this conflict, the episode is just a footnote. But let's hope an authoritative public account emerges, at least for journalistic, if not historical, reasons."

In the case of looting at the Baghdad museum, the level of destruction appears to have been far less than initially reported. In the heat of the event, staff there said 170,000 items may have been lost. However by April 30, according to *The New York Times*, museum staff had given U.S. officials a list of only twenty-nine artifacts that they definitely knew were gone.

The same sort of rolling refinement is underway with other aspects of the war, none of them flattering for the U.S. government. If the press willingly reported the Bush administration's allegations about Iraq's possession of weapons of mass destruction and, I'd argue, reporting such statements is obligatory, if only to establish a record for later comparison, they have also been keeping the so-far failed hunt for them in focus.

"The group directing all known U.S. search efforts for weapons of mass destruction in Iraq is winding down operations without finding proof that President Saddam Hussein kept clandestine stocks of outlawed arms, according to participants," *The Post*'s Barton Gellman reported on May 11. "The 75th Exploitation Task Force, as the group is formally known, has been described from the start as the principal component of the U.S. plan to discover and display forbidden Iraqi weapons. The group's departure, expected next month, marks a milestone in frustration for a major declared objective of the war."

Quoting one of the search team members, the story continues: "My unit has not found chemical weapons ... That's a fact. And I'm forty-seven years old, having a birthday in one of Saddam Hussein's palaces on a lake in the middle of Baghdad. It's surreal. The whole thing is surreal."

Chemical Ali proved as elusive as chemical weapons. On April 7, CNN reported British forces as saying the body of Chemical Ali had been found. "We believe the reign of Chemical Ali has come to an end," Defense Secretary Donald Rumsfeld told reporters a few days later. But on April 18, Irish press reports quoting interrogated Iraqi soldiers, hinted that the multi-million-dollar missile attack targeting Chemical Ali had failed to get the general. In June, the BBC, quoting U.S. military officials, said Gen. Al-Majid's fate was uncertain and that he could still be alive. Number five on the allies' most wanted list was nabbed August 21, 2003.

Regarding civilian casualties, the U.S. Department of Defense may not be planning to count, but *The Los Angeles Times* did. On May 18, staff writer Laura King reported the results of a database she assembled by canvassing twenty-seven Baghdad-area hospitals: around 1,700 dead and 8,000 wounded, a number she estimated to be low because of casualties that never made it into the official records. That sort of undertaking—trying to assemble facts that may not be available otherwise—hardly speaks of a press corps beholden to the government, or shackled by bias.

To argue otherwise is to overlook the commitment of money, resources, and effort that major U.S. print organizations made during the Iraq war; to say that the work is inherently flawed is to ignore what's there, in black and white.

CHAPTER 13

Of Journalists and Dogs: Tales from the Northern Behind

Maggy Zanger

For most journalists, comfortably embedded in the hotels of Kurdish-controlled northern Iraq, Gulf War II began with an early morning phone call on March 19. "It's started." Sleep and hang-overs were shaken off as remote controls were punched in to CNN and Thuraya satellite phones jammed up with traffic. They thought the long days of waiting were over.

Most of the perhaps 1,000[1] global media professionals—reporters, cameramen, producers, photographers, picture editors and technicians—had been in Iraqi Kurdistan waiting for the war for anywhere from a few weeks to a few months. They had done the anniversary-of-the-chemical-attack-on-Halabja story; the Kurdish-fighters-in-training story; the Turkey-threatens-to-interfere story; the Kurds-face-an-uncertain-future story; and the Iraqi opposition conference story. They had been scared to death by the mountain men of Ansar al-Islam, a radical group suspected of al-Qaeda connections. They had crawled around the mud of old airstrips in the dead dark of night, waiting for U.S. planes that never seemed to land with Special Forces.

In short, the pack had done it all. And they were restless by mid-March. Without stories to file, lobby lounging became a boring routine as all the rough and ribald tales of past adventures in Bosnia, Somalia or Afghanistan had already been swapped. Romances had bloomed, faded and died. The bar crowd at the main journalist's hotels expanded as closing hour grew later and later and the clouds of cigarette smoke grew to toxic levels.

News organizations represented in northern Iraq by the time the war started included (in broadcast) CNN, BBC World and Newsnight, Fox, ITN, the three U.S. networks including their several cable and satellite spin-offs, France's several television channels, Australian Broadcast Corp., Al-Jazeera, Abu-Daubi TV, AP Television, and NPR; and (in print) Reuters, Agence France Presse, Associated Press, Knight Ridder, *The New York Times*, *The Washington Post, The Boston Globe, The Los Angeles Times, Newsday, The Wall Street Journal, The Chicago Tribune, The Philadelphia Inquirer, The San Diego Union-Tribune, Pittsburgh Tribune-Review, Minneapolis-St. Paul Star Tribune, Toronto Star, Newsweek, Time. The Guardian, London Times, Sunday Times, Daily Telegraph, Scotsman,* and several Arabic, French, German, Italian and Spanish and Japanese papers. Also represented were the usual smattering of free-lance photographers and writers. Several "journos" were doing double time with both radio and television broadcasts, or with television and Web reporting.

Most journalists from large organizations had received "hostile environment" training and were armed with gas masks, bio-chem suits, body armor and helmets. Freelancers and those from smaller news bureaus were as unprotected as their Kurdish hosts.

By the end of February, drivers and translators had stocked their journalists-rented Land Cruisers with jerry cans of petrol, boxes of water bottles, extra tires, tents, bio-chem suits and gas masks. Hotel parking lots were jammed with trucks with huge "TV" taped to the top and sides. They were ready to move.

The journos were preparing to cover the Northern Front, which was to include 62,000 troops of the U.S. Army's 4th Infantry who would surge across the Turkish border (in exchange for a good $10 billion in aid and loans), move towards the northern city of Mosul and Kirkuk, then onto Tikrit, and finally meet the Southern Front from Kuwait in Baghdad for the final battle.

At least that was the plan.

CROSSING

Journalists had gone through hell and high water to get into Iraqi Kurdistan. Most *wanted* to be there for the war because they could operate Independently. There were no Iraqi government-minders to scare away sources, no embedding with military censors, no restrictions on movement. And, they soon found out, the Kurds were some of the few people in the Middle East who actually like Westerners—even Americans.

The Kurds of northern Iraq have great respect for the power of the international media as they credit the cameras with quite literally saving their lives in 1991 when they were huddled starving on the freezing but closed Turkish border trying to escape the wrath of the Iraqi regime after their 1991 Gulf War uprising.

The Kurds were the only people in Iraq able to speak freely. And they lost no time telling wide-eyed Western journalists that they absolutely supported the war; it would be a liberation, just as Bush and Blair claimed. Kurds told journos of the mass graves, massive ethnic cleansing, chemical attacks, torture chambers and raping rooms that were part and parcel of living under Saddam Hussein. And they talked of the of the heady sense of freedom they had experienced since 1991, when his regime withdrew from the northern governorates and left the Kurds to govern themselves under the protection of the U.S.-U.K.-enforced no-fly zone. Two Kurdish governments, which were as cooperative as any government journalists had experienced, controlled much of northern Iraq.

But the area was inaccessible from government-controlled Iraq, and neighboring Iran, Turkey and Syria tightly controlled their borders, especially for journalists and especially into Kurdistan, which was technically illegal since no Iraqi visa would be issued for this area.

Previously, Syria had been accommodating journalists, quietly allowing their passage into and out of Iraqi. But in mid-October, 2002, CNN broadcast a non-news, vanity story about how its huge crew with 3,000 pounds of gear had driven from the Beirut bureau across the desert width of Syria, and crossed the Tigris River in small boats into Iraqi Kurdistan.[2] Anyone with even a simplistic knowledge of the region would have known that media-paranoid Syria would react badly. And they did. The border was closed sometime in November to Westerners, leaving reporters around the world scrambling for alternatives. And there were few.

Iran was the most obliging, as long as the journo's organization had not published or broadcast a story that offended the government in some way and many had. Even with a clear record, it took from one to three months to get a visa. Then, a large group of reporters was held back in Tehran until early February, when it was suddenly allowed to cross the border and into the hotels of Sulaimania in eastern Kurdistan.

Turkey had long closed its border to journalists, but in late February announced it would allow journalists to cross for five days *only* to cover the Iraqi opposition conference that would take place near Erbil. Word spread quickly among the international press corp.

Betsy Hiel, Middle East correspondent for the *Pittsburg Tribune-Review*, and Cairo based free-lancer Gretel Kovach had arrived a week before the Turks agreed to the five-day exception and tried desperately to figure out some way of getting in. They finally agreed to pay a smuggler $5,000 to guide them through the mountains and across the river to Iraq—without benefit of boat, that is. They had their gear triple packed in zip-lock bags, laptops in backpacks to be held over their heads, ready to make the trip, when a fixer called to say the Turks had eased up and they needed to get on the good-for-five-days list. And they did—numbers 11 and 12 on the list that would expand to perhaps 200.

Paul McEnroe of the Minneapolis-St. Paul Star Tribune and his cameraman Paul Sennott took the plunge before the Turks started the list. They were smuggled across the border in a potato truck.[3] "A silent panic set in," McEnroe wrote afterwards. "There was barely room for two men to sit crossed legged under four ash beams braced to keep a half-ton of potatoes from caving in on us." After six hours and 100 miles, they arrived safely in Kurdistan; and after two months, they flew out with the U.S. military.

Another 200 or so journos waited on the Turkish border. And waited, as the five-day list grew and hotel prices grew with it.

Turkish officials were so determined that all the journalists would make the return trip to Turkey, they first said they would hold all passports. They relented under a shrill chorus of denunciation. Then they said the journalists had to leave behind all laptops and mobile phones. More denunciation. The Turks relented. But they stood firm on satellite TV up-link equipment. Journos 2—Turks 1.

A few days later, 175-250 journalists (depending on which of those 175-250 journalists you talk to) finally crossed the Ibrahim Khalil border into Iraqi Kurdistan to cover the opposition conference. Reportedly, 17 went back to Turkey at the end of it. The only ones who returned were people working for the large news bureaus in Istanbul and Ankara who had faced loss of their ability to operate in Turkey if they bucked the agreement. Everyone else went AWOL.

TALKING TURKEY

After escaping their Turkish minders, journalists quickly joined the huge pack of their colleagues already jammed into hotels in the Kurdish cities of Hawler, in Kurdish (or Erbil, Arbil, or Irbil, in Arabic) and Sulimani (or Suliamaniyah, or Sulaymania).

They were all ready to cover the Northern Front. The northern city of Mosul was a stronghold of the Ba'th Party and home to a large number of military top brass and intelligence operatives. Kirkuk lies in the heart of some of Iraq's most productive oil fields and had been subject to a ruthless ethnic cleansing campaign for many years. Even journalists who normally covered public transportation back home, had figured out that both cities—which each lay about 30 miles from Kurdish front lines—would be major benchmarks in the Northern Front.

But Turkey had other ideas.

In late February the Turkish parliament rejected U.S. plans to use its turf as a launching pad for the Northern Front. It was anticipated that some deal would eventually be struck before the war; negotiations between the U.S. and Turkey continued until March 22, even as coalition troops rumbled toward Baghdad. In the end, there was no agreement.

Plan B was for U.S. forces to lead the assaults against Mosul and Kirkuk with some of the 120,000 Kurdish peshmerga (fighters; literally, "those who face death," though once reported as "those who *fear* death"). Journos scrambled to buff up their contacts with peshmerga commanders and secure agreements to "embed" them with the Kurdish fighters when the big day came.

The notion of Kurdish troops moving on Mosul and Kirkuk sent Ankara into spasms. Turkey, which has long oppressed its own 15 million Kurds, feared that Kurdish control of the oil fields would empower the Kurds to seek an independent state, which would embolden Turkey's Kurds to want to join. Iraqi Kurds have not called for an independent state since the 1920s, but never mind.

It was this near-obsession to keep the Kurds from the two cities that propelled the Turks to announce in late February that they wanted send tens of thousands of their troops as far as 12 miles into Iraq to provide "humanitarian assistance" to Kurds who may flee the fighting and move toward the Turkish border.

The few journalists who understood the history of Iraqi Kurdish and Turkish relations knew this was a laughable ploy, and newcomers caught on quickly. But the Kurds weren't laughing. They hastily organized press conferences and made it clear they would fight the Turks. Journos excitedly covered Kurdish streets jammed with singing, marching Kurds with placards announcing: Yes to U.S. Liberation / No to Turkish Occupation.

The scene was set for a "war within a war," as the overused phrase went—Kurds fighting Turks with the U.S. in the middle of its two allies.[4] It made for great copy and kept the journos busy for a few days.

In the end the United States managed to keep the Turks at bay. Secretary of State Colin Powell made it clear that Turkish troops in Iraq would be unwelcome. The United States scrambled to assure the Turks that any advance on the cities would be strictly under U.S. command.

The Tora Bora of Kurdistan

Meanwhile, on the eastern border of Iraqi Kurdistan, where the rugged Shram Mountain fuses into Iran, journalists had been tracking an expected war with Ansar al-Islam (Supporters of Islam), a radical group that had been terrorizing the area for more than a year with assassination attempts and suicide bombers. Ansar controlled several mountain villages perhaps 50 miles southeast of Sulaimani, and was host to maybe 800 Kurdish militants, some trained in Afghanistan, and another perhaps 150 "Afghan Arabs" who fled Afghanistan in late 2001 when the United States attacked.

For months before the war, journalists had been stalking U.S. operatives in the area who were preparing for an attack against Ansar in conjunction with the Kurdish peshmerga, who journalists affectionately dubbed the Pesh or Peshy. While officials in Washington readily admitted that U.S. Special Forces were operating in Iraq, on the ground in Iraq they were a bit touchy about journalists' efforts to document their presence. In mid-February, for example, several western journalists, including ABCs Kevin McKiernan, had their tapes and film rolls confiscated after they filmed one of the U.S. teams in the valley below the Ansar camp, one of the very few such incidents in northern Iraq throughout the war period. Special Forces "came of the closet" only after the war began in mid-March.

Reporters found the Pesh far more accommodating than U.S. Special Forces, which went to great lengths to stay hidden and only came out of the closet after the war began. So the journalists frequently hung out at Pesh headquarters to watch for artillery shelling that occasionally rained down on them from Ansar heights. Many shared scary stories of the "shell that got too close," but they kept going back. It seemed to be enormously important to TV journalists in particular to catch on film artillery shells in the act of explosion.

Journalists and locals alike watched Colin Powell's February 5, 2003, speech to the UN on CNN via satellite, which is readily available in the Kurdish area but outlawed in Iraqi government-controlled areas.

Powell's targeting of Ansar as the crucial link between Osama bin Laden's al-Qaeda network and Saddam Hussein's regime, and his accusation that they were manufacturing "poison" in a lab in their mountain compound, sent journalists from Erbil running to Sulaimani, and Sulaimani journos shifting into high gear.

It also sent the more knowledgeable ones running for their maps because Powell apparently mistakenly labeled a satellite photo of the "poison lab" as located in Khurmal, a more populated village outside the Ansar area. He should have said Sergat, a tiny hamlet nestled in a stunningly beautiful canyon above Khurmal.

Powell's speech also prompted Ansar to invite journalists for the first time to their Sergat compound to prove the accusations false. The bright blue canyon sky and snow-capped Shram mountain rising behind Sergat looked like a Swiss Alps postcard and made for great pictures as reporters were shown an abandoned "media center" Ansar said Powell had identified as a poison's lab. The area had been evacuated, Ansar officials said, because they had feared a U.S. attack in the three days since Powell's speech.

Before leaving, the journalists were forced by gun-toting Ansar fighters to line up in front of Ansar's video camera and say, "I did not see biological or chemical weapons here." A few hours after reporters left the Sergat camp, Ansar members assassinated three Kurdish government officials, including a member of parliament, in a village near Sergat.

Kurdish officials posted even more Kalashnikov-armed Pesh in the main journalists hotels for protection, eventually demanding full searches of even journalists before entering. Journos took their own measures. Some stopped eating at the Ashti Hotel upstairs restaurant, which was ringed with large street-facing windows. Others stopped walking the two blocks between the two journo hotels, fearing a drive-by style attack. Others feared taxis drivers more and walked instead. And none argued with their Kurdish drivers, who always carried at least a sidearm and usually a Kalashnikov (AK-47) in their rented trucks.

A few days into the war, shortly after midnight, a BBC Newsnight crew was doing a live two-way from the roof of the Sulaimani Palace hotel when they heard missiles whizzing overhead. As many as 50 Tomahawk missiles pounded the Ansar mountain enclave. The only journalists who caught the assault on video tape were from the Kurdish satellite channel, Kurd-Sat, and there was a mad scramble to acquire copies.

Excited journalists spun out of their hotels that morning, flack jackets and cameras in tow, and headed east for the Ansar area to check out the damage. That afternoon, at a Kurdish checkpoint in the valley below Sergat, journalists stopped in the bright sun to interview civilians fleeing the villages near the Ansar stronghold. An Australian TV crew had finished up and were heading out. But cameraman Paul Moran decided to get one final shot of fleeing villagers. Near him, a sedan innocently pulled up to the checkpoint. A Kurdish guard leaned into the car to check the driver's ID when it exploded with 220 kilos of TNT, blowing body parts as far as 500 feet, and hurling a mushroom cloud of smoke and debris into the air cool spring air.

Moran and six others were killed. His reporter and translator were injured, along with as many as 24 Pesh and civilians at the checkpoint. The suicide bombing was a brutal message from Ansar to journalists working in the area.

The war had come home.

A few days later, on March 29, 10,000 freshly-armed Kurdish fighters advanced on Ansar in six simultaneous thrusts coordinated by perhaps 100 U.S. Special Forces and supported by intensive bombardment from mortars, artillery, B-52 bombs, cruise missiles and attack jets. The mountain villages controlled by the group fell like dominoes within 24 hours; perhaps 250 Ansar were killed; the rest fled into Iran. No one was sorry.

The next day, journalists rolled into the villages to find returning unveiled, cigarette-smoking residents happily cleaning up the wreckage. Almost to a single one, they told journalists that they would gladly lose everything if it meant being free of the oppressive control of the radical Ansar Islamists.

THE NORTHERN BEHIND

On the morning of March 19, with bombs falling on Baghdad, a perverse sense excitement buoyed the press corp. Newspaper reporters from Tokyo to San Diego and TV stars from Fox to al-Jazeera thought the Big Show was about to begin.

Antsy for action, a near caravan of journalists rushed half an hour west of Sulaimani to Chamchamal, a scruffy city of perhaps 60,000 that lies smack on the demarcation line with the Iraqi-controlled area. Iraqi troops and their bunkers are visible on the hills to the west of the city. As the journalists were filing in, the remaining Kurdish citizens of the city, fearing possible chemical attacks by Saddam, were filing out, seeking protection in Sulaimani or villages in the mountains beyond.

Some journos rented houses from fleeing residents so they had a place to hang out in or to set up cameras on the roof. From Chamchamal, any attack on Kirkuk, 30 miles away, just might be visible.

Alas, the only footage of fire journalists got that night were of a couple of stalwart Pesh dancing around bon fires in celebration of Nawrus, the traditional Kurdish New Year, which happily marks the beginning of spring. Kurds had something more to celebrate this year: for them the beginning of the war also signaled the end of their bloody 40-year struggle against the hated Ba'th regime.

For the next few days journos routinely trekked to Chamchamel only to come back empty-handed the next morning for showers and to exchange information over breakfast with those who stayed behind and watched TV.[5] The breakfast room of the Ashti Hotel became a morning briefing room.

Frustration soon saturated the morning briefings. On the third night in Chamchamal journos saw some distant glowing in the sky as Camp Khalid and the Republican Guard near Kirkuk reportedly came under some bombing. But a NBC producer reported that Chamchamal was basically, once again, quiet.

"Nothing but journalists and dogs," he grumbled. Kovach, the Cairo free-lancer who had come from Turkey, agreed, snorting, "I'm not shocked and I'm not awed." This prompted the *Christian Science Monitor* reporter at a nearby table to pick up the cue. "Yeah, where the hell is this Northern Front? We've been waiting all this time to cover the Northern Behind?"

But soon, it seemed everything was breaking open. Or so it seemed. Turkey's threats to send troops in to northern Iraq rose to a shrill. Some news organizations wrongly reported they had crossed the border. Journos debated whether to move to the western half of Iraqi Kurdistan to cover this possible action.

Meanwhile, on March 23, a couple thousand U.S. troops started parachuting and flying into Harir airstrip (often misreported as Bashur), and the cities of Kirkuk and Mosul came under near nightly bombardment. The bombing sent TV journalists to the front lines to stand in front of the cameras and say, "Behind me, U.S. bombs rain down on the northern city of ... " Not mentioning, of course, that it was *many miles* behind them.

For three weeks the Northern Behind moved in fits and starts. The tension was constant but nothing much really happened. Iraqi troops slowly began to abandon one checkpoint after another along the northern front line with Kurdistan—Qushtapa, Kalak, Taqtaq, Kifri, Chamchamal. As the Iraqis fell back toward Kirkuk and Mosul, the Pesh moved in to fill the void. U.S. Special Forces—hot from the success of working with the Pesh on Ansar—continued working with them, calling in air strikes on the new positions. After a while, in some areas, the Kurds and U.S. Special Forces came within a few miles of the cities.

Journalists too moved to the new "front" to see how close they could get and to catch video of "bang bang"—the sporadic U.S. bombardment of Iraqi positions and occasional and unpredictable artillery shelling by Iraqi forces of the areas they has just vacated. Print journalists collected exotic date-lines: Qara Anjir, Altun Kupri, Qadir Karam, and Maqloub.

However exotic sounding, these trips to the new front lines were also dangerous. A respected and well-liked BBC cameraman, Kaveh Golestan, was killed when he stepped out of his truck and onto a landmine west of Kifri. John Simpson's BBC World crew was traveling in a large convoy of U.S. and Kurdish forces when it was hit by "friendly fire" in an area of shifting frontlines 25 miles southwest of Irbil. Simpson's translator was killed along with some 17 others. But the crew did get dramatic footage of the immediate aftermath that the BBC milked to the fullest. Simpson's several errors in reporting during the war will no doubt be forgiven in the wake of his composed, professional piece-to-camera done shortly after the attack.

The remaining BBC crew in the north—from Newsnight—decided to pull out before their luck ran out. Unfortunately for them, Baghdad fell two days later while they were stuck in Tehran for 10 days straightening out visa problems. They watched the war from TV screens in their Tehran hotel rooms.

As weeks wore on and the Northern Behind went nowhere, reporters started talking of leaving, as much from dearth of story as from danger.

THE FALL

No one saw it coming. And no one who was there will ever forget it.

Midday, on Wednesday, April 9, the BBC reported that Baghdadis were celebrating the arrival of U.S. troops, and CNN aired the tearing down of the now-famous statue of Saddam in Baghdad city center.

In Sulaimani and Erbil, within minutes of the BBC report, people began to gather in the streets of the bazaars. And reporters gathered to capture it on tape.

Within an hour, Salim Street, which runs the length of Sulaimani, was jam packed with cheering, dancing, horn honking celebrators as far as the eye could see.

An American journalist, and a French documentary filmmaker in full traditional Kurdish clothing, climbed into a passing pick up truck with their cameras to shoot the celebrating crowd in the traffic circle in front of the Sulaimani Palace hotel. They, in turn, were shot and broadcast on local Kurdish television.

Iraqi Kurdistan needed no liberation from the Iraqi regime as it had been self-ruling, independent of the regime, since 1991. But the fall of Baghdad marked the end of its long bloody struggle against Saddam Hussein. It marked the end any possibility of more chemical attacks, more ethnic cleansing; another genocide. A people who had for decades collectively mourned, now moved spontaneously moved toward the city center to collectively celebrate.

For journalists who had spent months listening to their horror stories over little glasses of tea and meals of kebab and rice, it was an exhilarating moment

Early the next morning, about 500 Pesh snuck into Kirkuk to start an uprising that would soften things up for U.S. Special Forces to move into the strategically crucial city. But when they arrived, the Iraqi military, Ba'th Party operatives and security people were already gone. They had simply melted away. The Pesh met no resistance.

Around mid-day, disbelieving journalists in Sulaimani and Erbil watched a BBC "sat" phone report by Dumeetha Luthra, a print journalist working in the area who had just been hired on by the crew-short BBC: Kirkuk had fallen, she reported. Most thought it an exaggerated report. It seemed impossible that Kirkuk, the mighty northern oil city, epicenter of decades of ethnic cleansing, could have so easily unleashed it self from the grip of Saddam Hussein.

Nonetheless, they grabbed cameras, walkie-talkies, satellite dishes, tape recorders and sleeping bags, along with their translators, and leapt into their trucks that had been long well-stocked to follow the war. The waiting was over. Most went to Kirkuk, followed by Mosul, which fell the next day. Many went onto Tikrit and then Baghdad. Those with bureaus in Baghdad hung around to follow up on Mosul and Kirkuk and then melted away themselves.

By late April the hotels of Iraqi Kurdistan were empty of all but the most die-hard journalists, and were filling up Turkish and Iranian trade delegations, U.S. civil administrators, Arab tribal leaders, and curious Baghdadis seeking the cool climes of the north for the first time in many years. The Kurds welcomed them all.

ENDNOTES

1. Estimate based on the 700 journalists who were credentialed by the Kurdistan Regional Government, Erbil for the Iraqi Opposition conference in late February, plus

estimated numbers of those who did not attend the conference and those who arrived after the conference and throughout the war.

2. Brent Sadler's on-line version, "Crossing the river into Northern Iraq," October 11, 2002, http://www.cnn.com/2002/WORLD/meast/10/11/btsc.sadler/index.html

3. Paul McEnroe, "Star-Tribune journalists document Kurd's sorrows, hopes," April 20, 2003, http://www.startribune.com/viewers/story.php?template=print_a%story=3836288

4. "Before you know it, you would have a war within a war," a U.S. official told the *Los Angeles Times*. "U.S. Drops Its Bid to Base Troops in Turkey," *Los Angeles Times,* March 15, 2003, Richard Boudreaux and John Hendren. The "war within a war" scenario was repeated by numerous reporters, including this one.

5. This Chamchamal waiting game is also described also by *Guardian* journalist Jason Burke "Waiting for the war: Locals and journalists alike discuss when the bombing will start," *Guardian*, March 24, 2003. From Washington Kurdish Institute list-serve, March 25, 2003.

CHAPTER 14

Embedded Versus Behind-the-Lines Reporting on the 2003 Iraq War

Stephen D. Cooper and Jim A. Kuypers

A 2003 study by the Pew Research Center for the People and the Press found that "Most Americans (53%) believe that news organizations are politically biased, while just 29% say they are careful to remove bias from their reports ... More than half—51%—say that the bias is 'liberal,' while 26% discerned a 'conservative' leaning. Fourteen percent felt neither phrase applied" (Harper, 2003). Now add to this that even some academicians are finally accepting the idea that journalists, as a group, are more liberal than the population as a whole. However, whether political or other biases (Hahn, 1998) affect news coverage is still argued. We believe political biases do affect news coverage, in that reporters and editors select and frame news stories in a way that reflects their predispositions.

Regarding story selection, Bernard C. Cohen astutely observed the press "may not be very successful in telling its readers what to think, but it is stunningly successful in telling its readers what to think about" (1963, p.13). Maxwell E. McCombs and Donald L. Shaw found that voters learn about an issue in direct proportion to the attention given that issue by the press, and that voters tend to share what the media defines as important (1972, p. 177). This media effect is called agenda-setting. Subsequent studies of agenda-setting confirmed that the media can have enormous influence upon political decision making and that they are especially influential in telling the general population what to think about. In short, there is a correlation between the amount of news coverage of an issue and that issue's level of importance to the public.

Further, we find that the news media also suggest *how* to think about those issues. Jim A. Kuypers called this agenda-extension (1997), and it occurs when the media move beyond a neutral reporting of events. One way of locating instances of media bias—in the sense of non-neutral transmission of information—is by studying frames, which is one way the media provides its audiences with contextual cues necessary to evaluate the issues under consideration.

William Gamson asserted that a "frame is a central organizing idea for making sense of relevant events and suggesting what is at issue" (1989, p. 157). Facts remain neutral until framed; thus, how the press frames an issue or event will affect public understanding of that issue or event. On this point Gamson argued that facts "take on their meaning by being embedded in a frame or story line that organizes them and gives them coherence, selecting certain ones to emphasize while ignoring others" (p. 157). Framing thus elevates the salience of some ideas over others, while making some ideas virtually invisible to an audience.

Although it can be reasonably argued that providing contextual cues for interpretation of events is a part of media responsibility, when journalists infuse their political preferences into news stories the potential for manipulation increases. A powerful feature of frames is that they define problems, causes and solutions, although not necessarily in that order. They also provide the author's moral judgments concerning these problems, causes and solutions.

The power of frames to influence the way in which the public interprets certain issues was demonstrated by Paul M. Sniderman and colleagues. In one example, which involved the issue of mandatory HIV testing, researchers found that frames highlight some values over others, thus increasing or decreasing the saliency of these values: "[A] majority of the public supports the rights of persons with AIDS when the issue is framed to accentuate civil liberties considerations—and supports ... mandatory testing when the issue is framed to accentuate public health considerations" (1991, p. 52). When one considers the pervasiveness of the mass media in America, one must conclude that the potential power of framing is great indeed.

Comparative Framing Analysis: One War, Two Frames

Among the easiest ways to identify frames is through the use of comparative framing analysis (Kuypers, 1997, 2002; Entmann, 1991, 1993). To that end, this study looked for differences in war reporting between journalists embedded with combat units and journalists based behind the lines. The stories analyzed came from the *New York Times* and the *Washington Post*.

Choosing articles from these two papers created both a strength and weakness in the analysis. The strength was that both of these papers are still (recent *NYT* scandals aside) considered national papers of record. Both have extensive resources to support continuous coverage of any topic, so differences in framing observed in this study were unlikely to stem from limited staff or limited resources. The weakness was that the study analyzed news products of a limited number of journalists. Although unlikely, it is conceivable that differences in framing between the stories of embedded journalists and those of behind-the-lines journalists observed in this study were unrepresentative of news outlets in general, but instead, was an artifact of these two particular newspapers.

To the extent possible, stories by embedded reporters and behind-the-lines reporters were matched by date of publication. This was done to reduce the possibility that any framing differences observed were attributable to changes over time of actual conditions in the combat, rather than a property of the journalistic environment. As a practical matter, one day's difference in date was still considered a match. In all, 66 stories published between March 21 and April 10, 2003, were examined. Twenty-six were from embedded reporters and 40 were from behind-the-lines reporters. This study centered on two major themes in the war coverage: the strength of Iraqi army resistance and the response of Iraqi civilians to the Allied incursion. Space limitations in this volume prevent full discussion of the stories; the following two sections are intended to illustrate the framing differences as concisely as possible, and should not be taken as a complete exploration of the data.

Iraqi Military Resistance

Stories written by embedded reporters often reported Iraqi soldiers surrendering, Iraqi positions destroyed by artillery and aircraft attacks, Iraqi soldiers deserting and abandoning their uniforms and equipment, the superior force of the Allied units, and Allied officers surprised by the lack of Iraqi resistance. Behind-the-lines journalists wrote about Allied casualties and equipment losses, the potential for unconventional attacks by the Iraqi military, the ferocity of paramilitary or irregular Iraqi forces, the possibility of urban combat situations in cities such as Baghdad, and belligerent rhetoric by Iraqi officials.

The difference in framing became apparent in the early days of the war. Stories about the commencement of hostilities ran on March 21. In the *New York Times*, the headline of the story filed by an embedded reporter was, "G.I.'s and Marines See Little Iraqi Resistance" (Myers, 2003, March 21). Much of this story described how easily the Allied forces overran the Iraqi border defenses, and noted that "the first two border posts turned out to be empty, their soldiers having fled." The headline of the story filed from Kuwait was quite different: "16 die on copter; U.S. and British forces suffer first losses in crash in Kuwait" (Tyler, 2003, March 21). Two days later, a story by another embedded reporter described many Iraqi soldiers surrendering, and only limited resistance. This story framed the combat as "general retreat by the Iraqis with groups of fierce holdouts" (Filkins, 2003, March 23). In contrast, the headline story in that issue (Tyler, 2003, March 23), with a Kuwait dateline, emphasized Allied casualties and loss of vehicles, mentioned "heavy fighting and mortar exchanges" from the Iraqi forces, and commented that there was "no outward sign Saturday that either the government or military command of Mr. Hussein was wavering."

Directly contradicting the frame of the embedded reporter's story was the comment that "the mass surrender that characterized the 1991 Persian Gulf war had not materialized." In the next day's issue a front-page opinion piece (Apple, 2003, March 24), datelined from Washington, described the Iraqi resistance as stiffening, and tougher than Allied commanders had expected. An overview article (Collins, 2003, March 24) referred to the coming "showdown with the Iraqi Republican Guard," described the area around Baghdad as "intensely defended," and commented that on the prior day "allied forces faced the fiercest fighting of the war so far and suffered their grimmest casualty toll."

A week after the war started, a *New York Times* opinion piece written by a Washington-based journalist (Apple, 2003, March 27) framed Iraqi resistance as well-conceived and effective in its use of terrain features, and the Allied forces as highly vulnerable to unconventional tactics. Perhaps echoing reporting on the Vietnam War, the piece described the Iraqi war plan as "a kind of guerrilla defense," and predicted bloody urban combat in Basra: "the British and the American marines fighting with them are surely going to become involved in some kind of street-by-street, if not house-by-house, urban warfare." Another opinion piece in the same edition, datelined Kuwait, framed the war as "a tough fight," referred in the headline to Allied "setbacks," and asserted that "the Iraqi military's command and control system is still intact" (Gordon, 2003, March 27).

Reports from embedded journalists, however, were noticeably less pessimistic about the Allies' chances. In the next day's edition, one embedded reporter's story (Kifner, 2003, March 28) noted that irregular forces were slowing the advance of U.S. troops, but characterized the resistance as "nearly constant harassment and ambush by small bands of irregular Iraqi fighters and remnants of army units" perhaps receiving "rudimentary military direction from Republican Guard officers." Another embedded reporter described a surprise attack on Marine positions around Nasiriya (Wilson, 2003, March 28), which briefly threatened to overrun the command headquarters. The attack was repulsed, and the article ended by quoting an American officer saying, "We had a good day."

The contrast between the frames of the behind-the-lines journalists and the frames of the embedded reporters was, perhaps, even more striking as the serious fighting for control of Baghdad began. The headline of a hard news story by a journalist based in Baghdad (Shadid, 2003, April 3) referred to the coming "climactic defense" of the city. Iraqi officials were described as "defiant," and said to "boast that the country's most vaunted units are primed to repel an assault for which they have planned for years." This story continued the frame that the battle would become "block-by-block guerrilla warfare, with civilians caught in between." An analysis by behind-the-lines journalists (Ricks & Weisman, 2003, April 3) framed the situation as a "dilemma" for the Allied forces, who faced urban combat against "Hussein's most loyal fighters, drawn from the Republican Guard and his bodyguard Special Republican Guard," who might be planning to "hol[e] up in the city and wag[e] a grinding war of attrition." The lead story (Chandrasekaran & Baker, 2003, April 3), datelined Kuwait City, described resistance to the Allied advance as "only patchy," but nonetheless framed the situation as "the climactic battle—and the most dangerous."

This was in stark contrast to stories from the embedded reporters of the *Post*. One story (Branigin, 2003, April 3) was headlined, "No sign of capital defenses." This reporter's unit encountered "surprisingly little resistance," and the Republican Guard units were described as "disintegrating," with no sign of "the heavy Iraqi equipment expected to mount the main defense of Baghdad." Another story (Finer, 2003, April 3) described a unit moving "more than 70 miles through Iraq's central desert in an advance that met little opposition." These troops took control of an strategically-important airfield abandoned by a "fleeing Iraqi army."

The war front moved into Baghdad over the next few days. Stories from embedded reporters painted a mixed picture of relative quiet punctuated by firefights, but the stories from behind-the lines journalists—now close to the front lines!—tended to emphasize the intensity of the fighting. An embedded reporter described a unit searching for Iraqi troops in a suburb of Baghdad, but finding only abandoned positions (Finer, 2003, April 6). The army unit occupying the airport in Baghdad encountered only "sporadic" resistance (Branigin, 2003, April 6), but another brigade tasked with securing an intersection in the southern part of the city became involved in "five hours of killing and fiery chaos" (Branigin, 2003, April 7). An embedded reporter detailed a protracted firefight at a river crossing (Filkins, 2003, April 8), characterizing the Iraqi resistance as "tough, but uncoordinated."

Stories filed by behind-the-lines journalists framed the hostilities as being more intense. One described Baghdad as having become a "war zone," and referred to Republican Guard troops and armament having "poured into the capital," while irregular forces carrying rocket propelled grenades moved in the streets (Shadid, 2003, April 6). Another described the gun battles as "fierce" and the Allied advance as "grinding" (Tyler, 2003, April 7). As Allied forces began consolidating their control of the city, Iraqi resistance was still described as "fierce" (Burns, 2003, April 8; Shadid & Chandrasekaran, 2003, April 8), An analysis in the *New York Times* (Apple, 2003, April 9) characterized the resistance as "stubborn," and commented that "news of fierce fighting in Hilla ... belies talk of collapse."

In fact, Iraqi military resistance did collapse in the next two days. A story from a reporter embedded in a unit entering Hilla (Atkinson, 2003, April 10) referred to "shattered resistance" and "brittle defenses." A story from a reporter embedded in a unit entering Baghdad described a brief firefight and "mild resistance from snipers" (Finer, 2003, April 10). Stories filed by behind-the-lines journalists continued to highlight what resistance there remained, but acknowledged that the combat was essentially done. One described the extension of Allied control over the city as "halting," but noted that by the end of the day "Iraqi resistance—fought relentlessly but ultimately hopelessly with rockets, machine guns and other light arms—had died away" (Burns, 2003, April 9).

Iraqi Civilian Response to the Allied Forces

Another important theme in the coverage of Operation Iraqi Freedom was the response of Iraqi civilians to the incursion by Allied forces. Early reporting, both from embedded reporters and behind-the-lines reporters, dealt mostly with combat operations, but a distinct theme of civilian response developed after the first week or so of fighting. This first became an issue related to the adequacy of the war plans, which anticipated some degree of civilian uprising helping the Allied operations, and later was often linked to the restoration of civil order in areas where the Hussein regime's power structure had been displaced.

In general, the reporting from behind-the-lines journalists featured collateral damage caused by combat, privations suffered by Iraqi civilians after combat passed through their areas, and resentment toward occupation troops. In contrast, reports from embedded journalists described positive interactions between Allied soldiers and Iraqi civilians, Allied efforts to restore basic utilities to the civilian population, Iraqi civilians' fear of reprisals by Ba'ath Party and Saddam *Fedayeen* members, and civilians celebrating the collapse of the Hussein regime.

The cautious acceptance of Allied forces was a theme running through three reports from embedded reporters published in the March 31 *New York Times*. One characterized the first interactions between American forces and noncombatant Iraqis with the word "peacefully" (Filkins, 2003, March 31), and described how American troops helped an Iraqi civilian get his irrigation pump restarted. Another story used the word "warily" to describe the first contact between troops and civilians (Kifner, 2003, March 31). The wariness is attributed to memory of the brutal repression which followed the Gulf War, and one civilian is quoted as saying, "Don't make the mistake of 1991." A report filed from the outskirts of

Basra (Santora & Smith, 2003, March 31,) described civilians caught between British and Iraqi military units. In this story, fear and uncertainty were the predominant emotions, which bred mistrust of the Allied forces: noncombatant residents of Basra were "afraid of Saddam Hussein's troops inside the city who they said were executing people freely; afraid of the forces outside the city whose intentions they did not yet know; and afraid of what would come as their supplies of food and water continued to dwindle." A story from a *Washington Post* embedded reporter (Branigin, 2003, March 31) described a similar wariness as an armored column passed villages, prompting residents to raise white flags.

Civilian response to the troops grew warmer in the next few days, at least in the reports from embedded reporters. Two stories described Iraqis standing by the road and waving at convoys headed toward Baghdad (Branigin, 2003, April 3; Finer, 2003, April 3). A pair of stories from a journalist embedded with units entering Najaf (Atkinson, 2003, April 2; Atkinson, 2003, April 3,) likewise framed the civilian response as welcoming, even in the turmoil of war. In the first, civilians were described smiling at American troops, clapping, and "gestur[ing] impatiently for the Americans to press deeper into the city center." The next day's story framed the welcome as "jubilant," but noted residents' concerns that food and water had become scarce. Another reporter embedded with troops approaching Baghdad described civilians "cheering and encouraging the troops as they passed," framing what he saw as "one of the warmest receptions the Americans have gotten to date" (Filkins, 2003, April 4). An Iraqi civilian fleeing Baghdad was quoted as saying, "You have saved us, you have saved us from him."

Stories written behind-the-lines, covering the same time period, were strikingly different in their framing of the civilian response to the Allied incursion. One story described the burial of a young boy killed in Baghdad (Shadid, 2003, March 31). While the story noted that the boy may well have been killed by shrapnel from Iraqi antiaircraft fire, it framed the residents of the neighborhood as angry at the United States for civilian casualties and resentful at the prospect of an occupation. An analysis in the *New York Times* struck a distinctly pejorative tone when it referred to Iraqi civilians "cheer[ing] the invaders of their country" (Apple, 2003, April 4). The lead story in that same edition (Tyler, 2003, April 4) framed the civilian response in a similar way: "Allied forces had expected a more enthusiastic reception." The lead story in the next day's edition of the *Washington Post* (Chandrasekaran & Baker, 2003, April 5) framed civilians waving to passing convoys as a "surprise" to the troops. A story datelined from Zubair (Glasser, 2003, April 5), filed after the fighting had moved on to Basra, described civilians' "ambivalence" about the incursion in this way: "On the streets, children wave and smile at passing British troops. At the now-empty police station, a banner hangs. 'Shame on America,' it says."

Another analysis in the *New York Times* (Apple, 2003, April 6) referred to "the natural tendency of many Iraqis to feel their patriotic impulses bruised by the presence of heavily armed invaders in their midst." This is in stark contrast to the frame of an embedded reporter's story (LeDuff, 2003, April 8), about American troops entering a town of 45,000: "By noon it was apparent that the townspeople considered [the troops] liberators." The crowd's reaction is described as "euphoria," and a resident is quoted as saying, "you are owed a favor from the Iraqis. ... We are friends."

When the Hussein regime collapsed, the contrast between the framing by embedded reporters and by behind-the-lines journalists diminished somewhat, but did not disappear entirely. A story about American troops entering Hilla, written by the reporter embedded with the unit (Atkinson, 2003, April 10), described the residents as "jubilant," and "offering thumbs-up gestures and high-fives to infantrymen." The reporter commented that "the subsequent happy pandemonium had the distinct flavor of liberation." A story by a reporter embedded with troops entering Baghdad (Finer, 2003, April 10) described a similar response by civilians, "who lined the streets as if they were a parade route." The events were framed as "the most overt display of welcome the Marines had received since entering Iraq."

The two front page stories of the April 10 *Washington Post* carry headlines conveyed the celebratory frame, but included a substantial amount of copy supporting the frame of ambivalence and resentment. Both stories were written by the same behind-the-lines reporter, who was based in Baghdad throughout the war. The lead story (Shadid, 2003, April 10a) framed Baghdad residents as "celebrat[ing] the government's defeat and welcom[ing] the U.S. forces in scenes of thanks and jubiliation." Most of the description supports that frame, but in the second half of the article the reporter referred to the "conflicting emotions" of the moment, and the "hope that the U.S. presence would not become an occupation." The other story (Shadid, 2003, April 10b), also appearing above the fold, very strongly supported the frame of ambivalence. One Baghdad resident is quoted as saying, "You must bring these words to the American people. Thank you, thank you very, very much." Another is quoted as saying, "If they've come as invaders...nobody will welcome them." The crowd is described as having "erupted in cheers" at the sight of American military vehicles, and an Iraqi is quoted as saying, "It is a liberation." Another is quoted as saying, "This is my country and this is an occupation." The reporter summarized these sentiments with the comment, "a current of such ambivalence raced across Baghdad along with jubilation and surprise."

An analysis, on the front page of that day's *New York Times* (Apple, 2003, April 10), struck a decidedly negative tone about the fall of Baghdad. The event was framed as "the highwater mark for a new American determination to use the nation's military to project its power around the world." Near the end of the article, the reporter acknowledged that "some of the Iraqis in the streets were jubilant," but quickly tempered the bit of optimism with the comment that "many Iraqis resent America's Middle East policies as much as other Muslims do."

DISCUSSION

Stories about Operation Iraqi Freedom filed by journalists embedded with combat units differed noticeably from the stories filed by journalists working behind the lines, with regard to the framing of war news.

The embedded journalists often described the war in terms of the weakness of Iraqi army resistance, the frequency with which regular Iraqi forces deserted or surrendered, and the joy of Iraqi civilians at the demise of the Hussein regime. Their stories described the confusion and uncertainty of firefights, the tedium and fatigue inherent in warfare, the precise targeting of Allied ordinance, the pinpoint destruction such weapons produce, and friendly interactions between Allied soldiers and Iraqi civilians.

Stories filed by behind-the-lines journalists described the war in terms of the potential of Iraqi forces to mount significant unconventional counterattacks, the ferocity of the Iraqi irregular forces, the adequacy of Allied war planning, and the vulnerability of the Allies' long supply lines. These stories emphasized civilian anger at collateral damage, interruptions to utility infrastructure, and mistrust of American intentions. Journalists based in Baghdad usually included the statements of the Iraqi Minister of Information, Mohammed Saeed Al-Sahhaf. In the early stages of the war Al-Sahhaf's assertions about the war situation were repeated with little or no comment by the reporter. Only when the combat reached Baghdad itself did some journalists began to question the veracity of Al-Sahhaf's statements, particularly when Al-Sahhaf denied the presence of Allied forces which were visible from the hotel in which the reporters were staying.

In part, these differences in framing between embedded journalists and their behind-the-lines colleagues can reasonably be attributed to the activities and conditions they could directly observe. Embedded journalists, traveling with combat forces, directly experienced the tedium, intensity, danger, and uncertainty of those situations; they observed first-hand the dominance of Allied tactics and weaponry, and the elation of Iraqi civilians as the Hussein regime disintegrated. Behind-the-lines journalists witnessed different aspects of the war. At a physical distance from the actual fighting, their stories concerned the uncertainty and unpredictability of the war's course, the anarchy that sometimes developed when the control mechanisms of the Hussein regime collapsed, the potential—but not the actuality—for significant Iraqi military resistance and counterattacks, and the belligerent rhetoric of the Iraqi Minister of Information.

It is not plausible to attribute the framing differences to military control over the reporting of the embedded reporters. The Department of Defense directive establishing embedding as policy (U.S. Department of Defense, 2003) specifically ruled out any general review of the reporters' copy (para. 3.R), put interviews with troops on the record (paragraph 4.A), and narrowly specified what sorts of information could not be reported because of security concerns (para. 4.G, ff.). Although unit commanders did have the latitude to impose delays on the filing of reports from the combat theater because of concerns for operational security (para. 2.C.4), they were not allowed to exclude reporters from the scene of the fighting (para. 3.G). The directive also stated that the purpose of the embedding policy was to maximize reporters' access to information (para. 2.A), and that restrictions on the release of information in their possession had to be justified (para. 3.R). In sum, any notion that the copy of embedded reporters was censored by the military while that of behind-the-lines journalists was free from interference—and that the framing differences are attributable to the greater freedom of the behind-the-lines journalists—is not supported. It is also worth noting that, in general, journalists themselves were satisfied that their access to the combat theater was adequate (Cooper, 2003).

Although we cannot conclusively demonstrate this to be the case, we feel that the best explanation for the stark differences in the framing of the war stories is that behind-the lines reporters were heavily influenced by newsroom culture, and in the case of the *New York Times*, the paper's stated editorial opposition to the war. In the final analysis, embedded reporters were relaying their eye-witness accounts of events while behind-the-lines reporters could only relay second-hand accounts filtered through their preconceived understandings of the war.

REFERENCES

Apple, R.W. , Jr. (2003, March 24). Lowering expectations. *New York Times*, pp. A1, B2.

Apple, R.W., Jr. (2003, March 27). Iraqis learn the lessons of how U.S. fights wars. *New York Times*, pp. B1, B7.

Apple, R.W., Jr. (2003, April 4). U.S. commander, evoking MacArthur, hops past cities to Baghdad. *New York Times*, p. B8.

Apple, R.W., Jr. (2003, April 6. When to say war is won? *New York Times*, pp. A1, B2.

Apple, R.W., Jr. (2003, April 9). Bush's war message: Strong and clear. *New York Times*, pp. A1, B6.

Apple, R.W., Jr. (2003, April 10). In statue's fall, vindication of a strategy. *New York Times*, pp. A1, B4.

Atkinson, R. (2003, April 2). Army enters holy city. *Washington Post*, pp. A1, A22.

Atkinson, R. (2003, April 3). Jubilant crowds greet troops near shrine. *Washington Post*, pp. A1, A35.

Atkinson, R. (2003, April 10). Residents celebrate as U.S. forces take last of three key Shiite cities. *Washington Post*, pp. A1, A39.

Branigin, W. (2003, April 3). No sign of capital defenses. *Washington Post*, pp. A1, A26.

Burns, J.F. (2003, April 8). Capital has look of a battlefield. *New York Times*, pp. A1, B3.

Burns, J.F. (2003, April 9). Key section of city is taken in a street-by-street fight. *New York Times*, pp. A1, B3.

Chandrasekaran, R., & Baker, P. (2003, April 3). Baghdad-bound columns pass outer defenses. *Washington Post*, pp. A1, A27.

Chandrasekaran, R., & Baker, P. (2003, April 5). Marines on eastern outskirts; army in control of airport. *Washington Post*, pp. A1, A23.

Cohen, B.C. (1963). *The press and foreign policy*. Princeton: Princeton University Press.

Collins, G. (2003, March 24). Allied advances, tougher Iraqi resistance, and a hunt in the Tigris. *New York Times*, p. B1.

Cooper, S. D. (2003). Press controls in wartime: The legal, historical, and institutional context. *The American Communication Journal*, 6(4).

Entman, R.M. (1993). Framing: Toward clarification of a fractured paradigm," *Journal of Communication* 43, p. 51-58.

Entman, R.M. (1991). Framing U.S. coverage of international news: Contrasts in narratives of the KAL and Iran Air incidents. *Journal of Communication* 41, 4, pp. 6-27.

Filkins, D. (2003, March 23). As many Iraqis give up, some fiercely resist. *New York Times*, pp. B1, B4.

Filkins, D. (2003, March 31). U.S. troops meet Iraqis peacefully. *New York Times*, pp. B1, B4.

Filkins, D. (2003, April 4). Marines cruising to Baghdad. *New York Times*, pp. B1, B3.

Filkins, D. (2003, April 8). River is crossed after a day of fierce fighting. *New York Times*, pp. A1, B6.

Finer, J. (2003, April 3). Marines cross Tigris in big push. *Washington Post*, p. A26.

Finer, J. (2003, April 10). A few potshots, but mostly cheers. *Washington Post*, pp. A1, A35.

Gamson, W.A. (1989) News as framing: Comments on Graber," *American Behavioral Scientist* 33, p. 157-161.

Glasser, S.B. (2003, April 5). Until Hussein is gone, ambivalence about U.S. rules. *Washington Post*, pp. A1, A21.

Gordon, M.R. (2003, March 27). Allies adapt to setbacks. *New York Times*, pp. A1, B7.

Hahn, D. F. (1998). *Political communication: rhetoric, government, and citizens*. (State College, Pennsylvania: Strata Publishing, Inc.).

Harper, J. (2003, July 14). Public wants patriotic but unbiased reporters," *Washington Times* <http://washtimes.com/national/20030713-114140-6448r.htm>

Kifner, J. (2003, March 28). Constant Iraqi attacks are holding up the Allied forces trying to reach Baghdad. *New York Times*, p. B5.

Kifner, J. (2003, March 31). Warily, Iraqis get acquainted with Marines. *New York Times*, p. B4.

Kuypers, J.A. (2002). *Press bias and politics: How the media frame controversial issues*. Westport, CT: Praeger.

Kuypers, J.A. (1997) *Presidential crisis rhetoric and the press in the post-cold war world*, (Westport, CT: Praeger).

LeDuff, C. (2003, April 8). Troops bring home an Iraqi who fled in '91. *New York Times*, pp. A1, B8.

Maxwell E. McCombs, M.E. & Shaw, D.L.(1972) The agenda-setting functions of the mass media," *Public Opinion Quarterly* 36 (1972): 176-187.

Myers, S. L. (2003, March 21). G.I.'s and Marines see little Iraqi resistance. *New York Times*, pp. A1, B6.

Ricks, T. E., & Weisman, J. (2003, April 3). Advance's dilemma: Press on, or wait? *Washington Post*, pp. A25, A29.

Santora, M., & Smith, C. S. (2003, March 31). Fleeing civilians caught in the middle. *New York Times*, pp. A1, B3.

Shadid, A. (2003, March 31). A boy who was 'like a flower.' *Washington Post*, pp. A1, A18.

Shadid, A. (2003, April 3). Iraqis plan for a climactic defense of the capital. *Washington Post*, pp. A1, A28.

Shadid, A. (2003, April 6). Overnight, city turns war zone. *Washington Post*, pp. A1, A24.

Shadid, A., & Chandrasekaran, R. (2003, April 8). Fierce resistance seen in some street battles. *Washington Post*, pp. A1, A16.

Shadid, A. (2003a, April 10). Hussein's Baghdad falls. *Washington Post*, pp. A1, A33.

Shadid, A. (2003b, April 10). Iraqis now feel free to disagree. *Washington Post*, pp. A1, A32.

Sniderman, P.M., Brody, R.A., & Tetlock, P.E. (1991). *Reasoning and choice: Explorations in political psychology* (Cambridge, England: Cambridge University Press).

Tyler, P. E. (2003, March 21). 16 die on copter; U.S. and British forces suffer first losses in crash in Kuwait. *New York Times*, pp. A1, B8.

Tyler, P. E. (2003, March 23). Capital hit again. *New York Times*, pp. A1, B6.

Tyler, P. E. (2003, March 30). A shift in tactics. *New York Times*, pp. A1, B3

Tyler, P. E. (2003, April 4). Allies at airport. *New York Times*, pp. A1, B4.

Tyler, P. E. (2003, April 7). G.I.'s block roads. *New York Times*, pp. A1, B4.

U.S. Department of Defense (2003). Public affairs guidance (PAG) on embedding media. Retrieved May 7, 2003 from http://www.dod.mil/news/Feb2003/d20030228pag.pdf.

Wilson, M. (2003, March 28). A sudden Iraqi attack at sunset surprises a key Marine center south of the Euphrates. *New York Times*, p. B4.

CHAPTER 15

Allies Down Under? The *Australian* at War and the "Big Lie"

Martin Hirst and Robert Schütze

In the United States, Rupert Murdoch's Fox cable television network led the charge for patriotic journalism during the 2003 Gulf War.

Murdoch does not own a television station in Australia, but he does control two-thirds of the metropolitan daily newspaper market and over 75% of the lucrative Sunday market (ABC, 2000). With the two most popular papers—Melbourne's *Herald Sun* and Sydney's *Daily Telegraph*—and the only nationally circulating daily newspaper—the *Australian*—in his stable, Murdoch is without doubt the "Prince of Press" in Australia. Therefore, understanding how Murdoch's antipodean media empire tackled the war in Iraq is central to understanding how the conflict was framed for the Australian public.

This chapter takes a look at how his flagship masthead—the *Australian*—covered Iraq in the context of terrorism and the invasion hysteria surrounding asylum-seekers landing on Australian shores.

MURDOCH COMMITTED TO COALITION

From the start, the *Australian* was firmly committed to the coalition of the willing and the "war on terror," providing a well-orchestrated cheer squad for Prime Minister John Howard and the invasion of Iraq. This was obvious from the tone and content of both its editorials *(Australian*, 2002, October 12) and "straight news" pieces.

On one level this is not surprising given the global nature of Murdoch's $42 billion News Corporation empire and the likely economic benefits to big business from the Iraq war. Yet economic self-interest must be ruled out if we are to hold Murdoch to the public service rhetoric that marked the beginning of his rise to media power.

In 1961, shortly after acquiring his first Sydney newspaper, he said: "What rights have we to speak in the public interest when, too often, we are motivated by personal gain?" (Mayer, 1968, p. 51). Forty years later, the dichotomy between public and private interests somehow collapsed as Murdoch's *Australian* chief executive, Ken Cowley, told parliament:

> We take the view, as simple as it is and as corny as it sounds, that what is good for your country is good for your business and what is good for your business is good for your paper, its readers and our employees. (cited in Schultz, 1998, p. 102)

This argument underpins the "national interest" frame that the Murdoch press places over almost everything it does. Editorial writers have become particularly adept in framing economic liberalism, deregulation, privatization, tight budgets, and the user-pays principle as being not only good for the nation as a whole, but good for individual citizens.

So, perhaps there was more than just economic self-interest underpinning the *Australian*'s support for the Iraq war. Certainly the rhetoric employed by the paper invoked nationalist discourses that exploited the threat of global terrorism and historical fears of invasion to sell one of the most unpopular public policies in Australian history: the commitment of Australian troops to war.

Terrorism, Fear, and the Post-Cold War News Frame

Since September 11, 2001, the national interest frame has been subsumed by the new terrorism frame in the mainstream media.

In its moral simplicity, the terrorism frame is reminiscent of the old "Cold War news frame," which dramatized superpower rivalries and pitted East against West, capitalism against communism (Giffard, 2000, p. 389). Within the terror frame, bomb-wielding Islamic fundamentalists have replaced the "Reds under the bed" as the West's public enemy No. 1. While geography is not so clear—there is no Iron Curtain—the dichotomies are equally stark, as Christopher Kremmer (2002) noted:

> Media reporting on the war on terror is riddled with the simplistic notion that this is a battle between innately good, wise, Western, liberal, democratic paragons and dark-skinned, bearded, fanatical, evil-doers.

In this post-Cold War terrorism news frame, the battle lines are drawn between good and evil, us and them, with a jingoistic reassertion of nationalist pride. The *Australian*'s hawkish foreign editor embodied this perfectly in his response to the October 2002 Bali bombings:

> Just as we love Australia, the evil men who murdered our people and others in Bali, they surely hate Australia. And why do they hate us? They hate us not for our wickedness, which is occasional and undeniable. They hate us for our oddly persistent goodness. (Sheridan, 2002, October 17)

Murdoch's flagship newspaper might have taken the terror frame too far in early 2003 when it reported on a spate of bush fires in the eastern states under the banner, "Summer Terror." But otherwise, the selective articulation of facts and skewed perspectives that characterize writing within the terror news frame goes largely undetected. Yet the effect is palpable.

Passing off official versions of reality as common sense helps to sell "the big lie." In this case, "the big lie" is the notion that there is a war on terror that can be fought and won by invading Iraq.

"The Big Lie"

The notion that the war on terror can be fought and won by invading Iraq, a constant theme in the Murdoch press, has helped naturalize a piece of official spin and an otherwise problematic concept: that there is a tangible conflict which needs to be resolved (or at least approached) militarily.

The *Australian* began uncritically using this concept of waging war against an unspecified enemy soon after the terror attacks in the United States and has been feting Australia's need to fight in it ever since. Essentially it supported Prime Minister Howard's justification for sending troops into Afghanistan because everyone is susceptible to terrorism and what happens in the rest of the world affects "us." As the *Australian*'s own media columnist, Errol Simper (2002) notes: "The media has, more or less, tended to let the politicians run with the terrorism story."

But the Australian media, and the Murdoch press in particular, was pedaling fear long before the January 2003 "summer of terror." Ironically for a nation founded by European invasion just over two hundred years ago, invasion anxiety has been a strong and recurring theme in white Australian history. The notion of an amorphous external threat goes back to the influx of Chinese workers during the 19th century gold rushes, and later spawned the White Australia policy.

As Simon Philpott notes (2001, p. 376), fear of an imagined "Other," which for Australia has traditionally been Asia, helps galvanize political unity by locating threats to the national well-being beyond our borders. Fear of "being swamped by Asians" turned fish-and-chips shop owner Pauline Hanson into a runaway political success late in the 1990s and, more recently, the institutionalized fear of invasion has manifested as hysteria over refugees ("boat people," as they are referred to in the mainstream press) a level of public insecurity that Ghassan Hage calls "paranoid nationalism" (2003, p. 1).

BALI: AUSTRALIA'S SEPTEMBER 11?

Public terrorism fears were dramatically realized when two huge explosions ripped through Bali's tourist haven of Kuta in October 2002. The *Australian*'s first headline screamed, "TERROR HITS HOME," and the phrase stuck as the banner heading for all subsequent coverage.

Framing the bombings as an attack on Australia provided the key emotional link to September 11 and seemed to justify Australia's role in the "war on terror." As Errol Simper (2002) pointed out, amidst the grief and outrage that ran through the Bali coverage, there was an element of wish-fulfillment:

> To deny that segments of Australia appeared to crave at least a share of the adrenaline and global media attention that accompanied September 11 is to deny the nose on your face.

This was being played out, at least subconsciously, as Australia's September 11. As Labor's then leader Simon Crean told Parliament, "I think we get something of a better understanding as to what Americans must have felt on September 11" (Shanahan, 2002, October 18).

The link was also borne out in the rash conclusion from Day One that the Bali bombings were an attack on Australians, just as September 11 was an attack on Americans. As the *Australian's*foreign editor Greg Sheridan proclaimed on the first day of coverage, "There can be little doubt that Australians were specifically targeted." (Sheridan, 2002, October 14).

The conclusion is both hasty and vain. It highlights the perverse cultural imperialism that has transformed a part of Indonesia into an Australian territory. Perverse because Australia has persistently denied its geography and nurtured cultural links to Europe and North America rather than Asia. As the latest government White Paper on foreign affairs and trade states, "Australia is a Western country located in the Asia-Pacific region with close ties and affinities with North America and Europe" (Advancing the National Interest, 2003, p. 8). Asia, particularly Indonesia, has been the imagined "Other" in true Orientalist fashion. So to call this small part of Indonesia our "home away from home,"as Murdoch's national daily did in its first editorial after the bombing (*Australian*, 2002, October 14), is a paradox.

When the nationalist discourses in Murdoch's *Australian* are examined, the framing of Bali as an attack on Australia is hardly surprising. That many of the Australian victims were football players celebrating the end of the season was especially painful to a nation where "sport is the most universal of activities" (Fraser, 1971, p. 241). Old national character stereotypes of mateship, larrikinism, working-class perseverance, and sporting prowess pervaded the coverage, helping to frame the bombing as an attack on Australian values. Eulogies of the victims were perfect examples:

> He was a quintessential working-class boy. He loved his footy, his mates and betting on horses. But most of all, Adam Howard, a 27-year-old professional punter from Double Bay in Sydney, loved to party. (Bryden-Brown , 2002)

But from the barrage of emotive journalism sprang a more serious and sinister message in the *Australian*—that this was war and that a decisive campaign was called for. Greg Sheridan proclaimed, "The terrorist empire has struck back" (Sheridan, 2002, October 14), and said the "war on terror" had moved decisively into Stage Two.

A first-day editorial said Bali was a "wake-up call" to the civilized world that terrorism must be defeated. In language all but transcribed from a Bush or Howard speech, the Murdoch paper proclaimed, "Bali proves that all freedom-loving peoples are at risk from terrorism, at home and abroad" (*Australian*, 2002, October 14). This was a decisive moment for the saber-rattlers. Howard's central premise justifying action in Afghanistan and later Iraq was endorsed—namely, that terrorism affected everyone, so it was in the national interest to fight terrorism throughout the world, Iraq included.

The *Australian* roundly quashed the anti-war arguments that saw Bali as a payback for Australia's support for America in Afghanistan. But when Greens leader Bob Brown was pressed for his opinion on Iraq in light of the Bali bombing, his anti-war position was labeled "opportunistic" by political editor Dennis Shanahan (2002a, October 14) and sparked a wave of angry letters. The *Australian*'s bias was unmistakable the following day, when Shanahan (2002b, October 15) reserved judgment in reporting John Anderson's pro-war blather in light of the Bali attacks.

Instances of the newspaper's overt support for the "war on terror" and particularly for invading Iraq after the Bali episode are too numerous to list. Certainly, with the foreign editor (Sheridan, 2002, October 14) and editor-at-large (Kelly, 2002, October 19-20) talking up Australian involvement in Iraq, the pro-war lobby got a huge free kick.

But on a more insidious level, the *Australian* helped sell Howard's war by re-inventing him as a sensitive, trustworthy statesman in the aftermath of the Kuta attacks. In pictures, the usually wooden prime minister was shown hugging distraught mourners; in headlines he was given the heart to "weep" (Martin, 2002); and in stories he validated the nation's anger by saying, "We'll get the bastards" (Kelly, 2002, October 26-27). As Paul Kelly notes, "having divided the nation so bitterly for so much of his prime ministership, Howard is now a figure of unity. It is bizarre"(ibid).

Helped by the Murdoch press, Howard scored a major political boost after the Bali bombings—his approval rating soared seven points to 61% a week after the attacks (Shanahan, 2002, October 22). Even though intelligence reports and arguments for invading Iraq didn't add up, Howard's popularity and "track record" on security insulated him from an anti-war backlash. Even the vitriol of Bali victims and their families was muted when Howard explicitly linked his pro-war stance to the Bali bombings during a visit to New Zealand.

The anti-war *Canberra Times* led its March 11 edition with the backlash story, proclaiming, "Outrage at Bali linkage" (Peake, 2003). In stark contrast, Murdoch's paper picked up a wire story and tucked the embarrassing episode away on Page 5 (AAP, 2003). What this shows is that on both the op-ed and the news pages, the *Australian* manipulated the Bali bombings to plead the case for war in Iraq. Meanwhile, up to 75% of Australians opposed the war before the start of combat operations (Shanahan, 2003, August 5).

Allies Under Pressure

Despite its overt support for the war, there were plenty of divergent views in the *Australian*. This created the appearance of balance and objectivity, which underscores the values of a liberal-pluralist "fourth estate" defense of the media.

Just a week before combat began, the *Australian* was reporting the frantic attempts by President Bush and Prime Minister Blair to pull something out of the public relations disaster that was occurring in the UN. Blair was described as "bleeding politically" while the White House was claiming that any vote by the Security Council to support war would be a "moral victory," with or without a veto from China, Russia, or France.

A report from *USA Today* that the United States was threatening to withhold aid to recalcitrant Latin American nations unless they supported the war was buried in the last of sixteen paragraphs (Lusetich, 2003a). Prime Minister Howard's 20-minute phone conversation with George Bush was the second lead on March 13, 2003, saying Australian diplomats were "frantically lobbying" at the UN on the coalition's behalf (Shanahan, 2003, March 13). This story was reinforced by a UN "scorecard" on Page 8, outlining how former European colonies were being pressured for their crucial Security Council votes (Sutherland 2003a).

The *Australian* also reported the remarkable and dramatic resignation of Andrew Wilkie, a senior officer with spy agency the Office of National Assessments (ONA) a week before the fighting started. Wilkie cited his disagreements with ONA over their threat assessment of Iraq. He appeared all over the media for a couple of days and spoke at an anti-war rally in Canberra. Despite official attempts to discredit him, Wilkie stuck to his guns and denounced the government's decision to join the war:

> I have been following the flow of intelligence very closely and, as far as I am concerned, I have seen nothing that justifies a war against them (quoted in McIlveen, 2003a).

Yet despite the appearance of these divergent views on the news pages, the leader pages apparently "set the record straight" and put Murdoch's pro-war position in a loyal and succinct kind of way. The editorial, "French toast irrelevant UN" (*Australian*, 2003, March 13), makes it clear that the *Australian* regarded Chirac as a faded power living an "impossible dream" and whose arguments at the UN were "less weak than feeble." France, the editorial warned, could be accused of reducing "global politics to a competition between great powers in which a nationalist France cannot compete."

As usual, the *Australian*'s chorus of support for the Australian government was led by the very conservative and pro-Howard foreign editor Greg Sheridan. On March 13, 2003, Sheridan resolutely defended the morality of the war in the face of an "unreasonable veto" by one of the non-permanent Security Council members (Sheridan, 2003, March 13). Sheridan described the debate as "emotional and irrational," "hysterical," and then he restated all the well-rehearsed lines defending the morality of an attack on Iraq . Sheridan went on to cheer the psychological operations of the Americans, in particular "Shock and Awe," which he described as a "dislocation operation directed at the Iraqi leadership" (Sheridan, 2003, March 22-23).

To be fair, Sheridan's support for the war was tempered by two other opinion pieces on March 22. Washington-based commentator Harlan Ullman argued that U.S. unilateralism might have profound implications for the world geopolitical situation well into the future (Ullman, 2003). On the same page, Professor Paul Dibb (2003), a respected Australian commentator on defense issues, suggested that a likely outcome of the war was "a world divided and a return to the essentially tragic history of international affairs."

An Australian Interest?

Australian public opinion is sensitive to perceptions that its government might be accused of being a junior partner in America's imperial ambition. This has deep historic and cultural roots in Australia's colonial past and post-war reliance on America. There is still a memory of Australia's participation in Vietnam, summed up by the famous phrase of an otherwise forgettable Prime Minister, Harold Holt. During President Lyndon Johnson's Australian visit in 1966, Holt told the U.S. leader that Australia would go "all the way with LBJ."

Holt's political successor, John Howard, did not want to be seen in this unflattering light. It was therefore important that his government establish an independent rationale for supporting GWB's war against Iraq. Rather than merely being America's "loyal deputy," there needed to be some "national interest" in going to war.

The trump card was terrorism. Particularly in the aftermath of the Bali bombing, the successful argument was that terrorism could touch anyone, so threats to national security were global and required global solutions. This was reflected in the government's foreign policy white paper, released in early 2003:

> The terrorist attacks ... in the United States and ... Bali have been defining events. They have changed Australia's security environment in significant ways. They starkly demonstrated that threats to Australia's security can be global as well as regional. (Advancing the National Interest, 2003, p. 9)

The *Australian* firmly embraced this sentiment and linked the all-pervasive threat of terrorism after Bali to Saddam Hussein's fabled weapons of mass destruction:

> Gruesome as these terrorist outrages are, imagine what they would be like if they involved weapons of mass destruction. Iraq remains the most likely source of WMDs for al-Qaeda. (Sheridan, 2002, October 14)

National affairs editor Mike Steketee bolstered the *Australian*'s pro-war stance by trying to dismiss the "loyal deputy" label on the first weekend of war:

> Don't accept for one moment the propaganda that Australia is a lickspittle of the United States. Sometimes we get quite upset with the Americans. (Steketee, 2003)

The "propaganda" Steketee referred to here was the false argument that the anti-war movement was "anti-American" and believed that John Howard was merely following Washington's line. By highlighting Australia's mildly critical comments at the time of America's refusal to join international efforts to enforce an international ban on biological weapons in 2001, Steketee suggested that Australia was truly independent and by implication that support for the war against Iraq was good policy.

First Strike: Shock & Awe

In the first few days of the war there was plenty of patriotic footage and novelty stuff from the front of tanks.

The *Weekend Australian* (March 22) blared "PUNCH INTO IRAQ" over front-page stories about the military action (Eccleston, 2003) and published an opinion poll showing "support for war growing" (Shanahan, 2003, March 22-23). The key element of the *Australian*'s front page was the carefully staged photograph of an Iraqi soldier being given water while an assault rifle is aimed at his head and his hands are bound. This image was also on the front page of the *Sydney Morning Herald* the same day (Saturday March 22). While the Australian media's appetite for the "our troops in action" type of stories was satisfied by an easing of restrictions, the main game was still the coalition's confidence and apparent lack of resistance by Iraqi forces.

On the second day of coverage, the *Weekend Australian* reported American concerns that Iraqis would begin setting fire to oil wells, sparking "Fears of a new scorched earth" (Browne, 2003). It was another opportunity to quote from the briefing by Donald Rumsfeld, this time to the effect that by setting fire to oil wells

Saddam Hussein was "destroying the riches of the Iraqi people" (quoted in Browne, 2003). On the same page, Hussein is labeled a "master of propaganda" (Kerin, 2003, March 22-23), and a White House briefing paper, "Apparatus of Lies," is summarized without criticism.

This piece repeats the standard line from Washington: that Hussein is responsible for diverting food aid into "weapons programs and luxuries for himself" and lying to the Arab world. Throughout the military campaign, the *Australian* repeated these justifications almost daily.

It is worth noting here how commercial television in Australia approached the war. Immediately after the fighting actually got under way (as opposed to twelve years of bombing raids on soft Iraqi targets), broadcast network news presenters set a poor tone for the coverage that followed. On the first Saturday (March 22), some news anchors were smiling and almost cheering "our first strike" on Iraqi targets—a bombing mission by an Australian FA18 and some ship-to-shore fire at the Al-Faw peninsula.

The Nine Network, which is owned by Australia's second richest man, Kerry Packer, framed its coverage with a graphic rendering of the words "War on Iraq" that showed an uncanny resemblance to the title screen of George Lucas' science fiction classic, "Star Wars." Perhaps unwittingly, Greg Sheridan struck a similar chord when, after the Bali bombings, he wrote in the *Australian*: "The terrorist empire has struck back" (Sheridan, 2002, October 14). Episode Five in the Lucas epic is called "The Empire Strikes Back," a fitting allegory for the "war on terror."

Operation Mushroom: We Can Finally Tell You about It

On that first weekend, the Australian Broadcasting Corporation's (ABC) correspondent in Qatar, Peter Lloyd, unwittingly let the cat out of the bag about media control: the coalition forces were also conducting "Operation Mushroom" against the media.

In a frank exchange with Insiders host Barry Cassidy, Lloyd told of his frustration and that of the hundreds of reporters at the alliance military command center in Qatar (ABC 2003, March 23). They were not getting any information, the briefings were sporadic, and most of the stuff they were sending out in hourly "crosses" had actually been fed to them via fax, email, and Internet links from their home bases.

Early in the conflict, Australian reporters complained about the lack of information from their own national military sources. The *Australian*'s staffer in Qatar, Rory Callinan complained in print about being "cocooned from reality by the coalition's public relations machine" (*Australian*, 2003, March 22-23). Callinan said he was "locked into the multimillion-dollar press center ," he called "press conference central." Callinan said the press corps is unhappy: "We are a bit like mushrooms here, being drip-fed information."

The appearance of this brief piece signaled the emergence of a new genre of war stories: news and commentary on the media's broader role. Further attention was drawn to the media's role by Ashleigh Wilson's story about war coverage and comment on the Internet, "Conflict comes to a PC near you" (Wilson, 2003).

Complaints from Qatar and Canberra about the dearth of Australian information was not the harbinger of nascent anti-war sentiment among news reporters. It was really a plea for more color and background material to fill out the coverage and encourage a sense of Australian public ownership of the conflict. This was key to making the case for war in terms of the "national interest." Without a local angle, Iraq looked like someone else's war. Therefore, from very early on there was coverage of what Australian forces were doing, including frigates "in hunt for fleeing cronies" (Kerin, 2003, March 22-23).

To the media's relief, the Australian military PR operation allowed reporters to visit ships on search missions and mine clearing in the Gulf in the second week. And one ABC news crew was embedded with Marines as they entered Baghdad.

On the other side, Australian journalists operating behind Iraqi lines were confined to Baghdad and some were expelled. Ian McPhedran and other News Limited reporters were confined to a Baghdad hotel. McPhedran was also briefly accused of spying for the allies.

"Operation Mushroom" was not only going on close to the war-zone. On the home front too, the fog of war descended quickly on that first weekend. For many Australians watching the war unfold on television, it seemed like they were being carpet-bombed with expert opinion. Most commentators were pro-war, and very few anti-war or pro-peace voices were seen or heard.

PEACENIKS AND DEVIANTS: COVERING THE ANTI-WAR RALLIES

After the massive international rallies in February and March 2003, public sentiment in Australia was overwhelmingly against the war with up to 75% opposing it (Shanahan, 2003, August 5).

The anti-war marches were the biggest Australian mobilizations since Vietnam. Some estimate they were the largest political demonstrations ever in Australia—more people on the streets over a sustained period than during the anti-conscription mobilizations of World War I, and certainly bigger than the moratorium.

The marchers were a cross-section of ordinary Australians from every ethnic and religious background. There was a sense of purpose and strength in the crowds and sentiment way to the left of the official Labor opposition. In Brisbane, then Labor leader Simon Crean was booed when he addressed the crowd of about 80,000. His right-wing position of support for a "legitimate" UN-backed attack on Iraq was very unpopular.

High school students were mobilizing in impressive numbers in all major cities. Spontaneous walkouts, some supported by parents and the teachers' unions, saw several large student actions. Church groups, green, and peace groups worked with the various left groups and the unions to build the anti-war rallies.

As the war got closer the news media's attitude to the peace movement changed. The NSW police signaled a tough stand against student demonstrations and warned parents not to let their children get involved with anarchists and violent young men of a certain ethnic background (i.e., Arab-Australians). This policing action also sent a strong signal to the media that the gloves were off and the peace movement was no longer a "good" news story.

There is a formula for covering political demonstrations and if there is no strong violence—usually from the police—then it does not rate much of a mention. This approach was typified by a small piece in the Murdoch-owned *Courier-Mail* in Brisbane about an anti-war rally in Adelaide on March 14. The story, headlined "Eggs, tomatoes fly in Adelaide protest" (*Courier-Mail*, 2003), was only eight paragraphs and the "missiles" are mentioned in four of them:

1st par:	"demonstrators threw eggs and tomatoes at Howard's car";
2nd par:	"one protester was taken into custody after charging at a Commonwealth vehicle containing Mr. Howard";
3rd par:	"Earlier protesters pelted Mr. Howard's car with eggs and tomatoes";
4th par:	"One egg hit the rear window of the vehicle containing Mr. Howard";
5th par:	"Demonstrators chanting anti-war slogans and carrying placards were kept about fifteen meters from Mr. Howard by South Australian police";
6th par:	"despite the police barrier, protesters pelted three Commonwealth vehicles with eggs and tomatoes";
7th par:	"The protesters then left [the scene]";
8th par:	"When he left, one protester broke police ranks, charged at the vehicle containing Mr. Howard, and appeared to throw something. No charge was laid."

Apart from one mention of "anti-war slogans," this item did not say anything about the nature of the rally or the ideas behind it. Instead we got pointless repetition of two basic incidents: the "eggs and tomatoes" thrown at the car and one person running at "the vehicle containing Mr. Howard." This is a typical "news" report of the anti-war protests. The "deviant' nature of the smaller actions, such as confronting John Howard in Adelaide, is then applied to the movement as a whole.

This effect was also multiplied by the television coverage of the demonstrations. On the main television bulletins on the first Saturday of the war (March 22), the peace rallies held around the nation and globally got short shrift. At most, in a 90-minute bulletin the peace activists got a couple of short vox-pops. But they were bracketed with the violence of some protest actions in the Middle East. In Brisbane, the Channel 7 reporter sounded disappointed that there had been "scuffles, but no arrests" at that morning's rally and sit-in.

On the other commercial stations the same thing happened. The local peace rallies were always covered by long-distance camera, a few anonymous shots of the crowds, a couple of colorful banners perhaps and, on a slow news day, a grab from one of the speakers. The rallies overseas were most often covered with a reader voice-over that gave bare facts and where possible focused the shots on "disturbances."

Overall, the anti-war movement was reduced to inarticulate thuggery. Perhaps it is testament to the power of this and other elements of the pro-war coverage that by April, Australia's 75% opposition to the war had turned to 57% support (Shanahan, 2003, August 5).

Some Journalists Oppose the War

It would be unfair to characterize the Australian news media as solidly pro-war. Some, like *Canberra Times* editor-in-chief Jack Waterford, made their opposition clear, as did *Sydney Morning Herald* online political editor, Margo Kingston. Others took a similar stand and some held to a diminishing middle ground of critical distance and vague support for something to be done about Saddam Hussein.

Australian columnist Matt Price (2003) typified this latter position:

> Millions of Australians are despairing at this war. We want it to end quickly, even if this elevates Howard to short-term heroism and makes his slavish media cheer squad even more unbearable than usual.

Lies, propaganda, and deliberate misinformation should be expected in war. As British journalist and author Phillip Knightley (1989) says, the use of public information as a weapon of war is an honored tactic of presidents and generals. Only rarely do working journalists, particularly senior ones, acknowledge this openly; though many will say so quietly at dinner parties or in the bar after hours.

One rare editor in this category is Jack Waterford of the *Canberra Times.* He wrote a leader on April 5, 2003, detailing the countless lies we were told by "our own" side. He noted how Western journalists had been lied to about some events—the outcome of battles, the numbers of POWs, how civilian deaths had occurred at checkpoints. Waterford pointed out the deceptions in the Jessica Lynch incident, but pessimistically added that, in propaganda terms, when the truth finally emerged some time later, it didn't really matter:

> Surely the fact that the truth will usually emerge, often only in a day or so, might make some soldiers and politicians less willing to lie? Not necessarily, it would seem, if it serves some immediate purpose. (Waterford, 2003)

A direct propaganda hit on the news media won on the day in the Private Lynch affair and by the next day there was a new outrage, atrocity, or allied victory to take its place.

The Australian news media shared the pleasure of the allied victory in Iraq and carried most of the same packaged material seen everywhere—the toppling of the statue, the waving and smiling crowds, and the seeming celebration of Saddam's overthrow.

However, it was interesting to note how quickly this soured and how quickly we began to see cracks appearing in the coalition rhetoric.

Conclusions

It is not surprising Rupert Murdoch's *Australian* led the patriotic media brigades in Australia during the 2003 Gulf War. On the other side of the ledger, the *Sydney Morning Herald* and the *Canberra Times* both editorialized against Australian involvement in the anti-Saddam coalition. Cutting through what the popular press took to calling the "fog of war" was very difficult. As in the 1991 Gulf War, the American military controlled not only the air above Iraq but the airwaves as well.

The Doha briefing from the stage at press conference central produced more enhanced images of smart bombs, trucks exploding under bridges, and cruise missiles launched dramatically from the safety of the U.S. fleet. But television viewers saw much more intensive footage of the fighting and this impacted the language of the war, such as the Australian television news readers who excitedly reported that "our" fighters had had a "productive" day in the battlefield, or the one who smiled when announcing the RAAF had dropped its first bomb—like it was a birth or something to celebrate (ABC TV 2003, March 23).

The embedded media also showed us some horrible stuff: dead and wounded prisoners of war, bombed homes, a firestorm over Baghdad, and civilians dying in hospitals. British journalist John Simpson and his party were strafed by U.S. warplanes. His Iraqi translator was killed and viewers saw human blood dripping on the camera lens as it was carried by a wounded journalist.

We saw three civilians in Baghdad shot as their car tried to overtake an army truck in which an ABC crew was embedded. One of the few left-wing voices heard in the Murdoch press, Phillip Adams, described the barrage of gore as "pornographic violence" (Adams, 2003). Everything, it seems, was more bloody and extreme in the 2003 Gulf War.

In the new language of this war, extreme violence was commonplace. It shocked us momentarily, but then the relentless, more subtle language of war took over: "friendly fire," "smart bombs," "unfortunate" civilian deaths, the callous disregard for basic human rights and outright lies. It is easy to get angry about these obvious linguistic tricks of war; not so easy to decipher the more embedded language.

In the *Australian*, this amounted to a more purposeful, yet less obvious form of propaganda, known as "the big lie." It was the ideological appeal to nationalism, patriotism, and the myth of free markets and democracy. It is a lie because what it offered—so-called "Western liberal democracy" as the solution for Iraq and as the moral force behind the "war on terror"—was itself a deception.

The *Australian* and other Murdoch papers churned and spun this lie for all it was worth. They used it to link the Bali bombings with the invasion of Iraq by raising the specter of Armageddon: "Gruesome as these terrorist outrages are, imagine what they would be like if they involved weapons of mass destruction" (Sheridan, 2002, October 14). Then the spurious link between Iraq and terrorism is passed off as common sense:

> This week John Anderson told the Australian parliament what we all really know but try not to face, that there is a connection between terrorism and rogue nations with weapons of mass destruction. (Sheridan, 2002, October 14)

The alternative is never mentioned and so the lie appears to be the only possible version of the truth. This is an ideological swindle.

In the scramble to make sense out of complex and rapidly moving world events, journalists and editors fall back on simplistic generalizations and stereotypes. During the Iraq war, the "enemy" was demonized and opponents made deviant in terms of the "common sense" approach. This helped legitimize the use of force.

In the case of the military enemy—Iraq—Saddam Hussein's followers were constantly referred to as the Fedayeen. They were "thugs," they were vicious and criminal. This approach from the opinion writers and columnists justified the attacks and the killing, even though, according to these same apologists, any death in war is "regrettable."

At home, the effect was similar. Peace activists were derided as the "loony-left," the "peaceniks," or worse, manipulating communist cells operating clandestinely. Young working class students and teenagers from Sydney's southwest, angry about the war and clearly against it, were stereotyped as "hot heads," thugs, and "un-Australian." Their Arab-ness, not their Australian identity was what the pro-war press emphasized. In both cases—the Iraqi regime and Australian protesters—the media tended to fall back onto racist stereotypes, creating moral binaries.

This is exactly what the post-Cold War terrorism news frame is about—reducing complex geopolitical and cultural issues to simple questions of right and wrong, us and them. Within this frame, the 2003 Gulf War and the so-called "war on terror" are represented as battles between good and evil. George W. Bush talks about "freedom-loving people" and "evil men" and the Murdoch press regurgitates it in editorials as if this moral dichotomy was a natural category (*Australian*, 2002, October 14). This essentializes the "terrorist problem" in the same way that biological essentialism is used to justify sexism.

If the terrorists are defined as innately evil, then there is no need to look at how policies and practices in the Western world might contribute to the conflict, because innately "evil men" are beyond redemption. It's nature. Fighting the "war on terror" then becomes a matter of rounding up the evil men more than anything else.

In Australia, the agenda-setting Murdoch press employs this terror news frame and it sells newspapers. It sells because the frame is easy to understand. And it sells because it appeals to a sense of patriotic nationalism and an endemic insecurity based on the historical fear of invasion. In a multicultural country struggling to define its post-colonial identity, the moral certitude of the "war on terror" has obvious mainstream appeal, even if it somehow does not answer all the lingering questions.

During hostilities, support for war increased in the United States, United Kingdom, and Australia, which was to be expected in part because the news media popularized the war and dulled people's senses to the violence they portrayed. No doubt the Murdoch press played an important role in cohering what support there was for Australia's involvement in 2003 Gulf War.

REFERENCES

Adams, P. (2003, April 9). Pornographic violence and the games children play. *Australian*, p.11.

Advancing the National Interest: Australia's Foreign and Trade Policy White Paper. (2003). Canberra: Department of Foreign Affairs and Trade, Commonwealth of Australia.

AAP (2003, March 11) PM using victims, say Bali families. *Australian*, p. 5.

Audit Bureau of Circulation (2000). *Figures for Six Months Ending December 2000.* Sydney: Audit Bureau of Circulations Circulation History.

Australian. (2002, October 12-13). UN must take tough action against Iraq. *Weekend, p. 18.*

Australian. (2002, October 14). We must remain firm in the face of terror. Editorial, p. 14.

Australian. (2003, March 22-23). Journalists kept in dark. *Weekend*, p. 2.

Australian. (2003, March 13). French toast irrelevant UN. Editorial, p. 10.

Browne, A. (2003, March 22-23). Fears of a new scorched earth. *Weekend Australian*, p. 4.

Bryden-Brown, S., (2002, October 15). Sad palace goodbye to a working-class boy, *Australian*, p. 3.

Courier-Mail. (2003, March 15). Eggs, tomatoes fly in Adelaide protest. p. 4.

Dibb, P. (2003, March 22-23) Loud, and carrying a big stick. *Weekend Australian*, p. 11.

Eccleston, R. (2003, March 22-23), Allies race to key port. *Weekend Australian*, p. 1.

Fraser, B. (Ed.). (1971). *Australia: This land, these people.* Sydney: Reader's Digest.

Giffard, A. (2000). International agencies and global issues: The decline of the Cold War news frame, pp. 390-408. In A.K. Malek & P. Anandam (Eds.) *The global dynamics of news: Studies in international news coverage and news agendas.* Stamford: Ablex Publishing Corporation.

Hage, G. (2003). On Worrying: The Lost Art of the Well-Administered National Cuddle. *Borderlands* (online) 2 (1).
Kelly, P. (2002, October 19-20). The Islamic front is at our back door. *Weekend Australian*, p. 30.
Kelly, P. (2002, October 26-27). Hearts and minds, *Weekend Australian*, p. 19.
Kerin, J. (2002, October 14). PM calls review of security, *Australian*, p. 4.
Kerin, J. (2003a, March 22-23). Dark arts of a master of propaganda. *Weekend Australian*, p. 4.
Kerin, J. (2003b, March 22-23). Frigates in hunt for fleeing cronies. *Weekend Australian*, p. 4.
Knightley, P. (1989). *The first casualty: From the Crimea to Vietnam. The war correspondent as hero, propagandist, and myth maker.* London: Pan Books.
Kremmer, C. (2002). Reporting the "War on Terror." Internet. Australian Center for Independent Journalism. Retrieved October 21, 2002, from http://journalism.uts.edu.au/acij/forums/2002forum1.html..
Lusetich, R. (2003, March 13). Get off the fence, orders Bush. *Australian*, p. 1.
Martin, R. (2002, October 19-20). Howard weeps at "cruel view of humanity." *Weekend Australian*, p. 1.
Mayer, H. (1968). *The Press in Australia.* (2nd Ed.) Melbourne: Lansdowne Press.
McIlveen, L. (2003, March 13). Security analyst dismisses damage control bid. *Australian*, p. 6.
Peake, R. (2003, March 11). Outrage at Bali linkage. *Canberra Times,* p. 1.
Philpott, S. (2001). Fear of the Dark: Indonesia and the Australian national imagination. *Australian Journal of International Affairs 55* (3), 371-88.
Price, M. (2003, March 22-23).Bungler of Baghdad digs in for a long war. *Weekend Australian*, p. 40.
Schultz, J. (1998) *Reviving the fourth estate: Democracy, accountability and the media.* Melbourne: Cambridge University Press.
Shanahan, D. (2002, October 14). Deaths will not sway PM on Iraq stand. *Australian*, p. 4.
Shanahan, D. (2002, October 15). Anderson's warning of more dire scenario. *Australian*, p. 6.
Shanahan, D. (2002, October 18). Empathy brings us closer to U.S. *Australian*, p. 17.
Shanahan, D. (2002, October 22). PM soars in wake of terror. *Australian*, p. 1.
Shanahan, D. (2003, March 13). Howard called in to help White House. *Australian*, pp. 1, 6.
Shanahan, D. (2003, March 22-23). Support for war growing. *Weekend Australian*, pp. 1, 7.
Shanahan, D. (2003, August 5). Solomon's fillip for Coalition. *Australian*, p. 2.
Sheridan, G. (2002, October 14). A threat we ignore at our peril. Analysis. *Australian*, p. 11.
Sheridan, G. (2002, October 17). This nation we love must face the threat, and fight. *Australian*, p. 13.
Sheridan, G. (2003, March 13). UN power play cannot effect war's morality. *Australian*, p. 11.
Sheridan, G. (2003, March 22-23). Americans try to psych rational opponent. *Weekend Australian*, p. 11.
Simper, E. (2002, October 17). Tragedy calls for a responsible media. *Australian*, sec. Media, p.6.

Steketee, M. (2003, March 22-23) Buck the conventions. *Weekend Australian*, p. 40.
Sutherland, T. (2003, March 13). Council minnows resisting tug of war. *Australian*, p. 8.
Ullman, H. (2003, March 22-23). Pillars of security shaking. *Weekend Australian*, p. 11.
Waterford, J. (2003). Yes, they would lie to you. Canberra Times (online edition). April 5. Internet. Retrieved March 11, 2003, from http://canberra.yourguide.com.au/home.asp.
Wilson, A. (2003, March 22-23). Conflict comes to a PC near you. *Weekend Australian*, p. 4.

CHAPTER 16

U.S. and British Press Coverage of the Search for Iraq's Missing WMD

Kris Kodrich and Sweety Law

While the search for weapons of mass destruction in Iraq proved elusive for military and intelligence allies, newspaper readers hunting for accurate and unbiased news coverage in the U.S. and British press had a much easier task.

Media observers noted major differences between the British and the U.S. press as journalists covered the growing suspense involved in the WMD search. While world political intrigue was intense, media activity was gripping: was military intelligence about WMDs poor or, worse, faked? What political repercussions could befall Prime Minister Tony Blair or President George W. Bush (facing re-election in 2004)? Was the scathing British press working to bring down a prime minister? Was the lackadaisical U.S. press letting a popular president get away with an assortment of errors, misjudgments, perhaps even lies?

Washington Post media critic Howard Kurtz found the British press assault on Prime Minister Tony Blair to be relentless, with the press calling him a liar or worse. Kurtz said the U.S. media "pursue the weapons issue with tea-and-crumpets politeness compared with the screaming headlines inflicted on the prime minister along with his American counterpart" (Kurtz, 2003, June 16).

New York Times columnist Paul Krugman wrote that the British news media were not shy about implicating Blair and Bush in manipulating the evidence (Krugman, 2003). Syndicated media columnist Norman Solomon said the British media were "vehemently refusing to let Blair off the hook" and "were asking tough questions and demanding better answers. ... The willingness of the news media to challenge leaders is a vital sign of democracy. But overall, in the United States, the pulse is weak" (Solomon, 2003).

Commenting on the media coverage of the WMD search, Solomon found the mainstream British media to be much less narrow than in the United States, with nearly a dozen ideologically diverse national daily papers competing. "The people of Britain and the United States are living in parallel, yet substantively different, media universes" (Solomon, 2003).

This study attempts to determine just how different those universes are.

METHOD

Two influential British newspapers—*The Guardian* and *The Times* (of London)—are compared with two influential U.S. newspapers—*The Washington Post* and *The New York Times*.

The Guardian and *The Times* have good national and international reputations. They are considered two of the five quality British papers and are frequently quoted abroad (Stevenson, 1994). They differ substantially from the more numerous and well circulated British tabloids that sell sex and sizzle.

Similarly, *The New York Times* and *The Washington Post* enjoy national and international reputations. Nationally, *The Times* ranks third and *The Post* ranks fifth in circulation (Audit Bureau of Circulations, March 2003), preceded by *USA Today* and *The Wall Street Journal*.

The weekday circulations of the newspapers range from 381,000 for *The Guardian* to 714,000 for *The Post*. Like the British newspapers, U.S. newspapers in this study have also been in the business for more than a century.

This is primarily a qualitative study, with the authors examining news articles during a three-month period from March 19, 2003, to June 20, 2003—during the heat of the WMD search—for indications of bias and other differences. It focused exclusively on news or news analysis stories and excluded editorials or opinion columns.

The electronic database of Lexis-Nexis was used to find all news or news analysis articles related to the search for weapons of mass destruction in Iraq. Using a guided news search, the authors pulled all articles from the newspapers using "weapons of mass destruction" in the headline or lead paragraph, and similar terms such as "banned weapons" or "Iraqi arms." The authors excluded articles that did not mention Iraq.

FINDINGS: THE BRITISH PRESS

This analysis found that—despite T*he Guardian's* left leanings and *The Times'* right leanings—the two British newspapers studied both were dogged seekers of truth.

For many of the news stories, little bias or sensationalism could be detected, with headlines accurate and attributed, such as the March 25 *Guardian* headline, "U.S. accuses Saddam of chemical attack ploy," or the April 15 *Times* headline, "Saddam still hiding in Iraq, says Hoon." Even headlines that could have easily been sensationalized were restrained, such as "Missile cache could contain nerve gas, claims military," (*Guardian*, April 8, 2003) or "U.S. strikes at Saddam's hideout" headline (*Times*, April 8, 2003).

As the intensive search for WMD failed to turn up evidence, British newspapers began slamming the prime minister and the president. Every bit of evidence that did not add up, every piece of the puzzle that did not fit, became an opportunity for the press to question the rationale for going to war. The British press reminded readers time and again: the "coalition" invaded and defeated Iraq because of the regime's supposed weapons of mass destruction. When the weapons did not surface, the British press openly wondered why and repeatedly questioned Blair on the issue.

While the reputation of the British tabloids for sensationalism does not carry over to the respected Fleet Street newspapers, *The Guardian* and *The Times (*both broadsheets), both newspapers were skeptical of the U.S. and British claims and both bashed Blair routinely. While *The Guardian,* which opposed the war, led the way at first in the questioning of the administrations' policies and actions, *The Times,* which supported the war, quickly caught up and soon became even more aggressive as Blair was on the ropes. Perhaps some of this can be attributed to reversal of roles over the war. The more conservative *Times,* owned by media baron Rupert Murdoch, supported the war policies of the liberal Labor Party leader Blair, while the more liberal *Guardian* opposed Blair's war policies.

From March 19 to June 20, 2003, *The Guardian* published 134 news articles that mentioned the search for weapons of mass destruction in Iraq, while *The Times* and *Sunday Times* had 142 articles. Among these, fifty-one articles in *The Guardian* directly used the term, "weapons of mass destruction" in the first two paragraphs; sixty-five articles in *The Times* did.

A closer examination of how the two British newspapers covered the search for weapons of mass destruction reveals additional points of interest.

At the start of the war, *The Times* handled the existence of the weapons as more of a certainty, with one March 20 article saying that, "U.S. forces were ready to rush over the Iraqi border to seek and destroy any biological weapons that they find." That same day, *The Guardian* focused on UN weapons inspectors accusing U.S. officials of providing the mission with wrong and misleading information about Iraq's WMD program.

As the war continued, both *The Guardian* and *The Times* repeatedly printed stories that said WMDs had been found, only to have to report later that the evidence was not there. On March 24, for example, both *The Times* (p. 2) and *The Guardian* (p. 1) printed stories on troops discovering a suspected chemical weapons factory.

But also on March 24, *The Guardian* became the first of the two to emphasize the fact that WMDs had yet to be found. "There has been no sign of chemical or biological weapons," said one article. *The Guardian* the next day started using harsher language in describing the search. One story lead with, "Hopes of a much-needed propaganda coup for the United States seemed to be fading yesterday after reports of the discovery of an Iraqi chemical weapons plant appeared to be false." *The Times* first drew attention to possibly faulty British and U.S. intelligence on March 28 in a story headlined, "Washington hawks under fire for ignoring advice." The article said about shared U.S.-British intelligence on troop movements and WMD: "There are now doubts about the veracity of at least some of this information."

The Guardian on March 28 turned to Hans Blix, the UN weapons inspector, to cast doubt on the existence of WMDs. Blix felt he could do little to disprove British and American insistence that the weapons existed. *The Times* called more attention to the missing WMD on March 30, with the story "Hunt for banned weapons," which reported that American scientists were scouring the countryside. "Despite several potentially incriminating discoveries, a massive U.S. intelligence effort to prove Saddam Hussein has been lying about his weapons of mass destruction has failed to generate the early breakthrough hoped for by London and Washington."

The Guardian likewise emphasized the issue more. "Search for smoking gun draws a blank," *The Guardian* said on March 31, suggesting that Special Forces' failure to find WMDs undermined the coalition's main justification for war. It said "the failure to uncover weapons at sites identified by intelligence will be a severe blow to Tony Blair and George Bush, who attacked Iraq on the basis that Saddam Hussein has the weapons."

In early April, *The Guardian* took a stronger stand on the weapons in its news stories—an April 4 article questioned the existence of WMD. On April 5, a front page *Times'* story asked where Saddam was, but mentioned nothing about the weapons. Also on April 5, *The Times* had an inside story, "Frustration at lack of 'smoking gun,'" that signaled more doubt: "The first signs of exasperation among senior coalition officers began to show yesterday at the growing number of false alarms over "finds" of weapons of mass destruction in Iraq."

Another *Times'* inside story that same day describes the search as "desperate." On April 13, a front-page *Times* story reported that the arrest of Saddam's chief scientific adviser could play a key role in unlocking the secrets of Saddam's secret military programs.

The newspapers increasingly made it clear that the latest findings were not to be trusted. "The Pentagon claimed yesterday to have found a mobile biological weapons laboratory in Iraq," read the lead of a May 8 *Guardian* story. The *Guardian*'s headlines regarding the search for WMDs turned increasingly pessimistic over the three-month period. A *Guardian* headline on March 31, for example, indicated that the WMD search "draws a blank." On April 12, a front page story was headlined, "Weapons teams scour Iraq; Secret units in desperate hunt for banned arsenal."

The two newspapers were careful in their reporting of each latest finding. On April 15, a *Times*' headline said, "Troops find 'suspicious labs' buried near factory," while *The Guardian*'s said, "Buried vans could be chemical weapons labs, say U.S. troops." In a *Guardian* story on March 25 about a suspected Iraqi chemical plant, the headline read, "Report of arms factory may be bogus." In an April 17 *Guardian* story, the headline read, "Raid on laboratory of 'Dr. Germ' fails to turn up the smoking gun."

The most substantial differences in coverage came as pressure was mounting on Blair and Bush to produce evidence of WMDs, following several reports that questioned whether intelligence information was manipulated to make the case for war. The newspapers' tone and rhetoric began to heat up in mid-April as Parliament grew increasingly nonplused over the failure to uncover WMDs. "Prove Iraqi guilt, MPs tell Blair," read a front-page headline in *The Guardian* on April 19 over a story about members of Blair's own Labor Party demanding an inquiry to establish whether British intelligence misled ministers about Iraq's weapons programs.

Two days later, a *Guardian* news article reported that Conservatives said Blair had a moral obligation to investigate whether the intelligence services had misled the government. The next day, April 23, *The Guardian* reported Blix's condemnation of British and American intelligence to show that Iraq had WMDs. *The Times* published news stories about questionable intelligence on April 25, including one headlined, "Reports of weapons 'greatly exaggerated.'" Another *Times* story, however, reported on a Bush speculation that Iraq might have either destroyed or moved its WMDs.

On April 26, *The Guardian* published an 8,534-word special report on the government's road to war. The next day, *The Times* ran a story about troops searching for weapons that made it obvious the weapons were not being found. "Five weeks after the first bombs were dropped, not a single conclusive trace has been found of the 100-500 tons of toxic agents that U.S. Secretary of State Colin Powell described in February as a 'conservative estimate' of Iraq's chemical stockpile."

The newspapers put Blair on the defensive. "'Don't crow yet over elusive weapons,' says Blair," read an April 29 headline in *The Times*. The next day, in a front page story, *The Times* said Russian President Putin "mocked the coalition's failure to find any biological or nuclear weapons." *The Guardian*, in a story the same day, said Putin was "almost mocking Blair" in its story about the same event.

The headline on *The Times* article was, "Putin taunts Blair: Is Saddam sitting in a bunker ready to blow the whole place up with WMDs?" while *The Guardian* said, "Message from Moscow: We are not with you and we don't believe you." On May 1, *The Times* followed up with a story headlined, "Putin will soon eat his words, says Blair."

In late May, after accusations of falsified evidence and uncorroborated information, the newspapers began publishing several stories a day on the unraveling scandal. *The Times* headlines on May 30 included, "Britain and U.S. urged to show arms evidence" on page 1, "MPs react with fury at 'flimsy case' for invasion," and "No. 10 (prime minister's office) 'pressured' spies on damning evidence for war," while *The Guardian*'s headlines included, "Ministers 'distorted' UN weapons report" on page 1, and "MI6 (intelligence) led protest against war dossier."

Other strong headlines continued to flow, including the June 1 *Times* front-page headline, "No. 10 (prime minister's office) 'doctored' Iraq dossier," June 2's "Blair stands firm on weapons claim," and June 3's "Put up or shut up, Blair tells war critics" and "Criticism, contradiction, confusion and concern."

The Guardian, while not as strong as *The Times* in its attacks on Blair, had its share of strong headlines as well, but also focused on the Labor Party and the United States. A June 3 headline was "U.S. Senate inquiry into how case for war was made," while June 4 headlines included "Rogue spies out to get us Labor" on page 1, and "Labor gripped by paranoia as whips condemn hateful attacks." On June 7 *The Guardian* reported Blix's comments to the BBC that he was disappointed with the quality of the intelligence given to him by the United States and U.K.

Both newspapers focused more attention on the U.S. role in June. On June 9 *The Times* reported on members of the Bush administration accusing critics of distorting the truth. The next day, *The Times* reported on Bush trying to assuage the growing doubts about the credibility of American intelligence and his insistence that the weapons program would be unveiled. But *The Guardian* continued to pressure the Bush administration. A June 10 story said: "The debunking of the Bush administration's pre-war certainties on Iraq gathered pace yesterday when it emerged that the CIA knew for months that a connection between Saddam Hussein and al-Qaeda was highly unlikely."

The Times, on June 13, reported on Hillary Clinton's call for independent inquiries in Britain and the United States into the prewar intelligence on Iraq's WMDs. On June 14 *The Times* reported on Colin Powell's defense of the Bush administration by saying the pre-war evidence of such weapons was not a "figment of somebody's imagination." The next day *The Guardian* reported on specialist search teams sitting around in bombed-out palaces watching films because they have run out of places to look for WMD.

At one point, *The Guardian* seemed to have been too eager in trying to expose a weak intelligence case for going to war. In its June 5 edition it corrected a May 31 front-page lead story that claimed British Foreign Secretary Jack Straw and Secretary Powell had met in the New York Waldorf Hotel February 5 and expressed serious doubts about the reliability of intelligence on Iraq's weapons program. The correction, on page 25, stated that no such meeting took place. "*The Guardian* accepts that and apologizes for suggesting it did."

The next day, June 6, another correction ran on page 25 correcting a report that was posted on *The Guardian*'s Web site saying that U.S. Deputy Defense Secretary Paul Wolfowitz had said oil was the main reason for going to war in Iraq. "He did not say that," the correction stated, adding that the report had appeared only on the Web site and had been removed.

The following day Readers' Editor Ian Mayes wrote a column explaining the Web site mistake and calling attention to the correction. "That has not satisfied all the paper's critics. There is no total satisfaction in these situations. The story should not have run. In view of the significance of the statements attributed to Mr. Wolfowitz, rigorous checking should have taken place." The column then mentioned the earlier correction regarding Straw and Powell. "It has not been the best of weeks."

Stories about public opinion focused on the support for the war at first. On April 1, a *Times* article, "Voters believe war is being won," said support for the war was strong, with only a slight mention of the WMDs. *The Guardian*, meanwhile, was saying many people were conflicted over the war. Its story, "Divided views on coalition campaign from a town plagued by racial tension," talked with residents of a mill town and found both support and opposition to the war.

On June 1, in a story headlined, "Two-thirds say Blair misled public over Iraqi weapons," *The Times* reported on a new poll that reflected the growing political pressure on the prime minister. On June 14, *The Times* reported on a new opinion poll that showed he had lost the trust of one-third of British people as a result of his handling of the Iraq war. The poll indicated the controversy over the weapons of mass destruction had damaged Blair, but not sufficiently to cost him his job in 2004.

FINDINGS: THE U.S. PRESS

This analysis found that both U.S. newspapers studied adhered to high standards of journalistic practice on the WMD topic.

The New York Times was consistent for more than two months in its factual reporting from the front lines on the search attempts. *The Washington Post* also posted descriptive-narrative stories of the battles and the weapons search, but it also initiated a number of investigative stories on the weapons search.

All stories from the battle zone were highly descriptive and evocative, transporting the reader to the scene of engagement and action. Additionally, both newspapers included a homeland dimension by presenting stories on domestic crisis contingency plans and processes in the likelihood that the unconventional weapons were used domestically. These stories tangentially kept afloat the specter of the potential of weapons of mass destruction.

But *The Post* departed from plain reporting early on and started to ask more critical questions in its coverage of the topic of weapons of mass destruction and the rationale for war in Iraq. The number of investigative stories were almost as many as the regular reports.

Based on the articles reviewed for this study, it emerges that at *The Post*, there were constantly a number of reporters on the war-cum-weapons search assignment, and on different perspectives for the investigative stories. Several stories were collaborative work, suggesting perhaps one way the stories widened their scope and depth of reporting. Importantly, the reporters looked beyond official pronouncements and surface facts; they explored taken-for-granted assumptions on a number of aspects on the topic of weapons of mass destruction as rationale for going to war.

Within the time frame of this study, a total of 187 articles was selected by the authors that dealt with the WMD topic and the 2003 Iraq War. From March 19 to June 20, 2003, *The New York Times* published ninety-seven articles and *The Post* published ninety articles focusing on or referring to the weapons search. Among these, twenty-eight articles in *The Washington Post* directly mentioned "weapons of mass destruction" in the first two paragraphs, while only nine *New York Times* articles did.

The use of the term "weapons of mass destruction" in headlines of both *The New York Times* and *The Post* was quite restrained compared to many leading dailies in the United Kingdom and elsewhere. Either it was plain "weapons" or "banned weapons" or "illicit arms" or some other toned-down version. Neither in the days immediately preceding the war when conflict appeared inevitable, nor in the opening days of the war was the term itself (or WMD as it came to be popularly called) used to grab the headlines.

Both newspapers also appeared initially to speak with some certainty on the subject of the weapons, *The New York Times* more so than *The Post*. On March 19, the day before start of military operations, *The New York Times* carried a front-page story on the mission to eliminate weapons of mass destruction headlined, "Threats and responses: Disarming Saddam Hussein; team of experts to hunt Iraq arms."

In the 1,351-word article, its top reporter on bio-terrorism, Judith Miller, begins, "The Bush administration has deployed mobile labs and new specialized teams of intelligence officials and disarmament experts to Kuwait to help the military search for weapons of mass destruction, according to senior administration officials."

Similarly, on March 20, *The Washington Post* carried a 1,764-word front-page story by staff writer Barton Gellman on a top-secret Iraqi arms information-gathering initiative that yielded new valuable information. The overview of the U.S. plans of action for the weapons search—the agencies appointed and individuals involved—was as informative and detailed as later accounts on the progress of the war. It appeared that the reports were written on the assumption that the newspapers' readers wanted to know and learn about covert operations and military strategies and tactics as much of the information detailed used language such as that used by the military.

Additionally, both newspapers frequently reported press briefings and news conferences, from the administration and from the front-line, on the progress of the war and the weapons search, with *The Times* providing more verbatim excerpts frequently, such as quoting Defense Secretary Donald Rumsfeld on March 22: "Our goal is to defend the American people and to eliminate Iraq's weapons of mass destruction, and to liberate the Iraqi people." The article, "A nation at war: The White House says war is 'on track'; and " show of support" on March 29 gives another progress report.

On April 1, the article "A nation at war: For the record from the Pentagon 'Good progress so far; worse may lie ahead" is prefaced by "Following are excerpts from a news conference at the Pentagon yesterday by Victoria Clarke, Pentagon spokeswoman, and Major General Stanley McChrystal, vice director of operations of the Joint Chiefs of Staff.

After commencement of the military campaign, *The New York Times* mostly carried major stories reporting military maneuvers, achievements, and challenges, collectively titled "A Nation at War." The certainty about the existence of the weapons is reflected in nearly all its stories. A headline on March 21 reads, "Iraqi defenses: biological and chemical weapons would be likely to slow but not stop the invaders." Two days later, on March 23, another story was headlined, "Weapons allies say they took Iraqi posts to prevent use of chemical and biological arms."

The next day, March 24, *The New York Times* Miller stated in the lead, "Nothing distinguishes the complex of trailers parked at the edge of the desert. But the vehicles are at the core of the Bush administration's effort to disarm Saddam Hussein of biological, chemical and other weapons of mass destruction."

However, not until April 5 did *The New York Times* specifically report on the search for WMD by focusing attention on the enormous challenges involved in searching some estimated 1,400 sites suspected of housing weapons of mass destruction. The 1,146-word story by Miller with Douglas Jehl, "Illicit arms: U.S. forces have searched few Iraqi sites" mostly quoted Victoria Clarke, Pentagon spokeswoman, and defense and administration officials who chose to remain anonymous, to overview the huge task of searching "several hundred sites on a high-priority American list of those suspected of housing weapons of mass destruction."

On April 8 William Broad's story, "Chemical weapons on-site identification inexact" described the less-than-ideal conditions in the field that challenged the unconventional weapons search. Miller's April 12 story on the 75th Exploitation Task Force described how a plucky crew makes do in the field in the weapons search. Very likely reporters with *The New York Times* were hopefully convinced or sympathetically sanguine.

Or as Howard Kurtz, observed:

> A dustup between two *The New York Times* reporters over a story on an Iraqi exile leader raises some intriguing questions about the paper's coverage of the search for dangerous weapons thought to be hidden by Saddam Hussein. (Kurtz, 2003b)

On April 18, almost a month after the war started, *The New York Times* carried a story headlined, "Outlawed weapons; some skeptics say arms hunt is fruitless" by William J. Broad. Two days earlier, Broad's 1,144-word story—"Arms hunt; U.S. civilian experts say bureaucracy and infighting jeopardizing search for weapons"—described yet another perspective on the challenges surrounding the arms search. Perhaps the turning point came with the repeatedly futile searches at different manufacturing and storage plants. Other defining points might have been the April 13 surrender of Saddam Hussein's top science adviser who asserted that Iraq had no chemical or biological weapons, and—more likely—the end of major combat operations about the middle of April.

Still, *The New York Times* continued to carry primarily descriptive-narrative stories on the arms search until May 29, although around the third week of April, its reporting adopted an additional angle: the shift in focus from weapons to the people behind them. Additionally, it continued to recount the administration's reported difficulties in the search and its decisions to add specialists and expand the search teams. Unlike *The Post,* that raised early on in late March the questionable assumptions of the Iraq weapons hunt, *The New York Times* Foreign Desk's Sarah Lyrall filed a 659-word story May 31 in a series titled "After the war," that was headlined, "Intelligence—Blair denies Britain distorted reports on Iraqi weapons."

Then, on June 4, it carried a 1,236-word story by James Risen on the arms search: "Intelligence: Iraq arms report now the subject of a CIA review." Dana Priest and Walter Pincus had already reported this development earlier on May 23 in *The Post:* "CIA to review Iraq intelligence; Questions of accuracy, bias spur studies."

For nearly two and a half months—until the end of May—*The Times* seemed uncertain in its leads, editorials, and reporting assignments in its coverage of the WMD issue, the primary reasons for going to war. In contrast, *The Post* also recognized the difficult conditions and confounding realities of the war, but it seemed to have started out with healthy skepticism about the WMD issue.

Of the two newspapers, *The Post* was first to carry stories doubting the availability of WMD. Among their firsts was an 1,069-word article by Pincus on March 20—the day the war started—headlined, "Chemicals use considered less likely; Experts say Iraq does not have means to deliver them against invaders." Two days later, a 1,190-word story by Dana Priest and Karen DeYoung reported the CIA doubted the authenticity of documents claiming Iraq purchased uranium from Nigeria.

The next day—March 23—*The Post* headlined a 774-word story by Mike Allen and Dana Milbank, "Question of the day dogs administration: Where are

Iraq's weapons of mass destruction?" Four days later it ran a story by Joby Warrick, "Banned weapons remain unseen."

On March 30, *The Post* published Barton Gellman's 2,149-word story, "Special search operations yield no banned weapons." Four days, later in early June, another Gellman story was headlined, "Banned Iraqi weapons may be hard to find; Suspicious sites provide no proof yet." The story's narrative reported quite matter-of-factly on its extensive interviews with experts in and out of government, including experienced investigators and a former UN inspector from Britain.

After the start of war, *The New York Times* and *The Washington Post* ran several descriptive-narrative stories reporting military maneuvers, successes, and challenges. However, *The Post* significantly differed from *The Times* in its overall WMD coverage and reporting. Nearly every week from the beginning of the war, *The Post* ran at least one WMD story.

In addition to the early stories mentioned previously, *The Post* published, on April 10, following the quick collapse of Baghdad, a 1,381-word story by Glenn Kessler and Dana Milbank headlined, "Administration now turns to finding prohibited weapons; Discovery may soothe war's skeptics." On April 15, *The Post* ran a 1,091-word story by Vernon Loeb and Jonathan Weisman, headlined, "Military goals shift; Security efforts, weapons search are now priorities." *The Post* had several reporters assigned to cover the WMD topic from many different angles.

Following the end of the active military campaign, between May 31 and June 18, *The Post* continued to run WMD stories as a rationale for going to war. It started with a May 31, front page, first section story by Mike Allen, headlined, "Bush: 'We found banned weapons;' President cites trailers in Iraq as proof." A June 1, first section, 1,165-word story by Milbank, titled, "Bush remarks confirm shift in justification for war," the story described the administration's shifting focus from Iraq's weapons to Iraq's weapons programs.

Additionally, starting around the end of May, *The Post* also included more stories on criticisms of the British prime minister, such as "Blair accused of exaggerating claims about Iraqi weapons" on May 30 and "Blair feels heat at home over Iraqi arms allegations" on June 5.

Under increasing public and international pressure and questioning, most stories on the weapons thereafter focused on administration officials' and policy advisers' interviews such as, "Officials defend Iraq intelligence; Rice, Powell insist threat not inflated" on June 9. The same was true of *The New York Times*. Still, *The Post* continued to print investigative pieces on the WMD issue, such as the 1,405-word story on June 5 by Pincus and Priest, headlined, "Some Iraqi Analysts Felt Pressure From Cheney Visits" and the June 13 Gellman story mentioned earlier on a covert mission to hunt the weapons.

On the opening day of the war, while Dan Balz and Mike Allen's front-page 1,833-word story reported President Bush's vow of "No outcome but victory" that summarized his explanatory-motivational address to the nation, they also presented both statements of support as well as disagreement from congressional leaders. For additional balance to their story, they also quoted UN Secretary General Kofi Annan, who feared war would create a humanitarian crisis in Iraq. This policy of wide-ranging information-gathering from experts across professional boundaries and the political spectrum, even from abroad, emerged clearly in the in-depth and extensive quality of *The Post*'s reporting and coverage of the WMD issue.

The Post, also early on in its reporting, attempted to present a different rationale for going to war in Iraq: "to drive Iraqi President Saddam Hussein from power and eliminate the threat from the regime's weapons of mass destruction"—by including public opinion polls and by participating jointly in a series of polls with ABC News.

On March 19, 2003, *The Post* ran a story on the first polling information it had received. According to *The Washington Post*-ABC News Poll, 71% of Americans supported President Bush and his policy. The story also reported survey results from the Pew Research Center for the People and the Press in the United States (about 1,000 adults) and in Europe (about 4,500 adults). Broadly negative European views of Bush and U.S. policies contrasted strongly with the growing support for the president and his war policy among the American public.

Two days later (March 21) *The Post* carried another poll story based on a survey conducted the night before, primarily to gauge public opinion on whether for the United States and its allies to succeed, Iraqi President Saddam Hussein should be killed, captured, or merely removed from power. In the same poll, 53% said the war would be justified even if troops failed to uncover weapons of mass destruction—Bush's major rationale for the war. But more than a third said the United States and its allies needed to find the banned weapons to validate the use of force against Iraq.

On March 25 *The Post* reported another poll conducted the previous night in conjunction with ABC News: "War support persists as casualties grow; Public expects 'significant' losses." In yet another poll and follow-up interviews with survey participants, reported on April 5, *The Post* found that more than two-thirds of those interviewed 69% said that going to war with Iraq was the right thing to do even if the United States fails to turn up biological or chemical weapons. Perhaps these results partly explain why in the 2004 election year the Bush administration seemed to act as though it did not matter to Americans whether such weapons were ever found.

But, what if, after a long and unsuccessful occupation, with American combat casualties taking a toll on the national psyche, the question, "Why are we in Iraq?" becomes a modern equivalent of "Why are we in Vietnam?" Then the issue of the rationale for the war will inevitably come back to the fore (Weisman, 2003). Very likely, it was the twin goals of seeking truth and maintaining credibility that framed the stories from *The Post* on the WMD topic.

COMPARING THE BRITISH AND U.S. NEWSPAPERS

This study found that the two U.S. and the two British newspapers examined were all aggressive in seeking the truth about Iraq's alleged weapons of mass destruction.

The New York Times, more than the other newspapers, focused for nearly two months on describing the actual WMD search and the challenging field conditions of the search. The certainty and assumption about the existence of the weapons was also reflected in the beginning in the other newspapers but within days, they soon adopted a more investigative approach.

While their stories on the news pages helped foment political pressure, the newspapers did not cross the line and editorialize in news stories. The coverage of military operations to find the WMD reported on both suspected weapons and later admissions that the weapons had not been found. Any inaccurate attribution or incorrect fact was promptly handled up front, especially by *The Guardian*.

On the whole, coverage in all four papers was well-researched and various points of view were represented. Both countries' newspapers reported on controversies as they arose, and allowed different viewpoints to be heard. *The Washington Post* in particular appeared more interested in feeling the pulse of the people as well. It conducted or reported polls to gauge public opinion at various points.

But the more substantial differences in coverage are revealed in the intensity displayed by the British press concerning the issue. Between the two British newspapers, *The Guardian* took the lead, starting March 24, 2003, in stories questioning the motive for the war. Not long after, on March 28, *The Times* of London also cast doubt about the WMD threat. Their continuing aggressive coverage of the issue undoubtedly played a major role in the rising public questioning and dissatisfaction with Tony Blair and his administration.

In the United States, *The Washington Post* seemed to be the sole voice among all leading national dailies to ask for pause to consider both the possibility and probability of the existence and use of the weapons of mass destruction, one of the stated reasons for going to war in the first place.

Is there any truth to the remarks at the start of this chapter that the British and Americans live in two different media universes?

While there's no doubt that significant differences among the two media systems exist, this study suggests that, at least in terms of news coverage, the four newspapers studied all had the same goal: cutting through the fog of war and trying as best they could to accurately inform their readers on an important issue.

REFERENCES

Greenslade, R. (2003, June 9). Media: National newspaper circulation. *The Guardian*, p. 5.

Krugman, P. (2003, June 3). Standard operating procedure. *The New York Times*, p. A31.

Kurtz, H.(2003, June 16). For Blair and Bush, no Fleet Street credibility. *The Washington Post*, p. C1.

Kurtz, H. (2003, May 26) Intra-Times battle over Iraqi weapons. *The Washington Post*, p.C1.

Solomon, N. (2003, June 12). Britain Not quite a parallel media universe, syndicated Media Beat column, Retrieved June 19, 2003, from http://www.fair.org/media-beat/030612.html.

Stevenson, R.L. (1994) Global Communication in the Twenty-First Century New York: Longman

Weisman, S. (2003, June 8). The World: The why's of war truth is the first casualty, Is credibility the second?" *The New York Times*, Section 4, p. 3.

PART IV

THE WAR IN OTHER PLACES

CHAPTER 17

The Hong Kong Media During the 2003 Iraq War

Yoichi Clark Shimatsu

The Hong Kong media took a giant step in reporting the Iraq war as compared with their coverage of the Afghanistan conflict and other recent international wars. The stationing of reporters in Iraq, Jordan, Turkey, Kuwait, and Qatar was a major achievement for a press serving a region of only seven million inhabitants. During the Afghanistan War, in contrast, only one Hong Kong television network, TVB, sent a reporting team to Pakistan, and the *Yazhou Zhoukan* news weekly was the only magazine to have correspondents in the region, including the author of this chapter.

The reach of Hong Kong's media, of course, extends far beyond the boundaries of this former British colony, influencing as it does the gradual commercialization of the news media in mainland China. Eyewitness coverage by Hong Kong reporters in the Middle East immediately before the war spurred mainland China media to dispatch reporting teams to the region. For the first time ever, Chinese viewers saw foreign news from their own reporters through live television feeds.

Beijing officials have considered the Hong Kong media a model for commercializing the state-run media in the mainland. Their toleration of dissent has been largely motivated by China's wider regional plans of using Hong Kong's integration as a showcase for its unification campaign aimed at Taiwan.

Under the "one country, two systems" arrangement since the 1997 Handover to Chinese sovereignty, the Hong Kong press has been widely viewed as independent and free-wheeling, compared with the state-run media in China. Hong Kong editorialists have frequently challenged perceived meddling in local affairs by Beijing authorities.

Editorial opinion among the larger presses in Hong Kong is often aligned with the British and American media on international issues of democracy, market economies, and human rights. The Hong Kong press has lambasted and lampooned China's less-than-democratic allies such as Robert Mugabe of Zimbabwe and Kim Jong-Il of North Korea, and tilted in favor of the United States and the NATO case against Bosnia.

The Iraq crisis was a rare instance of the Hong Kong media not criticizing or even questioning the mainland's diplomatic strategy on a divisive foreign policy issue. In this former Crown Colony, Tony Blair's appeals for democratization of Iraqi society through regime change found no support, even though many residents have been urging exactly such a regime change in Hong Kong. In many instances, the net effect was that the *South China Morning Post* gave more coverage to the local protests by church-led coalitions and the predominantly Muslim South Asian community in Hong Kong, as opposed to the *Wen Weipo*, which focused on the peace movement in the United States and Europe. The *Post's* coverage took a straightforward look at the difficulties faced by would-be human shields, such as getting visas and finding "bombing targets worth dying for" (March 1, 2003).

In response to the Vatican's antiwar policy, Hong Kong's influential Catholic community sponsored antiwar rallies rather than its usual anti-China protests.

A Rush to Middle Ground

Traditionally pro-Western media groups such as the *South China Morning Post* and Chinese-language *Apple Daily* supported the multilateralist stance of favoring UN leadership, while China's diplomats were pushing the same course in the Security Council. The pro-Western media took the road of appealing to reason, pleading to the Bush administration to compromise with the UN. Using stronger rhetoric, the "pro-China" press in Hong Kong made similar arguments while also criticizing the coalition for threatening global order.

Some columnists in Hong Kong made painstaking efforts to spare the U.S. embarrassment for launching an unpopular war. Frank Ching, a columnist for the *South China Morning Post* and *Far Eastern Economic Review*, gave a tortured explanation on March 20, 2003, for the invasion: "The Bush decision was in a sense forced by France, which thwarted American hopes to win the security council's endorsement for an invasion of Iraq."

Despite the difference in tone, there were no substantive differences in editorial opinion in terms of support for the UN and calls for U.S. restraint. The spectrum of editorial opinion in Hong Kong was polarized into two camps: "pro-China" and "anti-China" (or pro-Western). The presses usually identified as "pro-China,"due to their funding by Beijing-linked business groups, are the *Takung Pao*, a general news daily, and *Wen Weipo*, a business-oriented daily.

The "pro-Western" pole includes the *Apple Daily* group, which also publishes the popular *Next* magazine, and the *South China Morning Post,* Hong Kong's largest English-language daily. If the political polarity is taken a step further, the pro-China camp would include the *Ming Pao*, *Sing Tao*, *Oriental Sun* group, and *Yazhou Zhoukan* (a news weekly jointly owned by the *Ming Pao* group and tycoon Li Kashing's *Tom.com* group), while the pro-Western bloc would include the *Hong Kong Economic Journal*, *Hong Kong Economic Times* and *The Standard*, the English-language daily of the *Sing Tao* group. Among the television networks and stations, ATV is considered "pro-China," while TVB and the Hong Kong government-financed RTHK are "pro-Western." Murdoch's News Corporation operations have different editorial tendencies. The English-language Star TV was pro-Western in outlook and style, while its Mandarin-language Phoenix TV was seen as "pro-China."

One reason for this rush to less-than-controversial middle ground was the fear that the war rhetoric of George W. Bush and Saddam Hussein might have an adverse effect on Hong Kong's trade-oriented economy. In the run-up to the war, commentary on the business pages centered on the possible economic impact on trade and tourism. As the war drums grew louder, however, editors stepped up the coverage of Iraq to scoop their rivals and grab a larger share of readership.

Market competition, rather than geopolitics or domestic politics, was the major factor that influenced Hong Kong news organizations to dispatch reporters in record numbers to the Middle East. The battle for readership is best exemplified in the longtime rivalry between Hong Kong's tabloid-style presses: the *Oriental Sun* group, publisher of two dailies, and the *Apple Daily* group, owned by Jimmy Lai, famed for his inflammatory jibes against Beijing leaders. Although both groups claim the largest circulation, *Apple Daily* has the edge after its *Next* magazine gained the No.1 position in news weeklies after its rival *East*, owned by the Emperor group, closed down in the wake of an uproar over its publication of nude photos of a Hong Kong actress taken when she was kidnaped by a criminal gang a decade earlier.

Locked in a circulation war against rival *Oriental Sun* group, *Apple Daily* aimed to boost its leading position in Hong Kong by taking on freelancer Susanna Chiu-yung Cheung in Baghdad, as well as sending its own reporters to Kuwait, Washington, and New York.

Cheung, one of the earliest arrivals to Baghdad, filed a series of ten articles for *Apple Daily*, the city's largest-circulation daily, and wrote a regular column for the *Hong Kong Economic Journal*. Hong Kong's only veteran war correspondent depicted a besieged city groaning under sanctions and imminent war through the voices of hospitalized children and ordinary Iraqis, as well as officials and government spokesmen. Hong Kong-based Cheung has covered the conflicts in Cambodia, Kosovo, East Timor, and Palestine/Israel as a radio correspondent for the BBC World News Cantonese-language section and freelance writer for several newspapers and Chinese United Press (CUP) magazine. Following the Iraq war's outbreak, Cheung wrote a column nearly every weekday until the fall of Baghdad. Her articles had a critical angle, focusing for example on the human shields arriving in Baghdad. Even though the *Apple Daily* usually takes editorial positions in favor of Anglo-American policies, the value of first-hand reporting to readers outweighed any political reservations in the editorial staff.

Cheung was ahead of the press pack as usual, but not by far this time around. By early March, several major dailies and the three major television networks—Phoenix, Asia TV, and TVB—had reporting teams in Iraq and the surrounding countries, if only for short stints.

Beijing's Policy U-Turn

As the crisis deepened with Bush's hardening rhetoric, Beijing distanced itself from its previously friendly ties with Iraq. At one point in early March, the official media even characterized Saddam as a dictator (Xinhua News Agency, March 6, 2003).

Within Beijing's press corps, the reason given for the policy U-turn was that domestic economic growth overrode any foreign policy concerns. When pressed with the inadequacy of that explanation, veteran Chinese journalists in Beijing conceded that China's Foreign Ministry did not want to be cornered into international isolation, as happened in the Kosovo-Serbia crisis.

In discussions with the author, one Xinhua editor who has extensive international reporting experience explained that the highly bureaucratic system of government gives the Foreign Ministry, rather than agencies overseeing the press or propaganda, near-total authority to determine the extent of Chinese reporting activity in other countries. In the Balkans crisis, China moved away from the Deng-era policy of avoiding conflicts with the United States and tested instead a proactive policy of supporting opposition to U.S. expansionism.

The NATO invasion of Kosovo, the U.S. attack on the Chinese Embassy in Belgrade, and the fall of the Milosevic government were serious setbacks to China's newfound activism. The sudden stationing of U.S. and NATO forces in Central Asia and Afghanistan after 9/11 further discouraged Beijing from confronting the United States.

China's emerging "neutralist" position exerted a restrictive influence on the Hong Kong media's coverage of Iraq. In an effort not to rile Washington, Beijing took a low profile on Iraq, leaving France and Russia to take the lead in the Security Council debates. Despite some anti-imperialist rhetoric from party organs, the mainland media avoided calls for anti-U.S. action, even largely symbolic measures such as an arms embargo by non-coalition countries. Beneath the veil of ambiguity, Chinese diplomatic establishment was making a policy U-turn from support to Iraqi sovereignty toward angling for a share of the spoils (postwar reconstruction contracts) from the United States.

Immediately after the U.S. coalition's final warning to Saddam, China's Foreign Ministry on March 17 advised the six remaining Chinese reporters in

Baghdad, one of them from Hong Kong, to leave Iraq out of concern for their physical safety (Xinhua News Agency, March 17, 2003). The evacuated reporters included two from Xinhua News Agency, three from CCTV and one from a Hong Kong media group. Reporters with *People's Daily* and China Radio International had already left by then.

Media executives in Beijing explained that reporters, including CCTV's popular Baghdad correspondent Shui Junyi, were pulled because hundreds of viewers called the network to express their fears for his physical safety. Chinese audiences were obviously haunted by vivid memories of the deaths of three Chinese reporters during the U.S. bombing of the Chinese Embassy in Belgrade May 7, 1999. *The New York Times* suggested that two of the killed trio were intelligence operatives working under cover.

The Belgrade embassy incident illustrated the threat to Chinese journalists reporting from war zones, since they could easily be targeted for "accidental bombing" and accused posthumously. The attacks on the Sheraton and Palestine hotels in Baghdad have shown that such fears among Chinese television viewers are not entirely unfounded. Jens Holsoe of the *Politiken* daily in Copenhagen and this author for the *Yazhou Zhoukan* magazine, wrote an investigative piece in 1999-2000, indicating that the Belgrade embassy bombing was not an accident.

China's low-profile stance gave the early advantage to Phoenix TV, News Corporation's Chinese-language satellite network based in Hong Kong. In contrast to Murdoch's English-language Star TV satellite channels, which simply picked up the war coverage from its affiliated Fox News, Phoenix took a highly critical approach to the American-British war effort. The Star TV operation in Hong Kong did not have an opportunity to cover Iraq because news-gathering assignments were divided between different regional bureaus. As a Chinese-language broadcast aimed at the mainland market, Phoenix TV can take on international news.

Though a Murdoch News Corp. operation, Phoenix TV has operated more like a joint venture since its founding in 1996 by Liu Changle, a former People's Liberation Army officer. Mainland Chinese executives and producers therefore have a large degree of editorial control.

The order to evacuate Baghdad meant that Hong Kong and Chinese media were completely dependent on Western news teams that were not expelled or removed from Iraq, such as the BBC, or the Arabic networks Al-Jazeera and Dubai TV. The pullout, of course, went against the competitive spirit of Phoenix TV and violated the journalistic instincts of its reporters, who were withdrawn to Amman, Jordan.

In late March, Phoenix business reporter Rose Luwei Luqui and her cameraman, Hong Kong native and former Star TV staffer, Cai Xiaojiang, made the decision to drive to Baghdad without obtaining permission from their editors. Their coverage of the bombing and humanitarian crisis electrified audiences in Hong Kong and the mainland. On March 29, after five days of war reporting, the team was ordered back to Amman by Phoenix TV executives on grounds of personal safety. *The China Youth Daily*, based in Beijing, conducted a Chinese-language interview of Luqiu Luwai on March 30. An English translation of her interview was posted by china.org.cn on April 7.

Since the Handover in 1997, Hong Kong officials have been quick to point out that foreign policy is made in Beijing. Though no similar guidelines exist for the Hong Kong media, Phoenix TV obviously had to toe the line on the unspoken rule to avoid Baghdad since its ad revenues depend on its continuing access to mainland audiences. The Iraq War turned the world upside-down: the Hong Kong media were being silently censored by Beijing so as not to offend Washington and London.

Although the Chinese news analysts appearing on Phoenix TV were vociferously critical of the U.S.-led invasion, most of the footage shown in Hong Kong and China came from Fox News and CNN. This amounted to a type of propaganda, produced by putting antiwar "spin" on pro-war video clips, all for the lack of original tape and eyewitness accounts of the actual horrors of battle. As a consequence, many Hong Kong viewers complained that Phoenix was parroting China's official network, when in many instances Phoenix TV reporters and editors were actually demonstrating to the Chinese media how to take a more aggressive stance in war coverage.

Since words could not be matched by deeds, the debate over the war was reduced to one of tone and emphasis rather than of substance. *Apple Daily* reporters embedded with the U.S. military in Kuwait conveyed their sympathy with American troops, while the *Ming Pao* newspaper gave inordinate attention to the human shield movement, even publishing the daily diary of one activist. Hong Kong published pictures of POWs.

The Hong Kong media's eagerness to scoop the competition vs. the mainland press' hesitation to offend American sensibilities came to a head on March 23, when Al-Jazeera broadcast scenes of dead and injured American POWs. Phoenix TV ran the gory scenes; the official network, CCTV, did not. On the following morning, the Hong Kong media—from the sensationalist *Apple Daily* to even the pro-China *Wen Weipo*—plastered photos of the POWs on their pages.

In contrast, the mainland press ran only a few stills of less gruesome shots several days later and most of these were taken from CNN re-broadcasts rather than the original Al-Jazeera footage. Ironically, the Hong Kong media turned out to be more anti-imperialist than Beijing, even though the motive was commercial rather than political.

The Hong Kong media also encountered the more mundane problems of scarce resources and "parachute journalism." Long-established presses, such as the *Sing Tao*, *Ming Pao* and *Hong Kong Economic Journal*, lacked the financial wherewithal to send reporters to the Middle East. Not even *Apple Daily* could afford the cost of keeping a long-term rotating team in Iraq or Kuwait. The *Hong Kong Economic Journal* made the best of its limitations by running insightful background commentaries from Chinese academics in Europe and the United States.

Many reporters, disoriented by the lack of action on the ground, grasped at any opportunity to dramatize the situation. The simplification and sensationalism culminated in the ludicrous when TVB's Raymond Wong, reporting from Kuwait, donned a protective suit with gas mask and goggles to illustrate the U.S. Army's preparations for biological and chemicals weapons attack, which had already been reported four days earlier. The South Asian community in Hong Kong was especially incensed by the TVB reports that exaggerated the Iraqi threat to Kuwait, although only one complaint was actually phoned into the station.

Before the fall of Baghdad, the Iraq War dropped off the front pages and TV news flashes as a threat closer to home, the "mystery" illness later identified as SARS, grabbed the spotlight and attention.

CHAPTER 18

Nowhere to Hide: South African Media Seek Global Perspective on Iraq War

Christine Buchinger, Herman Wasserman and Arnold de Beer

When the 2003 Gulf War broke out in March, coverage of the conflict swept through the continent's most diverse news media. Debates of media coverage in conflict situations, stories about spinning by governmental sources, allegations of a propaganda media war, and questions about media independence and conflicting interests also raged in the South African media.

Issues such as accuracy, truth and deception, objectivity, and social responsibility that were debated around the world also became burning topics in South Africa. Far away—both in a political and geographical sense and with only a small group of journalists actually "on the news scene"—South African media had to rely predominantly on U.S.- or U.K.-based news agencies for news on the progress of the U.S./U.K. led invasion into Iraq (Du Preez, 2003; Rettich & Prinsloo, 2003).

From Day One, media coverage by American outlets received in South Africa showed difficulty in attaining and maintaining editorial independence. The orthodox notion of objectivity and fact-based reporting became even more problematic when the media public started to realize that governmental public relations material was published and broadcast as news fact. As Engel (2003, p. 16) stated: "Unanimously, it is accepted that the Bush White House helped by his popularity, the post-September 11 mood, and the weakness of the Democratic opposition, has taken media control-freakery to unprecedented levels." Or, as Solomon (2002) has put it: "The fulcrum of supposed media balance is far into the realm of fervent militarism. Most public broadcasting in the United States seems to be cravenly licking the boots of Uncle Sam."

As was the case in previous conflicts in which the Unites States was involved, the debates in the public sphere centered on the choice between national security vi-à-vis the public's "right to know" and whether the media should merely report the news or should be actively involved in creating it (Wolfsfeld, 2003, p. 223).

However, where does this leave coverage in other parts of the world? Does the dominance of Western foreign coverage through international media outlets mean that British and American views were taken over elsewhere? This essay will focus on coverage of the conflict in Iraq in different media outlets in South Africa.

This will be done by reviewing content analyses of coverage across different South African media outlets and comparing these to analyses of coverage in similar outlets in the United States, Germany, and the Czech Republic. Such a cross-section will provide a basis for comparison between two developed countries and two developing countries, while the focus will fall on the South African media. The research data sets were obtained from Media Tenor Institute for Media Analysis.

This international media comparison will be undertaken against the background of debates around the ethical implications of war coverage and the media's role in South African society.

The main question of this study is one that has been asked by many South African critics concerned with the role of the media in society: "[h]ow has the South African media fared in its coverage of the war? Have we, in the process of feeding off the Western media, become collaterally embedded ourselves?" (Center for Civil Society, 2003, p. 1).

Media's Role in Conflicts

Although "media polarization is an almost inevitable function of war" (Stroehlein, 2002, p. 4), the social responsibility in conflict reporting and the extent to which journalists should involve themselves in such situations has led to a number of recent and ongoing debates in South Africa and elsewhere.

Some see the role of the journalist as either a detached observer—one who has the power to analyze conflict situations and facilitate resolution. Others see the journalist's role as a participant in conflicts (see, for instance, Lynch & McGoldrick, 2000).

The role of the news media in conflicts has in fact produced so much discussion and such a variety of viewpoints that these discussions have themselves become topics for news reports (Wolfsfeld, 2003, p. 223). One of the concepts emerging from the Iraq war was that of "embedded journalists." Traveling, living, fearing, and fighting together with allied forces, some of the reporters during the

Iraq war had a limited perspective of the war's larger issues at stake, but had valuable inside perspectives to offer. Although South African reporters were not offered this opportunity, the merits of embeddedness became a point of contention among South African journalists.

The South African National Editors' Forum invited comments about this matter and created a discussion forum on their mailing lists on the question of training and embedding journalists. Aakash Bramdeo, e-tv journalist, pleaded for the need of "journalists to remain independent" (Sanef, 2003) and said the process of embedding severely jeopardizes journalistic integrity and independence. Others, such as Paddi Clay, journalistic training and development coordinator at Johnnic Publishing Ltd., see these issues to be more a problem of the individual journalist and a hurdle good journalists should overcome or "they perhaps should not go into a war situation" (Sanef, 2003).

This discussion of embedded reporters followed debates around the newly established South African Presidential Press Corps, which also raised questions in the same vein around journalistic independence because of the closer proximity to the president this corps would afford reporters (see Wasserman & Van Zyl, 2003).

The editorial freedom and governmental control of American and British reporters did have some significance for South African media in as far as it affected the material received by South African audiences via international news providers. It is clear that the Bush administration set up a very effective and functionally perfect public-relations machine, and "turned the media into a weapon of war, using the information it provides to harass and intimidate the Iraqi military leadership" (Trustcott, 2003, p. 1). An example of this is one of the Bush administration's media bans on "news coverage and photography of dead soldiers' homecomings on all military bases" (Milbank, 2003, p. 1).

Although Pentagon officials have denied that this re-enforcement of a policy dating back to November 2000 has had anything to do with shaping public opinion, it also "previously acknowledged the effect on public opinion of the grim tableau of caskets being carried from transport planes to hangars or hearses" (p. 1).

In another example of U.S. media control, Ian Glenn (2003) referred to a text message that appeared on Sky News while images were shown of "Union Jack-draped coffins" that "reminded viewers," "that none of the dead soldiers had actually been killed by the enemy."

THE 2003 IRAQ WAR: ANALYSIS OF COVERAGE

Did coverage of the 2003 Iraq War differ so substantially in different contexts that one can say, as Harman (2003, p. 1) does, that "American audiences are seeing and reading about a different war than the rest of the world"? Did differences in reporting correlate with differences between countries, be they political, economic, or geographical, or did reporting within countries differ so markedly that the causes should be sought in other factors?

According to research done by Media Tenor (2003), journalists (especially in the Czech Republic and Germany) "enriched the coverage with extensive insights into their own working conditions," with the result that, "with audiences sensitized to the situation, correspondents no longer had to be sensitive about the sources of their information" (p. 11). Apart from the media only reporting on the war, the role of the media itself became a news topic on TV news broadcasts more frequently in German, Czech, and South African media (in that order) than in American and British media (p. 4)

In general, it seems as though U.S. media outlets (as could perhaps be expected) were less balanced and less critical in their coverage than their European and South African counterparts. This has been attributed partly by the fact that Europe is closer to the Muslim world (Harman, 2003).

Not only was the progress of the war itself reported differently in different media, but reporting on opinions about the war and its legitimacy also differed—the latter seemingly under-reported in the United States media (Harman, 2003).

The content analysis (Media Tenor, 2003) of South African media reporting on the Iraq conflict suggests that not only did America watch a "different war than the rest of the world," but there were clearly two different views of the war presented within South Africa.

The South African broadcasting market is dominated by the public broadcaster's—the SABC's—four channels, but has two private channels: e-tv, a free-to-air, private broadcaster, and M-Net, a cable-subscription channel. e-tv positioned itself openly against the conflict as clearly critical of the United States with a peak of 28% negative reporting of the Iraq war (during the second week of the war); the SABC "remained clearly ambivalent in its evaluation of American military actions" throughout and had a peak of 7% negative reporting (during the second week of the war) (Media Tenor, 2003, p. 22).

This critical stance of the private broadcaster e-tv vis-à-vis the public broadcaster SABC is also evident from its greater focus on the United Nations (p. 43) and far greater interest in political background issues, with almost double the share of visuals devoted to the UN than the SABC (p. 45). This is, however, in far greater contrast to the overwhelmingly positive tone of newscasts in the USA (p. 20).

Such broad support for the war among American media has led media commentator Matt Zoller Seitz (2003, p. 1-2) to remark: "Correspondents and anchors of the ABC News, Fox News Channel and CNN (among others) have succumbed" to a "reflexive embrace of core emotions and received political wisdom" and "have flipped out to varying degrees, delivering coverage that advances the medium's logistical and technical reach while reinforcing persistent stereotypes of TV news as impatient, simplistic and slanted" (p. 2).

These reporters were further seemingly "mesmerized by 'smart missiles' and 'surgical bombing'" (Rostron, 2003, p. 23), despite already having heard and reported U.S. government announcements during the first Iraq war that, similarly, turned out to be incorrect.

The clear support for the U.S. government is also evident from the amount of coverage given to the allied protagonists (60% of the coverage on ABC, NBC and CBS alike) against the roughly 30% to 40% of coverage given to Iraqi antagonists.

Because of the impression that the American media has become "a dog that never bites, hardly barks but really loves rolling over and having its tummy tickled" (Engel, 2003, p. 16), the South African public broadcaster, the SABC, decided to supplement material received from CNN with material from ZDF, Al-Jazeera, and the BBC just before the start of the war (Schreiner, 2003, pp. 1-3). This was highly disputed, but Peter Matlare, the SABC's CEO, defended the decision by referring to the "sneaking feeling that all might not be well in the objectivity department" and identifying the need for "balance in the global media industry" (Engel, 2003, p. 6).

The SABC's decision to draw on a larger variety of news providers in its coverage of the Iraq conflict is supported by a statistical analysis of the coverage: the SABC used only 3% of Al-Jazeera and an insignificant percentage of footage from U.S. networks, instead opting to balance in-house correspondents' material with ZDF, BBC, and other network materials to gain a well-balanced, total coverage (Media Tenor, 2003, p. 9).

The Media Tenor study (p. 8) shows that both the South African broadcasters, the SABC and e-tv, relied on journalists reporting from Baghdad (12% and 2%, respectively) more than on embedded (and possibly biased) reports (4% and 1%, respectively). Both these broadcasters gave at least some air time to worldwide anti-war protests. SABC gave 4.4% and e-tv gave 7.8% of its total coverage. The analysis also found that in general, South African TV news stood out in international comparison in covering civilian and military casualties (SABC 14% and e-tv 12% of total coverage) (p. 31).

As Tawane Kupe, a South African columnist and academic, points out, however, there were "precious few local commentators and analysts and even less special debate programed" (Kupe, 2002, p. 38). Also, the analysis shows that, in SABC and e-tv Iraq war reporting, military actions were indeed the "focal point of the coverage" with 53% and 41% respectively, while the consequences of the war only took up 21% and 20% of the total reporting respectively (Media Tenor, 2003, p.18).

Although South Africa was not directly involved in the conflict, South African broadcasters displayed much more emotion in their coverage than their non-U.S. counterparts abroad: the SABC "got emotional" about the war in 2.9% of the total coverage, while e-tv did the same in 1.6% of theirs. On e-tv, much of this emotionality was displayed by journalists (9%), a peak value by comparison to Czech, German, British, and American media (0-1%, 0-6%, 4% and 0% respectively) (p. 30).

SABC and e-tv also tended to remain superficial in their coverage by portraying it as a private struggle between the two personas of Bush and Hussein: SABC devoted 1.5% of its total coverage to Bush and 4.5% to Hussein, while e-tv used Bush footage in 2.5% of its coverage and Hussein footage in 3%. This is relatively high when compared to American NBC, which used Bush and Hussein footage in 0.4% and 1.8% of its coverage and CBS, which used such footage 0.6% and 1.9% of the time, respectively (p. 23).

Such findings are not only surprising, but an indication of the shallowness to which conflict reporting has succumbed in South Africa broadcasters.

CONCLUSION

Often there was little sign of anything but sensationalist, "feeding-frenzy" reporting during the Iraq war in the U.S. media. "All in all, TV has delivered a confused (and confusing) morass of coverage—technically and logistically breathtaking, but undermined by what seems like an institution-wide case of tunnel vision" (Media Tenor, 2003, p. 3).

"The American broadcast media have failed to present a rounded view of this war" (Spira, 2003, p. 40), but the Arabic media has been accused of heavy bias as well: "Al-Jazeera is no less partisan than its American counterparts" (Spira, 2003, p. 40). The non-U.K., European media generally took a clear stance against U.S. and British military action. South Africa, on the other hand, seems to have positioned itself somewhere in-between. And, although the amount of emotional coverage aired by the SABC and e-tv is an indication of sensationalism and irresponsible conflict reporting, the bias is clearly less developed.

With a subject as complex as this, it is difficult to draw lines that determine the borders between objective, aloof, detached, subjective, partisan, propagandist, and fair and balanced reporting. The European press has often been (and still often is) accused of being partisan, while British and American media outlets were until recently seen as being fairly objective.

What is often neglected in this discussion, however, is to what extent media should still be considered partisan if the different political stances of each separate medium are known and publicly announced. Is it, then, still considered biased reporting? Or does freedom of expression also include "a news organization's right to decide what position it will take on an issue such as the war in Iraq and a broadcaster's right to choose the subject matter of a current affairs program or documentary. Each product carries the accent that the producer and director have chosen" (Matlare, 2003, p. 6).

REFERENCES

Center for Civil Society (2003, March). The Great Media War Debate. CCS Online [Organizational Homepage, selected articles online.]. Retrieved 5 November 2003 from the World Wide Web: http://lists.nu.ac.za/pipermail/ccs-l/2003/001429.html.

Du Preez, M. (2003, March). Maximum headroom media key to guide world view. *Cape Argus*.

Glenn, I. (2003). Media coverage of the Iraqi War. Transcript of speech delivered at the 25th anniversary of the Department of Journalism, University of Stellenbosch.

Engel, M. (2003, January 17-23). Bushwhacked. *International Mail & Guardian,* p.16.

Harman, D. (2003, March). World and America watching different wars. CNN vs. Al Jazeera: Seeing is often believing. *The Christian Science Monitor* [Institute Homepage, selected articles online.]. Retrieved April 11, 2003,from the World Wide Web: http://www.csmonitor.com/2003/0325/p01s04-woiq.html.

Kupe, T. (2003, May). Local TV's wide angle on war in Iraq. *The Media,* p. 38.

Lynch, J. & McGoldrick, A. (2000). Peace journalism How to do it. Retrieved September 9, 2003,from the World Wide Web: www.mediachannel.org/atissue/conflict

Matlare, P. (2003, June 1). What's needed is a wide choice of`freedoms . Media coverage of the Gulf war raised many questions about press responsibility. *The Sunday Independent,* p. 6.

Media Tenor (2003, May). The War in Iraq on television: A split reality. Media Tenor Report, Bonn, Germany: Media Tenor Institute.

Milbank, D. (2003). Curtains ordered for media coverage of returning coffins. The Washington Post Company. Retrieved November 5, 2003, from the World Wide Webhttp://pub12.ezboard.com/fpoliticalpalacefrm21.showMessage?topicID=94.topic.

Rettich, M. (2003). The war on TV: "Better" is not good enough. *Media Tenor Quarterly Journal,* 2, 39-43.

Rettich, M. and Prinsloo, S.. (2003). War is not popular. *Media Tenor Quarterly Journal,* 10, 1-2.

Rostron, B. (2003, April 29). Wars bring out the worst in media. Journalists absorbed by propaganda machine. *Cape Times,* p. 23.

Sanef (2003). South African journalists debate the Iraq war: To train or not to train? Sanef Web site. [Media Organisation, selected comments online.] Retrieved April 22, 2003, from the WWW: http://www.sanef.org.za/default.asp?ID=79&subclick=yes&parent_id=78

Schreiner, W. & Prinsloo, S. (2003). Iraq the turning point for Bush? Coverage on U.S. President internationally and locally more negative. *Media Tenor SA Research Journal, 3*(4), 1-3.

Solomon, N. (2002, January). The discreet charm of the straight spin. Media Beat. Retrieved October 9, 2003, from the World Wide Web: http://www.fair.org/media-beat/020103.html

Spira, T. (2003, May). Slices of war. *The Media,* p. 40.

Stroehlein, A. (2002). The Propagandists of War. Is there space for objective reporting in global conflict? Online *Journalism Review*. April. Retrieved October 9, 2003, from the World Wide Web: http://www.ojr.org/ojr/ethics/1017781981.php.

Wasserman, H. & Van Zyl, L. 2003. Independent or embedded? An exploration of views of the Presidential Press Corps. *Communicare 22*(1), 117-130.

Wolfsfeld, G. (2003). The role of the news media in unequal political conflicts. In N. Palmer (Ed.). *Terrorism, war and the press.* Hollis, NH: Hollis Publishing Company.

Zoller Seitz, M. (2003). Tuning in and flipping out. Poynter online. Retrieved September 9, 2003, from the World Wide Web: http://www.poynter.org/column.

CHAPTER 19

Arab Satellite TV News: Up, Down and Out

S. Abdallah Schleifer

Although more prominent TV news broadcasters were based in the Dubai/Abu Dhabi UAE sector of the Gulf Emirates than in Doha,[1] the capital of Qatar, the dynamic for "off shore" war coverage was centered in that tiny Gulf county with a curious media-mix triangle of Al-Jazeera, the Coalition Central Command headquarters (Centcom), and the dozens of TV news people covering the daily Centcom briefings.

Jehane Nujaim, the amazing Egyptian-American documentary film maker, whose first venture "Startup.com" was such an extraordinary success, called my attention to that curious dynamic (or field of force) when I had suggested she might leave Doha and visit Al-Arabiya in Dubai and nearby Abu Dhabi TV. She had come out to the region right after Startup.com had premiered in Spain to do something about war coverage. She sensed, as did *The New Yorker* and so many other publications, that this war was as much about television and its role in reporting on war and making war as it was about the oft-cited reasons for going to war: weapons of mass destruction, taking care of unfinished business (the 1991 betrayal of a popular Iraqi uprising), ending an oppressive regime, making a grab for Iraqi oil, serving Sharon's interests, or any combination of the above, depending on one's political persuasion.

What made the Doha field of force even more pronounced was its curious contrast to the mood outside this Electronic Triangle in those parts of the Gulf, including Doha, where I touched down during the first weeks of the war. So much of the population of Dubai, Qatar, and Abu Dhabi is expatriate—a high percentage of which are non-Arab, largely from the Indian subcontinent, or British—that the war seemed barely of concern on the Arab streets. There were none of the street tensions displayed in Cairo or even more so, Amman, where everyone seemed to be waiting for the next street demonstration or possible riot.

If there was a concern outside of the Electronic Triangle, it was about commercial implications: less tourism and empty hotels, apart from the local expatriate special weekend trade at the more spectacular seaside/pool side hotels. This was particularly the case in Dubai, where the non-Arab expatriate population was nearly overwhelming in numbers. Yet within the force field—with the foreign correspondents at Centcom and Al-Jazeera (and by metaphorical extension, in the news centers at Al-Arabiya in Dubai and ADTV in Abu Dhabi) the mood was one of adrenaline-enhanced war fever.

From the beginning everything about the war seemed exaggerated. Early on, there were claims of captured southern Iraq cities in which resistance continued for days afterwards. Later, a very sympathetic military spokesman explained that what I took for exaggeration had to do with nomenclature; that "secured" didn't mean "safe." But even the earliest descriptions out of Centcom's briefing room reeked of exaggeration. The only exception was the briefing room itself—the Hollywood set allegedly designed in the states and flown in at high cost—which was smart, effective, and functional but didn't seem as far over the top as had been reported.

It was as if this war was being fought in a vacuum without any sense of context or history. That was understandable when it came from the Iraqis. They had every reason to exaggerate the impact of the bombings, and the access they provided for still and video photographers of terribly burned or maimed children resulted in claims that the coalition was intentionally targeting civilians. Understandably, Baghdad was doing all it could in the first week to stoke the fire of an all-pervasive anger in the Arab world and among anti-war elements in the West in hopes that such anger would translate into unrest or even civic upheavals, which would buy the Ba'athist regime a cease-fire and a reprieve.

That also explains why Baghdad threw its most committed "paras," the Saddam Fedayeen, and the party militia into the southern cities to provide unexpected resistance that pinned down coalition forces for more than a week. News media in Dubai and elsewhere swallowed the bait and started talking about "quagmire," "bad intelligence," "another Vietnam," and drew parallels to the Soviets in Afghanistan in the pre-Taliban era. And then suddenly the war (the first phase—the successful liberation or occupation of Baghdad) was over.

And while coalition spokesmen at Centcom soldiered on, reasonably denying that anyone was intentionally targeting civilians, the telecast images continued to fuel a fire that only could have been doused by a single, brave Arab intellectual who could have stood up and told the inflamed millions watching Arab television that this was simply crass manipulation of the unintended and remarkably limited tragedy of any war. In fact, the 2003 Gulf War will go down in history as having the fewest civilian casualties in relation to ordnance (bombs and missiles with measurable destructive capacity).

It could have been pointed out on Arab TV that if the Western powers wanted to target civilians, they would have been able to wipe out Baghdad in one day with less ordnance than was dropped on selective targets (underscored by incredulous reports by the press in Baghdad of how normal life went on and on). One only needed to recall 50,000 German civilians who died in one RAF fire-bombing of Dresden in retaliation for the German bombing of peaceful Coventry, England, or the 100,000 Japanese civilians fire-bombed in just one U.S. air raid over Tokyo in World War II. What was needed was for a brave and prominent Arab intellectual to have stood before the cameras of Al-Jazeera, Al-Arabiya, Abu Dhabi, and Al-Hayat/LBC—the big four of serious Arabic broadcasting—and declare that if the Coalition were intentionally targeting civilians they could have leveled all of Baghdad in one night without using a single WMD.

But the hype and the exaggeration weren't just disseminated by Iraqis and bought into by what appears to have been the entire Arab world (save the Kuwaitis and the Iraqis themselves, both of whom were in the unique position of having experienced the Ba'athist regime and did not see it through glasses tinted by either Arab Nationalism and Islamism or a liberal/left-wing Western perspective). The hype also came from the American broadcasters. On the eighth day of the war Jonathan Mann of CNN talked about "The enormous human cost—350 civilians killed, according to the Iraqis and forty coalition troops killed, according to coalition HQ."

Three hundred and fifty civilians killed—that's terrible, but after eight days of war? That's two big apartment houses brought down in a lone night's surprise air raid in some other time or place. What are forty troops killed (half by friendly fire or accident)? That's three minutes of combat, storming ashore at Normandy or trying to hold the line in the Battle of the Bulge. Perhaps the problem is that I am simply too old; I can remember WBT—War Before Television—and I have read history all my life.

Neither Al-Jazeera nor CNN holders of super assets, if not "the franchise," in the 1991 Gulf War and Afghanistan had the field to themselves any longer. But Al-Jazeera somehow dominated its crowded field more than CNN dominated its English-language arena. CNN was challenged by the fluency and observational skills of BBC World Service correspondents like Rageh Omaar and John Simpson, and the surprisingly enterprising reporting of Sky News. Even for all the embarrassing cheer-leader enthusiasm, Fox demonstrated vital energy and coverage that was both gutsy and interesting despite its seeming attempts at times to become the Iraqi TV of Anglo-American journalism. Nor did it help CNN to have been thrown out of Iraq by the regime in the earliest days of the war—a strange event that might, if one favored conspiracy theories, be considered Peter Arnett's Revenge.

But Al-Jazeera dominated the Arab competition. It had correspondents all over Baghdad and the rest of Ba'athist-controlled Iraq and at the same time it had more journalists embedded within coalition forces than the other Arab satellite channels. One would have expected Abu Dhabi, Al-Arabiya, and Al Hayat/LBC to have been given priority by the coalition in that they had presented themselves as more detached, more professional in producing news, and more fact-driven than Al-Jazeera.

Al-Jazeera had mellowed and matured, as well as prospered, since I last visited during the earliest days of the Afghanistan War. At that time Al-Jazeera was overwhelmed by the presence of the international media, television crews in particular, crowding around the relatively small news center, waiting to interview director Mohammed Jasim Al-Ali. This time around the Al-Jazeera environment was much more orderly and outside crews were banned. There was only a BBC crew doing its quick news-oriented documentary about Al-Jazeera and Jehane with her field producer and cameraman.

There is no doubt in my mind that Al-Jazeera does not make up facts or hide them and there is also no question in my mind that many of Al-Jazeera's presenters indulge their emotional commitments as Arab nationalists to such a degree that at times the spin they put on the facts can be scandalous. One example: a few days after British forces took over the siege of Basra, an Iraqi tank column burst out from the southern edge of town—everywhere else, exit was barred by the siege. Abu Dhabi and the other channels reported that fact, nothing more, since the intentions of the column commander were known only to God and perhaps Saddam Hussein. There were half a dozen possibilities that became idle speculation when the column was decimated by the British, but the Al-Jazeera presenter noted with certainty that the tank column had launched the counter-attack to drive the coalition forces out of Um Qasr and southern Iraq. Clearly a case of wishful thinking.

But if Arab channels, on the one hand, must grapple with demons in the form of their urge to subordinate news to propaganda in this war, American television coverage has its own resident imp too, in its seemingly irrepressible drive to turn the war up to the fall of Baghdad and before the post-war resistance and terrorism into an entertainment, in which all of the many complex issues and options for Iraq were subsumed.

The problem of ideological spin is not uniquely Al-Jazeera's. Even Abu Dhabi, which is directed by one of the most detached and professional of all Arab broadcasting news directors, Nart Bouran, was not initially able to get the sort of reports one would expect of it, despite the prospects for private Centcom briefings and interviews with coalition military spokesmen. That is because, dipping deep into the pool of available journalists, Abu Dhabi came up with a reporter who did not hesitate to tell me, as he had earlier told U.S. military spokesmen, that he put his duty to his people, to the Arab nation, above his duty as a journalist. I told him to lighten up, which he didn't take too kindly, so I changed tack and suggested that if he was serious about his duty to the Arab people, then he would do everything he could to make them conscious of simple facts rather than making easy and sweeping judgments. Later, Abu Dhabi moved in a more professional correspondent and their Centcom reporting—already excellent from the war zones—improved significantly.

Another reason why Al-Jazeera so dominated its field was because everyone's favorite as the main contender for title of Arab satellite TV news broadcasting—Al-Arabiya—simply wasn't up to speed. The channel had only made its hard launch a few weeks before war began and, despite lots of serious preparation and rehearsal it was still, in the words of Fadi Ismail, MBC's head of Current Affairs and Documentaries, "obligated to run before we could walk." As Ismail observed, off-air rehearsal is different from on-air experience. He continued:

> Our biggest challenge was to get the experts, the talent, by which I mean correspondents. We had to use our most experienced correspondents, but on the other hand you cannot drain the major news centers, the global political capitals where reaction is a critical part of the story, so we had a real human resources problem. In retrospect, our equipment (which we initially worried about) was more than adequate but our problems were on the human level.

Al-Arabiya also ran into problems that could only be described as political. Due to its association with Saudi Arabia the channel simply could not get equal treatment in Baghdad from Iraqi authorities. In their love-hate relationship with Al-Jazeera, Iraqi authorities reportedly gave Al-Jazeera a tape of the first American dead and the four POWs under interrogation even before Iraqi TV had aired it. Al-Arabiya had sent two satellite news-gathering facilities (SNGs) to Baghdad, but the regime took one away, claiming it was trying to ensure equality among the news organizations. The government also expelled one of Al-Arabiya's three correspondents in Baghdad.

When it was all over Al-Arabiya's seasoned news director Saleh Negm summed it up:

> We simply had too many problems in deploying our people. Perhaps because we were new operators or whatever the Iraqi government did not allow us as they did other broadcast news organizations, to operate outside of Baghdad. And in the south we had managed to get ourselves embedded with the coalition forces, but we were allowed only one crew even though we were providing two different channels (the older MBC and the new all-news Al-Arabiya) with news. But the one team we had operating in the south with the coalition was kidnapped by the Iraqi Army a few days after the war began in the course of a counter-attack, and we couldn't replace them; the embedding process was over by then. They were kept by the Iraqi Army and then handed over to a tribal chieftain to keep them under lock. But it was the tribal chieftain himself who smuggled them out. I think he realized the regime was going to collapse soon so there was no point in his playing jailer for it.

It was curious that the Pentagon only offered Al-Arabiya one embedded position and still more curious that the station did not move aggressively to get a bigger allocation. It was particularly strange given the difficult reaction it could expect from the Iraqi authorities and its inability to function at Centcom because of Qatar's hostility to the channel due to its Saudi associations. Certainly Centcom was more than ready to admit Al-Arabiya to its briefings regardless of how the channel might manage to get a news team past the Qatar accreditation process, but Al-Arabiya never took any of the classic evasion tactics that, admittedly, often border on misrepresentation; tactics that competitive journalists have always taken when faced with similar discriminatory situations.

America's Neo-Conservatives—who were expecting the majority of Iraqis (the Shi'ites alone are 80% of the population) to throw roses at the Coalition forces as they stormed into Iraq—erred in forgetting how badly we had betrayed the Iraqi Shi'ites and Kurds back in 1991, and how badly all Iraqis (except Ba'ath party militants and their family/tribal networks) had suffered from twelve years of UN sanctions. Arab public opinion and the Arab satellite anchors who fed that public opinion lived in a parallel ideological dream world in which "the Iraqi people" were resisting the coalition occupation—which they clearly were not. Six months after the fall of Baghdad they still were not resisting the occupation, unless the 20% of Iraq that is Arab Sunni—many of whom were beneficiaries of the regime—is effectively "the Iraqi people." In the end, Arab nationalism might come down to a nearly universal Sunni Arab supremacy, and as such be the same sectarian poison that has wrecked so much damage and fed the condition that has led both the anchors and their overwhelmingly Arab Sunni audiences to such distorted perceptions.

ENDNOTE

1. This included such Al-Arabiya, Abu Dhabi TV, Dubai Business Channel, MBC News (not to mention all the individual UAE emirati state channels).

CHAPTER 20

Move Over CNN: Al-Jazeera's View of the World Takes on the West

Catherine Cassara and Laura Lengel

While discussing international news coverage, one regularly encounters the comment "what the 1991 Gulf War did for CNN, the 2003 Gulf War has done for Al-Jazeera." Several aspects of this truism bear scrutiny and discussion. \

First, this chapter will argue that Al-Jazeera's impact on public diplomacy is far less than CNN in one way, and far greater in another. Beyond that we are concerned with the entry of Al-Jazeera into the global arena of public diplomacy, particularly with regard to what has been called tele-diplomacy—"the conduct of diplomacy in real time through the use of CNN or some other medium" (Strobel, 1997, p. 84).

Al-Jazeera clearly challenges the monopoly on international news by CNN and other Western broadcasters, especially in the Middle East, Africa, and other places where audiences and broadcasters seek alternative views of world events. In South Africa, for instance, Al-Jazeera broadcasts now fill the overnight hours when state television is off the air, a privilege that used to belong only to CNN and BBC World. Certainly, Osama Bin Laden's choice of Al-Jazeera as his media outlet of choice made the station a household word in American homes.

Bin Laden aside, the impact Al-Jazeera actually has on Western audiences is minimal. While Western television operations use Al-Jazeera footage in their broadcasts, and newspapers and international news agencies cite Al-Jazeera as a source for facts in their coverage of news events, Western news consumers never actually have access to the Qatari station's telling of a story (Najjar, 2003, June 23). Western news outlets use Al-Jazeera as a convenient source of information in the Middle East, but rarely convey its take on any of the stories they use. Experts who watch both American networks and Al-Jazeera note that the former overlook the Qatari channel's value as a source of breaking news.

For instance, Al-Jazeera was first with the story of possible nuclear contamination after villagers looted a top-secret production site in Iraq, but the American networks did not pick up the story. "[The Western channels] have Al-Jazeera running twenty-four hours a day, but they don't seem to be paying attention to what's running there" (Najjar, 2003).

If there are questions about the true power of the "CNN Effect" when the media involved are American networks and newspapers publishing in English (Strobel, 1997; Robinson, 2002; Seib, 2002), then there can be little question that by standard definitions there could be anything close to an "Al-Jazeera Effect." As used here, the CNN Effect refers not only to the Cable News Network, but also to other satellite-distributed news channels such as Fox, SkyNews, BBC World, and MSNBC. In some usages, the term is also used to refer to print as well as broadcast media.

However, before CNN or Al-Jazeera effects are completely discredited, it is necessary to reconsider how the effect is being defined.

The "CNN Effect" might seem straightforward, but it is actually an expression with vastly different meanings depending on who is using it. For hoteliers, for example, it might be defined as the dynamic that keeps Americans at home glued to their TV sets during crisis, thus emptying restaurants and resorts. For people concerned with the intersection of global media and foreign policy, the term also might have a wide range of meanings.

In its early, news-related uses, it described the belief that during international crises the political actors on both ends, their advisers, and the public were all glued to the television set to find out what had or might be happening. An illustration of this occurred during George Herbert Walker Bush's presidency when the new CIA chief, William Colby, is said to have entered the agency on his first day to find everyone watching television. As the story goes, he ordered the sets turned off immediately, noting that the CIA didn't need CNN to tell it what was happening.

The CNN Effect also has been defined as including everything from the impact that graphic pictures of human suffering can have on television audiences, to the apparent power to speed up the diplomatic decision making process because of the short news cycle. It has also been defined as the increasingly frequent examples of heads of state using the convenience of global news coverage to communicate directly to the opponent, bypassing standard diplomatic communication channels.

The studies analyzing the purported power of the CNN Effect to drive policy decisions—either to intervene in humanitarian crises or to withdraw from them—suggest that what power media have is differential and limited. The decision to intervene—or withdraw—is found most often to have been driven by the policy goals of an administration, which have been formulated prior to television's blanket coverage of a crisis. Where the media do appear to have some impact is in those situations where the administration or regime is unsure of which action to take and is open to pressure (Strobel, 1997; Robinson, 2002).

This chapter suggests that an important aspect of the "CNN Effect," present from the earliest reports of its existence, has to do with the ability of real-time coverage to transfix audiences during crises. Impacted is anyone with access to twenty-four-hour news channels that broadcast seemingly endless discussions and analyses about what the policy response is and what it should be. In other words, real-time media coverage of crises has made the public a party to policy discussions that once were conducted behind the closed doors of foreign ministries, consulates, and executive offices. While those high diplomatic discussions still happen, increasingly policies are being made in venues and during events likely to be covered and analyzed by global news media.

In this arena of public diplomacy in the Middle East there can be little question of the impact first of CNN and now, of Al-Jazeera. While governments have always engaged in some form of public diplomacy, nothing compares with the immediacy or impact of a nation's chief executive wagging his finger on television—literally or figuratively—at the leader of another country. Elected or unelected leaders involved in world crises have become masters of the television image game. Some have required coaching to improve their TV presence, while others seem to have come to it naturally. So have the networks.

During the 1991 Gulf War, CNN broadcast images of Saddam Hussein engaged in one-sided, "friendly" conversations with his "human shields." After 9/11, Al-Jazeera broadcast Bin Laden's anti-sound bytes—lengthy lectures set against unidentifiable rocky backdrops—and during the 2003 Iraq War, Al-Jazeera broadcast exclusive pictures of dead and captured U.S. soldiers. Often these attempts at public diplomacy backfire when unintended consequences result because of cultural misperceptions.

Under this definition of the "CNN Effect," Al-Jazeera is fundamentally redrawing the map of the Arab world—both the West's understanding of the region and the region's understanding of itself—both impacting the 240 million residents of the Middle East and North Africa, and the millions more in the Arab Diaspora around the world. As noted elsewhere in this book, the upstart Qatari network has challenged the tradition of state-controlled television in the Arab world and, in the process, threatened government interpretations of news in the region. In that reach and significance, Al-Jazeera became an important player in public or tele-diplomacy.

Al-Jazeera emerged in Arab and Western consciousness as the result of its coverage of the second Intifada (Al Nawawy & Iskandar, 2003). While CNN and other U.S. networks provided little coverage of the Palestinian unrest in Gaza and the West Bank—and what little coverage there was slanted toward Israel—Al-Jazeera offered comprehensive coverage with an Arab perspective. North

American satellite viewers came to know Al-Jazeera because of the Bin Laden tapes, but Arab audiences had already become familiar with its gloves-off coverage of religious, political, and international issues of interest to Arab audiences. This aspect of Al-Jazeera has yet to penetrate the consciousness of the mainstream Western media, even though American policy makers have come to recognize the channel's reach and power.

As virulently antagonistic as the Bush administration's domestic, public rhetoric about Al-Jazeera may be, the president's closest advisers are eager to appear on the Qatari channel to make the case for their policy positions. Donald Rumsfeld, Colin Powell, and Condoleezza Rice have all appeared on the network's interview shows to express the Bush administration policy positions.

By the time the first Bin Laden tape appeared on Al-Jazeera on October 7, 1991, policy insiders in the West already knew about Al-Jazeera. They might not have grasped the full magnitude of it existence, but then it is arguable that the Qataris were also slow to understand themselves what they had created. The emir himself is said to have wondered aloud about the unexpected global phenomenon of the channel that originally was intended as a national television station with regional pretensions.

Certainly journalists like Thomas Friedman of *The New York Times* noticed the presence of the station and argued that its philosophy of vigorous and outspoken press freedom was a valuable addition to the region. In fact, given its record as a gadfly to the conservative, autocratic regimes of the Middle East, it is ironic that Al-Jazeera came to the attention of broader Western audiences as the representative of the most extreme forms of Islamic reaction.

American audiences who know nothing else about the network, can, nonetheless, identify it as "Osama's mouthpiece" or "Taliban TV." During the 2003 Gulf war, Al-Jazeera came under fire from the West for its footage of Iraqi casualties, as well as its use of footage of Alliance casualties and prisoners. These criticisms seem odd when one considers that the network only reaches an estimated thirty-five to forty million Arabic-speaking viewers, and is only accessible to American and British viewers who subscribe to Arabic satellite TV packages. Networks buying Al-Jazeera's feed chose for themselves what footage they would use.

Al-Jazeera's employees suggest, with some apparent justification, that footage of Bin Laden that they ran would have been used by CNN or any other American news outlet that was lucky enough to get it first. At the same time American commentators were loudly criticizing Al-Jazeera for running footage of U.S. casualties and prisoners, American media were running pictures of dead Iraqi soldiers and captured Iraqi soldiers. In fact, Al-Jazeera Washington bureau chief Hafez Al-Mirazi suggests that Al-Jazeera told a more balanced story of the war since it made a point of covering the casualties and prisoners on both sides. In fact, the crisis had passed before it was noted publicly that when the U.S. Defense Department asked Al-Jazeera to withhold footage until next of kin were notified the station willingly complied, according to Al-Mirazi (2003, April 3).

In a similar vein, while American officials were still complaining publicly about the network's airing of the latest Bin Laden footage in the spring of 2003, they conveniently failed to acknowledge that Al-Jazeera had at least provided the footage to the U.S. government several days before it aired.

The preoccupation of policy insiders—whether journalists or others—with the power of the media to drive policy is understandable. Each new medium or medium innovation has been met with a mixture of skepticism and fear as technology seemingly opens new Pandora's boxes. But given time the segments of society most affected by the innovation adapt and the power of the immediate effect subsides. That might be the case with the CNN Effect. Policy makers might well have learned how to turn it to their advantage and to dodge its impact when no advantage is forthcoming. Hence, the conviction that real-time news coverage impacts policy actions has been overstated.

What cannot be argued away, however, is the fact that CNN and Al-Jazeera both cover live and breaking news for their audiences. Both also provide political actors with an opportunity to directly address world audiences, bypassing career diplomats and equally pesky journalists. While the power of such coverage cannot be easily measured it should not be underestimated.

There is no question that CNN and other channels are willing to pay Al-Jazeera for audio-video feeds when they have nothing immediate of their own. This fact illustrates one of the interesting contradictions of Al-Jazeera's rise to fame in the United States. While networks have been using news and footage from the network for years, and American news makers have been seeking air time on its talk shows, it was only Bin Laden's exclusive choice of Al-Jazeera after September 11 that brought the network to the attention of most Americans.

Criticism of Al-Jazeera by those same news makers made Al-Jazeera a household name across the United States. In one news cycle it was possible to find Western news operations citing Al-Jazeera as the source for breaking news, while at the same time they carried stories critical of the Arab broadcaster. Simultaneously, high-ranking members of the Bush administration were arranging to be interviewed on Al-Jazeera in Qatar while administration spokespersons at home were demonizing the network.

Whether there is merit to Western criticism of Al-Jazeera is arguable. Some of these differences in reporting techniques might be accounted for by culture or custom. Al-Jazeera is carving out an identity for itself as an unrestrained medium in a region where neither public diplomacy nor a free press has a tradition. The channel is known for its sensationalism that offends some, and the vigorous and unrestrained discussions and disagreements on its talk shows, that offend others. It has offended and alienated many by its commitment not to bend to regional government restrictions or preferences that it mute criticism of autocratic regimes.

Time's James Poniewozik pithily observed that there is little difference between CNN and Al-Jazeera. "In fact, Western and Arab media are driven by the same imperative—to feed the hunger for human interest. Their interests are simply in different humans" (Poniewozik, 2003). Different audiences aside, there seems to be validity to Al-Jazeera's response to criticism from the West: the interviews it airs would be carried by CNN or other Western networks if they had gotten the footage first.

On the very day that American politicians and journalists were criticizing Al-Jazeera for using of footage of captured British soldiers, *The New York Times* ran a large, color photograph of a dead Iraqi solider at the top of its front-page—a picture so detailed that a family member or acquaintance would certainly have recognized the unnamed soldier. It is understandable that Arabs claim Western critiques of Al-Jazeera are hypocritical, and should be read as American discomfort with others exercising the very freedom and democracy the United States holds up to the world as a model.

Criticism aside, observers note that Al-Jazeera has produced another effect: It has given the "Arab street" its first regional—if not global—media presence (Kifner, 2001):

> The "Arab street," once all but powerless, may be taking on a new importance. The "street" (that is, views of Arab public opinion) has become a real force: now exposed to more sources of information that repressive governments do not control, harder to rein in once inflamed, and more susceptible to radical Islam, Arab rulers no longer have a monopoly on information and can no longer shape public opinion. Particularly with the existence of Al-Jazeera, an explosion of information has occurred that has defined the debate (Hachten & Scotton, 2002, p. 20).

REFERENCES

Al-Mirazi, H. (2003, April 3) Interviewed by Charlie Rose, PBS.

El-Nawawy, M. & Iskandar, A. (2002) *Al-Jazeera: How the free Arab news network scooped the world and changed the Middle East.* Cambridge, MA: Westview Press.

Hachten, W. A. & Scotton, J. F. (2002) *The world news prism: Global media in an era of terrorism.* Ames, IA: Iowa State University Press.

Kifner, J. (2001, Nov. 11) Street brawl; the new power of Arab public opinion. *The New York Times,* Sec. 4, p. 1.

Najjar, O. (2003, June 23). Personal communication with authors.

Poniewozik, J. (2003, April 7) What you see is vs. What they see. *Time 161*, pp. 68-69. Retrieved May 3, 2003, from the Business Source Premier database.

Robinson, P. (2002) *The CNN effect: The myth of news, foreign policy and intervention.* New York: Routledge.

Seib, P. (2002) *The global journalist: News and conscience in a world of conflict.* Lanham, MD: Rowman & Littlefield.

Strobel, W. (1997) *Late-breaking foreign policy: The news media's influence on peace operations.* Washington, DC: U.S. Institute of Peace.

CHAPTER 21

Indian Media Coverage of the 2003 Iraq War

Janet Fine

> "The 'liberation' rhetoric is not unfamiliar here. In 1917, Lt. General Stanley Maude, then leading the Anglo-Indian Army of the Tigris, used that very term after invading and occupying Iraq. He declared: 'Our armies do not come into your cities and lands as conquerors or enemies but as liberators.' A terrible spell of colonial tyranny followed. The Iraqis learned never to trust imperial powers."—Indian media personality Praful Bidwai from an essay "Revulsion, Disgust in India at The Iraq War"

Although the war in Iraq might have ended, the real battle just began in the Indian media when the Americans requested India send 15,000 combat troops to Iraq as part of the U.S.-led "stabilization force."

This opened up old imperialistic scars of British rule with U.S. financial implications. Indian media covered the issue constantly showing that in an election year, the ruling Indian BJP party would have difficulty justifying any death of an Indian soldier in Iraq (a Marketing Development Research Associate poll found 69% of Indians were against sending troops to guard Iraq). Yet there was approval for India's initial offer of $20 million for humanitarian relief in Iraq.

A *Times of India* headline on July 15 read: "India Rejects U.S. plea for troops in Iraq." Other papers declared: "India will not send troops to Iraq" (*Indian Express*), "Dear Uncle Sam, No!" (*Asian Age*), "Mission Iraq not without UN mandate, avers India" (*The Free Press Journal*) and "Bush irked by Indian refusal—but decision does not affect Washington-New Delhi relations" (*Afternoon*).

Indian TV news reported the gesture as a reconfirmation of India's ambivalent position of bridging east and west in the region. At a seminar for government and military officials exploring the Indian Iraq military question, Indian Admiral Madhvendra Singh concluded, "On the end gains by the U.S. forces, it is difficult to impose foreign value on people who are part of an ancient civilization and who have a sense of nationalism."

Indian media coverage of the Iraq war and its aftermath brought on a wide-ranging diversity of opinion in India. In the world's largest democracy—consisting of an estimated one billion people—television, rather than the print media, developed as the visual platform to understanding the war.

Indian entertainment, in its own non-"imperialistic" empire, is acknowledged as the world's largest producer of cinematic films, churning out an estimated 850 movies annually. India has jumped into TV with the same passion for the entertainment of the masses. There may not be running water in some villages, but cable TV appears to be an essential commodity. The town hall discussion format is popular on most channels. Often, TV personalities achieve the same level of deification as movie stars.

In this context, for the first time, Indian TV reporters became personalities in their coverage of the war rather than their embedded and better-financed western counterparts. Satish Jacob and his cameraman Syed Nooh Nizami of government-run Prasar Bharti channel Doordarshan (DD) had a providential escape of U.S. aerial bombing on the journalist-inhabited Palestine Hotel and dramatically reported it on the hotel roof-top. It was a scoop for Doordarshan and brought the war directly into homes across India to suggest that Americans may have been targeting civilian locations.

Star News sent three reporters to cover the war, with a daily 9 p.m. prime time bulletin "Iraq Report." Star News reporter Gaurav Samant discovered an Indian who had languished in an Iraq jail for the past nine years. After leaving the jail, Star News arranged for the man to speak to his family back in Mumbai, India, on the reporter's satellite phone. Star News ratings jumped 20% during the coverage.

TV news competition has become more intense due to rapid expansion of news stations. India is reportedly the second largest provider of original TV programming at 40,000 hours. Satellite news channels in India are making "news" with growing regional and national channels. Between March and April 2003 more than six News channels started, including Sahara Samay Rashtriya, Headlines Today, NDTV 24x7 and NDTV India (which split with Star in March). War coverage was standard fodder for these channels.

2003 War Had Greater Impact than 1991 War

The Iraq war coverage on TV also had a bigger impact in India than the 1991 Gulf War due to an increase in TV penetration and expansion of cable. Half of all Indians have TV sets in their homes and reports indicate that there will be a growth of 35% for TV cable subscribers in the rural and semi-urban areas by 2006, indicating an increasing penetration of cable into less populated regions.

An India National Readership survey found that the four main Indian metro cities (Mumbai, New Delhi, Chennai, and Kolkata) command 6.7 million cable subscribers, 15% of total cable TV households of 44 million.

Hindi language channels naturally dominate with Aaj Tak (India Today News) leading cable viewership at 38%, according to an A.C. Nielsen TAM media May 10, 2003, survey; with Star News at 25% (which has grown 70% since March 30 this year when it launched its all-Hindi formatting); Zee News at 19%; followed by new entrants Sahara Samay at 10%; and NDTV Hindi at 6%. What is most surprising is the marginalization of news in English with channels like NDTV 24X7 and TV Today's Headlines making no mark in the ratings, and international English news channels like CNN, CNBC, and BBC scoring a low 2% viewership.

Although coverage of the war by foreign satellite channels naturally brought in more viewers, many Indians said their perception changed. As one prominent Indian businessman said, "We all watched CNN, CNBC, and BBC, but their coverage seemed more propaganda like tuning into CBC (Christian Broadcast Channel) whose telecasts portrayed the war to 'destroy the Iraqi heathens in Bush's crusade' and restore the 'ancient Mesopotamian kingdom to its Christian rightful place.'"

SURFING THE WAR

Anil Wadhwani, founder and CEO of *Indiantelevision.com*, a leading TV consultant group monitoring Indian TV, commented that, "We found that most Indian viewers channel-surfed during the Iraq war, but I think Doordarshan TV had the best coverage with its updates three times a day with live coverage.

Western channels like German, Italian, and French TV offered new information, but CNN and BBC seemed for us too nationalistic. Pakistan TV was banned in India and Al-Jazeera was only seen on STAR once a day. Lack of access and media management perhaps hampered Indian journalists who are used to reporting more on home issues."

Bringing the war into Indian homes in fact presented its own unique dilemma. India was in an ambivalent position in its Iraq war coverage, perhaps due to regional interests and past experience. Parts of India, such as the south and especially Kerala, have a huge portion of its labor force living in the Gulf region, including Iraq. They are affected by what happens in the Middle East. During Desert Storm in 1991, India took the unpopular position of supporting Saddam Hussein, invoking Kuwait's ire and resulting in the expulsion of the many Indian citizens living there while India retained Iraq's friendship and continuous working relationship.

Ensuing years have brought closer ties with the USA and Israel and thus some shift in vision. More than in other countries, the announcement of the contracting of American companies to rebuild Iraq inflamed Indian commentators, since this was one of the carrots dangled in front of India by the United States in return for its support. The huge Indian work force assumed they would be involved in the reconstruction of post-war Iraq due to its proximity and experience. Reality proved crushing to some and it was reported cynically in the media that Americans were giving themselves all the contracts, even excluding loyal allies.

Overall, Indians took the nebulous position of supporting Western efforts while denouncing the war. This impacted the way the conflict was portrayed, especially on Doordarshan, which had been heavily influenced by CNN during India's early satellite telecasts of Iraq's invasion of Kuwait in 1991. This influence resulted in modernized facilities and better training for DD's news arm, including its international satellite news channel.

India also has a special relationship with the BBC, dating back to British rule, when BBC radio news provided a window to the world for most Indians. Indeed, in India good English usage is called "BBC English." Yet this time around, the BBC in India did not seem as "plucky" in its coverage as in past wars, a difference that may be attributed to Britain's role as an integral partner in the war and its consequent constraints. BBC Asia takes the region into consideration, but Indians seem to prefer to watch war coverage from an Indian point of view.

According to a TV ratings survey, viewers ultimately seemed to prefer the comfort of regional channels in local languages like Hindi (in the north), Telegu (Andhra Pradesh), Malyalam (Kerala), and Tamil (Tamil Nadu), which also telecast to the Gulf region, where a majority of the labor force from these states works. Indian satellite television news coverage obviously could not compete with more established channels covering the war that had correspondents embedded with military units in the field.

What they did was to offer their own perspective and more coverage of local reactions, including those of the large Muslim population. According to one executive of an Indian TV company, "War is a serious issue, but it has its novelty value for TV channels and audiences, too, what with the latest gizmos and weaponry on display and being utilized."

Since the onset of the war coincided with the Cricket World Cup, in which India was a finalist, the early reports from the battlefield did not lure viewers away from the game, which is a national passion. Satellite television vied for these same audiences, especially with advertisements committing themselves to war coverage.

The TV reality show of war quickly became a fix on the news but did not displace American movie channels or Bollywood film channels offering alternatives to war watching in India.

DOORDARSHAN OUTSOURCED WAR NEWS

As terrestrial TV, Doordarshan still claims an estimated 70% of viewers in India who do not have satellite television. With government funding, Doordarshan contracted out its war coverage to a private company, Saeed Naqvi's Third Eye production house. This well-regarded journalist has always paid attention to the Muslim and Hindu perspectives in his work and he is known for resourceful, investigative reporting.

Third Eye produced a daily half-hour show for DD, at an estimated cost of $10,000 a day for every half-hour slot and inputs for the daily bulletins. Of this, about 35% up-linked one of the teams in Kuwait, with additional feeds sent through satellite used for its various news bulletins and translated for the DD regional channel. The urgency for Doordarshan in its Iraq coverage was not to repeat the Afghanistan experience of the U.S. war against the Taliban regime.

"After the embarrassment we faced over not covering the Afghanistan story, we decided to be well-prepared this time round," said Doordarshan Director-General, S.Y. Quraishi. "However, on realizing that we did not have the necessary experience to cover such a story, we decided to give it to an outside agency. Third Eye TV was hired to provide coverage of the Iraq story from the Indian perspective. Though Doordarshan had considered using footage of foreign news channels, the need to show the Indian angle was apparent on the daily show, 'Gulf War II: India Cares, India Counts.'"

Some of the reporting had been faulted, with DD and Third Eye sometimes not always "seeing eye to eye." One reported discrepancy, according to *Indiantelevision.com*, occurred when Sasi Kumar for Third Eye reported Indians in Kuwait had decided to stay in Kuwait with their Kuwaiti friends, while a DD news team immediately afterwards broadcast images of Indians returning by the planeload from the Gulf. The feeds were compiled in Moving Pictures Studios in New Delhi; its CEO Ramesh Sharma who produces "India This Week" news program said, "This was a first for India to have live coverage of a war and broadcast daily. It was a learning experience. But it brought a voice to India news."

Saeed Naqvi wrote cynically about the experience of covering the war in an article "Media as Soldier's Assistant." He said that "once President Bush issued the ultimatum from the Azores, the journalistic population in the Iraqi capital began to thin out. Needless to say, there were no Indian journalists to cover the war from Baghdad except for my colleague, Satish Jacob and myself, on an assignment for Third Eye-TV Doordarshan. My return left Satish as the sub-subcontinent's eyes and ears in Baghdad, even more so since Brij Tyagi, India's ambassador, reluctantly shut shop and drove to Amman. One questions why journalists did not leave Baghdad in the first Gulf War."

Third Eye gained credibility for its eyewitness Iraq coverage, as did leading news channel Aaj Tak's reporting. Some viewers in India have always preferred the more feisty news channels, like the twenty-four-hour Hindi channel Aaj Tak (translated as "Today There") of TV Today Network, which has often reported controversial stories. The channel linked an exclusive deal with another hard-hitting channel, Al-Jazeera, for footage of the Gulf War. "The entire coverage philosophy in the Iraq war was designed to give access to the Western media," said Uday Shankar, chief executive producer of Aaj Tak. "A good chunk of the Western media's contemporary coverage celebrating 'the Allies' triumph, based on 'embedded' correspondents, falls in the category of crude war propaganda. Regrettably, there were not too many Indian channels which used Al-Jazeera or Abu Dhabi TV as feed."

Aaj Tak sent three teams to countries around Iraq, including anchor Deepak Chaurasia in Kuwait, as well as tying up with local TV stations there and international agencies like APTN and Reuters for footage. Interspersed with war coverage were discussion panels and groups, a technique of which Indian viewers are fond, and which gained a viewer following.

Father of Indian TV Weighs in

"It is sad that even though we had so many news channels covering the Iraq war, most were not present either in Baghdad or elsewhere to give a clear-cut, honest-to-God report on the war scenario from an Indian journalist's eyes and ears," said Prem Prakash, chairman of Asian News International (ANI), who is considered the "father of Indian TV News" as a pioneer in Doordarshan and founding member of Visnews, Reuters Television. He continued:

> I fully appreciate that the coverage of war is a dangerous and expensive affair. But the channels should have come together along with a premier TV news agency like ANI to bring about pool coverage from a totally Indian view point.

The cost factor did affect Indian war coverage. Estimates included CNN allocating $25 million (incurring an expenditure of $1 million a day); BBC allocating $15 million; and Britain's ITV allocating £5 million, while Indian channels spent an estimated $10,000 to $12,000 a day. Most of the Indian channels used footage from international networks, like Star News, which took visuals from sister networks Sky News and Fox News.

Indian channels said they did not show ads when important news broke. "We cut our ad-breaks whenever there had been important war news breaks," said G. Krishnan, chief executive officer at TV Today. According to an analysis by TAM Adex, inventory levels of break duration comprising promos and advertising went down substantially in India. CNN's inventory levels came down by 30%, while BBC's were down by 39%. This contrasted to Indian channels reporting an increase in inventory levels. Aaj Tak rose almost 25% along with its new channel, Headlines Today, while Zee News was up by 5%. Star News also reported an ad rise.

Third Eye correspondent, V.K. Shashikumar, said the real media battle was fought in the shadows, where there are neither embedded reporters nor independent journalists. "The only access to southern Iraq was through Kuwait, where coalition officers formed an invisible barb wire fence," said the intrepid Shashikumar. "They take calls, are patient, answer queries with 'there is nothing on that yet' or 'you will have to keep calling to find out.' The U.S.-led coalition's military planners had 'out-thought' every opportunity in which journalists might take recourse in order to get inside southern Iraq."

A Jordanian journalist, representing an Indian news channel disparaged, "There is hardly any coverage for us Indian correspondents. We have never been allowed in. To be honest, most of us are relying on Arab TV networks. We were told to be patient, in accordance with the adage, 'Your access is dependent on the troops you have on the ground.'"

The only Indians who were embedded with coalition troops were Ajai Shukla and Vishnu Som of New Delhi Television (NDTV), but they did not get into Iraq as the war was virtually over by the time the Germany-based regiment into which they were embedded even arrived. TV reporter Shukla said after the war, "The biggest challenge for a journalist reporting the Iraq conflict was in bypassing the sophisticated American media management campaign. Journalists must now consciously divert their attention away from the easily available stories of soldiers and military success and focus instead on the more difficult stories of human beings caught up in a war."

Perhaps one could say that the Iraq war and its war coverage in India opened a more obvious east-west divide since Rudyard Kipling and "the white man's burden." Memories of the Raj and occupying British troops in India were rekindled by the Iraq war and reinforced by nationalistic reporting of western journalists embedded with troops. By presenting the war and ensuing debates afterwards on their own terms, Indian media coverage remained more pertinent to its viewers and values.

Part V

THE WAR IN CYBERSPACE

CHAPTER 22

Iraq War Ushers in Web-based Era

Naila Hamdy and Radwa Mobarak

Although the Internet was popular during the Bosnian ethnic conflict from 1992 to 1995, it was used mainly for news and statistics (Allen & Seaton, 1999). In contrast, the Internet bustled with proactivity during the 2003 Iraq War.

People went online to share opinions about the conflict, to send and receive e-mails mobilizing others to oppose or support the war. Some Internet users went further and used the technology as an instrument of war. A variety of Web sites offered news, pictures, analysis, discussions, and live audio and video feeds to satisfy needs that traditional media failed to satisfy. Some journalists, like Rodney Weidemann of IT Web, even termed the 2003 Iraq War the "First Internet War," with competing Web sites on both sides of the issue in the lingua franca of the combatants, English and Arabic.

WEB SITES CHOOSE SIDES IN COMING WAR

Many Web sites supported the coalition, saying it was necessary to protect America from "the terrorists." Some thought it was the only way to liberate Iraqis from the tyrant, Saddam. Other Web sites portrayed the war as a plot to control Iraq's vast oil reserves. Still others, particularly Arab Web sites, saw it as a war against Islam or as a plan to divide the Arab States for the benefit of Israel.

Web sites supporting the war gave reasons why the war was necessary. The White House's official Web page, titled "A Decade of Defiance and Deception," argued for "Operation Iraqi Freedom," providing all types of reasons why the war was necessary, from saving the poor Iraqi people to protecting Americans from expected terrorist attacks. In a similar conservative pro-war tone, "Defend

America," the official U.S. Department of Defense Web site, provided information about the war under the title, "Iraq: Facing the Threat." As expected, the information varied from Iraq's nuclear weapons to biological and chemical weapons that Iraq presumably possessed. Articles sported strong ideas varying from Saddam as "a madman and a danger to the world" to Iraq deceiving UN inspectors about biological weapons.

Other pro-war Web sites were entirely devoted to criticizing war protesters, led by journalists such as Bill O'Reilly of Fox News. "From boycotting French products to implying that anti-war protestors are terrorists, count on Bill O'Reilly to give you the conservative take on the war and everything else!" " O'Reilly and the entire Fox News network take their right-wing timbre from the boss, Rupert Murdoch," stated Irene McDermott, a librarian who writes about Internet issues (2003, March 31).

Meanwhile, anti-war Web sites were taking their positions on the field, declaring that war was not a solution. "United for Peace and Justice," for example, is "a national campaign to bring together a broad range of organizations throughout the United States to help coordinate work against a U.S. war on Iraq" (*www.unitedforpeace.org*). It provides links to news outlets, resources for organizing protests, and contacts for those who want to take action.

But perhaps the most prominent anti-war Web sites were independent media or Indymedia, which consist of organizations and journalists offering alternative coverage and news of anti-war protests around the world. Ken O'Keefe, a former Marine and veteran of the 1991 Gulf War, posted a message on *www.indymedia.org* bulletin board announcing he would go to Baghdad to act as a human shield. Later, when he arrived at Baghdad, he started his own e-diary. He wrote his day-by-day experience as a human shield, trying "to make the West understand that the Iraqi people are people, just people" (O'Keefe, 2003).

Mini-war Declared in Chat Rooms

But the real cyber war was only warming up. The real heat didn't begin until the coalition forces attacked Iraq on March 20, 2003.

Chat rooms and discussion forums that examined news from the scene of the war became a trend. With traditional news media so strictly controlled by either governments or their own conventions, the Internet represented the differing realities of war from diverse perspectives. During the allied bombing campaign, Web sites featuring chat rooms and e-mail forums on both sides of the issue started competing vigorously. A group that calls itself Abu Banan Global Islamic Media Group operated a Web site that presented a series from a volunteer who went to fight in Iraq, as well as publishing reports on Islamic *fatwas* (religious rulings) disputing those by government-appointed sheikhs in Saudi Arabia, who had argued against fighting to save Saddam's regime" (*boston.com*).

Arabic chat rooms, meanwhile, flamed with insults aimed in every direction. Opinions swung wildly from putting the U.S. forces on a pedestal to mocking the war and the Iraqis who rejoiced over the tumbling of Saddam's statue. "Iraq is now finally free," said a joyful KB, who identified himself as Iraqi. Yet Samantha, also self-described as Iraqi, disagreed. "Iraq is not freed," she wrote. "It will fall under another oppression: the American oppression" (Associated Press, 2003).

With much controversy surrounding this war, sites such as Yahoo Groups site featured slogans such as "Come to jihad" and pictures of Osama Bin Laden flashing alongside images of machine guns and fighting. An article posted by an Egyptian Islamist conceded that coalition forces were in control of Baghdad (El Deeb, 2003). "But Ilham, who said she was from Egypt, condemned celebrating Iraqis for selling out their country. A Syrian chatter signed in under the name Failasoof warned that other Arab and Muslim countries are on the hit list. But Ro'a, a Lebanese chatter said she could understand why the Iraqis were happy after they have finally got rid of Saddam's dictatorship rule" (Associated Press, 2003).

Similarly, Americans were joining Yahoo chat forums to express their opinions about the war, ranging from sympathetic comments to racist statements. In one of the chat rooms, Jessica, who used a bright pink font to attract attention, opined that Iraqis did not deserve to live in the first place. "You know the difference between an Iraqi infant and an Iraqi man? When he is a man, he wears the diaper on his head instead of you know where," she wrote.

But a man who identified himself as a U.S. Marine who claimed to have been in the 1991 Gulf War deemed the war as a "big hoax." He wrote: "You think that Iraq is a threat to Americans? You don't even know where Iraq is. This has nothing to do with your safety. In fact you will pay the price. I know it, 'cause I have been there before and I know that the Marines are the ones who are hurt most, not Saddam or anyone else."

The main motivations of those who visit chat rooms are seeking conversation, experimenting with a new communication media, and initiating relationships with other people (Peris et al., 2002).

When Arabs and Americans joined the same chat rooms it was like burning down the house. Arabs belittled and ridiculed the United States and Americans claimed the Middle East encouraged terrorists. After one heated exchange on one of the sites, Americans and other supporters virtually rejoiced about making one of the Arabs leave the chat room after swearing at him or her. The Arabs, on the other hand, were easily enraged and would swear back just the same, so that the discussion was almost diverted from the issue of the war to the lingering tension between Arabs and Westerners left over from September 11.

War boosts Internet traffic to record highs

The start of the war led to a greater flow in Web traffic on news sites as Internet users searched for the latest breaking news and updates. According to Web monitoring company Hitwise, traffic to news sites had risen by 6% in the two weeks following the first attack on Iraq. Traffic had particularly mounted during daytime, as more people checked for the latest developments by visiting various news Web sites from work.

According to the Los Angeles Times, major news sites on the Web reported from 30-100% more traffic since the war started. In fact, Reuters reported that in Britain, the top Internet service, Freeserve, noted that the war had beaten Britney Spears and even sex to being the most popular search term, while the term Iraq had shot up to No. 1 on the weekly Yahoo search list up from No. 42 in just one week.

BBC and CNN reported a dramatic rise in the number of users visiting their international sites. Unofficial figures showed there were 150 million visitors to BBC's World site during the final two weeks of March—more than double the corresponding period in February. As for its new international site, BBCnews.com, it received more than 130 million hits in March, compared to 72 million in February, while its Arabic site had 150% more traffic than the normal 15 million hits.

Likewise, CNN had witnessed a huge growth on its international Web sites with the highest ever traffic on *CNNArabic.com* and its international site. The main *CNN.com* also achieved record usage figures. According to Nielsen NetRatings some 78 million users logged on over the weekend of March 22-23 (Kornblum, 2003).

AL-JAZEERA GOES INTO CYBERSPACE

Yet, one of the most remarkable developments in the news media was the launch of the Doha-based, much talked-about channel Al-Jazeera's English language Web site. Because not many Westerners can read Arabic, this Web site was an opportunity for the West to gain awareness about Arabs' views. Thus, despite being forced offline, the Web site has shot up sixty-three places in the news service rankings. Web portal Lycos reported that Al-Jazeera became its most searched site during the first weeks of the war, generating three times as many search requests as sexually-oriented sites.

Although Al-Jazeera was accused by the Western media of bias by showing pictures of dead coalition soldiers and POWs, it showed similar pictures of Iraqis. The front page of the Web site had a flash presentation of pictures of dead and injured Iraqi children. When clicking on a grotesque picture of an Iraqi child whose eye is dripping blood, another page with more pictures of the sort is displayed. Some people thought the images portrayed reality, but to others the pictures were offensive.

ENTER THE LARGE MEDIA CORPORATIONS

American network news broadcaster ABC News (a division of Walt Disney Co.) and Web Portal Yahoo Inc. had teamed up on a subscription-based broadband Internet news service, also launched days before the outbreak of war.

Both *CNN.com* and *ABC.com* also offered streaming video for a premium fee. CNN, however, took it a step further through CNN Radio, which broadcast updated headlines and stories about the war. Similarly, BBC World used multimedia in the form of BBC radio, which presented reports about the war, as well as three-minute streaming videos filmed every weekday evening that discussed the next day's headlines. But the most popular online radio during the war was NPR (National Public Radio), which produced complete transcripts of shows about the conflict without charge.

MSNBC.com, the NBC/Microsoft hybrid, delivered the latest war news headlines. It also featured "Target: Iraq" hyperlinks and free video feeds, including "a live downtown Baghdad-cam with sound: Boom! Boom!" (McDermott, 2003). The Web site also offered links to its other partners: *Newsweek*, *Washingtonpost.com*, and Microsoft Encarta articles about war and the Middle East. Not surprisingly, *MSNBC.com* reported roughly one million more users a day since the war began. In fact, *MSNBC.com* figures for the Tuesday before war formally broke out showed that the site served 2.5 million video screens; within days, the number had rocketed to 6.1 million and topped 10 million (Kornblum, 2003).

The New York Times International Special edition of the Times Web site was devoted to complete coverage of the Iraqi conflict. It provided a summary of the day's war-related events, followed by reports from correspondents and photographers from *The New York Times* as they covered the war from all around the Middle East.

Guardian Unlimited in England was the most visited newspaper site, with 107 million hits during March alone, followed by sites operated by *The Financial Times*, *The Sun*, *London Times* and the *London Telegraph*.

Bloggers Add Something New to the Internet

But checking news was insufficient when the world buzzed about such a massive and controversial conflict. Unlike other media, the Internet is not only a newsroom, but it is also a living room-type of medium, where people can interact with others. Because of increasing cynicism about both American and Arab news media coverage of the war, Weblogs became increasingly popular (individual Web sites commonly called "blogs"). Blogs became useful sources for posting opinions and diaries about the war. Bloggers often publish alternate views absent from Fox, Sky, CNN, and the Middle East channels.

Blogs are a way for Internet news to compete directly with television. You can turn on CNN to find out what the latest headlines are, but you may have to wait through a cycle. But while people are at work in front of their computers, it is fairly convenient to find out the latest news from blogs. In fact, the uncertainty about what is really happening in Iraq brought blogs into the light, stressing opinion, debate, and the seeking of information from alternative sources.

One popular blog was called, "Where is Raed?" by a gay Iraqi architect, "Salam Pax." Writing in English from the heart of Baghdad, Salam provided accounts of daily life in a city under U.S. bombardment. Salam was the only Iraq resident known to be filing accounts from Iraq directly to the Web. Traffic on his Web site was so great it caused the server to go down, reports Sapa-AFP (*The Guardian*, 2003, February). On March 22, he wrote:

> Half an hour ago the oil-filled trenches were put on fire my cousin came and told me he saw police cars standing by one and setting it on fire. Now you can see the columns of smoke all over the city.

Salam was one of the first to produce a book on the war. A collection of his writings hit the bookstores in late summer 2003.

During the war on Iraq a variety of people wrote blogs, including reporters from prestigious news outlets like The Associated Press and *New York Daily News*, military men and women deployed in the Middle East, and families of soldiers and Arab civilians living near Iraq.

Bloggers used sites that allowed subscribers to easily publish on the Web. That makes them immediate and uncontrolled. By their nature, blogs are unmediated opinion, biased, and often unfair. They are also difficult to find unless bloggers register their sites in search engines and/or are linked by other blogs and Web sites. Still a Weblog can be a source of timely information and many of them were expertly done.

Despite the virtues of the Internet and the ease with which information can be accessed, people have become more critical and increasingly skeptical of the medium. People realize that reports can be easily faked—that the Internet is not an inherently pure news and information channel, but can be used by all sides to spread propaganda. Cyberspace may be the place an information war might happen. In fact, those who claimed in chat rooms to be Iraqi or U.S. soldiers were not guaranteed to be so. Anyone can fake an identity on the Internet and say anything and other people know it because they do it themselves.

Chris Hables Gray, University of Montana-Great Falls professor and author of *Postmodern War: The New Politics of Conflict*, said in an interview:

> [T]he Internet has always been as good place as any to put out white, black and gray propaganda. But in moderated list serves and chat rooms there is more chance of feedback so that a careful reader can actually get better information than one can from print media, by tracking down sources and interrogating rumors ... It's one thing to resist a handful of reporters to sanitize news opportunities; it's another to keep all soldier/civilian accounts off the Internet. Impossible really (McClellan, March 8, 2003).

All this makes the credibility of the Internet questionable.

HACKERS, VIRUSES AND WORMS: CYBER WAR'S WEAPONS

The war was not only a war of words, but a war for hackers, who targeted Islamic and Arabic Web sites, as well as American and British sites. New agencies reported that the attack on Iraq:

> has stirred up computer virus writers and malicious hackers, who have apparently decided to vent by defacing Web sites and releasing e-mail worms that prey on people's fears and curiosity. Antagonists and activists based in the United States, Europe and the Middle East are engaged in their own form of war games. Some are vandalizing Web sites, particularly government sites, scrawling scornful cyber graffiti urging people to "make love not war." (Delio, March 21, 2003).

With the Internet, opinions that previously would have had just an audience of friends and acquaintances can spread to thousands of readers. And with the Internet it has become much easier to damage someone's Web site than make the effort to change their opinions.

At *Islamonline.net*, one of the most popular Web sites for news and analysis on Islamic and International affairs, traffic doubled after U.S. forces attacked Iraq (Rageh, April 17, 2003). "So did cyber attacks, which reached 250 a day," according to Mutiualiah Ta'eb, the site's general co-ordinator. Another attack targeted *Arabia.com*, a Dubai-based Web site, by the third day of the war. However, it is unclear how many sites have been targeted by hackers, who typically sought to alter Web pages or bring a site down altogether.

The highest profile Arab Web site targeted by hackers was Al-Jazeera's new English language site in the early days of the war. Almost as soon as it came online, hackers attacked the Al-Jazeera site. As a result, the site's English and Arabic pages could not be accessed or were referred to a page with a notice that read: "Hacked by Patriot, Freedom Cyber Force Militia" on a stars and stripes background.

Soon after, hackers who claimed to be members of Islamist groups, defaced some U.S. and British Web sites and swamped others with anti-war messages. An American site that showed pictures of dead U.S. troops was taken down after individuals bombarded the Web host with complaints (Krebs, 2003). Anti-war hackers employed similar tactics. In Spain, activists crashed the ruling party's Web site with e-mails to protest Prime Minister Jose Maria Aznar's support of the war.

Obviously, hackers of all kinds had seized the opportunity of war to cause chaos online. More than one thousand Web sites had been hacked as a reaction to the Iraq conflict, according to a BBC Online report, citing information from security firm F-Secure. Web sites of the U.S. National Center for Agricultural Utilization Research and the U.S. Navy were also among hacked Web sites, F-Secure told the news organizations. The Web site of the city of Pacifica, California, "was defaced with anti-Bush, anti-war and anti-American messages,"

InternetWeek.com reported. Unix Security Guards described as a "pro-Islamist hacking group" broke into some four hundred Web sites and scrawled anti-war slogans in both Arabic and English, *washingtonpost.com* reported.

Also, hackers had targeted a public affairs Web site of the National Security Agency, according to Security Focus, a California-based Internet security company, owned by anti-virus company Symantec. The hackers' motives were unclear, but may be related to the U.S. military action against Iraq, "which like past conflicts has already spurred a rash of protest Web site defacements" (Security Focus, 2003). The hackers' e-mail included a distribution list of about five hundred e-mail addresses, most of which belonged to the U.S. military," Security Focus said.

Messages posted on hacked sites said that vandalizing those sites was the beginning of the "new era of cyber war we promised! More is coming, just like the United States do [sic] what it wants to the world, we will do what we want to the Internet. Stop the U.S. terroristes [sic] and we will stop! Viva Iraq!" (Krebs, 2003).

Similarly, computer worms and viruses took their rounds, hiding in war-related attachments with titles like "Go USA" aimed at pro-war types or "Make Peace" aimed at anti-war types. These viruses capitalized on people's interest in war news and messages about the conflict, disrupting their files and e-mail accounts.

The best-known worms during the war on Iraq were the e-mail viruses, Ganda and Prune worm. These two viruses came with subjects and messages about military action and the political situation in Iraq (F-Secure). Messages ranged from claims that the attachments contained pictures of Iraq taken by U.S. spy satellites, to pro-American or anti-Bush screen savers. Once the attachments were opened on PCs running Windows, the worms e-mailed themselves to addresses in the infected computer address book lists. While camouflaged as war-themed messages, security experts warned that many might be fake.

Comic Relief

Despite all the worms and the hacking, the war had its humorous moments on the Internet.

Many Web sites made fun of the war, Bush, Saddam, and others who were involved in the war. *Welovetheiraqiministerofinformation.com* was one of the most visited sites using humor. This Web site is a tribute to one of the funniest and most liked people who appeared in the media during the war: Mohammed Saeed Al-Sahhaf, the Iraqi minister of information. The comment "People want to see him in Hollywood" greeted visitors, followed by comic caricatures, and manipulated pictures of Al-Sahhaf.

Other Web sites made clever use of computer software Flash such as animation, like Mark Fiore's, that had a funny cartoon where Bush and Blair were trying to find weapons of mass destruction in Iraq. The Onion, "America's Finest

News Source,"delivered satire like no one else can. Fake headlines such as "Dead Iraqi would have loved democracy" and "Bush asks Congress for $30 billion to help fight war on criticism," cast a goofy liberal light on the real stories of the day.

The White House Newsroom is another Web site that has an address exactly like that of the White House, except for the .org and the .gov difference. Funny flash posters like the campaign stickers that read "Bush Christ" and "Bush 4 more wars!" are as clever as the headlines of the Onion. And at a press of button, a set of articles under the title "Target: Iraq. Taking out the Evil-doer" pops up. These articles are in the form of radio statements by Bush, starting with statements like, "Good morning people of Texraq. This is your superior white liberator speaking."

Experienced Internet users know they don't have to search for such Web sites. Every day they find attachments clogging their e-mail boxes full of humorous stories and pictures about the war, especially altered reality pictures. Saddam and Bush are usually the main players in such photos, followed closely by Blair. Oscar award winners for Male Terrorist to pictures of Bush and Saddam getting married became common in everyday e-mails. Also Flash is sometimes used, like the video showing Bush and Blair singing a duet, "My Endless Love." These dark-humor touches gave the war comic relief that often masked the reality of death and destruction.

Whether the 2003 war on Iraq was truly the first Internet War will be debated for years to come. What is certain is that future wars will be fought in virtual space as well as real territory acquired through blood and fortune.

References

A Decade of Defiance and Deception. The official White House Web site. Accessed August 22, 2003, www.whitehouse.gov/iraq

Allen, T. & Seaton, J. (1999) *The media of conflict: War reporting and representations of ethnic violence.* New York: Zed Books.

Defend America. U.S. Department of Defense News about the war on terrorism. Www.defendamerica.mil

El Deeb, S. (2003, July). Islamic Web sites bemoan 'occupation' of Bagdad, Arabic chat rooms flame with opposing views. *The Associated Press.*

Delio, M. (2003, March 21). War worms inch across Internet. *Wired News.* Retrieved August 23, 2003, http://www.wired.cm/news/print/0,1294,58143,00.html.

Independent Media Center. Accessed July 14, 2003,http://www.indymedia.org

Kornblum, J. (2003, March 26). War brings a surge of traffic on the Internet. *USA Today.* Retrieved August 23, 2003, from http://www.usatoday.cm/tech/world/iraq/2003-03-26-warweb_x.htm

Krebs, B. (2003, March 20) Web sites vandalized with antiwar messages. *Washington Post.*

Lycos search reports Al-Jazeera tops Web searches for second straight week; urban legends surround war in Iraq surface online; SARS enters the Top 10. (April 8, 2003). Www.finance.lycos.com/home/news/story.asp?story=33757927

McClellan, J. (2003, March 8) Bullets over broadband. *The Age.* Retrieved August 24, 2003, from http://www.theage.cm.au/articles/2003/03/07/1046826526197.html

McDermott, I. (March 31, 2003) Iraq around the clock: the first Internet war. *Searcher,* 10704795:11 (6).

O'Keefe, K. Diary of human shield. Retrieved July 3, 2003,from www.counterpunch.org/okeefe02262003.html

Peris, R., Gimeno, M.A., Pinazo, D., Ortet, G., Carrero, V., Sanchiz, M.,& Ibanez, I. (2002). Online chat rooms: Virtual spaces of interaction for socially oriented people. *CyberPsychology & Behavior, 5,* 43-51.

Rageh, R. (2003, April 17). Arab Web sites plagued by attacks. CNEWS World. AccessedAugust 22, 2003, http://cnews.canoe.ca/CNEWS/World/2003/04/17/67613-ap.html.

Security Focus. www.securityfocus.com

United for Peace & Justice. www.unitedforpeace.org

War on the Web (2003, February). *The Guardian.* www.guardian.co.uk.

Weidemann, R. (2003, March 25). War redefines role of the Internet. ITWEB. Retrieved August 23, 2003, from http://www.itweb.co.za/sections/internet/2003/0303251100.asp?Q=E

CHAPTER 23

The First Hours of Online Coverage of "Operation Iraqi Freedom"

Daniela V. Dimitrova, Lynda Lee Kaid and Andrew Paul Williams

President George W. Bush announced military action in Iraq on March 19, 2003, at 10:19 p.m. EST. This chapter analyzes the coverage of online news sites from around the world in response to this attack. It focuses on the immediate coverage of the event by looking at how the Iraq War was framed on the home pages of leading international news Web sites.

While there were some differences in the framing of the event, the majority of the coverage focused on the military conflict frame. However, U.S. online news sites did not incorporate prognostic and responsibility issues as often as their international counterparts. Journalists around the world abstained from using value-laden terms such as "aggression" or "invasion" but often incorporated more subtle cues in their visuals and choice of themes.

WAITING FOR WAR

In the beginning of 2003 the topic of war, military build up, and weapons of mass destruction saturated the news cycle (Raspberry, 2003).

Iraq and its program for weapons of mass destruction were discussed widely, both within and outside the United Nations. On March 17, 2003, Bush presented Saddam Hussein with an ultimatum: Saddam must give up power and leave Iraq or the United States would use military force to achieve a regime change. Saddam Hussein had forty-eight hours to comply with the ultimatum. Hussein chose to stay in Iraq, and the "coalition of the willing" decided to enforce UN Resolution 1441 (Balz & Allen, 2003). With that, the forty-nine-day war began.

Even though the world press was awaiting Bush's reaction on March 19, 2003, as the ultimatum expired, they were not expecting the war to begin as quickly as it did. The press would later report that the war began days earlier than planned because U.S. Central Command (CENTCOM) wanted to seize a "target of opportunity," which contained intelligence of Hussein's whereabouts (Gellman & Priest, 2003).

Yet it was fascinating to observe how the leading international news Web sites responded almost immediately with substantial coverage of the Bush announcement. One of the central questions addressed in this study was not only how quickly this coverage happened, but also how the Iraq War was framed in relation to national policy stances.

How Media Frame War

News media play an important role in framing public issues or events. Framing theory posits that media transfer the salience of specific attributes to issues or events.

While there is no one universal definition of framing, several common key elements are evident. Gamson (1992) defines framing as "the central organizing idea or story line that provides meaning to an unfolding strip of events" (p. 15). According to Entman (1993, p. 52), "to frame means to select some aspects of perceived reality and make them more salient" in the media text. For instance, in the case of war, the media can frame the event as an invasion versus attack, or suggest a positive versus negative attitude toward the war.

Framing is visible through the choice of actors and themes present in the media coverage. Past research shows dominant frames for war coverage to be the conflict frame and the responsibility frame. One of the few studies examining the coverage of the 2003 war in Iraq was conducted by Media Tenor (2003). The study found differences between the TV networks in five countries: the Czech Republic, Germany, Great Britain, South Africa, and the USA. For example, the BBC often reported problems with journalists' working conditions, whereas American TV did not concentrate on this as a big problem. The study also observed that American TV news rarely showed dead or wounded members of the Allied forces. The opposite was true for dead, wounded, or missing Iraqis.

Studies of the coverage of the 1991 Gulf War also provide interesting background of how media cover military conflict. Kanjirathinkal and Hickey (1992), for example, have identified four stages in the mythical drama of the first Gulf War: (1) hero's quest; (2) the encounter with evil; (3) fulfillment of the mission; and (4) return.

Kelman (1995) criticized public discourse during the 1991 Gulf War, noting the framing of self-glorification, neglect for the human costs of the war, and the call for rallying around the flag as things to avoid when framing the issue for the American public.

In a study of the coverage of the first Gulf War, Kaid, et al. (1993) found that there were substantial differences in themes chosen by five leading international newspapers from France, Germany, Great Britain, Japan, and the United States. They also found that the papers tended to focus on different actors and settings, thus localizing the event and making war a "national" story.

SIGNIFICANCE OF INTERNET COVERAGE

The Internet became a critical information source during the Iraq War.

According to Pew Internet and American Life Project data, the number of online users significantly increased right before the war (2003). In fact, 77% of U.S. Internet users went online in relation to the war, and more than half of the American online population visited a Web site specifically to get information about the war in Iraq.

Researchers have been taking note of how people use the Internet to gather information and news (Flanagin & Metzger, 2001) and how newspapers use the Internet to disseminate the news they report (Dibean & Garrison, 2001). Research findings suggest that people use the Internet to further their existing interests; with regard to news, people are looking for more information about a topic that they are already interested in. In the case of a major conflict such as war, many people are likely to turn to the online news environment as a supplement to traditional media.

As the Internet has become a more accessible information source, studies on the effectiveness and use of online newspapers, magazines, and television news Web sites have increased. Such studies review the work of journalists (Deuze, 1998), the use of the Internet for information gathering (Garrison, 2000, 2001), and coverage of national news events (Dimitrova et al., 2003), as well as online staffing and reporting (Singer, 2001; Singer et al., 1999). Such research provides insights into how online newsrooms operate and cover major news events.

STUDYING THE WEB COVERAGE OF THE WAR

The Iraq War was, without question, a major news event internationally. The research reported here was designed to explore the characteristics of international online news site homepages in the aftermath of Mr. Bush's war announcement. We focused on the question of how the event was framed around the globe and how the war was justified.

To answer these questions, a content analysis of leading international online newspapers was conducted. The list of online news Web sites included the following: BBC (*http://www.bccnews.co.uk*), CNN (*http://www.cnn.com*), *The*

New York Times on the Web (*http://www.nytimes.com*), *The Washington Post* (*http://www.washingtonpost.com*), France's *Le Monde* (*http://www.lemonde.fr*), Spain's *El Pais* (*http://www.elpais.es*), Argentina's *Clarin* (*http://www.clarin.com*), Brazil's *Globo* (*http://www.globo.com*), Egypt's *Al-Ahram* (*http://www.ahram.org.eg/weekly*), Turkey's *Aksam* (*http://www.aksam.com.tr*), Russia's *Izvestia* (*http://www.izvestia.ru/*), as well as the Web sites of the major U.S. television networks.

The sample of international Web news sites chosen was based on the national reputation of the news publications and their availability online. The goal was to represent news sources from the countries most involved in the Iraqi conflict. We collected a total of 185 Web sites from forty-three countries in the hours immediately after President Bush's speech.

We analyzed the content of the home pages of all Web sites. The coding categories included pre-defined frames based on Li, et al. (2002) and Semetko and Valkenburg (1999). Web sites were coded by trained coders who were fluent in the language of the site, and intercoder reliability averaged +.88 across all categories, using the formula developed by Holsti (1969).

Characteristics of Immediate Web Coverage

Using the potential of the Internet, the majority of the online news sites offered substantial coverage of the Iraq War just hours after the Bush announcement.

Specifically, 119 of the 195 Web sites had war-related coverage on their home pages. Of those 119 Web sites, 56% had a "breaking news" or "latest developments" section regarding the war. The Iraq War was by far the leading story across all news sites. Many of the international sites provided links to additional coverage related to Iraq and the war build up. Special sections about the conflict in Iraq were common across all Web sites.

Even though "Operation Iraqi Freedom" was the leading story around the world only hours after the war began, we expected to find some differences in the way the war was framed, especially since the prior debates about possible war were highly controversial.

First, we examined whether six pre-defined frames were present in the news coverage (see Table 23.1). The most common frame in the world coverage overall was the military conflict frame (94%). Reports on the troops, military strategies, types of military equipment, and future attacks were common. The agenda-setter for the U.S. media—*The New York Times*—provided an interactive map of Iraq on its Web site, with additional coverage of the air raid and military analysis of the strike. The second most common frame was the human interest frame (74%). Human interest themes focusing on the families of U.S. soldiers as well as stories about the lives of ordinary Iraqis were quite common. The BBC, for example,

TABLE 23.1 WEB SITE FRAMING OF THE IRAQ WAR

Frame	Present across all news Web sites	U.S. Web sites	International Web sites
Military conflict*	94	96	86
Human interest	74	79	68
Diagnostic frame	33	33	32
Media self-reference**	25	35	11
Responsibility frame**	22	15	36
Prognostic frame*	16	11	26

a. N=119; Numbers in table are percentages.
b. * and ** indicate statistically significant differences between international and U.S. news Web sites at the .05 and .01 level respectively, using chi-square comparisons.

had an interactive essay about the plight of Iraqi civilians on their home page. Many of the U.S. online sites had stories about the lives of U.S. soldiers.

A distant third was the diagnostic frame (33%), which basically discusses the reasons why the conflict occurred. Our findings showed that deep analytical coverage of the roots of the conflict was rare. The media self-referential frame was present in a quarter of the home pages (25%), followed by the responsibility frame (22%), and the prognostic frame (16%). Early reports on the Iraq War failed to provide forecasts for the future development of the conflict.

What was the dominant reference to the event in this immediate online coverage? Was it an attack, an invasion, a military action, "Gulf War II," or "Operation Iraqi Freedom"? Different news sources used a mix of these terms, not only during the initial hours of the coverage, but also throughout the entire war effort.

Most reporters, however, referred to the event as an attack or strike (59%). Less than a quarter of the home pages labeled it a war (23%). Journalists around the world tried to remain objective and use non-value-laden terms to describe the attack during the initial hours. Terms such as invasion and aggression were the exception rather than the rule.

We also examined whether the major reasons given for the war were different domestically or internationally. By far, the removal of Saddam Hussein/regime change was the dominant reason across the sample publications

(64%). (In a way, the justification to attack Iraq was personified by Saddam.) The second most common reason was weapons of mass destruction, which was dominant in 31% of the Web sites. Despite prolonged discussions at the UN about weapons of mass destruction, this was not portrayed as a dominant reason for the war. There were few references to American world domination or oil as main reasons.

We asked who was to blame for the attack by offering different individuals, countries, and groups as possible answers. Blame for the attack was attributed to the U.S. in 61% of the cases. Even though the United States was part of the "coalition of the willing" participating in the war, most reports attributed blame for the war directly to the United States. No blame was assigned in this initial coverage in 19% of the Web sites. Interestingly, almost 11% of the homepages pointed fingers at President Bush as personally responsible for the attack.

Of the six major frames described above, two were similar and four were different when comparing domestic and international Web sites. The U.S. Web news sites emphasized more the military conflict frame and the media self-referential frame. Media covering itself—the difficulties journalists faced in reporting on this story, for instance—were common for the U.S. news sites.

Non-U.S. Web sites, however, emphasized the responsibility frame. For example, *Le Monde* blamed the United States for the failure of diplomatic efforts in the conflict. The French online newspaper cited the Iraqi leader as saying on television that this attack was a "crime against humanity." It was also interesting to observe that international Web sites had more stories about the long-term effects of the conflict, discussing such issues as the rebuilding of Iraq and the future of the region as a whole.

Each national news site also had more extensive news coverage of their own involvement in the war efforts. As might be expected, local political figures and other national actors were mentioned. For instance, the Turkish online newspaper had more extensive discussion of the controversy regarding giving airspace to the coalition forces. This topic was not present in most of the other news sites.

Another noteworthy characteristic of the Web coverage of the Iraqi War was the use of photos to frame the event visually. Several Web sites used images of Bush and Saddam literally facing off against each other, which implies a personal type of battle, instead of one between two countries. Also, many of the Web sites in our sample quickly uploaded photos of Baghdad city, shots of Iraq being bombed, and of U.S. military carriers launching missiles.

This emphasis on the actual weapons and explosions is somewhat noteworthy, as it focuses on the actual violence and military conflict, literally, exploding. Strangely, the *China Daily* used a file photo from the 1999 U.S. bombing of Yugoslavia. Most Web sites, however, had either live pictures from the bombing or mug shots of Bush or other political figures.

In the aftermath of the military conflict, it became obvious that the media—and the Internet in particular—had a tremendous impact on world opinion about the Iraq War. A subsequent poll conducted by Pew examined global attitudes and revealed clear divisions among the publics in different countries (Pew Charitable Trusts, 2003). For example, when asked if the use of military force against countries that threaten your own country is justified, the vast majority of the Palestinian and Lebanese public said it is never justified (57% and 65%, respectively).

Many countries in the Arab world and elsewhere also blamed the United States and its allies for not trying hard enough to prevent civilian casualties in Iraq (79% in Brazil, 74% in France, 52% in Germany, 67% in Italy, 72% in Russia, 88% in Turkey, 74% in South Korea, 83% in Indonesia, 81% in Nigeria, 91% in Morocco). Even among the coalition of the willing, the survey shows some doubt that the attack on Iraq was justified.

The majority opinion in Spain showed regrets about the decision to go to war (62% say the country made the wrong decision) with 37% of Australians feeling the same way. The differences in world opinion about the war and its consequences may be at least partly attributable to the differences in the local news coverage of the Iraq war. The differences in framing, in particular, are likely to have contributed to such diverse attitudes around the globe.

CONCLUSION

The conflict frame and the human interest frame dominated the international Web news coverage immediately after the war began.

Our analysis also shows that there were some important differences in the framing of the Iraq War between American and international online news sites. We found that U.S. Web sites had a stronger conflict and media self-referential focus. On the other hand, the responsibility frame and the prognostic frame were more common in the coverage of foreign Web sites.

This study is limited because it focused on the immediate coverage of the Iraq War. Future research should encompass a longer time frame and examine whether the frames emerging in the early coverage remain the same over time. Also, comparison with the online coverage of other breaking news events would be important.

REFERENCES

Balz, D., & Allen, M. (2003, March 19). U.S. names 30 countries supporting war effort. *The Washington Post,* A01.

Deuze, M. (1998). The WebCommunicators: Issues in research into online journalism and journalists. *First Monday, 3*(12). Accessed Sept. 15, 2003, online:

http://www.firstmonday.dk/issues/issue3_12/deuze/

Dibean, W., & Garrison, B. (2001). How six online newspapers use Web technologies. *Newspaper Research Journal, 22*(2) 79-83.

Dimitrova, D. V., Connolly-Ahern, C., Williams, A.P., Kaid L.L., & Reid, A. (2003). Hyperlinking as gatekeeping: Online newspaper coverage of the execution of an American terrorist. *Journalism Studies, 4*(3) 403-414.

Entman, R. (1991). Framing U.S. coverage of international news: Contrasts in narratives of the KAL and Iran air accidents. *Journal of Communication, 41* (4), 6-27.

Entman, R. (1993). Framing: toward a clarification of a fractured paradigm. *Journal of Communication. 43* (4), 51-58.

Flanagin, A. J., & Metzger, M. J. (2001). Internet use in the contemporary media environment. *Human Communication Research, 27*(1) 153-181.

Gamson, W. A. (1992). Talking politics. New York: Cambridge University Press.

Garrison, B. (2000). Journalists' perceptions of online information-gathering problems. *Journalism & Mass Communication Quarterly, 77* (3), 500-514.

Garrison, B. (2001). Computer-assisted reporting near complete adoption. *Newspaper Research Journal, 22* (1), 65-79.

Gellman, B., & Preist, D. (2003, March 20). CIA had fix on Hussein; Intelligence revealed 'target of opportunity." *The Washington Post,* A01.

Kaid, L.L., H, B., Ballotti, J., and Wawrzyniak, M. (1993). *Telling the Gulf War story: Coverage in five papers. Desert Storm and the Mass Media,* Greener, B. and Gantz, W. (Eds.). pp. 86-98. Creskill, NJ: Hampton Press.

Kanjirathinkal, M., & Hickey, J. V. (1992). Media framing and myth: The media's portrayal of the Gulf War. *Critical Sociology, 19* (1), 103-112.

Kelman, H. C. (1995). Decision making and public discourse in the Gulf War: An assessment of underlying psychological and moral assumptions. *Peace & Conflict, 1*(2), 117-130.

Holsti, O.R. (1969). *Content Analysis for the Social Sciences and Humanities.* New York: Longman.

Li, X., Lindsay, L.F., Mogensen, K. (2002). Media in a crisis situation involving national interest: A content analysis of the TV networks coverage of the 9/11 incident during the first eight hours. Paper presented to the annual convention of the American Educators and Journalists in Mass Communication, Miami, FL.

Media Tenor. (2003). Media Tenor's international news monitor. Accessed November 5, 2003, from http://www.mediatenor.com/index1.html

Pew Charitable Trusts. (2003). Global attitudes. [Online] Accessed September 15, 2003, at http://www.pewtrusts.org

Pew Internet and American Life Project. (2003). The Internet and the Iraq war: How online Americans have used the Internet to learn war news, understand events, and promote their views. Accessed September 15, 2003, online: www.pewinternet.org;reports/pdfs/PIP_Iraq_War_Report.pdf

Raspberry, W. (2003, January 6). Congress's rollover on war. *The Washington Post* A15. Accessed September 15, 2003, online:www.washingtonpost.com/wp-dyn/opinion/columns/raspberrywilliam/

Semetko, H.A., & Valkenburg, P.M. (1999). Framing European politics: a content analysis of press and television news. *Journal of Communication,49*(50), 93-109.

Singer, J. (2001). The Metro Wide Web: Changes In Newspaper's Gatekeeping Role

Online. *Journalism & Mass Communication Quarterly, 78*(1), 65-72.

Singer, J., Tharp, M.P., & Haruta, A. (1999). Online staffers: Superstars or second-class citizens? *Newspaper Research Journal, 20*(3), 29 48.

Thussu, D. K. (2002). Managing the Media in an Era of Round-the-Clock News: notes from India's first tele-war. *Journalism Studies, 3*(2), 203-212.

CHAPTER 24

Digital Deconstruction: Indymedia as a Process of Collective Critique

Lisa Brooten

> "The directors governing media conglomerates also sit on the boards of the military weapons manufacturers and all of the other industries in an interlocking directorate of power. So it is not really accurate or enough to just say, 'the corporate media is biased.' In point of fact, the corporate media IS the war, is the military, is the destruction of the environment, is the gentrification of our cities, is the criminalization of the poor and non-Aryan and foreign-born ... it is everything that we loathe about this society."—Quote from the San Francisco Indymedia site, March 2003

This chapter examines how the Independent Media Center (IMC) targets mainstream media for public scrutiny by promoting a collective, public process of critique. Instead of seeing mainstream media as government watchdogs, the IMC suggests that corporate media need watchdogs themselves, and, more importantly, that this role can now be decentralized and put into the hands of millions of media-savvy citizens.

In addition, the global nature of the IMC engages individual participants with other people from around the world. In the context of the 2003 Iraq War, IMC features and discussions created a rhetorical binary between the United States and the rest of the world, promoting a process of public introspection on the part of IMC participants in the United States.

This process provoked two very different forms of response: isolationism and apologetic engagement. The apologetics centered on the inadequacy of mainstream media to provide the information necessary for the U.S. polity to become responsible world citizens.

Development of an Independent Media Network

The Independent Media Center (IMC), often referred to as Indymedia, began as a coordinating mechanism for independent media groups that wanted to provide alternatives to mainstream media coverage of the protests against the World Trade Organization (WTO) in Seattle in November 1999.

Since that time, the IMC has grown to include more than 120 local chapters worldwide and describes itself as "a network of collectively run media outlets for the creation of radical, accurate, and passionate tellings of the truth." IMC chapters have been formed on every continent, and organization of new local chapters is ongoing.

As members of this decentralized network, each local IMC collective has control over its own mission statement, finances, and decision-making processes. The thousands who work with and post onto the IMC Web sites around the world are volunteers who receive no financial compensation.[1] IMC's global Web site (*http://www.indymedia.org*) offers feature stories culled from local IMC Web sites worldwide, each linked to the global site. According to the global Web site, the Indymedia network as a whole receives an estimated 500,000 to 2 million hits a day, depending on what is occurring worldwide at the time. During the first few days of the Iraq war in March 2003, some local IMC sites (such as IMC Italy) were receiving about half a million page hits a day.

The Independent Media Center network challenges the structures of corporate media by encouraging people to "be the media" by participating in an open publishing system. In open publishing, the process of creating news is transparent to the readers, who can contribute a story and see it instantly appear in the pool of stories publicly available. Those stories are filtered as little as possible to help the readers find the stories they want. Readers can see editorial decisions being made by others, and can see how to get involved and help make these decisions (Arnison, 2001).

This chapter assesses whether those using the Independent Media Center Web sites are practicing a rhetorical strategy that supports their goals of media transparency and personal involvement with media production. A critical focus on media practices and how they are discussed will help to clarify how those who use the IMC understand the role of the media and their own involvement with it.

To understand the functions the IMC global Web site serves for those who use it, a subset of the features on the site, the links within these features, and the discussion threads that follow them were analyzed from February through May, 2003. This time frame includes analysis of the features and discussions during the build up to the U.S. invasion of Iraq, the conflict itself, and its immediate aftermath.

The focus is on those specific stories and discussions that deal with the coverage of the war by mainstream or corporate media. While the essay concentrates on content originating on IMC Web sites, some of the stories published on other Web sites and linked to IMC features are summarized. The various ways IMC writers represent themselves, those with views opposing their own, mainstream media coverage, and the IMC were also examined. An analysis of these texts revealed clusters of ideas that shed light on how those people writing for and responding to IMC perceive the practices of the corporate media and the effectiveness of IMC's challenge to it.

THE CHALLENGE: "BE THE MEDIA"

> To all those who complain about IMC content, remember that IMC is you. Don't complain, get off your asses and participate.—A post to a discussion of the state of journalism on the global site, April 2003.

Most of the local IMC sites included a main column running down the center of the page with a set of feature articles, a set of links to all the other IMC Web sites running down the left side of the page, and a column on the right featuring the open publishing newswire, where anyone with a computer and Internet access could post information. Features on the global site were drawn primarily from the different local sites, usually consisting of a short summary text with a series of links to a longer feature and to sources of information related to the topic at hand. Each feature ended with the option to "add your own comment," and often this discussion section is the lengthiest part of the final mediated text.[2]

By encouraging people to "be the media" by offering an open access newswire and the opportunity to react publicly to any article, IMC challenges the traditional relationship between media producer and consumer and promotes media literacy. It also challenges traditional approaches to journalism and "objectivity," and offers a forum for first-hand and eyewitness accounts of events by those not formally trained in journalistic practices.

Because there is no attempt to control the process of message production on the newswire or in discussions after features, the IMC does not profess to be objective. In fact, the global Indymedia information page suggests that there is no such thing as objective journalism—that all reporters have their own biases. A page on the IMC global site devoted to frequently asked questions suggests to readers that "You should look at all reports you read on the Indymedia site with a critical eye, just as you should look at all media before you in a discerning manner." This role as a promoter of careful reading, analysis, and judgment and as an outlet for the expression of critique—whether it be against the corporate media or the IMC—is perhaps the most significant contribution IMC makes to the development of media savvy reader/producers.

The collective process of media critique promoted by the interactive uses of IMC content parallels the "ideological turn" in communication studies, in that the IMC challenge to "be the media" challenges the concept of objectivity and encourages a critical approach to media consumption. This approach, within the IMC as well as within communication studies, values the search for alternatives to "the existence of powerful vested interests benefitting from and consistently urging policies and technology that threaten life on this planet" (Wander, 1983, p. 18). In doing so, the IMC and communication scholars have similarly argued that "objectivity" as a concept is as ideologically driven as the work it critiques (Crowley, 1992).

The search for alternatives, then, begins with an understanding of what these alternatives would be opposing, which in the rhetoric of the IMC is clearly defined as corporate media.

THE CORPORATE MEDIA MACHINE

Mainstream or corporate media is a central concept in the ideology of the IMC, for it is in defining its nemesis that the IMC defines itself.

"Corporate media," represented as the cornerstone of the military-industrial-media complex, is most often contrasted with independent media, or media not owned or controlled by government or corporate interests. The corporate media are "cheerleaders for the war" that "control the people" through "lies" emerging from the "military mouthpiece" that they have become. They are "tools for those in power," "echo chambers" for "the 'decision-makers' running the world who refuse openness to our scrutiny."

Corporate media are profit-driven to expand their networks and increase their ratings. They seek shows that "look good" but often cross the line between news reporting and news creation. Corporate media are at times labeled "right wing media" by people posting to IMC, especially during discussions after IMC feature stories, when the construction of a right wing/left wing political binary becomes most pronounced.

Corporate media are described on IMC posts in contrast to an ideal media system, which would be "responsible" in reporting "the history of this conflict and other interests involved." The ideal media would present "a wide range of views from a wide range of sources," and practice "impartial journalism" with an "even-handed, respectful" debate that would be "ethical" and "actually refreshing."

INDYMEDIA

In contrast to corporate media, the IMC is defined in these features and discussions as a decentralized, transparent system of information sharing.

When a writer was criticized for something left out of a story, discussion participants urged the critic to post an alternative, or add more information to further the discussion. When the need for "objectivity" was raised, other participants retorted that "all media are biased" and that the answer was to read many views on an issue before coming to conclusions. The degree to which multiple perspectives were considered became a way to judge the value of a news source, as this participant argued:

> The European and Asian press has voluntarily and repeatedly aired unedited statements from American military and political officials as well as Iraqis and other national/global figures. They have also aired footage from journalists in Iraq who are both affiliated and unaffiliated (explicitly at least) with a particular nation, military, or cause. The U.S. media [air] only [their] own footage and [feature] commentary from only a limited range of public figures.[3]

The IMC's dominant ideology challenges free-market capitalism and encourages critical assessment of mainstream media as capitalism's lapdog. In doing so, the IMC creates a new marginalized group within the confines of its Web sites, yet incorporates their discourse of rebuttal (vocalizing society's dominant ideology) in ways that, in fact, support the IMC's dominant ideology.

By promoting the idea that mainstream media do not tackle difficult issues, those who promote the IMC's dominant anti-war, anti-free market ideology can represent those who oppose it as "uninformed," "ignorant," "sad brainwashed pinhead Bush lackeys," who raise their "sarcastic, patriotic, cynical, pro-war voices" and are accused of seeming "more at home in a totalitarian society by the manner of [their] diatribes." Those opposed to the dominant IMC ideology are often labeled "right wing nuts" who support "an artificial, unsustainable mass-consumption lifestyle of SUVs and endless suburbs," that will require that "our children and grandchildren deal with the mess."

By defining their political foes in these terms, those who promote the dominant IMC ideology can identify themselves as "true Americans" who "do not sit still while being spoon-fed information," but instead see the development of media savvy as a responsibility.

> If you sort through the information given by both sides, remove any bias, check all the facts, and divorce yourself from what you want to believe, you can come up with an opinion that is uniquely your own. This is the responsibility of any American, or indeed any world citizen....Only when all Americans do this can we truly say that our government is ours. Until then, we are owned by our government.[4]

Critics argue that IMC's "left-wing, anti-American" stance resulted in "totally absurd and sometimes criminally flawed reporting of the war by its opposers." One writer argued, "You people ... you are all like a disease that keeps infecting other helpless people," while another states that "this Web site is a rag ... the Fox News of the left."

Those who opposed the dominant IMC ideology label other IMC contributors "moonbats" and "liberal pathetic wankers" with "brilliant conspiracy theories," urging them to "be part of the solution not the problem, like you freaking parasites." They also argued that writers to IMC "deserve a medal for stupidity" for "opinions based on pure emotion, a few half-digested Noam Chomsky books, and very little substance." Perhaps most telling, IMCers were also labeled as people who did not "live in the real world" but instead promoted "high-minded collectivist ideals, [a] tone of moral superiority, [and] condescending attitudes toward anyone not goose-stepping to your lefty agenda."

What is at stake here is how the "real world" is represented in the media, by whom, and for what purposes. By challenging the practices of corporate media, Indymedia acts as a training ground for those who challenge either the mainstream media or the IMC itself through their own writings. It has also become a source of alternative information for people around the world who have become disillusioned with corporate media news coverage.[5]

INDYMEDIA CONTENT

Indymedia offers readers both an alternative source of information and a means to critique that information, add to it, or reject it.

By encouraging first-hand accounts posted by readers, the IMC promotes a respect for story and interpretation that challenges traditional approaches to "objective" journalism. The capacity to link to other sources of information also makes the IMC an especially potent tool for identifying patterns of events: activities of protestors, responses by the authorities, and coverage of these events by corporate media. IMCers have developed their own collective media critiques that resemble the media's traditional watchdog function.

This chapter will demonstrate that the Indymedia has become a watchdog of the corporate media.

Indymedia reports often focused on issues writers felt were not being adequately covered by corporate media. One key focus of Indymedia's global features in the lead up to and during the war was the attempt to address what many activists claimed was an under-reporting by corporate media of the size and impact of anti-war protests around the world. The focus on protest coverage was prominent in January and February, before the attack began, especially after the February 15, 2003, global day of protest against an impending war.

Reports of protests were accompanied by lengthy lists of links to on-site, first-hand accounts from around the world, often accompanied by photographs and by differing crowd estimates by both organizers and local police. Surfing these links provides an unparalleled view of the extent of opposition to the war worldwide.

Another central focus of Indymedia texts, especially after the bombing of Iraq began, was how corporate media coverage differed from what alternative reports were conveying about the situation on the ground in Iraq. Indymedia offered numerous links to other media sources, including Al-Jazeera, but relied primarily on first-hand accounts provided by independent reporters, activists, and others in Iraq. This was true even before the attack began.

Once the United States began bombing Iraq in March, the IMC openly contrasted eyewitness accounts of the violent consequences of the bombing for Iraqi people with reports by the corporate media's "embedded reporters." Indymedia reports in February, March, and April included many first-hand accounts in e-mails and diaries sent home (to places around the world) by eyewitnesses in Iraq, including, as one report put it, "independent information agents, freelance reporters ... human shields and some Baghdad inhabitants who work with them."

The IMC also invited readers to post links to other alternative news sources, and so became a hub with links to articles from both independent and commercial sources, advocacy groups, peace coalitions, and independent observers.

The shaping of public opinion was also a focus of Indymedia coverage, which questioned "the line between news reporting and news creation in the corporate media." A link in an IMC feature story in March questioned the accuracy of opinion polls and presented a critique of misleading headlines that the author argued were derived from inaccurate interpretation of public opinion polls measuring support for the war among U.S. citizens. An IMC feature in February reported that editors of *The Wall Street Journal*'s European edition had solicited from leaders of several European nations a letter of support for Bush's plans for an imminent attack on Iraq, a letter that then appeared on the paper's editorial page.

After its publication, the op-ed became "news," appearing in WSJ's news pages, in *The New York Times* and other corporate media. The IMC story featured a link to *The Wall Street Journal*'s "brash defense" of this practice, in which they indicate that such solicitation is a regular practice by mainstream U.S. papers. While this may be the case, it becomes clear from reading the comments in the discussion after the IMC article that if this was a regular practice, it was not common knowledge to many of those who read the story.

Discussions like this made IMC more than just an alternative source of information. The IMC network also became a tool for exploring the process of media representation itself. This is clear when the IMC investigated alleged misconduct or dangerous carelessness by corporate media, and the relationship between corporate media and the military, government, and industrial elite. In some of these stories and the comments that follow them, mainstream media and the U.S. government were represented as interchangeable, especially when mainstream coverage looked suspiciously staged.

A May 23 global IMC feature entitled "Corporate Media Promoted Phony Stories in Iraq" provided a series of links to exposés of what the writer called "bogus news stories" such as "the staged toppling of Saddam's statue," and the allegedly staged rescue of Private Lynch as reported by the BBC. The BBC article, "Saving Private Lynch Story Flawed," described the episode as "*one of the most stunning pieces of news management ever conceived*" in which "the American strategy was to ensure the right television footage by using embedded reporters and images from their own cameras, *editing the film themselves* [italics added]."

IMC made possible a collective process of visual image analysis that was especially popular. A May 23 IMC feature, for example, included a link to a story in which the writer challenged a comment he reportedly heard from Diane Sawyer, comparing the fall of Saddam's statue with the fall of the Berlin Wall. "The entire event is being hailed as an equivalent of the Berlin Wall falling ... the long-shot photo shows something more akin to a carefully constructed media event tailored for the television cameras."

This writer, who chose to use the name "against occupation," used visual imagery to suggest the event was carefully staged. He juxtaposed several pictures he says he "grabbed off of Reuters" to show the fall of the statue alongside a text describing the involvement of Ahmed Chalabi and his group, the "pro-American" Free Iraqi Forces Militia, reportedly flown into Iraq by the U.S. Pentagon three days prior to the fall of Saddam's statue. The author claimed these militiamen made up the bulk of the "crowd" that cheered the toppling of the statue in Baghdad, an event he argued was overblown by mainstream media coverage.

To support his argument, he posted several photos for discussion. He compared two shots, claiming both showed the same man: one photo of a group of Chalabi's militiamen who arrived in Baghdad on April 6, with one of the men circled for identification, and another photo of an Iraqi cheering at the fall of Saddam's statue on April 9 who resembled the identified militiaman.

In a long shot of Fardus Square in Baghdad where this event took place, the photo was circled in four places to show where a U.S. mechanized vehicle pulled down the statue with a cable and three U.S. tanks surrounded the square. This long shot showed a small crowd of people. "The toppling of the statue was promoted as a massive uprising ... does this event look massive to you?" the author asked.

This story produced a lengthy discussion, with people analyzing and debating the meanings of the images. Some people questioned aspects of the story itself, others argued that the long shot was too blurry and distant to be decipherable. Others posted more shots of the event, analyzed them, and were challenged in turn. The central issues became the number of people who actually attended, and the ways the media were framing the event. Despite the inconclusive nature of a debate about the honesty of how this event was framed in mainstream media coverage, the critiques presented by participants were themselves a form of collective criticism that called for a more sophisticated engagement with media than is the case with less interactive media.

IMC also promotes public activism against questionable media practices. A link from a May 2003 global feature reported the doctoring of a front page photograph that appeared in London's *Evening Standard* on April 9, 2003, showing cheering Iraqis ostensibly welcoming the U.S. and U.K. troops. The writer posted a scan of the cover photograph and then systematically showed how it had been doctored by placing two or more photographs together to create what seems like a large crowd.

In the discussion that followed, others added to the analysis, some reproducing the photograph highlighted with additional circles and lines to point out specific people and patterns repeated within the photograph. Someone called the *Evening Standard* and reported, "a picture editor [there] ... said he was 'aware' of the picture and that it 'had been a mistake.'

"When I asked him how a mistake like this could happen, he put the phone down on me." This person then reportedly complained to the press commission and provided the commission's Web site address in their post to the IMC, encouraging others to contact them as well. Posts following this one indicated that other people did call the paper and file complaints. Another person copied his letter of complaint about this case to the Press Complaints Commission (PCC) onto the discussion page, and later the reply from the PCC requesting further information.

Someone else later posted an article from *The Guardian* that reported the accusations and the response by the *Evening Standard*, which defended its photograph by claiming that it "grabbed" the photo from video provided by the BBC, removed the BBC's logo and, using a "standard practice," replaced the removed logo with a bit of repeated background image. In the remaining comments, the credibility of both papers was questioned by several discussants, who argued that those who wish to should "just keep swallowing the pap the media and government throws at you like good little sheep."

While there were a few who defended the papers and made derogatory comments about those making accusations, the majority of the discussion participants either expressed surprise and anger, or denied surprise at such media practices. As one summed it up, "More important than catching the particulars, is developing a complete distrust of corporate media amongst our fellow humans." It was the misleading nature of corporate media, they argued, that had created such a schism between the U.S. and the rest of the world.

The U.S. vs. "The Rest"

By comparing U.S. and European coverage of the war, the IMC promotes critical examination of the U.S. self-image.

When discussing mainstream media texts produced before or during the war, the rhetoric in IMC posts often create a binary between U.S. vs. European media or U.S. vs. the rest of the world's media. In these cases, U.S. media is represented as providing coverage of the war that focuses on its mechanics and hardware rather than its human costs. U.S. media is represented as practicing deception by failing to present its audiences with any real alternatives to the war before it began.

One writer argues that the lack of contrary opinions in U.S. media is comparable to "the lack of opposing opinions in Nazi German media." U.S. media "no longer represents a diverse set of views," but overwhelmingly represents the United States as "heroic and triumphant" in the aftermath of the bombing. IMC features and many of the comments that follow them suggest that for this act of "hubris," and for its reported deception of viewers around the world, U.S. media's credibility has suffered in Europe and elsewhere.

Indymedia focused a good deal of attention on coverage in European media that was more critical than mainstream U.S. media of both the war and of the United States. A March 19 feature on the IMC global site, for example, provided a link to a Washington, D.C. Indymedia story quoting veteran BBC war reporter Kate Adie. The story discussed a report by Ms. Adie, entitled "Pentagon threatens to kill independent reporters in Iraq," which quoted a Pentagon official discussing the possible bombing of the satellite uplink positions of independent journalists in Iraq. Ms. Adie was quoted as saying that the Pentagon's attitude was "entirely hostile to the free spread of information."

A link from another IMC global feature on March 25, titled "Resistance Continues Despite Media Blackout," leads to an article on the Web site of the politically progressive news service, Common Dreams.[7] The article, "TV Avoids Showing Deadly Side of War," was originally printed in the *Toronto Star*, and focuses on the lack of corpses in U.S. corporate media coverage of the war. The February 11 feature mentioned earlier (that questions the WSJ's practices in engineering an editorial in its European edition) includes a link to a British critique of U.S. newspapers on an anti-war Web site.[8] This critique includes a discussion of the U.S. media's tendency to expect and rely solely on hard facts:

> In its reliance on "hard news," the American media makes itself an easy target for government manipulation. A plethora of data, coupled with a dearth of critical analysis, make for reports that are essentially devoid of meaning or other nutritional value : in other words, McNews.[9]

In a firsthand account linked to an April IMC global feature entitled "Journalism Under Siege," a writer using the name Randy Repost compared the U.S. and European coverage he had seen of the war from where he lived in Granada. This writer presented some interesting perspectives on the differences between U.S., Spanish, French, and British television news, and provoked a lengthy discussion. The author used many examples to make the point that European media's framing of events leading up to the war made it astonishing to Europeans that the U.S. self-perception was one of heroism and victory. He summed up:

> In the eyes of non-American media it took the world's most powerful and wealthiest nation months of planning, the deployment of hundreds of thousands of troops, and the launching of thousands of missiles at a cost of tens of billions of dollars to topple one dictator in a country already crippled by two earlier wars and ten years of international sanctions, defended by a third-rate army almost entirely bereft of advanced armaments who put up no coordinated resistance. Not an impressive feat.[10]

The language used in this firsthand account established a distinct binary between U.S. media (in one sentence identified as U.S. and Israeli media) and their accounts of the war, described as almost entirely military in nature, and the rest of the world's media and their version of events that presented the war "in unrelenting human terms." This "U.S. vs. the rest" binary is associated in this essay with the theme of compassion, or more accurately, the lack of it, in the United States. The American people have become "inured [sic] to human suffering."

The author observed that European broadcasts often juxtaposed headline stories of U.S. military mishaps and civilian deaths with the "typically immodest statements of Rumsfeld that American missiles were 'the most precise ever seen in human history' or that 'everything is going exactly as planned.'" He described the reaction of one Spanish TV commentator he saw, after "a series of unrelenting images of civilian wounded and dead (far more graphic than would ever be allowed in the U.S.)," who "looked directly into the camera, shook his head sadly and mused, "One wonders what type of human being can refer to the death of a child as 'collateral damage.'"

The article described how, during the war, European media critically examined the relationship between U.S. media and the U.S. government. Several focused on the state of the U.S. media after journalist Peter Arnett was fired by NBC for his statements critical of the war to an Arabic satellite channel. The author described "commentary by multiple political and academic figures [that] made it clear that America no longer has a free press in the true meaning of the term." Especially galling to European viewers, he argued, was the prevarication of U.S. officials after American troops fired directly into the hotel housing many of the international journalists in Baghdad, killing an Al-Jazeera reporter. Captured on film, this event was aired on European media, including footage of people screaming and searching the rubble for bodies.

Critical examination of U.S. media, according to Repost, led many European commentators to openly "compare Iraqi and American [media] sources as being equally tendentious and unreliable." In summary, he argued, "the credibility of the American government all but disappeared and that of the American media crumbled." Repost concluded that, by and large, Americans are uninformed because their media provides them with very little valuable information, and no real discussion of foreign policy options. Media elsewhere in the world, he argued, presented several different possible approaches to dealing with the rogue Iraqi regime.

Many Europeans could not understand U.S. aggression and unilateralism, and came to one of two conclusions: either Americans are a violent people, or Americans are largely uneducated about the rest of the world. Repost added a third possibility: that Americans learn virtually nothing about the rest of the world from their media. He related the words of a Spanish man who told him, "I don't believe the polls. I don't think Americans really do support the war, no people can be in favor of war, but they don't really see the war, do they? They just believe what the American media tell them."

This feature elicited a long discussion among people all over the world, including some rabidly anti-American messages, many comments expressing concern with the U.S. image abroad, and a few dismissing the importance of such concerns. Anti-American messages in this discussion represent the people of the U.S. as "opinionated, hyper-arrogant" people who are "forcing their global hegemony down the world's throat." One anti-American post, entitled, "When will Babylon Fall?" argued that the "U.S. is sleeping," while another maintains that "the Americans will eat their lead" since the "real world ... [will] unite against the oppressors." One writer compared the United States to the schoolyard bully who yells that "you'd BETTER like [my propaganda], else I'm gonna call you names and turn everybody else in the playground against you while I steal your lunch money and let my fat ass get fatter."

In response, several people expressed hopes that the rest of the world doesn't judge all U.S. citizens as "scum bags," or too harshly, or as people asleep, or as passive "spectators" rather than participants in life. Others argued that U.S. citizens are unaware because they are offered no real "mainstream media choices" and therefore "don't even realize that their news is being sifted to only show the 'positive' things the government is doing." Questioning the accuracy of opinion polls, one person wrote that those in the United States who support the war do so not out of "bloodthirsty barbarianism," but because, "a huge proportion of the information available does not clearly explain what is happening, and has not for years." As another person wrote:

> I couldn't understand how my American friends could not see my point of view about why the war was/is so tragic ... Now I realize they didn't see the footage of maimed children in hospitals, they didn't see the cameraman wipe the blood off his lens when an interpreter got hit by an American bomb, they probably didn't even see footage of people weeping and howling at the loss of their loved ones. And they probably didn't get much critical commentary about what was happening.[11]

Others represented Americans as limited in their understanding of what's happening globally, as people whose "brains no longer function," or as victims of a media system intending "to blind us with coverage that says Iraq is happy we've come." These and other images suggested a process of decay in the health of the U.S. democracy and its people due directly to the limitations of corporate coverage. Those expressing concerns about the U.S. image abroad encourage readers to seek out information beyond U.S. mainstream media to understand the effects of U.S. policies abroad.

Such concerns, however, were countered by those who argued, in essence, that "most Americans know what the average Swede or Swiss or Frenchman thinks of them as a world citizen and quite frankly does not care.... Why do I have to be some kind of world citizen? I am a citizen of the United States." Several people posting comments in this vein asked, if the United States was so terrible, why do so many foreigners "want to come here to travel or study?" Others evoked a higher judge: "If you wish to complain about America, do so to God, for he has been with us in every war (except Vietnam, our big mistake ...)." Quite a number of people referred to the views expressed in this feature as evidence of "wacko conspiracy theories" and "liberal media crap."

These posts were answered by those who refuse to accept an isolationist stance from U.S. citizens, and argue that "yes, you do have to be a global citizen, because your goods and services are produced by, paid for, or imported from areas all over the globe, and your financial and political decisions (or your complicity in the decisions of others) directly affect the health and well-being of people all over this planet." This person went on to argue that to refuse to acknowledge this global interconnection "is the rough equivalent of showing up at a neighborhood cookout, eating your fill, ignoring everyone present, and pissing in the grill without any willingness to be held accountable."[12]

Summary

In defining itself in opposition to the corporate media machine, IMC attempted to provide alternative views of the war and a transparent process of news reporting that promoted the personal involvement of the reader. How well did the rhetoric of IMC features and discussions promote these goals? The open publishing system does provide a process whereby anyone with Internet access can post a comment or additional information after stories. For those with access, this process did provide a forum for personal involvement, as evidenced by the level of discussion following many of the features.

IMC makes two important contributions to the development of media-savvy readers/writers that become clear in this textual analysis of IMC content. On the one hand, IMC has begun to develop a collective process of mainstream media criticism. That this process is inclusive can be seen to the extent that those practicing critique on the site are not only critiquing mainstream media, but also IMC itself, and that those from all political persuasions are gaining critical skills in the process. This phenomenon of collective media critique is transferring the expectations of transparency beyond the confines of IMC, challenging many of the practices of corporate media directly, and in some cases requiring them to respond to accusations of misconduct.

In addition, the features and discussions encouraged an awareness among U.S. contributors to IMC of their place within a larger world, providing insight into how others elsewhere in the world hold a very different view of them than mainstream U.S. media would have them believe. IMC offers a forum for engagement with the larger world. While some U.S. participants rejected the need to see themselves in the context of this larger picture, a larger number of participants in the IMC discussions laid the blame for this lack of engagement squarely at the feet of the corporate media. In this process, corporate media have become the target of a new public watchdog practice that has highlighted their inability to carry out a function that has served as a traditional cornerstone of media legitimacy.

ENDNOTES

1. The IMC has no central organizing body and no regular source of funding. Donations to the global IMC network fund are distributed in the form of grants or loans to support local collectives through an online global finance group that uses a consensus decision-making process.

2. Each collective determines its own newswire policy, but the general agreement is that anyone can post non-commercial information without being edited. Duplicate and commercial posts are usually the only material removed. Each local chapter also has its own policy regarding how features are posted to the central column of its Web site. In many instances, those who post to the newswire forward their stories to an editorial board at one or many local IMCs, each of which then works on a consensus basis to determine whether or not a submitted story qualifies to be posted as a feature. While the makeup of the editorial team and the process through which they edit and approve stories are determined by each individual IMC collective and therefore vary in terms of their

openness, each local Web site also hosts the unedited, open publishing newswire and a comments section after each feature article.

3. Available at www.nyc.indymedia.org/front.php3?article_id=57339&group=Webcast

4. Ibid.

5. I do not mean to discount the seriousness of the divide between those with and without access to computers and the Internet around the world, but the number of existing IMC chapters in the global South and the fact that new ones continue to form indicate that the IMC is indeed a global phenomenon.

6. Available at http://news.bbc.co.uk/2/hi/programmes/correspondent/3028585.stm

7. Available at http://commondreams.org/views03/0323-01.htm

8. Available at http://www.antiwar.com/orig/deliso67.html

9. Ibid.

10. Available at www.nyc.indymedia.org/front.php3?article_id=57339&group=Webcast

11. Ibid.

12. Ibid.

REFERENCES

Arnison, M. (2001). Open publishing is the same as free software. Retrieved July 22, 2003, from http://www.cat.org.au/maffew/cat/openpub.html

Crowley, S. (1992). Reflections on an argument that won't go away: or, a turn of the ideological screw. *Quarterly Journal of Speech, 78,* 450-465.

Wander, P. (1983). The ideological turn in modern criticism. *Central States Speech Journal, 34,* 1-18.

CHAPTER 25

Iraq War News: Were Young Audiences Bored with the News or the Media?

David Weinstock and Timothy Boudreau

Young people do not find the news as interesting as they once did, studies show. It might be that life is just too good, or that there are too many other diversions, distractions, or pleasures available to them from other sources.

The outbreak of the 2003 Iraq War presented an unusual opportunity to study how and whether young people read/watch/listen/consume news media. It was like a giant TV sweeps week, except the stories and images were international, rather than local or national, and all media—not just TV—were getting more attention than usual. The daily fare was more compelling than usual.

With this increased attention, especially from younger adults who normally are less attentive to news, it was a good time to ask them why they liked or disliked what they saw/heard/read/surfed.

MAINSTREAM MEDIA AUDIENCES SHRINKING

What we know to be true about U.S. mainstream news media—and perhaps wish we didn't—is that their audience sizes are either shrinking, or, at best, holding steady with population growth.

As the new millennium arrived, boredom with news media seemed a general trend. In 2000 the Pew Research Center found the number of persons identified as regular watchers of network TV news had slipped to 30% of the U.S. population, down 8% from six months previously. In 1995, 54% of Americans said they preferred network news programming. Three years later that percentage dipped to 50%, and in 2000, it fell to 45% (Pew Research Center, 2000).

This audience slide is not unique to TV news. From 1945 to 1970, the number of daily newspaper readers steadily increased to about 50% of the U.S. households. From 1970 to the early 1990s, that number did not increase at all.

Then, in 1992, a funny thing happened. National dailies—*The Wall Street Journal, USA Today* and *The New York Times*—experienced circulation growth while regional papers—such as the *Los Angeles Times, New York Daily News,* and the *Chicago Tribune*—saw a circulation slump (LaRose & Straubhaar, 1997).

As it turned out, this was a minor fluctuation in what has been an overall trend of total morning and evening newspaper circulation hovering around 60 million since 1960 (Whelan, 2001).

AGING READERS, VIEWERS POSE ADVERTISING CHALLENGE

Publishers and academics alike take small comfort that the newspaper industry is still profitable, even though circulation growth remains flat.

It should be small comfort, because today's average newspaper reader is forty-four years old and an aging demographic is buoying readership. Soon these Baby Boomers will retire and newspapers will either have to reinvent themselves into a channel that can effectively and profitably service the elderly loyalists, or reinvent itself to reach youth. At best, the former proposition is difficult since most elderly people live on fixed incomes and are an audience unattractive to advertisers, who seek potential customers with buying power.

Future profits in the newspaper industry, and all media for that matter, clearly lie with younger audiences. Currently, the electronic media—TV, radio, and the Internet—do well with youths, though news offerings do not seem much of a lure to these channels.

Perhaps the newspaper industry is the best indicator of this. Newspapers are the closest of all media to being a pure news channel, yet studies in the mid-1990s showed that fewer than 40% of adults under the age of thirty subscribed to a newspaper (Jeffries & Atkins, 1996).

Overall, newspaper readership hasn't changed significantly in the last four decades, making it the world-champion, no-growth industry on a planet whose population and literacy rates are ever-increasing.

That should tell us something.

YOUNG PEOPLE ONLINE BUT ARE THEY SEEKING NEWS THERE?

The only bright spot in news media, according to media analysts, is the Internet. But audience numbers might be deceiving. Make no mistake, young people are online, but news is not what is pulling them there.

According to a February 2003 Gallup Poll taken a month before the Iraq war, teens who were online for five or more hours a week said the major online activities in which they were involved included e-mail (95%), instant messaging (83%), and downloading music (73%). Ninety-six percent said they used the Internet to "find information" (Hanway, 2003). While the category "find information" might very well involve online news, it could also embrace a wide variety of other activities, ranging from homework research, to checking concert schedules for their favorite bands, to seeing what movies are playing in local theaters.

Just as network TV news watchers are a fraction of general TV viewers, so, too, are online news seekers a fraction of all Internet users. Taken another way, news is only a fraction of radio and TV programming and Internet content. More likely, activities such as e-mailing, downloading music, and instant messaging show the most promise for youth-generated profits within the Internet. Indeed, others have recognized this potential, releasing e-mail and instant messaging client software that displays advertising banners above and below e-mail and IM windows.

The Internet music downloading service Kazaa now claims its client package has surpassed ICQ as the most popular file-share in the world, with more than 230.3 million downloads worldwide (*Kazaa.com*, 2003). Its Web site has its share of advertisers, too. News executives know that in the future they must attract young people to build audience numbers.

Young consumers have demonstrated that when they earn money they will spend it; wisely or foolishly, it doesn't matter from a media executive's point of view as long as they spend it on the goods and services advertised in their media. Chances are good young people today will earn even more money than their parents did at the same age. These once-youthful consumers will have homes and spend what money they earn on themselves, their spouses, and their children. Advertising will influence those purchases.

The buying power of mass media's audience follows a progression from young to old. From un-moneyed to moneyed, from having it bought for them to buying it themselves, the progression begins when they are young and continues through life.

Yet newspaper publishers know their forty-four-year-olds, in time, will age to a point where their eyes will not slide so easily over their newsprint, just as TV and radio executives know their eyes and ears won't so easily hear and see the messages brought to them on TV. As a group, they will eventually retire and move from being moneyed to not-so-moneyed and their abilities to purchase advertisers' goods and services, cable, satellite TV, and even newspaper subscriptions will diminish.

But young people have youth on their side. If eighteen-year olds begin to steadily consume news, they will do so for twenty-six more years before they turn forty-four, but in twenty-six years, forty-four-year-olds will be five years past retirement age, with many of them heading toward the media audience bone-yard where elder readers who lack purchasing power go.

It is this progression that drives media's interest in youthful audiences. The more eyes and ears on news programs, newspapers, and Web sites, the easier it is to sell subscriptions and advertising—the twin sources of profits—and the continued programming, posting, and printing of the news product. It's a cycle: more eyes mean more money; more money pays for more media, which, in turn, should attract more eyes. And yet, it is the "more eyes" part that seems problematic, especially more youthful eyes. Young people today do not seem as interested in classically defined "news" as were previous generations. And no one seems to have a clear idea why.

A study by the Pew Center for People and the Press in 2000 noted that news consumption is event-driven and that half of those who watch news programs tune in only to get news about significant or important events like wars and disasters, especially if the news affects them. That finding was supported by research we conducted at Central Michigan University during the 2003 Iraq War.

Youth Reading Patterns of 2003 Iraq War Studied

If the 2003 Iraq war had lasted for months or years instead of weeks, young people likely would have been called to fight. Since no one knew how long the war would be last, young adults' interest in war news should have been very high. In our study, nearly 40% of our sample reported having a family member in the U.S. armed forces at that time. Together, these two factors should have pushed their interest up off the charts. To an extent, it did.

In a survey on media preferences during the Iraq war, more than 90% of college students at a medium-sized, public, mid-western U.S. university said they were interested in war news. In a statement sure to warm the hearts of any publisher, more than three in four (77%) said they were actively seeking news when they last read, watched, or listened to it.

The students were surveyed April 21-24, 2003, (Weinstock & Boudreau, 2003), as U.S. forces were struggling to restore order in Baghdad. Fighting continued in parts of northern Iraq and coalition forces had stepped up the search for weapons of mass destruction, Saddam Hussein, and the former leaders of his regime in the infamous deck of playing cards.

A total of 244 college students responded to the survey that examined wartime media use, preferences, and attitudes about news media. The sample of students was overwhelmingly white (93%) and skewed slightly toward females (65%), with 97% of the sample being of traditional college age, 18-25.

YOUTHFUL NEWS-SEEKERS QUICKLY SATISFIED

Interestingly, these same students followed a trend well known to those in the newspaper business: people who read news, spend less time doing it than they once did (Barans, 1999). For example, a 1989 study found that people read only about 20% of a newspaper (Bogart, 1989). These results were echoed in our findings that almost three in four (74%) surveyed reported they spent an hour or less acquiring news the previous day.

Similarly, Web news readers seemed to progressively lose interest in the news the deeper they mined for it. About 30% of our sample said they only read the blurbs on Web news sites while nearly 60% clicked through to the full story. Once they got to the story, only 40% said they thoroughly read it, while a little more than half (53%) only scanned it. Of those who claimed to have read the stories, more than half (55%) read at least half the story. Four in ten (40%) said they read less than half the story.

More than 90% of those surveyed stated an interest in the Iraq war, yet 75% spent less than one hour finding and reading the news, while only 24% read all of what they found. Whatever interest our students had in war news, stories failed to hold their attention beyond the immediate context of the conflict. Nearly one in three students (29%) said that on an average day they had little or no interest in the news, and another 38% reported only some interest. Only a third said they had "quite a bit" or "a great deal of interest" in other events of the day.

WAR NEWS PREFERRED ON TELEVISION

Reflective of the general population, students in the study relied heavily on television for news about the Iraq war.

They not only turned to television for most of their news about the war, but they also saw television as more convenient to use, more credible, and more informative than other media. More than half (57%) of students surveyed said television was the most convenient medium, although almost a third chose the Web. Only 6% selected newspapers as easiest to use.

More than three in five (61%) in the survey said television was the most informative medium, compared to newspapers (21%) and the Web (17%). Television was also seen as the most credible medium by 57% of the students, compared to newspapers (24%) and the Web (11%).

These findings were similar to those in the Pew Internet and American Life Project's The Internet and the Iraq War (Rainie, et al., 2003). That study surveyed a homogeneous U.S. population group of Internet users. According to that study, most Internet users tuned into TV for the bulk of their war news. Similar to our study, its respondents placed online news at the end of their list of most important media. The Pew Study found 17% of its respondents used online news as its major source of war news. We found 19% of our sample preferred Web sources.

OLD AND YOUNG SHARE SIMILAR ATTITUDES, PREFERENCES

From this, a pattern emerged. Young people in this country immediately before and during the Iraq war shared many of the attitudes and preferences held by their parents and older Americans.

According to the Gallup Youth Survey, immediately prior to the Iraq War, American teens' ratings of George W. Bush as president mirrored that of U.S. adults (59% overall approval vs. 63% for teens). Nearly two-thirds of American teens favored a U.S. invasion of Iraq to remove Saddam Hussein from power, compared with a general population invasion approval of 59%.

Mainstream news media might try to take advantage of young people's heightened interest in the war-time news, calamity, or other crises. Though it cannot be confirmed without a peacetime post-test, we think these times represent a space when mass media may truly send out a one-size-fits-all message to the U.S.(if not global) market and expect a hit.

Interestingly, we also found our survey respondents showed a willingness to venture beyond their traditional sources of news with more than a third of them (34%) seeking out new sources of information since the war in Iraq had begun.

WHAT CONVERGENCE?

Few students in the survey reported taking full advantage of the convergent features of the Internet.

A vast majority (89%) looked at photos, and 87% read the photo captions. But their fascination with the multimedia aspects of the Web seemed to end there. Less than a third clicked on video links that accompanied news stories they accessed, and even fewer—just 22%—clicked on audio links.

Any discussion of Web-based multimedia must consider access. More than half the study sample reported accessing Web news sites at home, where dial-up connections are the norm. One-third of the sample accessed online news at school via faster T1 Internet connections. The Pew study noted in its findings that at-home broadband access seems to go hand-in-hand with higher income and education levels. Our surveyed students were firmly entrenched within the lower-income and less-educated categories that go hand-in-hand with dial-up access, though the greater majority will one day have more broadband access.

Whether access-driven or not, students in this study effectively deconverged multimedia news sites to traditional media forms viewed on a monitor. In effect, they discarded the higher-end multimedia aspects of online news sites and turned multimedia news fare into a traditional mix of print and photos viewed on a TV screen. It serves as a possible explanation of the matching 19% war-time Internet news source preference in the Pew study with our survey's 18% newspaper share.

How to Capture Youth Media Market

Heading off this de-convergence may not be as challenging as we might think. Perhaps online news producers could learn from online advertising techniques and use pop-up windows for pages that lead to story links. Certainly, if slow dial-up connections are the most prevalent access methods, the amount of filmed and taped content can be dramatically reduced to only the "punchiest" quotes or the most telling infographics or taped sequences.

They might even auto-run, as software CDs do when loaded into CD drives on computers, as long as file size is minimized. Page downloads might be sequenced so that readers might first be confronted with photos, headline and deck blocks, and pulled quotes, while higher bandwidth content loads to buffers. In pursuit of younger audiences, they might also want to consider limiting story size to a single computer screen that can be read without scrolling,.

Newspapers, too, should find more ways to increase their visual content. Though some journalists might resist the notion of "dumbing down" their medium, newspaper publishers might consider packaging news products for younger audiences who are more visual and less text-block oriented. Story components might be presented as pulled quotes usually are, but instead of presenting the same text from the story, this copy could be complementary material that does not appear elsewhere.

In effect, the headline, the deck, the text, the featured quotes, the pictures, and the captions would all combine to tell the story quickly with no single element being redundant. This would be a more compartmentalized approach of delivering news aimed at news browsers rather than news readers, an audience that would read only part of what it was offered.

Younger audiences are news browsers and not necessarily news readers in a traditional sense. Our study raised questions about how attentive students are when they say they are actually looking at or listening to news. Almost six in ten students (59%) admitted to some form of media multi-tasking while acquiring news about the war. Among the media they reported using: playing computer games, listening to music or surfing the Web while they were acquiring news.

In many cases, students said they were tending to more than one other medium while they were ostensibly reading/watching/listening to the news. More than half of our respondents (56%) reported a night-time habit of acquiring news from 8 p.m. to 4 a.m. The Pew study also reported its users claimed they were online longer to get war news, but were they multi-tasking?

Again, this must give us pause to consider. For news that they are interested in, younger audiences stay up later, stay online longer, and multi-task with other media while they are acquiring news. Certainly, this speaks to shorter attention spans and less concentration on the subject matter.

The medium reporting the highest use and preference for war news television is the same medium that presents the least amount of information in the shallowest depths. Newspapers, the medium that requires single-minded attention while providing the greatest depth of coverage, ranks lowest with younger audiences in preference and use.

DISINTERESTED YOUTH WILL GROW OLDER THEN WHAT?

The inescapable fact about younger audiences is that they will get older. The question that remains unanswered about them is: will they retain their current news browsing behaviors or will they age into more traditional news consumers?

Only the passage of time and their entrance into middle age will answer that. Until then, mainstream media must continue to search for ways to entice younger audiences into developing news consumption behaviors if the media are to survive. Ultimately, it seems it is not news that is putting younger audiences off, but the way that news is presented.

REFERENCES

Barans, S. J. (1999). Media, Media Industries and Media Audiences: Newspapers. In *Introduction to Mass Media: Media Literacy and Culture* (p. 102). Mountainview: Mayfield.

Bogart, L. (1989). *Press and public: Who reads what, where, when and why in American newspapers.* Hillsdale: Lawrence Erlbaum Associates.

Hanway, S. (2003, May 5). What are teen Webheads doing online? Gallup News Service. Retrieved June 30, 003, from Gallup.com: http://www.gallup.com/

Jeffries, L. W., & Atkins, D. (1996). Dimensions of Student Interest in Reading Newspapers. *Journalism and Mass Communicator Educator, 51*(3), 15-23.

Kazaa Media Desktop. (2003) Sets Most Downloaded Software Record.. Retrieved July 8, 2003, from Kazaa Media Desktop: http://www.kazaa.com

LaRose, R., & Straubhaar, J. (1997). *Communications Media and the Information Society.* (Updated Version). Belmont: Thomson.

LaRose, R., & Straubhaar, J. (1997). Print Media: Newspapers, Books and Magazines. In R. LaRose & J. Staubhaar (Eds.) *Communications Media and the Information Society*, p. 158. Belmont: Thomson.

Pew Research Center for People and the Press (2000) Internet sapping broadcast news audience. [Survey Report] Retrieved July 10, 2003, from http://www.people-press.org/

Rainie, L., Fox, S., & Fallows, D. (2003). The Internet and the Iraq War: How online Americans have used the Internet to learn war news (chap.) Retrieved May 1, 2003, from http://www.pewInternet.org/

Weinstock, D., & Boudreau, T. (2003). [Media Preferences of Younger Audiences During the Iraq War] Unpublished raw data, Central Michigan University.

Whelan, D. (2001). Who's Reading the Paper? *American Demographics, 23*(7), 32-34.

CHAPTER 26

Weblogs as a Source of Information about the 2003 Iraq War

Barbara K. Kaye and Thomas J. Johnson

The most celebrated reporter during the Iraqi War was not a clever wordsmith from a major national news magazine, nor was he a stunning "scud stud" from one of the twenty-four-hour news channels. He was Salam Pax, a twenty-nine-year-old gay Iraqi architect whose Warblog (a war-oriented Weblog)—*Where is Raed?*—offered first-hand, clandestine observations of the bombing of Baghdad.

The site attracted not only 100,000 visitors a day, but also profiles from several leading media outlets, including *Time*, (Hamilton, 2003), CNN (Hill, 2003), *Business Week* ("Wild World," 2003), *USA Today* (Kornblum, 2003), *Maclean's* ("Surfing the Warblogs," 2003) and NPR (Simon, 2003). Salam's Weblog (or blog) became so popular that his Internet host upgraded his account for free so he could continue posting stories and photos.

Just as the first Iraqi war popularized newsgroups as a way to share news and personal information (Ashley, 1992), Warblogs, such as those posted by Salam Pax, boosted the popularity of Weblogs—diary-style Web sites that offer frequently updated observations as well as news stories, commentary, and recommended links (Palser, 2002; Seipp, 2002). Supporters argue that blogs provided some of the most thoughtful analysis of the war and provided it on a frequent and consistent basis, with many blogs providing updated news and commentary every fifteen seconds or so. Indeed, CNN staffers often updated their link to *The Command Post*, a major Warblog, for news and analysis they didn't see on mainstream sites (Ryan, 2003).

PURPOSE OF THIS STUDY

This study of Weblogs paints a picture of the type of individual who relied on Weblogs to follow the Iraqi War. More specifically, this study investigates demographic characteristics of blog readers, as well as how often they relied on blogs compared to traditional media for war information.

This study also examines the major reasons why individuals visited Weblogs for information about the war and how credible they viewed the information they found on blogs and other sources of news. This study was conducted by posting a survey on 139 Weblogs, including several of the more popular ones such as *InstaPundit*, *Drudge Report*, *Metafilter*, *homelessguy.net*, *JoanneJacobs.com* and *AndrewSullivan.com*. The survey was also posted to fourteen blogging news groups and mailing lists and by asking respondents to send the survey to their friends who blog. The survey was online from April 23 to May 22, 2003. Overall, 3,747 people completed the survey.

Analysts suggest that Warblogs gained popularity for several reasons. First, they put a more personal face to the war by presenting eyewitness reports of the conflict ("Surfing the Warblogs," 2003). For instance, in his Web postings, Salam Pax described the columns of smoke rising from the burning of oil-filled trenches in Baghdad (Hastings, 2003).

Second, while most media feature one-way communication, readers of blogs can comment on items appearing on the page, fostering a healthy debate about the progress and purpose of the war (Hastings, 2003), and because blog readers can comment on news items on the page as well as to each other's messages, regular users of a blog may develop a sense of community by reading the views of like-minded individuals they feel a connection with (Carver, 2003; Katz, 2002; Seipp, 2002).

Third, the traditional media presented a narrow, pro-American perspective, while blogs featured scribes with a variety of political perspectives, as well as from different geographical areas of the world, who brought different insights than the largely American traditional media (Hamilton, 2003; Hastings, 2003).

BLOG READERS

Blog readers who filled out the online survey were very interested in the War on Iraq and its aftermath. Almost nine out of ten (87%) of the respondents claimed a high interest in the war and only 3% were not very interested at all.

Further, just over three-quarters (77.9%) of the respondents agreed or strongly agreed that they accessed Weblogs to get more information about the war.

There are many reasons why the respondents chose Weblogs over traditional media for war news. One respondent commented, "Bloggers I read either are military personnel or have relations in the war and that gives a different, more human perspective than news reports." Another wrote, "A lot of Warblogs give good summaries of what's going on while giving links to traditional media for substantiation and depth. Another blog reader claimed, "A few Webloggers had compiled the most comprehensive, up-to-date news and analysis from all over."

The common thread among almost a thousand comments was that blogs are an alternative source of news and information that is not filtered by traditional mass media. Blog readers commented that blogs provided more accurate, in-depth, and often first-hand accounts of the war from those who are more knowledgeable and more in touch with realities of war than traditional media reporters who may not be schooled in military matters or who may be reporting second-hand or news wire information. Additionally, many respondents commented that blogs delivered thoughtful analysis of the war which was sorely lacking in traditional media, provided links to traditional mass media stories to compare accounts, and rescued them from what they perceived as the "liberal media."

Little hard research is available to paint an accurate portrait of the average blog user, but evidence suggests that those who access Weblogs resemble the veteran Internet user or the average user of the Internet for news on the 2003 Iraq War: young, white, affluent, and well-educated conservative males. Pew Research found that 4% of Internet users had used Weblog sites to glean information about the war. Although the percentage of those who had used blogs was too small to draw statistically meaningful conclusions about who frequented blogs, their data suggested that active Internet users and those under the age of thirty were the most likely to have visited blog sites. Active users were more likely to be upscale males with higher levels of education and income (Rainie, Fox, & Fallows, 2003).

Andrew Sullivan conducted a survey on his popular conservative news blog, andrewsullivan.com, and his results confirmed that blog readers are hardly mainstream. More than eight in ten (85.2%) are male, and 50% had earned a graduate degree; another 37.6% had graduated from college. Sullivan's readers are wealthy—more than a third (34.6%) earned at least $100,000—and just over six out of ten (60.3%) said they were conservative or leaning toward conservative. Finally, his readers were relatively young, with more than half (55%) being between the age of twenty-five and forty-five.

More impressionistic observations about the blogosphere also suggest that bloggers hardly resemble the American population as a whole. For instance, *New York Times* reporter Lisa Guernsey (2002) claims blogging is a man's world, although the number of women bloggers is growing. Most high profile blog users are males. They are more drawn to politics than women, which accounts for their predominance in the blog world.

Seipp (2002) notes that blogs tend to attract lawyers, scientists, and journalists, which would suggest that the average blog reader is well-educated and has a high income. The most common observation is that the blogosphere is dominated by conservatives (Cavanaugh, 2002; Levy et al., 2002; Seipp, 2002), which parallels the Pew Research finding that Internet users in general were more likely to support the war and the way President Bush handled it than non-users (Rainie, Fox, & Fallows, 2003). But because of the wide range of blog subject matter and viewpoints voiced on blogs, there may not be such a thing as a typical blogger.

In describing who visits his blog, a Los Angeles blogger claimed his most avid readers were "a gay conservative bed & breakfast owner; a retired Republican cop in Pomona; a Naderite expatriate in New Zealand; a liberal literature professor fed up with campus radicalism; a music freak from Minnesota; a thoughtful, pessimistic lefty housewife in Nebraska; a pissed-off quatrilingual Czech-born grad student in Berkeley; [and a] top editor at a major science-fiction publishing house"(Seipp, 2002). While some Weblogs may indeed draw diverse readers, the respondents to this study's Weblog survey are more like those found by other researchers: war supporting, conservative, highly educated, white males. The war on Iraq was supported or strongly supported by three-quarters of the respondents, and almost half (48.1%) were affiliated with the Republican Party. Only one out of five (20.1%) claimed independent party status, while 14.3% were Democrats and 7.3% were Libertarian.

The blogosphere is dominated by white (89.3%) males (76.5%); just less than 1% are Black and 23.5% are female. Just over nine out of ten (92.6%) report that they have some college or higher, and four out of ten (41.8%) claim they make more than $65,00.00 per year. Additionally, respondents average 38.9 years of age, have been blogging for about 1.9 years and spend 9.1 hours per week on Weblogs. About one-third are active participants who often send comments and links to bloggers, about one-third sometimes participate, and about one-third are content to just read Weblog comments.

CREDIBILITY OF WEBLOGS

Observers debate the credibility of Weblogs. Critics note that most blogs are operated by armchair observers who are not bound by the same ethics and standards observed by trained journalists. For instance, Sean-Paul Kelley, the host of one of the most popular Warblogs, *The Agonist*, was accused of lifting information from Stratfor, a subscription intelligence service, and posting the information to *The Agonist* without attribution (Ryan, 2003).

Many bloggers do not use their own names, making it difficult for readers to judge the credibility of the blogger (Bedell, 2003). For instance, Salam Pax was a pseudonym meaning "peace" in Arabic and Latin. When his transmissions mysteriously ceased on March 24, online speculation was rife about whether Pax was indeed an Iraqi who may have been silenced by Saddam loyalists, whether he was a hoax located stateside who was presenting a fictionalized account of the war, or whether he was a CIA agent spreading anti-Saddam propaganda (Bedell, 2003; Hill, 2003).[1]

On the other hand, Weblog proponents note that the most popular Warblogs were hosted by journalists such as CNN's Kevin Sites, *Time* freelancer Joshua Kucera and former Associated Press reporter Christopher Allbritton, who all strictly adhere to journalistic standards (Ryan, 2003), or were first-hand accounts from soldiers stationed in the Middle East who may be better trained to offer opinions and personal observations than the reporters who covered the war (Bedell, 2003; Hamilton, 2003). As Julia Hayden, who regularly posted her daughter's e-mails from the front to Warblog *Stryker's Daily Briefing*, contends, "The very good Warblogs are people who are experts right down to their bones, and they can write about it" (Bedell, 2003).

Also, while blogs may not go through the gatekeeping process of an editor, they rely on peer review to point out errors (Carver, 2003), and mistakes on blogs can be immediately and prominently corrected (Seipp, 2002). Finally, because blogs normally exist independently of major media organizations, readers may find them more credible because they do not serve corporate interests, and are therefore more likely to take on sensitive topics the mainstream media will not touch (Blood, 2002; Lasica, 2002a). As researcher Hope Cristol argues, "They aren't censored by advertisers or constrained by editorial policies and they are therefore a more democratic publishing medium" (Cristol, 2002, p. 9).

Almost three-quarters (73.6%) of this study's respondents judge Weblogs as the most credible source of news and information, followed by printed news magazines (56.4%) and printed newspapers (46.5%). Broadcast television news and bulletin boards/lists and chat rooms are judged the least credible sources. Blog readers trust that Weblogs deliver accurate, unbiased, believable, and in-depth accounts of news events, especially about the war on Iraq. These readers have little trust in chat rooms and bulletin boards/lists, which also provide interaction between users and postings of opinions and other information. It could be that blogger oversight and management of information and links to other sources adds an air of authenticity, which leads to perceptions of heightened credibility. Indeed, analysts indicate that the measure of how credible and authoritative a Weblog is viewed by fellow bloggers is the number of them who want to link to that site (Lasica, 2002b).

While observers may argue about how credible readers should view blogs, there is little debate how blog readers themselves feel about the media: they have little faith and considerable contempt for the traditional media, which the predominantly conservative blog readers judge as elitist and liberally biased.[2] Indeed, bloggers see themselves as the opposite of traditional journalists: independent, unedited, opinionated and personal. As *Online Journalism Review* senior columnist J.D. Lasica argues, "Where the editorial process can filter out errors and polish a piece of copy to a fine sheen, too often the machinery turns even the best prose limp, lifeless, sterile and homogenized. A huge part of blogs' appeal lies in their unmediated quality. Blogs tend to be impressionistic, telegraphic, raw, honest, individualistic, highly opinionated and passionate, often striking an emotional chord" (Lasica, 2002b).

Commentators claim that the rising popularity of blogs is linked with a growing distrust and dislike of the traditional media (Amis, 2002; Lasica, 2002a). The events of 9/11 served as a wake up call to bloggers who were dissatisfied with traditional media coverage that they viewed as over sympathetic to Islamic terrorism; blogs were transformed from online diaries "typically concerned with boyfriend problems and technie news" (Seipp, 2002, p. 43) to ones that regularly commented on the news and those who create it.

Bloggers became "angry ankle-biters who ferociously snipe at traditional media" (Levy et al., 2002). As columnist Catherine Seipp put it: "Bloggers see the traditional media as The Great and Powerful Wizard of Oz manipulated by a snake-oil salesman behind the curtain. Blogs pull aside that curtain, pointing out logical flaws, incorrect facts and occasionally the self-important approach of the reporter" (Seipp, 2002).

But although credibility (i.e., the more people rely on a source, the more they judge it as credible) is linked to use of traditional media, the link does not appear to exist for blog readers. They may see traditional journalists as snake-oil salesmen, but that does not mean that they do not buy their elixirs.

Reliance on Weblogs

Bloggers lean heavily on traditional media for information they post on their sites, and to be a critic of the media, one must be a voracious consumer of it. "Why do you become a critic of the media? At least in some sense it's because you like it," says *InstaPundit*'s Glenn Reynolds. "If you don't read the paper, you don't get mad at the paper" (Seipp, 2002).

Just as this study's blog readers judge Weblogs as credible, they also relied on them as sources of information about the Iraqi war. Just over three-quarters (76.9%) of the respondents answered that they rely or heavily rely on Weblogs. In contrast, cable television news and printed newspapers were the next most relied upon media, but by only 47.4% and 40.1% of the respondents, respectively. Weblog users very much relied on these sites to deliver credible war information.

WEBLOGS AS A SUBSTITUTE FOR OTHER NEWS SOURCES

Many media analysts fear that the more people rely on the Internet the less time they have to spend with traditional sources (Dimmick et al., 2000; Kang & Atkin, 1999; Lin, 2001a, 2001b; Vitalari, Venkatesh & Gronhaug, 1985) and they could be shifting their use from more established online resources, such as Web sites and bulletin boards, to Weblogs.

An online survey of politically interested Internet users found that about half of the respondents have not changed the amount of time they spend seeking political information from traditional media since they started using the Internet; however, of those whose media habits have changed, many more of them claimed they have decreased rather than increased the amount of time they spend with traditional non-online sources (Kaye & Johnson, 2003).

On the other hand, because the Internet at large has been found to supplement rather than replace traditional media (Kaye & Johnson, 2003; Pew Research, 1999), it could be that Weblogs also act as a supplement to, instead of a replacement for, traditional media and other online resources.

This survey of Weblog users found that since respondents first started using Weblogs changes in media use has been largely dependent on the medium examined. For instance, a greater percentage (45.7%) of respondents report a decrease in the amount of time they spend watching broadcast television news; online broadcast television news sites appear to have taken a hit as well, with 38.9% of the respondents claiming to spend less time on those sites than before.

However, just less than half report that their use of broadcast television news and online broadcast television sites has stayed the same. It could be that Weblogs are taking the place of over-the-air television and accompanying Web sites, especially as these sources are not relied upon or deemed very credible.

Weblog use does seem to supplement face-to-face discussion, online newspapers, and to a lesser degree cable television. Slightly more than half (52.2%) of the survey respondents are spending more time in face-to-face discussion since they first started using Weblogs. Presumably, Weblogs spark an interest in current events such as the Iraqi war, provoke thought, and stimulate blog readers to discuss what they have read with their friends and family. Weblog users could feel confident and knowledgeable enough to enter into in-depth discussion with others.

The interactive nature of Weblogs allows users to compare traditional and online accounts and provides links to more in-depth information. Just over four of ten respondents (42.4%) spend more time reading online newspapers than before they started accessing Weblogs. Bloggers often provide links to online newspapers and traditional newspaper Web sites that provide in-depth coverage of some issues. It could be that just following the links to information of interest may land blog users on newspaper sites, thus increasing their use.

Although almost half (45.5%) of the survey respondents have not altered the amount of time they spend watching cable television news and almost one-quarter (24.3%) have decreased the time they spend on these channels, three out of ten (30.1%) have increased their viewing time. Conservatives who bristle at the so-called liberal leanings of traditional media are taking refuge in cable channels such as Fox News, which has aligned itself right of center. Fox News likes to "wave the flag, give'em an attitude and make it lively," and to position itself as an opinion page (Johnson, 2002), somewhat like Weblogs, which often represent a particular ideological standpoint.

It is not surprising that because almost two-thirds (63.6%) of the survey respondents access conservative or very conservative Weblogs, they would also increasingly turn to cable news networks, especially those that deliver information that agrees with their political perspective.

SUMMARY

This survey of the uses of Weblogs for information about the War on Iraq was one of the first studies of its kind. While the popular press abounds with stories about Weblogs and bloggers, little attention has been paid to blog readers. The purpose of this paper is to create a profile of blog readers and discover what draws them to Weblogs, and more specifically to understand their reasons for turning to Weblogs for information about the war on Iraq.

This study found that the blogosphere is primarily visited by white, Republican, conservative, war-supporting, highly educated, high income males who strongly distrust and who have turned their backs on the mainstream media for delivering what they perceive as liberally biased news and information, especially about the war on Iraq. The survey respondents were very interested in the Iraq war and had a thirst for in-depth coverage and analysis that traditional media could not quench. Blog readers were searching for information and points of view about a war that they were already in agreement with and thus, mostly sought support from conservative Weblogs.

Blog readers judge Weblogs as the most credible source of information, followed by printed news magazines and newspapers. Blog readers have little trust in online bulletin boards and chat rooms. Although bulletin boards and chat rooms are also forums of public debate, they are not moderated by a trusted blogger and they often offer a variety of opinions. On the other hand, though Weblogs may be very different from each other, each tends to present homogeneous viewpoints, making it easy for blog readers to find a home among like-minded people.

The survey respondents relied on Weblogs more than any other non-online or online source to keep abreast of the war. To a lesser degree, they also favored cable television news and printed newspapers. Some cable television news outlets, particularly Fox News, are known for slanting news right-of-center so it is not surprising that Weblog users look to cable television news for support of their positions.

Blog readers do not hold the broadcast media and their accompanying Web sites as very credible and thus have turned away from those sources in favor of Weblogs for information about the war. Although Weblogs may be supplanting broadcast media, they may be supplementing cable television, online newspapers, and face-to-face discussion. Blog readers are attracted to cable news because of its conservative bias, and readership of online newspapers may have increased largely due to bloggers posting links to newspaper sites. It seems that Weblogs empower blog readers with information and support for their opinions, which may enhance feelings of self-confidence and make them more likely to enter into political and war-related discussion with others.

Overall, Weblogs became homes for those who supported the war and were looking for confirmation of their conservative viewpoints.

ENDNOTES

1. Pax emerged from hiding in June 2003. Pax worked as a translator for freelance journalist and author Peter Maass during the war and later signed on with the British *Guardian* as a columnist (Pillar, 2003). Salam's collection of Weblogs, *Salam Pax: The clandestine diary of an ordinary Iraqi*, was published in October 2003 by Grove Press.

2. The contempt between bloggers and traditional media is mutual. Mainstream journalists blast blogs for being politically biased and because they lack editors to provide quality control. As *American Journalism Review* writer Catherine Seipp claims, "Just as many bloggers view the mainstream media as elitists, mainstreamers generally look upon bloggers as a bunch of mutts crashing the dog show."

REFERENCES

Amis, D. (2002, Sept. 21). Web logs: Online navel gazing. [Online]. http://www.netfreedom.org.

Ashley, C. (1992). Internet groups allow for productive information gathering. *Online Review, 16,* 157-159.

Bedell, D. (2003, April 7). War blogs add personal edge to news. *The Dallas Morning News.* [Online] http://www.dallasnews.com

Blood, R. (2002). Weblogs: A history and perspective. In *We've got blog: How weblogs are changing our culture,* pp. 7-16. Cambridge, MA: Perseus Publishing.

Carver, B. (2003). What would Dewey do? Librarians grapple with Internet. *Library Journal, 128,* 30-32.

Cavanaugh, T. (2002). Let slip the blogs of war. In *We've got blog: How weblogs are changing our culture,* pp. 188-197. Cambridge, MA: Perseus Publishing.

Cristol, H. (2002, September). News in the digital age. *Futurist, 36*, 8-9.

Dimmick, J., Kline, S., & Stafford, l. (2000). The gratification niches of personal e-mail and the telephone. *Communication Research, 27,* 227-248.

Guernsey, L. (2002, Nov. 28). Telling all online: It's a man's world (Isn't it?). *The New York Times,* p. G1.

Hamilton, A. (2003, April 7). Best of the war blogs. *Time, 161,* p. 91.

Hastings, M. (2003, April 7). Bloggers over Baghdad. *Newsweek, 141,* p. 48-49.

Hill, E. (2003, March 26). Blogging for a better view. [Online] Available at http://www.cnn.com/2003.tech.

Johnson, P. (2002). Fox News enjoys new view - from the top. *USA Today*. pp. 1A - 2A.

Kang, M., & Atkin, D. J. (1999). Exploring the role of media uses and gratifications in multimedia cable adoption. *Telematics and Informatics, 16,* 59-74.

Katz, J. (2002). Here come the weblogs. In *We've got blog: How weblogs are changing our culture,* pp. 17-24. Cambridge, MA: Perseus Publishing

Kaye, B. K. & Johnson, T. J. (2003). From here to obscurity: The Internet and media substitution theory. *Journal of the American Society for Information Science and Technology, 54* (3), 260-273.

Kornblum, J. (2003, March 24). Web logs convey 'raw stuff' of Iraq War. *USA Today,* [Online] http://www.usatoday.com/tech

Lasica, J.D. (2002a). Blogging as a form of journalism: Weblogs offer a vital, creative outlet for alternative voices. In *We've got blog: How weblogs are changing our culture,* pp. 163-170. Cambridge, MA: Perseus Publishing.

Lasica, J.D. (2002b). Weblogs: A new source of news. In *We've got blog: How weblogs are changing our culture,* pp. 171-182. Cambridge, MA: Perseus Publishing.

Levy, S, Figueroa, A., Campo-Flores, A., Lin, J., & Gossard, M.H. (2002, August 26) Living in the Blog-osphere, *Newsweek,* pp. 42-45.

Lin, C.A. (2001a). Audience attributes, media supplementation, and likely online service adoption. *Mass Communication & Society, 4,* 19-38.

Lin, C.A. (2001b, August). Online use activity and user gratification-expectations. Paper presented at the Association for Education in Journalism and Mass Communication, Washington.

Palser, B. (2002, July/August). Journalistic blogging. *American Journalism Review, 24,* p. 58.

Pew Research Center. (1999). The Internet news audience goes ordinary. [Online] Available: www.people-press.org/reports.

Piller, C. (2003, June 4). Iraq's mystery man steps in the light. [Online] http://www.latimes.com

Rainie, L., Fox, S., & Fallows, D. (2003). The Internet and the Iraqi War: How online Americans have used the Internet to learn war news, understand events, and promote their views. [Online] http://www.pewInternet.org/reports.

Ryan, M. (2003, April 17). Blogs' rise stymies old media. *Chicago Tribune.* [Online] http://www.chicago.tribune.com.

Seipp, C. (2002, June). Online uprising. *American Journalism Review, 24,* 42-47.

Simon, S. (2003, March 29). Analysis: Web logs the newest way to convey war information. National Public Radio.

"Surfing the Warblogs for news from the front." (2003, April 1). *Maclean's,* 116, p. 28.

Vitalari, N. P., Venkatesh, A., & Grohaug, K. (1995). Computing in the home: Shifts in the time allocation patterns of households. *Communications of the ACM, 28,* 512-

522.
"The wild world of 'open source media.'" (2003, June 10). *Business Week.* [Online] http://www.businessweek.com/technology

Part VI

THE WAR FOR HEARTS AND MINDS

CHAPTER 27

Cognitive and Emotional Effects of Media Coverage of the 2003 Iraq War

Glenn G. Sparks and Will Miller

In many important respects, news coverage of the recent war in Iraq was unprecedented. Self-conscious about their own presence on the battlefield, network and cable newscasters repeatedly reminded viewers about the unique show they were seeing and how the consequences of such global, non-stop coverage of the conflict were surely profound. Indeed, viewers were encouraged not to just "watch" the war, but to "experience" the war as it happened. Of course, the news coverage was unique in the sense that more than six hundred journalists from the United States and elsewhere were permitted to travel with the military and file reports from various battle stations.

The Bush administration seemed intent on having the whole world witness what was really happening, partially out of the desire to thwart any attempts on the part of Iraq to disseminate false and misleading information about the course of the conflict. This was especially important given the unpopularity of the war among many of our traditional allies and the perceptions of a fragile domestic public when it came to the prospects of a military invasion.

While there can be little doubt about the unique nature of the news coverage that the world witnessed during the war, we propose that, in the final analysis, some of the major cognitive and emotional consequences of all of this ground-breaking coverage were strictly old-hat. In this chapter, we argue that:

1. The well documented process of selective exposure tended to minimize significant changes of opinion about the war;
2. Well established individual differences in emotional coping helped to determine people's patterns of exposure to news coverage;
3. Younger viewers tended to suffer the same emotional consequences to the news coverage about the war that they have suffered on other occasions that are documented in the literature.

Although considerable attention has been devoted to the novel qualities of war coverage in Iraq and the potential consequences of this coverage that were new and unanticipated, much can be gained in terms of understanding the effects of the war coverage by emphasizing the traditional scholarship about theory and effects of media messages.

Selective Exposure

The principle of selective exposure to communication has been formally articulated in the scholarly literature for over a half-century. Its pivotal role in understanding the effects of media messages has been recognized for nearly as many years.

In their book devoted to the scholarly literature on selective exposure, Zillmann and Bryant (1985) defined the concept as, "behavior that is deliberately performed to attain and sustain perceptual control of particular stimulus events" (p. 2). Perhaps an easier way of articulating the notion was the way it was expressed by one of Adolph Hitler's film-makers, Fritz Hippler, in an interview that he gave to Bill Moyers in the ninth episode of the PBS TV series, "A Walk Through the 20th Century." Hippler noted the Germans carefully designed their propaganda films according to the principle that, "people only want to see things that they find to be agreeable." The basic idea is that exposure to various forms of communication is deliberate and motivated to bring about the most pleasant experience possible. In the context of media messages, the application of the principle is clear: people will systematically tend to avoid messages they find to be disagreeable in favor of ones that they like.

There is no need to review here the exhaustive empirical evidence in favor of the fact that people actually do selectively expose themselves to messages they find agreeable. The existence of this basic tendency among news viewers suggests that for all the various stories that were reported during the Iraq war, the tendency for people to significantly change their basic views about the necessity or desirability of the conflict as a result of this coverage was probably minimal. In opposition to this view, some scholars have recently argued that relative to interpersonal sources of contact, the media are especially good at exposing people to a diversity of political viewpoints. Such exposure presumably leads to change.

Diana Mutz and Paul Martin (2001) report research in support of the idea that when people rely upon the media for their information, they acquire exposure to a greater diversity of political opinion. However, Mutz and Martin point out that this conclusion is tempered by the nature of the media environment. When that environment is more partisan, their data clearly show that consumers are more likely to exercise selective exposure, consuming only the news sources that they find to be consistent with their own views. In our view, the media environment during the coverage of the Iraq war was seen by supporters and critics alike as highly partisan.

With the recent proliferation of cable news channels that competed for ratings during the weeks of heaviest fighting, highly publicized controversies emerged about the differing nature of the coverage from network to network. Predictably, the Fox News Network (FNN) was seen by many as offering a far more conservative account of the news coverage than CNN or stations affiliated with National Public Radio. An August 2001 report on the FNN from FAIR (Fairness and Accuracy in Media) documented the general glee on the part of political conservatives about how Fox covered various events. The report called FNN "the most biased name in news" and chastised it for its "extraordinary right-wing tilt."

Of course, we suspect that FNN and Brent Bozell's conservative Media Watch would accuse FAIR of being political liberals and biased in their perspective. While we await the results of systematic content analyses of the media coverage that might or might not document actual bias in news coverage from different stations or newspapers, there is no question that the charges of bias from both liberal and conservative camps certainly fostered a general perception that news coverage of the Iraq war was distorted according to the political ideologies of individual news organizations. News consumers, who were conscious of these charges—whether they were themselves liberal or conservative—were undoubtedly affected in the way that they went about consuming news.

A loyal democrat, upon hearing about the strict conservative FNN bias, was more inclined to avoid that coverage than a Republican supporter of George W. Bush, who heard that Fox was the only network worth watching because it wasn't trying to bash the president's good faith efforts to lead the country down the right path. At the very least, all of the charges of political bias in the news coverage about the war helped to contribute to the sort of partisan media environment that Mutz and Martin associated with selective exposure behavior.

According to this analysis, were American political liberals likely to deliberately expose themselves to FNN news coverage and consequently change their attitudes about the war? As we've already suggested, we think not. Were the political conservatives who preferred Fox coverage likely to consider news reports from NPR worth their time? Probably not. The same questions could be asked of Middle East media consumers about their news channel selections.

Instead of the news coverage promoting attitude change among people with prior views about the war, we believe that in the vast majority of cases, people followed the selective exposure principle and viewed news programs they found to be most agreeable with their own attitudes and outlooks. If any attitudinal change took place, our suspicion is that, in the main, it was by way of weakening or strengthening beliefs that were already in place at the beginning of the war coverage.

In support of this general stance, we point to the recent survey data reported by the Gallup Organization in response to the question, "Do you favor or oppose the U.S. war with Iraq?" The results revealed that the percentages of respondents who expressed either support or opposition remained virtually constant during the entire month of the most intense U.S. news coverage of the conflict (March 22 through April 23, 2003). At the war's beginning, 72% of the respondents expressed support and 25% expressed opposition. One month later, these percentages were 71% and 26% respectively. Moreover, during the month-long period, opposition remained between 25-28% and support remained between 68-72%.

In short, the stability of opinion about the war was well documented—at least at the level of the overall sample. If our view about selective exposure processes is correct, it would not, of course, be the first time that such processes operated. Lazarsfeld, Berelson, and Gaudet (1948) uncovered this same effect in their often-cited study on political attitude change in Erie County, Ohio. Naturally, our analysis remains subject to the scientific data that might emerge in the literature over subsequent months and years. But at this point, our best guess is that despite the novelty and innovation of news coverage, not many people changed their essential views about the war as a result of their news consumption.

Selective Exposure Based on Emotional Coping Styles

While we believe that selective exposure based on one's general predisposition definitely governed patterns of news exposure during the Iraq conflict, we also note that another type of selective exposure undoubtedly took place: exposure that was based on one's preferred way of coping with stressful news events. Sparks and Spirek (1988) published data showing that people's exposure to news coverage of the space shuttle *Challenger* explosion was a function of their general tendency to cope with stressful events by employing one of two different strategies.

These individual coping strategies have long been observed by Suzanne Miller in her research in the health setting (Miller, 1987). "Monitoring" is a coping strategy that seeks to maximize information pertaining to the stressor. When monitors find themselves in a stressful situation, they want to know every detail about the situation that is possible to know. Presumably, for these types of individuals, knowing about traumatic events helps them cope effectively with the reality of the stress.

Alternatively, "blunting" is a coping strategy that seeks just the opposite with respect to information. When blunters find themselves in a stressful situation, they seek to block out information pertaining to the stressor, perhaps in an attempt to distract themselves and think about more pleasant thoughts. Both strategies appear to be effective in reducing stress. One's prior socialization and biological temperament may help to determine which strategy is preferred for a given individual.

Clearly, these differences in preferred coping style hold implications for understanding patterns of media exposure. Sparks and Spirek (1988) showed that monitors were much more likely than blunters to want to: a) see replays of the astronauts' family members watching the launch sequence of the *Challenger*; b) see the astronauts' family members talking about their own reactions to the explosion; and c) see news coverage that focused on children's reactions to the explosion as they watched the event live in their school classrooms.

Over a decade later, in a serendipitous diary study of news exposure that began on September 10, 2001, Spirek (2002) found that monitors and blunters differed markedly in their self-reported news consumption levels following the terrorist attack on the World Trade Towers. In the twenty-four-hour period following the attack, monitors increased their exposure to TV news reports from about one hour on September 10 to over four hours on September 12. In contrast, blunters did not increase their level of news exposure at all. When Spirek examined exposure to entertainment programming during this same period, she found that monitors had reduced their exposure to entertainment by a factor of five. In contrast, blunters had nearly doubled their reported exposure to entertainment programming.

Given the fact that differences in monitoring and blunting have been observed with different news stories in two different decades, we feel confident in speculating that these tendencies also governed patterns of news exposure during the Iraq war. Viewers who found the reality of the conflict to be stressful were likely to implement their preferred coping style. Some viewers found themselves watching more news, while other viewers found themselves watching less. The consequences of these different tendencies for changing political opinions have not yet been studied.

However, focusing on changes in political views may miss the point. These coping strategies are employed mainly to cope with the emotions that a person might feel regarding the news. It seems possible to us (even likely), that the major effect of individuals using these strategies is not to be found in the realm of cognitive or attitudinal change. Instead, since the coping strategies are designed primarily to manage emotion, we suspect that studies of emotion management during exposure to the news coverage would yield more interesting data than studies that focused on changes in attitude.

Children's Emotional Reactions to Tv Coverage of the War

In general, we believe there is a need to counter-balance the focus among scholars upon important topics like the political ramifications of news coverage about war, how the structure of news organizations influences war coverage, how governments influence news coverage, and how people's attitudes might be affected by war coverage. Often lost in this smorgasbord of scholarly reflection is how news coverage of war emotionally affects our children. Fortunately, there is a growing literature on children's emotional reactions to frightening or upsetting media.

Based on this literature, it is relatively easy to engage in informed speculation about how news coverage of the Iraq war might have affected children. In a recent survey of parents about their children's reactions to coverage of the terrorist attack on the World Trade Towers (Smith, Moyer, Boyson & Pieper, 2002), parents were asked to describe specific dimensions of TV news coverage that, "concerned, frightened, or upset your child." Prior to this question, nearly half of the parents of children five to eight years of age reported that their children experienced a fright reaction while watching some aspect of the news coverage. For older children, the percentages were even larger (65% for parents of nine to twelve-year olds; 67% for parents of thirteen-seventeen-year olds).

Examples provided by the authors of the things that parents mentioned as being particularly upsetting to their children were "explosions," "seeing the burning of the buildings," and "planes going into the building." In addition, parents mentioned that their children reacted to verbal reports that expressed concern for those who had died or who were missing, future attacks, and the future possibility of war.

These data provide a firm grounding from which to speculate about the emotional effects of the war coverage in Iraq. First, the fact that the coverage was so prolific and constant increased the probability that children would be exposed to some portion of the coverage during the most intense days of fighting. Second, since the content of war coverage contained ingredients that were similar conceptually to those of the 9/11 coverage, it seems safe to speculate that images of explosions, bombings, fires, and human suffering had the same general effects on many children who were exposed to these images.

One implication of this is that older children were more likely to be emotionally affected by news of the war than younger children. This tends to run counter to the conventional wisdom that parents use when they decide whether they should permit their children to watch certain media events. In general, parents are more permissive with their older children and more protective of their younger ones. While older children may have an increased awareness and interest in war coverage, they are also more emotionally vulnerable. Instead of assuming a generally permissive attitude with respect to older children's news consumption, the data suggest that parents ought to be more concerned about what children in these age ranges are thinking and feeling about the coverage that they see.

Our advice to parents about how to deal with media-induced fears from war coverage and our advice to media organizations covering these events is the same as that given by Joanne Cantor (*www.joannecantor.com/terror_adv.htm*), the researcher who pioneered studies on children's fright reactions to media and continues to research in this area. Cantor emphasizes limiting children's exposure to war news by not leaving the TV set on for unrestricted viewing. She also advises parents to recognize that children are often simply seeking reassurance from them and she suggests emphasizing the good than can come from tragic events.

For media organizations, she urges those who make programming decisions to make war coverage predictable so that parents can be forewarned about disturbing reports and images that may be upcoming. She also asks stations to resist the temptation to replay disturbing scenes over and over again. The research evidence suggests that younger children may believe that each time they view a replayed event, they believe that it represents another new occurrence.

One interesting issue that we would highlight for future research in this domain has to do with the nature of the reports about war casualties and how these reports might emotionally affect viewers. Based on the news coverage that we saw, it seemed clear, for example, that Al-Jazeera tended to cover civilian casualties and suffering, while U.S. news outlets tended to focus on military casualties. What sorts of differences might such coverage produce in emotional reactions among children who saw images of each type? We hope that future research on emotional reactions to news coverage might take up this sort of question.

In concluding this brief essay, while we sincerely hope that our future news reports will not have to carry reports of war, we suspect that the best predictor of future news coverage is past news coverage. As researchers rush to investigate the various nuances and particulars of the coverage as it emerges around the globe, the point of our essay is to call scholars and observers back to some of the basics. There is a considerable amount to be learned about the effects of news coverage of any war by studying the research that has already been conducted.

Our focus in this essay upon selective exposure processes, individual coping styles, and children's emotional reactions does not begin to exhaust what we already know about how news coverage affects people. In attempting to learn about the effects of global media war coverage, we would do well to begin our quest for knowledge by studying the bountiful evidence that already exists.

REFERENCES

Ackerman, S. (2001). The most biased name in news: Fox news channel's extraordinary right-wing tilt. A special FAIR report. Available on-line: http://www.fair.org/extra/0108/Fox-main.html

Gallup Organization. (2003). War with Iraq: The latest polls and analyses on the conflict with Iraq. Available online: http://www.gallup.com/poll/focus/sr030224.asp

Lazarsfeld, P.F., Berelson, B., & Gaudet, H. (1948). *The people's choice: How the voter makes up his mind in a presidential campaign.* New York: Duell, Sloan & Pearce.

Miller, S.M. (1987). Monitoring and blunting: Validation of a questionnaire to assess styles of information seeking under threat. *Journal of Personality and Social Psychology, 52,* 345-353.

Mutz, D.C., & Martin, P.S. (2001). Facilitating communication across lines of political difference. The role of mass media. *American Political Science Review, 95* (1), 97-114.

Smith, S.L., Moyer, E., Boyson, A.R., & Pieper, K.M. (2002). Parents' perceptions of children's fear responses. In B. S. Greenberg (Ed.). *Communication and Terrorism,* pp. 193-208. Cresskill, NJ: Hampton Press.

Sparks, G.G., & Spirek, M.M. (1988). Individual differences in coping with stressful mass media: An activation-arousal view. *Human Communication Research, 15*(2), 195-216.

Spirek, M. M., Fitzpatrick, C., & Bridges, C. R. (2002). Tracking media consumption among monitors and blunters. In B. S. Greenberg (Ed.). *Communication and Terrorism,* pp. 75-86. Cresskill, NJ: Hampton Press.

Zillmann, D., & Bryant, J. (1985). *Selective exposure to communication.* Hillsdale, NJ: Lawrence, Erlbaum.

CHAPTER 28

Propaganda and Arab Audiences: Resisting the "Hearts & Minds" Campaign

Makram Khoury-Machool

For the traditional and new Arab media, the toppling of Saddam Hussein's statue in Fardus Square on April 9, 2003, evoked a different reaction than the West expected. Baghdad, it turned out, was no Belgrade.[1]

The Iraqi capital of seven million people did not erupt in jubilation, as Western news organizations implied: not one million of them, not even one thousand (Al-Hassan, 2003). Indeed, there were hardly two hundred people in Fardus Square that day, and the majority of those were foreign journalists.

From an Arab perspective, the toppling of Saddam's statue was a production directed and stage-managed by the international media and the U.S. military, which were well prepared and equipped with even the old Iraqi flag,[2] and who challenged a handful of Iraqi youngsters to attack the statue. It was the opening salvo in the battle for "Iraqi hearts and minds."

Just a few hours after the transmission of these "euphoric" images, it became clear that the fighting in Baghdad was continuing, and was harvesting even more Iraqi civilian casualties. Far from signaling Iraq's liberation, the fact that U.S. forces had given "permission" for the destruction of the Iraqi president's statue gave the go-ahead for much of the looting, anarchy, and destruction of the Iraqi national heritage that followed.

McOccupation

Having witnessed the chaotic human crisis unfolding in Baghdad, Arab public opinion, as represented in the Arab media, now seems more convinced than ever that the Anglo-American slogan of "winning Iraqi hearts and minds" was mere cynicism, or a strategy for mass deception.

Voices across the Arab media have even expressed doubt at the Western coalition's success in selling this concept to its own public, let alone to the Arabic-speaking world. In the view of the Arab media, both the slogan and the concept behind it were little more than propaganda and demagogy, for "hearts and minds" in the Arab culture have a particularly distinguished status and cannot be won easily, especially by those employing a foreign language.

Coalition spin-doctors targeted Western public opinion by suggesting that to "win the hearts and minds" of the Iraqi people was to liberate them from the tyranny of Saddam and his regime. Convincing the newly-occupied Iraqis by using the established Israeli line of "enlightened occupation," raised altogether different considerations.

Founded on an American consumerist expectation of "fast" liberation—what we might call "McOccupation"—this is a concept far removed from everyday Arab realities, and reveals an Orientalist perception of Arabs and Arab culture.

Propaganda and the Palestinianization of Iraq

If Eugene Ionesco is correct that the aim of propaganda is to "destroy the clear conscience of the rival and strengthen one's own"(Ionesco, 1968, p. 93), then Anglo-American propaganda against Iraq (even without the counter-propaganda of Iraq's infamous Information Minister Mohammed Saeed Al-Sahhaf)[3] stood no real chance of meeting its aims.

This applied as much to the Arabic-speaking world as a whole as to the citizens of Iraq themselves. For, besides the traditional media, the overwhelming majority of Arab households, both in the Middle East and in the Arab diaspora, have access to new media, among them the Arab satellites MBC, LBC, Al-Jazeera, ANN, Al-Manar, Al-Arabiya, Future, and Abu Dhabi, alongside numerous Arab newspapers available on the Internet, such as *Al-Quds Al-Arabi, Al-Sharq Al-Awsat, Al-Hayat, Al-Nahar, Al-Ahram,* and others.[4]

Because of the rapid and expansive growth of such technology, these new Arab media have leveled the playing field with Western media in their capacity to present alternative forms of coverage, news counter-framing and multiple opinions, and to reach audiences of a previously unimaginable size. One need look no further than the traditional and new Arab media to see the contempt and anger expressed at the Anglo-American public relations effort in Iraq. Having differing patterns of ownership and supporting often opposing ideologies, no single Arab media was in favor of the U.S.-led war, although some supported deposing the Iraqi Ba'athist regime.

From those who explicitly opposed the war in both their news terminology and views, to those who aimed to strike a balance in their news coverage but opposed the war through editorial comment, to those who attempted neutrality by giving a podium to the chief propagandists of both the occupying powers and occupied Iraq, the Arab media have expressed a plethora of opinions and have helped shape wider Arab public opinion in turn. Yet they have been united in conveying the over-riding message that the coalition members are "invaders," and in representing the Iraqi people as an aggrieved Arab nation alongside the Palestinians: unjustly occupied, humiliated, and suffering under siege.

Writing in the cultural supplement of the Beirut-based *Al-Nahar*, Palestinian novelist Ziyad Khadash published a short story during the 2003 Iraq War, titled: "As if I am in Basra, as if you are in Ramallah" (Khadash, 2003). Highlighting the perceived "Palestinianization" of Iraq, Khadash describes an imagined telephone conversation between him and a Basra-based Iraqi novelist. He writes that he finds it hard to distinguish between the sound of the Apache helicopters attacking Ramallah and those attacking Basra.

In a column headed "Lies are the Salt of War," journalist Amjad Nasir wrote in *Al-Quds Al-Arabi* that "it is widely assumed that the politician is a professional liar." Referring to the coalition's military spokespersons, he continued: "The assumption is to attach to the military person characteristics such as honor, self-control, and respect. But the current war on Iraq gives us an example of the military person who outdoes the politician in his lies" (Nasir, 2003, p. 20). Such a viewpoint was clearly not conducive to the attempts of the Anglo-American coalition to create a positive "spin" on its actions.

The News in Arabic

Arab newspapers, radio stations, television, the Internet, and especially satellites now play a pivotal role in presenting to the Arab world and beyond uncensored coverage that the American and other Western media often do not show. Key to the success of the Arab new media in particular is the "gratification" element: Arab audiences seek the new media out since their governments could not openly oppose U.S. policies leading to the war against Iraq. Furthermore, the new media are active in countering Anglo-American propaganda by giving air time to Arab voices overlooked by the Western media.

Then there is the significance of the shared language of Arabic, with its thousands of years of collective history. In particular, Arabic is viewed as the sacred language of the Qur'an, revealed to the Prophet Mohammed fourteen centuries ago, and which has 300 million speakers worldwide.

Daily, throughout the 2003 Iraq War, the Arab media set out to expose the "constant lies, rumors and disinformation of the invading powers" in the world's media, and to show how the invaders' information campaign was losing credibility by the hour. As such, it gave maximum coverage to the "heavy" Iraqi civilian casualties incurred in the war, and the situation of anarchy and lawlessness that followed. In a news item from Al-Jazeera's Web site, one (uncredited) headline reads: "The Iraq war is filled with the invading powers' false arguments" (*Harb al-Iraq tahfal bi'l-maza'im al-zai'fa li''l-quwwat al-ghaziyya*). Quoting the Iraqi poet Mohammed Nasif Jasim, the Saudi-owned *Al-Sharq Al-Awsat* wrote: "A thirty-five-year nightmare has been removed, only to be replaced by a worse one" (Juwda, 2003, p. 1).

Despite the huge pressures placed on them in the Iraq war, the Arab media did attempt to provide credible coverage in the eyes of both Arab and world opinion. Bush administration criticism of Al-Jazeera,[5] and the later bombardment of its office that killed reporter Tariq Ayyub, were seen in the Arab world as methods for concealing, if not silencing, the truth (Al-Ahmad, 2003).[6] Undaunted, the Arab media's terminology was frequently subversive, with Arab journalists, writers and artists openly resisting the Western "aggressors," "invaders" and "occupiers." In his live TV show, ANN presenter Hisham Diwani claimed:

> As an Arab journalist, once you have discovered the truth and given an accurate account of events, you cannot stay aloof and not condemn the actions of the occupation. This is your role as a journalist: it gives the occupying coalition forces no hope of winning the Iraqis' hearts and minds.[7]

Another Arab columnist, writing in the Egyptian *Al-Wafd* newspaper, warned that official U.S. media policy would have to "use Arab voices and Arab pens" to promote its imperialist agenda, since "Arab audiences suspect any direct American media" (Ghadban, 2003, p.10).

Poetry and Propaganda

Early in the 2003 Iraq War, the two most eminent living Arab poets, Palestinian Mahmud Darwish[8] and Syrian Adunis,[9] joined Egyptian poet and folklorist Abd Al-Rahman Al-Abnudi[10] in publishing three powerful polemical poems in the Arab press. These three poems, "Only Iraq" (Darwish, 2003), "A Greeting to Baghdad" (Adunis, 2003) and "Baghdad" (Al-Abnudi, 2003), lauded Iraq's contribution to the rich Arab culture and heritage, and called for Arab solidarity and fraternity with Iraq.

The prominent role of the modern Arab poet should be seen here in its traditional, culturally-specific context. Historically, the ruler in Arab culture secured the minds of his citizens through oaths of allegiance, respect, and other coercive means. To win their hearts, he enlisted the services of a co-opted poet laureate.

During his invasion of Kuwait in August 1990, Saddam Hussein would most certainly have recruited poets to his palace, but he found no Arab poet to rally the Arab masses behind him. In the 2003 Iraq War, the situation was different. It was U.S.-led assaults on "Iraqi honor; the land and the human," as described by one Arab interviewee (Qara'uni, 2003, p. 1)[11] that truly succeeded in capturing the Arab mind. And it was the committed Arab poets who truly captured the Arabs' hearts by describing the sufferings and sentiments of their fellow Iraqi Arabs with an eloquence and artistry that made full use of the rich semantic possibilities and socio-cultural power of the Arabic language.

By contrast, Anglo-American propaganda directed primarily at the Iraqis was far less successful. Among these this were the speeches of Prime Minister Tony Blair and U.S. President George W. Bush on "Towards Freedom TV" that was transmitted from an American Hercules airplane.[12] This was an attempt to affect Iraqi behavior on the ground and to persuade the Iraqi people to accept the "invading/liberating" powers. The coalition's line of winning Iraqi hearts and minds aimed to bring about permanent behavioral change, yet this was unlikely to occur, since the Iraqis—of all Arabs—had long experience with propaganda.

In a society such as theirs, it had long been recognized that messages are invariably propagandistic, even when biases are unconscious. In Iraq—as elsewhere—propaganda emerged as an essential element of warfare. Moreover, it had become a major weapon in ideological struggle, both before the outbreak of these hostilities and after. Having already been engaged in a propaganda war for some thirty years, it was never going to be easy to change Iraqi attitudes and behavior.

As has been demonstrated by the Arab media, the overwhelming majority of Arabs and Iraqis saw no substance to the coalition's campaign to "liberate" the Iraqis and "win their hearts and minds." In their view, the coalition's prime concern was Iraq's natural resources, namely oil, as had been the case since Britain's first occupation of Iraq in the early 20th century.

Having seen the results of this invasion both on the ground and through the media, many have asked how the coalition could secure Iraq's oil fields and its oil ministry, yet could not prevent the destruction and looting of its national heritage. Their questioning grew even louder when an Al-Jazeera crew filmed British soldiers openly pillaging truckloads of Iraqi oil.[13]

In the view of most Arabs, had the Western preachers of democracy and freedom been at all concerned for the plight of Arabs living under oppression, they would have liberated the Palestinians, rather than the Iraqis, who have been enduring the longest occupation in modern history. Rather, they are confronted by scenes of Palestinians meeting their deaths at the hands of a state backed by U.S. money and arms.

INVADING HEARTS

"Hearts cannot rest quickly in peace, for in order to accept you have to re-trust the one who killed your father, wife or children," wrote the Christian Arab Bishop George Khudhur (2003, p.12).

As the example of the Arab media shows, no amount of Anglo-American sloganeering will ever be sufficient to convince the relatives of those Iraqis killed in the U.S.-led war of 2003. Nor will it ever be possible to market the coalition's propaganda to those who were injured in that war, or those who found their property looted, or who were harassed while U.S. occupying forces stood by. In short, the battle to "win Iraqi hearts and minds" has become a slogan too cynical for Arabs to believe.

The overall mood of the Iraqis and Arabs, as reflected in the various forms of Arab media, suggests that the coalition's propaganda and its techniques have been weak weapons. Indeed, the Arab media express the view that the Arab world remains overwhelmingly in sympathy with the citizens of Iraq. In this war, it was the suffering Iraqi people who gained possession of the majority of Arab hearts and minds.

In the 1991 Gulf War, following the Iraq's invasion of Kuwait, the collective Arab "heart" felt broken by events. Although some Arab regimes rallied behind the Western coalition forces in their bid to liberate Kuwait, the Arab "mind" felt disrespected, both by Iraq's invasion of another Arab capital, and by the fact that "the imperialists," who were the driving force behind Kuwait's liberation, had attacked a leading Arab country in order to secure their own national interests in the Middle East.

And yet, unlike in 2003, the Arab world did not throw its weight behind the citizens of Iraq, because their president had occupied another Arab country.

As the Arab media charge, in order to "win the hearts and minds" of the people of Iraq the Western coalition should not have bombarded and slain them, denied them necessary medical aid, or cut off their water from the nation's two main rivers (then offering them limited supplies of mineral water). In their view, by such methods the coalition could have hoped for little more than to temporarily silence a handful of Iraqi stomachs before these hungry stomachs became even angrier minds.

Hitler's chief propagandist Joseph Goebbels argued that it is relatively easy to influence a people's mood (*Stimmung*), but that it is far more problematic to change their behavior (*Haltung*) (Hale, 1975). Although signs of visible, if temporary, relief were expressed by Iraqis after Saddam Hussein's removal, this began to shift negatively with the continued scenes of civilian killings and national devastation. Hence, there has been no real evidence a year after the war of a mood change in Iraq, and it is hard to foresee that any real behavioral change will be witnessed in the near future.

Although difficult to establish whether it was merely an unfortunate translation error rather than a Freudian slip, the official BBC Web site in Arabic translated the coalition's campaign to "win" Iraqi hearts and minds as an "invasion" (*ghazw al-qulub*).[14] In matters of warfare, as well as matters of romance, the Arab heart is never won through aggression or by depriving it of its basic human rights, but through relentless, gentle action.

As with human beings everywhere, the Arab mind is won only through appreciation and respect. All of this was absent in the U.S.-led occupation of Iraq, and so the coalition's battle for hearts and minds may never be won.

ENDNOTES

1. This refers to the events of October 2000, when a huge crowd from across Serbia marched on and stormed Belgrade's Yugoslav Parliament building, proclaiming opposition leader Vojislav Kostunica as the new Yugoslav president and presenting serving president Slobadan Milosevic with an ultimatum to surrender his post. See:
http://news.bbc.co.uk/onthisday/hi/dates/ stories/october/5/newsid_2493000/2493021.stm.

2. Initially, U.S. soldiers placed the U.S. flag over the face of the Iraqi president's statue, then replaced it with an old version of the Iraqi flag, one which did not bear the phrase *Allahu akbar* ("God is Great"), added by Saddam Hussein after the 1991 Gulf War.

3. Iraqi Minister of Information 2001-2003, who became one of the best known faces during the U.S.-led war on Iraq due to his often sensational counter-propaganda role and style.

4. For more on the various Arab satellites and newspapers, plus comments, see www.bbc.co.uk/hi/arabic/talking_point/newsid_2910000/ 2910597.stm
www.Al-Bawaba.com, and www.arabia.com

5. See Colin Powell"s comments to the media on March 26 and 27, 2003.

6. For more, see http://www.aljazeera.net/news/arabic/2003/4/4-8-18.htm and http://www.aljazeera.net/ news/arabic/2003/4/4-8-14.htm

7. Arab News Network, April 28, 2003.

8. Mahmud Darwish (b. 1942) became a so-called "internal refugee" after his village of Birwa was razed by the Israelis alongside five hundred other Palestinian localities, during the Nakba (Catastrophe) of 1948. Darwish was discovered, adopted by, and joined the Israeli Communist party and worked for its press until his voluntary exile from Israel in 1971. His works, alongside those of his mentor Imil Habibi and comrades such as Samih Al-Qasim, Salim Jubran and Tawfiq Zayad, reached the Arab world after the Israeli occupation of the second part of Palestine in 1967. Committed to the Palestinian cause, he became known as the Palestinian "poet laureate" and is now one of the major proponents of modern Palestinian and Arabic poetry.

9. Adunis (Ali Ahmad Said, b.1929) is a Syrian-born poet and was a member of the Syrian Nationalist Socialist Party. He took Beirut as his center of academic study and political activity. He was a leading light in the evolution of Arabic free verse poetry, and is seen as the most prominent modernizer of Arabic poetry. He was a founding member of the Shi"r group in 1957, and in 1968 he established his own cultural and literary

magazine, *Mawaqif.* He has taught Arabic literature in Arab and European universities.

10. Al-Abnudi is one of the better-known living poets of the so-called "Sixties Generation," and is one of Upper Egypt's best-known writers and public figures. Writing in colloquial Egyptian Arabic, he is famed for his resistance poetry, such as his songs for the Palestinian Intifada.

11. See *Al-Quds Al-Arabi* and Reuters, April 1, 2003.

12. For more on "Towards Freedom TV," see http://politics.guardian.co.uk/iraq/story/0,12956,934290,00.html and http://www.pm.gov.uk/output/Page3469.asp

13. For more on this episode, which took place on 27 April 2003, see http://www.aljazeera.net/economics/ 2003/5/5-14-4.htm

14. http://news.bbc.co.uk/hi/Arabic/news/

References

Adunis (2003, April 1). Tahiyya ila Baghdad [A Greeting to Baghdad]. *Al-Quds Al-Arabi,* p. 1.

Al-Abnudi, A.A-R. (2003, April 16). Baghdad. *Al-Quds Al-Arabi,* p. 3.

Al-Ahmad, U. (2003, April 8). Al-sahafiyyun hadaf Al-ghuzat li-takmim afwah Al-shuhud 'ala Al-jarima [Occupiers targets journalists to silence witnesses to the crime]. Available June 15, 2003, from http://www.aljazeera.net/news/ arabic/2003/4/4-8-14.htm

Al-Hassan, B. (2003, April 13). Bad isti'mar Al-'Iraq wa'l-ati a'tham [Iraq's colonization has started and the worst is yet to come]. http://www.asharqalawsat.com/view/leader/2003,04,14,165312.html.

Darwish, M. (2003, March 29). Laysa siwa al-Iraq [Only Iraq]. *Al-Quds Al-Arabi,* p. 1.

Ghadban, A-S. (2003, 22 April). Kalam fi'l-i'lam [Rhetoric in the media]. *Al-Wafd,* p. 10.

Hale, J. (1975). *Radio power: Propaganda and international broadcasting.* London: Paul Elk.

Ionesco, E. (1968). *Fragments of a journal.* (J. Stewart, Trans.). London: Faber.

Juwda, A. (2003, April 13). Jawla fi'l-Basra wa Um Qasr [A Tour of Basra and Um Qasr]. http://www.asharqalawsat.com/view/Currentissues/2003,04,13,165357.html.

Khadash, Z. (2003, April 6). Ka-anni fi'l-Basra, ka-annaka fi Ramallah [As if I am in Basra, as if you are in Ramallah]. *Al-Mulhaq Al-Thaqafi,* p. 4.

Khudhur, G. (2003, April 13). Simfonia Al-'arab [Symphony of the Arabs]. *Al-Nahar,* p. 12.

Nasir, A. (2003, March 28). Al-Kadhb milh Al-harb [Lies are the salt of war]. *Al-Quds Al-Arabi,* p. 20.

Qara'uni, M. (2003, April 1). Mutatawi'un 'arab yatawajahun ila Al-'iraq li'l-difa' 'an Al-ard wa'Al-sharaf [Arab volunteers head for Iraq to defend land and honor]. *Al-Quds Al-Arabi,* p. 1.

CHAPTER 29

News Credibility During the 2003 Iraq War: A Survey of UAE Students

Muhammad I. Ayish

The Anglo-American invasion of Iraq in March 2003 spawned worldwide debates about how coalition governments handled political and military affairs, and how news media communicated different aspects of the conflict.

As much as U.S. and U.K. governments were criticized for intelligence manipulation, news media were also taken to task for their perceived one-sided and inadequate reporting of military and political realities in Iraq. U.S. media coverage has been described as "simplistic, unapologetically patriotic, and generally unquestioning of military pronouncements." It was noted that the war's terminology shifted in news reports from "war on terror," to an "invasion," to a "liberation" of a people (Sanchez, 2003). Some critics argued that the role of the Western news media was to objectively cover the war, but they fell short after a slew of false reports, embedded reporters "playing by the rules" to which they had agreed with the Pentagon, and pro-war sentiment ringing through cable news networks (Sanchez, 2003).

In the Middle East, public perceptions of Western media biases in the war on Iraq seem to have given more credence to regional Arab media players such as Qatar-based Al-Jazeera satellite Channel (JSC), Abu Dhabi Satellite Channel (ADSC), Lebanese Broadcasting Corporation (LBC), and Al-Arabiya Channel.

Internet-based news operations like Jazeera.net and IslamOnline were also important sources of information on war developments in Iraq. JSC's chief Baghdad correspondent was killed during the U.S. Army's thrust into Baghdad while crew members of other TV channels experienced certain hardships as they covered military developments.

Unlike 1991 Operation Desert Storm in Iraq, the 2003 Anglo-American invasion marked the meteoric rise of a select group of pan-Arab media with Western-style news-gathering practices. Broadcast media reporting of Iraqi civilian casualties and destruction, as well as daily press briefings from Central Command Headquarters (Centcom) in Qatar and from Iraqi information officials in Baghdad, were the staple of daily Arab television coverage.

Print media, on the other hand, made up for their relatively "outdated" news by publishing more viewpoints and analyses on the Iraqi crisis that were unanimously negative toward the coalition's efforts before, during, and after the war. The daily appearances of former Iraqi Minister of Information Mohammed Saeed Al-Sahhaf, with his seemingly credible tone of voice, turned him into a popular figure among Arab audiences and a pop culture figure in the West.

Arab media performance during the Iraq war was credited with the flow of information about the developing crisis to a pan-Arab audience in deep shock over the relative ease a fellow Arab country was invaded by foreign forces. At least one credible public opinion poll seemed to reflect growing anti-American sentiments in the Arab world in pre-conflict times (Telhami, 2002). Hostile U.S. attitudes towards Iraq and anti-war governments worldwide seemed to have aggravated an already tarnished official U.S. image in Arab minds, resulting mainly from systematic support of Israeli policies in Palestinian lands and unfriendly post-9/11 policies toward Arabs and Muslims.

Five days into the U.S. invasion of Iraq, Arab foreign ministers described the attack as "a violation of international law and legality, a threat to international peace and security and a challenge of the international community and public opinion." They also called for "immediate and unconditional withdrawal of U.S.-British invading troops from Iraq" and renewed the Arab world's "commitment not to participate in any military actions that would undermine Iraq's sovereignty and security and international legality." With growing perceptions of the Bush administration's manipulation of American media, Arab viewers seemed more predisposed to trust their trans-national media.

An exploratory study was conducted on a random, convenience sample of students at the University of Sharjah in the United Arab Emirates (UAE) that found students perceived Arab media as more credible than Western media in handling Iraq war developments. The study was based on a survey of students in different colleges at the university on their media exposure patterns and media credibility perceptions during the invasion. The writer argued that due to existing public anti-U.S. sentiments and mistrust of Western media reporting of the Iraq situation, Arab audiences were more likely to trust Arab-based media services. Two research questions are addressed in this study:

RQ1. How do media exposure patterns during the Anglo-American invasion of Iraq relate to audiences' credibility perceptions?

RQ2. How do credibility perceptions vary across different media?

MEDIA CREDIBILITY: LITERATURE OVERVIEW

The question relating to perceptions of media credibility has been a recurring issue in mass communication scholarship since the mid-20th century. While Hovland and Weiss's seminal work on this issue (1951) concentrated on dimensions of source credibility, more contemporary literature has highlighted variations in credibility perceptions of different channels (Rimmer & Weaver, 1987).

Westley and Severin (1964) are credited with conducting the first comprehensive analysis of news credibility across media outlets. In their classic study, the authors noted that certain demographic variables (such as age, education, and gender) mediate people's perceptions of news credibility. Several analysts indicated that television news was more credible than newspapers (Carter & Greenberg, 1965; Lemert, 1970; Gaziano & McGrath, 1986). Other researchers have traditionally related credibility perceptions to media political and ideological leanings, especially in election times.

Past studies suggest that how credible one views a medium is strongly related to how often one relies on it (Wanta & Yu-Wei Hu, 1994), with relationships proving stronger for reliance measures than general use ones (Gaziano & McGrath, 1986). It has also been suggested that people judge their preferred medium as the most credible, with television gaining the highest ranking (ASNE, 1985). Research findings suggest that those who are older, wealthier, and better educated are least likely to view media as credible, while males judge media as less credible than females (Westley and Severin, 1964).

Since the mid-1990s, with the proliferation of new media, credibility research has been broadened to include audience perceptions of Internet-based news. Johnson and Kaye (1998) note that the Internet, with its potential for free access features, might affect the credibility of the medium as a source of information. Flanagin and Metzger (2000) pointed out that while newspapers, books, and television undergo a process of information verification before they reach the public, Internet sites do not always use such measures.

Abdallah et al. (2002) analyzed news credibility components for a range of U.S. newspaper, television, and online sites and found similarities in how each medium was perceived. The study revealed some fundamental differences as respondents evaluated newspaper and television news credibility more similarly than they did online news credibility.

While traditional news sources and their online counterparts are subject to both professional and social pressures to provide accurate and unbiased information, such constraints do not exist for the Internet.

In their study, Flanagin and Metzger (2000) compared perceptions of Internet information credibility to other media. They concluded that the Internet was as credible as television, radio, and magazines, but not newspapers. They found that credibility varied by medium and types of information sought by audiences, such as news and entertainment. Kiousis (1999) found perceptions of news credibility to be influenced by media use and interpersonal discussion of news.

Internet studies also suggest that how credible people judge the medium to be depends on how often they use it. Johnson and Kaye (1998) found that reliance on the Web for political information was correlated with how credible they judged online newspapers, news magazines, online candidate literature, and issue-oriented sources.

However, hours per week on the Web and on political sites in particular, as well as the number of times the Web has been accessed, were unrelated to media credibility. Similarly, the Pew Research Center found that while 55% of Americans in general rated the Internet as accurate as traditional media, 69% of Internet users considered it as equally credible (Bromley & Bowels, 1998).

THE UAE COMMUNICATIONS SCENE

The United Arab Emirates has one of the most developed and diverse media infrastructures in the Arab world region (UNDP, 2002). In mid-2003, there were nine television channels (terrestrial and satellite), in addition to thirteen local and international radio stations operating from the UAE. Six daily newspapers and four weekly magazines are also published in the UAE.

On the other hand, telecommunications continues to be the sole domain of the UAE's telecommunications service provider "Etisalat," which has enjoyed a monopolistic status in this area since its establishment in 1976. The UAE has over a million Internet users with free access to regional and international online media resources (Etisalat, 2001). A free-market economy has provided media with an appropriate environment for development and expansion.

Television was first introduced into the UAE in August 1969 in black and white from Abu Dhabi. In 1972, Dubai had its first channel, followed some years later by the launch of Channel 33, a foreign program channel that combined with Abu Dhabi's second channel to reach out with mostly English-language programming to members of the large UAE expatriate community. In 1989, another television station with mostly cultural programming was launched in

Sharjah.

In the 1990s, the introduction of satellite television broadcasting was instrumental in changing the face of UAE television broadcasting. In 1992, Abu Dhabi Television began its satellite transmissions, followed by Dubai Television in the same year, and by Sharjah Television in 1999 (Boyd, 1999).

The UAE broadcast media scene also witnessed the launch of Dubai's Business and Sports Channels, and Abu Dhabi's Emirates and Sports Channels. In Abu Dhabi, Emirates Media Inc. (EMI) was created in January 1999 by Federal Law No. 5 to succeed the UAE Radio and Television Corporation and Al Ittihad Press, Printing and Publishing Company. The UAE also allows free access to a wide range of regional and global satellite television broadcasters on free-to-air or subscription bases.

As for print media, the first publication in the UAE dates back to the 1950s; however, it was not until 1969 that periodical publications became an established institution with the launch of *Al-Itihad* newspaper by Al-Ittihad Publishing and Printing Company in Abu Dhabi. In 1971, *Al-Khaleej* newspaper was launched, but failed after a year. It was launched again in 1980 by Al Khaleej Publishing and Printing Company and has become one of the most respected publications in the Gulf region.

In 1980, with a clear business orientation, Al-Bayan Publishing and Printing Company established a third Arabic newspaper, *Al-Bayan*, in Dubai. *Akhbar Al-Arab* was launched in 2001 as a national Arabic daily newspaper published in Abu Dhabi and distributed countrywide. Two English language publications are also published: *The Gulf News* and *Khaleej Times*. UAE residents also have access to a wide range of international and pan-Arab publications.

In terms of Internet-based media, the UAE is the "most wired" country in the Arab world (Ayish, 1999). Data on information technology diffusion in the UAE show that the country is well ahead of other Arab states in terms of Internet availability, computer usage ratios, and information technology applications.

For the past few years, the UAE has embarked on a long-term policy of diversifying its economic production base to include non-oil sectors like trade, tourism, media, and information technology. The launch of Dubai Internet City (DIC) in early 2000 marked a quantum leap in the UAE information technology landscape. Residents now have access to a wide variety of Internet-based media outlets such as electronic newspapers and online news portals.

Method

This study is based on a survey of a student sample randomly selected from the University of Sharjah enrollment lists. Data were collected using a ten-item questionnaire distributed to students representing seven university colleges in different study levels, conducted during May-June 2003.

A total of 150 interviews, equally divided between males and females, were completed. Twenty students (half male) were selected from each of the seven colleges (except for the College of Arts and Sciences whose share was thirty, in proportion to its large student body size). Each student in the sample was assigned a number that was blindly and randomly drawn.

The survey instrument included a news credibility scale adapted from Gaziano and McGrath (1986). A Likert-type scale developed for this study views credibility as a multidimensional construct. On a scale from -5 to + 5, the survey was based on five items: timeliness, professionalism, objectivity, accuracy, and balance. Respondents were asked, "How would you rate this medium's objectivity, professionalism, accuracy, timeliness, or balance?"

Scores for the five measures of credibility were combined into a credibility index for each medium. From each of these credibility scores, a summated mean was computed and the scales were analyzed for similarities and differences. Scale mean summations for three media (television, newspapers, and online news) were correlated with media exposure levels.

Based on respondents' selections of favorite media outlets used during the conflict, media outlets were identified for analysis in each media category as follows:

- Print Media: *Al-Khaleej, Al-Ittihad, Al-Bayan, Akhbar Al-Arab*, and others.
- Broadcast Media: Al-Jazeera, Abu Dhabi, Al-Arabiya, MBC, and others.
- Online Media: *Al-Jazeera.net*, *IslamOnline*, *BBC.com*, *CNN.com*, and others.

Media exposure data were broken down into ten time-range categories (10-28 hours per week or 40-112 hours for the whole period). The number of hours a week spent by respondents in their exposure to different media was coded.

FINDINGS AND DISCUSSION

Sample members represented balanced national backgrounds comprising UAE and Arab students attending the University of Sharjah (55% UAE nationals and 45% Arabian expatriates). Following is an overview of the study findings:

Media Exposure Levels

The data show that during the first four weeks of the military conflict (March 20-April 9), respondents spent a total of 3,452.8 hours a week with different media. Television got the lion's share of that time (39.78%), followed by newspapers (21.47%), online media (12.44%), and a host of other media that included radio, magazines, mobile phones, and interpersonal communications

(26.31%).

The average exposure time for each member of the sample was twenty-three hours or 3.5 hours a day. By normal standards, time devoted to following up on war developments was quite high and seemed to reflect rising tensions among Arab populations as they coped with war developments. The fact that television took first place is not surprising since satellite television broadcasting has increasingly become an integral part of daily communication experiences of Arabs (Berenger & Labidi, 2004). In the UAE, satellite television is obtained through subscription and free-to-air services like Al-Jazeera, Al-Arabiya, and Abu Dhabi television. There are scores of other channels operating in the area, but these three seem to be the leaders.

Lower exposure to newspapers may be because print media are less timely than TV broadcasts that carried war developments live. Respondents might have read papers more for analysis and insight into what was happening in war. Online media, though gaining ground in the UAE, seem to have a long way to go before they can match the power of television as a source of wartime information.

Perceptions of Media Credibility

Respondents rated television news highest in credibility. Data in Table 29.1 show TV news received a mean score of 68.61 for credibility, followed by daily newspapers (42.8), and online media (20.96). With its timely and visual approach to war developments, television news seemed to have won greater trust than print media news.

Online news had the lowest credibility with respondents. Among the print media, *Al-Khaleej* ranked first with a credibility mean score of 103.49—over three times more credible than any of its competitors—*Al-Bayan* (38.23), *Al-Ittihad* (36.54), and *Akhbar Al-Arab* (15.62). The remaining newspapers received a combined credibility mean score of 20.12.

This variation among respondents' perceptions of newspaper credibility during the Iraq conflict may reflect different media exposure habits that seem to have a bearing on how readers view their favorite newspaper. All four newspapers, in fact, devoted full coverage to war developments and to reporting both Iraqi and Anglo-American views of the war.

Among television broadcasters, Al-Jazeera satellite television channel scored the highest credibility score among respondents (118.74), followed by Abu Dhabi satellite television (105.12), Al-Arabiya (64.99), MBC (24.62), and other broadcasters with a combined mean of 20.12.

As a regional broadcaster with professional capabilities, JSC seems to have convinced Arab audiences that this satellite channel was a powerful match for CNN and BBC television. In 1991, Operation Desert Storm in Iraq was a CNN

TABLE 29.1 CREDIBILITY MEAN SCORES

Medium	Mean Score
Newspapers	
Al-Khaleej	103.49
Al- Ittihad	36.54
Al- Bayan	38.23
Akhbar Al-Arab	15.62
Others	20.12
Newspaper Credibility Mean	**42.8**
Television (terrestrial and satellite)	
Al-Jazeera Satellite Channel	118.74
Abu Dhabi Television	105.12
Al-Arabiya Satellite Channel	64.99
MBC	24.62
Others	29.62
Television Credibility Mean	**68.61**
Internet	
Al Jazeera.net	65.49
IslamOnline	1.87
BBC.Com	6.37
CNN.COM	1.87
Others	29.24
Online Media Credibility Mean	**20.96**
Total Media Credibility Mean Score	**44.12**

news exclusive, but since the launch of JSC some six years ago, the preference among Arab audiences has been shifting to pan-Arab television broadcasters like Al-Jazeera. In Operation Desert Fox in 1998 JSC was in Iraq, dispatching live reports about air strikes in Baghdad and other cities. In November 2001 JSC was also a central media player in Afghanistan.

Yet JSC's most reputed role was during the 2003 Iraq War when the network dispatched three television crews to the battlefield. One of its correspondents, Tareq Ayyoub, was killed by U.S. fire as he covered U.S. Marines' push into Baghdad.

Abu Dhabi satellite television has risen to prominence as a leading television broadcaster in recent years, with live coverage of regional and international events in Iraq, Palestine, and other locations. Al-Arabiya satellite channel is a newcomer to the media scene. However, its third-place ranking seemed to indicate its growing role in Arab world broadcasting. MBC, a sister company of Al-Arabiya, was launched in 1991 as a variety channel with an important news and public affairs dimension. But, with the pooling of its resources with Al-Arabiya, this channel seemed to have scaled down its news operations to enhance its sister news channel's regional standing.

Online media, despite the proliferation of Internet services in the UAE, continued to play a minor part in media usage. *Al-Jazeera.net* has been chosen as the most credible source of online news during the Iraqi war, far exceeding similar services like I*slamOnline*, *CNN.com*, and *BBC.com*. It seems that while young generations in the UAE are increasingly using the Internet for different purposes, its use as a source of news and analysis during critical times is still far from being realized. *Al-Jazeera.net* received a 65.49 credibility score, far ahead of other online news sites.

The fact that exposure to online media requires connectivity to an Internet service could account for low use. Users might have to choose between live audio-visual reporting of war and multimedia presentations. In times of crisis, visual news immediacy dominated as an exposure criterion compared with "outdated" print media coverage or "less than live" online reporting of ongoing developments. Audiences' thirst for news in war times seems to propel them to go for timely news sources, and television seems to be the most favored medium as it combines audio-visual and timely features.

Relating Media Exposure to Credibility Levels

Those who spent more time with different media were more likely to perceive them as more credible, the study showed. The zero-order correlation was .98 ($p<.001$).

This finding supports other research projects that have found a positive correlation between media exposure levels and news credibility perceptions. In times of crisis, heavy media usage usually suggests some sort of attachment to media outlets to quench audience thirst for information.

Common sense dictates that people ascribe their favorite news medium with having high believability, otherwise they could not continue use it. However, one should note that people tend to expose themselves to selected media simply because they have no other alternatives. In this study, however, respondents had an abundance of media resources they could draw on for news about the war. UAE audiences had access to over three hundred television channels, scores of local and regional radio broadcasts, and hundreds of conventional and online news sources in different languages.

Although extended exposure to media outlets would reinforce audience credibility perceptions, one should note that coverage of the Iraq conflict invoked considerable patriotic feelings in both Arab and Western media organizations. U.S. TV network logos were draped in red-white-and-blue bunting as anti-war voices were subdued by what could be perceived in the Arab world as a government/media front to promote the cause for war. Given this Arab world perception of U.S. media as propaganda machines in Pentagon hands, they had no choice but to fall back on Arab world media that possessed professional news standards.

It was in this context that Arabs rated a TV network like Al-Jazeera as the most credible among all media. For many Arabs, JSC and Abu Dhabi satellite channel were powerful matches for Western networks like CNN and BBC. Arab broadcasters were lauded for their insightful reporting of issues independent of government influence. JSC's reporters who were killed, injured, or roughed up by U.S. forces were viewed as heroes with legitimate professional and patriotic causes.

CONCLUSION

This study was an exploratory effort to investigate public perceptions of media credibility in times of crisis. University students with different Arabian national backgrounds represented a young generation who reflected their familial and broad societal values and attitudes about the 2003 Iraq War.

Western media and governments were viewed with suspicion in Arab countries and, hence, were perceived as less credible. This guilt-by-association argument goes back to the mid-1960s when Voice of America broadcasts were received negatively by Arab audiences that considered the radio services as the propaganda arm of what was perceived as a hostile foreign government.

In this Iraq war, U.S. and British media were viewed as co-culprits in the conflict with their governments. The rise of pan-Arab media like JSC, Abu Dhabi TV, and Al-Arabiya was a timely development for Arab audiences deeply shocked and offended by the invasion.

Online media, on the other hand, lagged in exposure levels apparently because of the recency of these services. Yet, the heavy use of the Al Jazzera.net portal seems to auger well for online news media in an Arab world as Internet usage increases. Because of their timely and visual limitations, newspapers trailed television broadcasters in both preference and credibility. Print media were used mainly for analysis and commentary.

Although the four UAE newspapers studied have online versions, respondents were more inclined to opt for conventional exposure to print media in paper form. Electronic newspaper versions were transcriptions of conventional papers; therefore, they were not as useful as specialized news portals that furnish users with continuously updated news developments.

The findings also support other studies regarding positive relationships between exposure levels and credibility perceptions. However, it would be inaccurate to think of this relationship outside mediating variables like communitarian sentiments on the part of pan-Arab audiences who were nearly unanimously negative toward the coalition strategy in Iraq. Credibility perceptions might have developed in reaction to antagonism toward both the Bush and Blair prosecutions of the war and the Western media that seemed to support those governments.

REFERENCES

Abdulla, R., Garrison, B., Salwen, M., Driscoll, P., and Casey, D. (2002, August 9). The credibility of newspapers, television news, and online news. A paper presented to the Mass Communication and Society Division, Association for Education in Journalism and Mass Communication, annual convention, Miami Beach, Fla.

American Society of Newspaper Editors (1985). Credibility: Building reader trust. Washington, DC: *American Society of Newspaper Editors, 63.*

Ayish, M. (1999, December). Trends in communication technologies in the GCC states. In *Scientific and Technological Developments in GCC Region,* (in Arabic). Abu Dhabi: Emirates Center for Strategic Studies and Research,

Berenger, R.D., & Labidi, K. (2004). Television in Egypt. In A. Cooper-Chen, *Global Entertainment Media: Content, Audiences, Issues.* Mahwah, NJ: Lawrence Erlbaum.

Boyd, D. (1999). *Broadcasting in the Arab world: A survey of electronic media in the Middle East.* Ames: Iowa University Press

Bromley, R. and Bowles, D. (1995, spring): Impact of Internet on use of traditional news media. *Newspaper Research Journal 16,* 14-27.

Carter, R., & Greenberg, B. (1966). Newspapers or television: which do you believe? *Journalism Quarterly, 42,* 29-34

Emirates Telecommunications Corporation. (2001, December). Annual Report.

Flanagin, A.J., & Metzger, M.J. (2001, January). Internet use in the contemporary media environment. *Human Communication Research, 27*(1), 153-181.

Gaziano, C., & McGrath, K. (1986, Autumn). Measuring the concept of credibility. *Journalism Quarterly, 63*(3), 451-462.

Hovland, C.I., & Weiss, W. (1951). The influence of source credibility on communication effectiveness. *Public Opinion Quarterly, 15,* 633-650.

Johnson, T. J., & and Kaye, B.K. (1999). Using is believing: The influence of reliance on the credibility of online political information. Paper submitted to the Mass Communication and Society Division for the AEJMC annual convention, New Orleans, August 1999.

Johnson, T. J., & Kaye, B. K. (1998, Summer). Cruising is believing: Comparing Internet and traditional sources on media credibility measures. *Journalism & Mass Communication Quarterly, 75*(2), 325-340.

Kiousis, S. (1999, August). Public trust or mistrust? Perceptions of media credibility in the information age. Paper presented to the Mass Communication and Society Division, Association for Education in Journalism and Mass Communication, New Orleans.

Lemert, J.B. (1970). News media competition under conditions favorable to newspapers. *Journalism Quarterly, 33,* 330-339.

Rimmer, T. & Weaver, D. (1987). Different questions, different answers: Media use and media credibility. *Journalism Quarterly, 64,* 28-36, 44.

Sanchez, M (2003). Patriotism shaped war coverage, foreign journalists assert. The Kansas City Star, retrieved July 14, from: http://www.kansascity.com/mld/kansascitystar/news/opinion/6303511.htm

Schweiger, W. (2000, March 1). Media credibility experience or image?: A survey on the credibility of the World Wide Web in Germany in comparison to other media. *European Journal of Communication, 15,* 37-59.

Telhami, S. (2003, March 16). Arab public opinion: A survey in six countries. *San Jose Mercury.*

United Nations Development Program (2002) *Arab Human Development Report.* New York: United Nations.

Wanta, W. and Yu-Wei Hu. (1994, Spring). The effects of credibility, reliance, and exposure on media agenda-setting: A path analysis mode. *Journalism Quarterly 71*(2), 91.

Westley, B. H., & Severin, W.J. (1964). Some correlates of media credibility. *Journalism Quarterly, 41,* 325-335.

CHAPTER 30

War Against Media During the 2003 Iraq War

Abdullah Al-Kindi

War activities against media during the 2003 Gulf War began before Anglo-American soldiers invaded Iraq on March 20, 2003.

The term "war activities" refers to practices and actions carried out by the warring sides against journalists and broadcasters and considers the effects these practices might have on media behavior and performance. War activities focus on the following practices:

- Imposition of military control over media coverage. Examples include military practices of preventing journalists' access to some locations or enforcing information blackouts. The system of "embedded journalists" in military units will be explored.
- Harassment of journalists and, in a few cases, banishment from further war reporting.
- Criticism of media war coverage, particularly from politicians and military officials.
- Killing of journalists by bombarding their media centers or by "friendly fire."

Prior to the American/British attack on Iraq, world public opinion and expectations were cultivated and shaped to accept a new war through around-the-clock news coverage. Yet there seemed to be some predetermined selectivity of what the public should or should not receive.

Despite this selectivity, the information and news flow was very high compared with previous conflicts such as the 1991 Gulf War, the wars in the

Balkans, and the invasion of Taliban-controlled Afghanistan.

This surge in news flow shaped public expectations regarding when the war would start, what kind of strategies the warring sides would employ, and who the loser or winner would be. The intensive flow of information led politicians and military officials to attack media performance and to "[turn] their tanks on the reporters" (Knightly, 2003).

A cursory comparison of the 1991 and 2003 Gulf Wars would illustrate how the media environment, especially Arab media outlets, had changed in the intervening twelve years. CNN was the media star of the 1991 Gulf War, providing exclusive news feeds from Baghdad only a few hours a day, but narrowcasting news to cable customers around the clock. Despite CNN's limited coverage and its occasional lapses of journalistic proficiency, analysts observed that CNN played an extraordinary role in that war by offering news that was "faster, more continuous, less polished, and less edited" (Zelizer, 1992).

CNN was alone in covering the Gulf War without any true international or regional news competitor. BBC World, for example, would not be a competing factor for another decade, and Arabic language satellite channels were only far-off dreams. Because of that, the information flow was a trickle compared with today's news inundation. And global public's opinion measurement and reporting, especially from within the Arab world, was virtually nonexistent.

War activities enforced against news media in the 1991 Gulf War included press pools, military censorship, and official military briefings from designated spokesmen such as General Norman Schwarzkopf and from Colin Powell, Chairman of the Joint Chiefs of Staff, the most powerful military position in U.S. government. Even before that war started, journalists were warned by President George H.W. Bush that he "[didn't] want another Vietnam in the Gulf."

Media in the United States and in some of the coalition countries got the message and were dependent on military and official sources when reporting the war activities. In this way, media provided mostly positive news and avoided negative images and evaluations, thereby mobilizing public opinion in support of coalition governments' objectives. The control over reporters and information flow in 1991 war was massive. Accordingly, international media consumers received little unbiased information about the conflict upon which to form an opinion.

In the 2003 Gulf War, the world media environment had changed dramatically. However, war activities against news organizations and reporters increased and became more aggressive and restrictive. When this war started, media outlets around the world found themselves competing not only among themselves as media organizations, but also with the military units that first invaded Baghdad.

Although an estimated 1,400 journalists gathered to report the 1991 Gulf War, 5,000 journalists covered the 2003 war. After twelve years of CNN dominance, the world audience followed the 2003 war over a variety of international media outlets, ranging from electronic journalism and broadcasting via the Internet, to printed media along with around-the-clock TV news coverage. This time the significant change in the media environment came from the Arab world.

Arab media coverage of the 1991 Gulf War illustrated the global information gap between the Arab world and the West, the imbalance of news flow between the East and West, and more importantly the news manipulation by international wire services and CNN. In this context, it was rare to find any correspondent working for any Arab media outlet who reported from the war zone.

This situation changed completely in the 2003 Gulf War. Some Arab media organizations were in Baghdad before the rest of the international media organizations, and they had exceptional access to Iraqi news sources. Furthermore, some of these organizations—mainly Al-Jazeera, Abdu Dhabi, Al-Arabiya, and Future TV—competed not only with their Western counterparts as well as politicians and military officials, but with themselves. A scoop was a scoop, regardless of the language in which it was reported.

Because of their twenty-four-hour news broadcasts (covering different regions in Iraq) Al-Jazeera, Abu Dhabi, and Al-Arabiya became important news sources for other international news agencies as well as Arab audiences. They were not only sources for television images, but some daily newspapers in France (*Le Monde*) and England (*The Guardian*) devoted daily spaces to tell their readers what Al-Jazerra had said about the war the previous day. Debates about the performance of these Arab TV channels, particularly Al-Jazeera, raged among politicians, government officials, and media specialists.

Changes in the Arab media environment and work styles were expected after the 1991 war, and many new media channels were introduced to the Arab world by private investors. These new media outlets included private TV channels, pay TV, controversial channels and progra3ms, twenty-four-hour news programs, and the Internet (Alterman1998).

WAR AGAINST MEDIA (2003)

Documentation and narratives of the war activities against media in the 2003 war will be in a question/answer format. Some war activities against media are not peculiar to the latest war and have been recorded before. However, some of them, such as the apparent deliberate killing of journalists, are specifically attributed to the latest war. This chapter focuses on two major questions:

Q1: What are the main types of war activities against media during the 2003 Gulf War, and to whom are they attributed?

Q2: How did the war activities shape media content and reporters' attitudes?

Q.1: Main Types of War Activities

The primary war activities against media in the third Gulf War are:[1]

1. Military control over news and information feeds in different war zones. Both warring sides employed this type of control. On the coalition side, this control was embodied in the news briefings in the headquarters of the U.S. Central Command (Centcom) in Doha, Qatar, which was built and prepared a short time before the start of the war. The coalition also replaced the technique of "news pools" employed in the 1991 Gulf War with a new system called "embedded journalists." According to some estimates, around six hundred journalists, mainly American and British, were attached to military units in the Gulf. The U.S. Department of Defense justification for this technique was clear:

> [T]his holds true for the U.S. public; the public in allied countries whose opinion can affect the durability of our coalition; and public in countries where we conduct operations, whose perceptions of us can affect the cost and duration and our involvement.[2]

Embedded journalists were part of military units, sharing the same circumstances as soldiers, and they were guided by military commands. After journalists became part of the military units it could be argued that they turned into military spokesmen rather than independent journalists, especially when what they reported was self-censored for "military reasons." Of course, it can be equally argued that embedded journalists had extraordinary access to military personnel in the field, which they would not otherwise have had. Both Western and Arab reporters were embedded with coalition forces.

Following the lead of Centcom in Doha, Qatar, the Iraqi regime adopted the technique of news briefings conducted by the Iraqi information minister Mohammed Saeed Al-Sahhaf. Through his news briefings, the minister countered coalition military speakers and attempted to limit journalists' movements in Iraq by controlling the information and news flow. Al-Sahaf's role in attempting such control was confirmed after the war in a series of TV interviews he gave to Abu Dhabi television.

The coalition's military was accused by both reporters and organizations defending press freedom of mistreating reporters, targeting non-embedded journalists, and practicing prior restraint by screening some films and images from the battlefield. For example, the International Federation of Journalists (IFJ) accused U.S. military commanders of targeting non-embedded journalists, especially after the death of three journalists in American attacks in Baghdad on

March 8, 2003. Prior to that date, the Reporters Sans Frontieres (RSF) accused U.S. and British forces in Iraq of mistreating independent or non-embedded journalists. RSF accusations came after U.S. military police arrested four journalists. According to RSF's secretary general, these journalists were mistreated, beaten, and humiliated by the forces.

2. Harassing journalists and their news organizations.

The two warring sides subjected journalists and their news organizations to all sorts of annoyances and humiliations. Before detailing such activities—which took place over a period of just twenty days—it is worth noting here that actions against media and reporters began before the "actual war" started on March 20, 2003, and continued after that.

On February 16, 2003, the Iraqi government ejected four journalists from the Fox News crew following the U.S. expulsion of an Iraqi journalist from New York. Prior to the war, the Bush administration claimed that CBS TV's interview of Saddam Hussein by anchor Dan Rather allowed the Iraqi leader to set the agenda by refusing a right to reply by the administration. The White House offered to make available a spokesperson who would appear intermittently throughout the network's broadcast of Saddam's interview to comment on the interview. CBS accepted the administration's proposal on the condition that the president himself would be the guest, which the White House refused.

This example illustrates how the Bush administration, even before the war, tried to manipulate the media to alter its professional values. On September 22, 2003, Iraq's governing council threatened to take action against the Arabic television networks Al-Jazeera and Al-Arabiya because of "incitement to violence" in their reports about Iraq. During the war period in Iraq, the following activities against media were taken:

- The Iraqi government asked Nic Robertson, a CNN correspondent in Baghdad, to leave the country on March 21, 2003.
- Two correspondents for *Newsday* disappeared in Baghdad for nine days, after Iraqi authorities arrested them.
- New York Stock Exchange and NASDAQ ejected Al-Jazeera reporters on March 25, 2003.
- Hackers attacked the English-language and Arabic Web sites of Al-Jazeera on March 26, 2003.
- Military missiles hit the Iraqi information ministry headquarters three times: March 25, March 29, and March 30-31, 2003.
- Hackers again attacked Al-Jazeera's Web site and hijacked the Arabic news broadcaster's domain name and redirected users to an American patriotic Web site on March 28, 2003.
- NBC news sacked its reporter in Baghdad—Peter Arnett—on March 31, 2003, after he gave an interview with Arabic language channels and said the military

effort had bogged down after ten days of war. Arnett, who was in Baghdad during the 1991 war and drew criticism for his reporting for CNN, covered the rest of the war for a London newspaper.

- Iraqi authorities on March 31, 2003, ordered Reuters not to supply CNN with pictures from Iraq.
- U.S. military officials told Fox News channel to remove its reporter Geraldo Rivera from Iraq on April 1, 2003. The demand came after officials became concerned when, during a report from Iraq, he drew a map in the sand showing military positions.
- The Basra Sheraton, where Al-Jazeera journalists were staying, received four direct hits on April 2, 2003.
- Iraqi officials expelled one of Al-Jazeera's correspondents in Baghdad and asked another to leave the country on April 2, 2003.
- A U.S. tank shell hit the Palestine Hotel in Baghdad, which housed foreign media, particularly the offices of Al-Jazeera and Abu Dhabi TV April 8, 2003.
- A Detroit crowd—most of them Iraqi-Americans—attacked an Al-Jazeera crew on April 9, 2003, accusing the channel of supporting Saddam's regime.

These activities and others confirm that both warring sides were deliberate in their attacks against the mass media and reporters. Some of these actions were attributed directly to authorities from both sides, and others were attributed to the general public affected by media coverage of the war. Part of the harassment came from within the news organizations themselves, as in the case of Fox News and NBC. Such harassment by news organizations of their own reporters was indicative of the level of cooperation these organizations forged with the government to support its war efforts.

One could also note that most of the harassment was directed at Al-Jazeera, suggesting how influential and even controversial this channel has become. It could be argued that actions against Al-Jazeera during the 2003 war was an indication of how seriously it was taken by Western forces. One analyst described Al-Jazeera as the only "winner in the war."

3. Criticizing media coverage, particularly by politicians, military officials, and journalists.

Criticism of media coverage of the war came from two main sources. First, politicians and military commanders' reactions to coverage of war displayed negative tones and rejection of the media's work styles. One of the strongest criticisms came from Prime Minister Tony Blair on March 26, 2003, after Al-Jazeera screened footage of dead British soldiers.

According to 10 Downing Street's spokesman, Blair expressed "horror" at the deaths and the broadcast images of the soldier's bodies on Al-Jazeera TV. The British Ministry of Defense criticized Al-Jazeera for the same reason, pleading that media not become tools for Iraqi propaganda by re-broadcasting such material. The British Home Secretary David Blunkett launched another "vitriolic" attack on media coverage on April 4, 2003. Blunkett was critical of how media gave equal importance to reports from behind Iraqi lines and to those coming from the front line. He stated, "those of a progressive or liberal bent, in my view, are egged on into believing that this is the right way to get the true facts." These criticisms reflected the official's attitudes toward information control by suggesting what media should and should not cover.

Second, there was some criticism of media war coverage directed by journalists at their own news organizations. MSNBC reporter Ashley Banfield was reprimanded for an April 25, 2003, talk at a Kansas university, wherein she criticized the U.S. government and news organizations. Coverage of the war, she said, "was not journalism." An equally strong attack came on September 15, 2003, from CNN's veteran war reporter Christiane Amanpour against her organization; she claimed that the network was "intimidated" by the Bush administration in its coverage of the war in Iraq.[3]

Then-BBC Director General Greg Dyke attacked U.S. media on April 24, 2003, describing its war coverage as "unquestioning." But American columnist Michael Wolfe accused the American TV networks of "kissing ass" when they were reporting the 2003 war.[4] Furthermore, BBC officials warned the British government of "Americanizing" the British media. At one point during the war, several British warships changed their in-ship television from BBC's News 24 to Rupert Murdoch's Sky News. The HMS Ark, on April 8, 2003, was one of the first ships making the switch, but the BBC claimed the change was only temporary.

To media scholars, journalists' criticism of their news organizations is often more highly regarded than official criticism. This is because journalists tend to reflect "real" worries about media performance, credibility, and ethical dilemmas. Moreover, such criticism could help the media see their quality judged by media experts in the field.

4. Killing journalists individually or by bombing their media centers.

The 2003 war has been described as the most dangerous war for journalists since the war in Afghanistan, where casualties among international journalists for weeks into the conflict exceeded those of all coalition forces combined. In a twenty-day period during the Gulf conflict—March 20-April 8, 2003—sources confirmed that fourteen journalists were killed, two were missing and nine were detained in Iraq.

In the 1991 Gulf War only four journalists were killed.[5] Most of the dead journalists in the 2003 Gulf War were killed by military from both sides, but especially by U.S. forces. The U.S. military apparently targeted some media centers in Baghdad, such as the Palestine Hotel, which housed Al-Jazeera and Abu Dhabi TV offices, on April 8, 2003. The U.S. military repeatedly has denied targeting journalists offices.[6] That day was called "Journalism Black Day" by Arab media. The death of journalists during the conflict could explain how the news media and reporters were usually identified as the "third fighting group" beside the two warring sides.

Media outlets in the 2003 war were not just witnessing and recording the events as they happened. They also created their own realities and events—often becoming a part of the story—so the governmental strategy of how to deal with media totally changed. This is not meant to justify the killing of reporters in a war, but it might explain the high number of journalist casualties.

Q2: Media Content and Journalists' Attitudes

Talking about the pressures on media during the 2003 war does not mean that everything was gloomy and negative. There were some positive outcomes. Starting with the negative effects, media analysts strongly criticized the submission of some news organizations to governments or officials. Most criticized U.S. TV networks. The pressures of war activities also forced some news organizations—such as CBS, ABC, and NBC—to pull their journalists from Baghdad just before the war.

Media critics during and after the war blamed the system of embedded journalists and military news briefings as primary sources of news. These systems forced news organizations to favorably slant coverage toward one side, rather than focusing on the events of the conflict and the war's consequence on ordinary people. In addition, some media outlets chose to ignore some events and images that were available from other news organizations. This issue was explained and later criticized in many articles comparing the war coverage between Arab and Western media as "two different wars."

Contrary to the negative effects generated by the war, some news organizations took advantage of the precarious atmosphere against the media and practiced its own brand of journalism. Al-Jazeera was a clear example. During the 2003 war, this Arabic channel challenged both warring sides with its reports from the war zone. It refused many demands from the coalition to stop airing provocative images, particularly those of dead coalition soldiers.

Because the channel ignored most of these requests, it was accused of being used by Iraq for propaganda purposes, a charge often leveled against the Western media. Al-Jazeera also challenged Iraqi authorities after that government expelled a JSC correspondent in Baghdad and asked another to leave the country. As a reaction, Al-Jazeera suspended its live broadcast from Iraq until it received a reasonable explanation of why the expulsions had occurred. Two days later, the channel was back on the air after Iraq rescinded its decision.

Despite all the war actions against media in the 2003 Gulf War, the conflict was a "good" chance for some Arabic news channels. Al-Jazeera, Abu Dhabi, and

Al-Arabiya—whose launch was months before the war started—were practicing new media work styles and techniques to the extent that they became reliable news sources for some "traditional" international news organizations. Their performances in reporting the war in the Gulf led Arab audiences to follow their "own" media, speaking their own language. It had been a long wait for the Arab audience, but its patience finally paid big dividends.

ENDNOTES

1. Most of these activities and actions are listed in http://media..guadian.co.uk

2. See U.S. Department of Defense, "Indemnification, and Hold Harmless Agreement and Agreement Not To Sue." The full text of this release could be find in: http://cpj.org

3. Amanpour is of Persian descent and is married to a former Clinton Administration official.

4. Wolfe frequently wrote an Internet column in 2003 on Islam, to which he has converted.

5. The list of names can be found in "War toll: journalists killed, missing and held in Iraq." Available at http://media.guardian.co.uk

6. Some skeptics note that Al-Jazeera's office in Kabul was also bombed twice during that military excursion in 2002.

REFERENCES

Alterman, J. (1998). *New media, new politics from satellite television to the Internet in the Arab world.* Washington: The Washington Institute for Near East Policy.

Knightly, P. (2003, June 15). Turning the tanks on the reporters. *The Observer.* Accessed at http://media.guardian.co.uk

U.S. Department of Defense. (2003). *Indemnification and hold harmless agreement and agreement not to sue.* Washington: GPO. Full text available at http://cpj.org

Zelizer, B. (1992). CNN, the Gulf War, and journalistic practice. *Journal of Communication, 42*(1), 66-81.

AFTERWORD

Media Monitoring: Watching the Watchdogs

Kaarle Nordenstreng

Almost every page of this book invites the reader to reflect upon the role of media, not only in the Iraq war, but in society at large. Regardless of how strongly one shares the perspective of political insanity and even despair exposed in Cees Hamelink's *Preface* and John C. Merrill's response to it in the *Foreword*, one is inspired by such a rich collection of chapters to critically assess the status and tasks of media in the contemporary world.

This *Afterword* leaves it up to each reader to draw conclusions and do further homework in the spirit of critical analysis, which logically follows from all that stands above. Instead, I use the case of the 2003 Iraq War and its coverage to highlight an old idea whose time has really come: systematic monitoring of media performance in matters of global importance. I shall present below first the idea, then its rationale, some concrete examples of its implementation, and finally a proposal to go ahead.

THE IDEA

The idea of monitoring media performance is a logical extension of the methodological approach in communication research known as content analysis. The classics of content analysis, notably Bernard Berelson and Harold Lasswell, did not introduce the method for its own sake, but as an instrument to *assess* what the media are really doing and to define *policy* for various aspects of social life—including media themselves. It is indeed paradoxical that while content analysis has been a central part of the empiricist and positivist tradition in media studies, it has also nurtured a policy paradigm, inviting us not only to discover the reality but to change it. This is the paradigm that was already promoted by Max Weber in his legendary speech to the first German congress of sociologists in Frankfurt in 1910 (see Hardt 1979, pp. 174-182).

Historically speaking, we should recall Karl W. Deutsch, the political scientist known for his paradigm of seeing communication as "the nerves of government" (the title of his book in 1963). In the first volume of the *Journal of Conflict Resolution* he proposed "an early warning system" to register the amount of media attention given to a conflict area or an enemy country, because "continuing hostile attention in the mass media may tend to harden public opinion to such a degree as eventually to destroy the freedom of choice of the national government concerned" (Deutsch, 1957, p. 202). His idea was "to measure quantitatively the relative shares of attention allotted to particular interstate conflicts and issues in the general flow of news, the extent to which these are retained or forgotten by leaders, and the extent to which they have cumulative effects" (p. 204).

It is interesting to compare this proposal with what we can read in the MacBride Commission's report:

> The primary function of the media is always to inform the public of significant facts, however unpleasant or disturbing they may be. At times of tension, the news consists largely of military moves and statements by political leaders, which give rise to anxiety. But it should not be impossible to reconcile full and truthful reporting with a presentation which reminds readers of the possibility, indeed the necessity, of peaceful solutions to disputes. We live, alas, in an age stained by cruelty, torture, conflict and violence. These are not the natural human condition; they are scourges to be eradicated. We should never resign ourselves to endure passively what can be cured. (*Many Voices, One World,* 1980, p. 177)

Both are outspoken in their normative positions on behalf of peace and against war and violence, but Deutsch's proposal is more concrete than any of the recommendations by the MacBride report (for a detailed examination of the latter, see Hancock & Hamelink, 1999).

Deutsch' s vision has never been realized, but in these times of Bosnia, etc. in the Balkans, Rwanda, etc. in Central Africa, and the new CNN-type of media diplomacy, it has become ever more topical. The current relevance of the idea is reflected in a recent proposal by Cees Hamelink (1997), suggesting that an International Media Alert System (IMAS) to monitor media content in areas of conflict. "This system would provide an 'early warning' where and when media set the climate for crimes against humanity and begin to motivate people to kill others" (p. 38).

Reviewing the history of ideas, we cannot overlook Walter Lippmann, who in 1919 wrote of the idea of a "pseudo-environment" created between people and the world, largely by mass media and the idea of the "manufacture of consent" as a system of manipulating public opinion (Lippmann, 1995 [1920]). It is clear that recent critical thinking about media performance in books by Herman and Chomsky (1988), Parenti (1993), Hackett and Zhao (1998), and the numerous studies of the Glasgow Media Group (Eldridge, 1995; Philo, 1995; Philo, 1999), build from a relatively long history of attention to media artifice and representation.

Yet we have never before faced conditions in which industrially produced media are such a global presence in every day life and provide such a vast range of people with what Lippmann called the "picture in their heads" of the outside world. The globalization of media not only involves the geographical extension of distribution and transmission, but the homogenization of media forms within a commercial corporate model (Herman & McChesney, 1997). The continued expansion of transnational commercial media, both by means of new technology (especially satellite telecommunications and the Internet) and through the ever-larger scale and longer reach of ownership and control, has extended and accelerated the blurring of classical definitions of news, entertainment, and advertising. The commercial imperative has made "information" a more highly ambiguous term than ever before, as Merrill points out in this book's Foreword, and the "information industries" encompass media commodities of every stripe.

Media monitoring as an international project is highlighted with over twenty examples in a reader that I initiated in the 1990s (Nordenstreng & Griffin, 1999; referred to below as *IMM*). While the idea builds on modern approaches to content analysis (McQuail, 1992), it implies that the ultimate frame of reference is democracy (cf. Nordenstreng, 2000a). Accordingly, Peter Golding and his colleagues have suggested that the idea is properly designated as "an audit of democracy." (See their chapter in *IMM*.)

The Rationale

The idea of media monitoring has a simple four-step logic that proceeds along the following path:

> 1. Mass media play a vital role in (post)modern societies and in the surrounding global culture, which makes them a backbone of a pervasive cultural environment—the media have *influence*. The assumption is that mass media will continue to be important instruments to address vast audiences and to shape public and private minds at the national and international levels. Contrary to what many today suggest, new media technologies will not bring about an end of mass media and an "end of journalism." New means and practices will emerge, but the basic characteristics of mass communication will remain and even increase in socio-cultural influence.

2. Mass media, in particular the printed press, enjoy a special constitutional status (based on Article 19 of the Universal Declaration of Human Rights and of the International Covenant on Civil and Political Rights), which protects them from many conventional social policies—the media have *freedom.* This freedom is vital to a democratic society—a safeguard of human rights in civil society. The special constitutional status of the media that provides them with autonomy must be respected and defended as an essential part of the monitoring idea.

3. Mass media not only enjoy an exceptional degree of autonomy, but also carry duties and responsibilities (based on the same international instruments) that call for normative regulation of this sphere of "cultural ecology," both on legal and ethical levels—the media have *accountability.* It would be both sociologically and politically naive to place media outside of any social control. Accountability can conceptually be divided into various levels and aspects, including law and ethics. The aspect related to the present monitoring idea is focused on an analytical appreciation of media content, thus largely bypassing all the well-known normative and structural aspects, including those media accountability systems that are implemented through professional codes of ethics or media councils (see Nordenstreng, 2000b). Thus, the monitoring idea being pursued here has a limited scope—limited, but still significant, if its potential is fully utilized.

4. Mass media are regulated by legal and financial means to a degree determined by the political balance of power prevailing in each society. There is little the professional and academic community can do about it, but there is an untapped potential for indirect participation in the democratic process of media accountability—through *media criticism.* The media criticism called on here is not the kind of more or less politically motivated interest group advocacy that is well known everywhere. What is meant here is scientifically-based description and assessment of media performance, mainly carried out by methods of content analysis. And the epistemological paradigm is one of conventional realism rather than postmodern phenomenalism. Thus, it is assumed that an objective reality exists, and it can be discovered more or less accurately, although in practice the media coverage may be far removed from true reality. In other words, the reasoning typically follows the correspondence theory of truth: comparing media coverage with extra-media data. However, truth checking can be left aside, and monitoring may be focused on tracing the trends and interests of the content alone—the ideological narrative of the media discourse that is customary in cultural studies.

This rationale not only renders support to media monitoring, but it even calls forth, indeed demands, some sort of an institutionalized accountability system. The system would not be a legal or administrative mechanism by official powers (governmental, parliamentary, or judiciary) but something that falls within the non-governmental civil society sphere. However, the system suggested is not another form of straight self-regulation by the media because the content analysis is supposed to be carried out by independent scholars, and the overall media performance is supposed to be assessed by panels that would also be relatively independent from the media—otherwise the idea of accountability would be missed.

Obviously this is a line that is quite similar to the reasoning of the Hutchins Commission over a half-century ago. The same rationale about social responsibility is more or less shared by a number of later initiatives that do not only reflect narrow academic or social interests, but are indicators of a fundamental tendency in contemporary society to see the ever-larger role played by the media as needing new ways their accountability can be defined and monitored.

Although scientific content analysis constitutes a cornerstone of the media monitoring idea, it does not suggest new, elaborate, and expensive research to be conducted. A lot of content analytical research is already being carried out all over the world—as master's theses and doctoral dissertations by students, academic contributions by scholars, administrative exercises by authorities, and, in some cases, as international joint ventures. The monitoring idea does not advocate any more such cumbersome projects that tend to consume a lot of mental and material energy, often with marginal outcomes. Instead, it is suggested to pool existing research and to invest energies into digesting accumulated research evidence that already exists.

A host of content analysis exists, especially as case studies, and from such events as the 1991 and 2003 Iraq Wars (see, e.g., Nohrstedt & Ottosen, 2000; Kempf & Luostarinen, 2002). There is a huge accumulation of evidence from numerous small and large projects, both national and international. The problem is, however, that these exercises are seldom pooled to facilitate an overall review and assessment of media performance—neither in a single country, nor internationally. If done on a permanent basis such overviews could help identify neglected areas, not only in media coverage, but in studies of media content that too often are based on a haphazard choice of topic and media. In such a manner one could counteract the tendency to end up with abundant piles of disjointed data, and one could also encourage young scholars to focus on content areas that are strategically important, but neglected in the research carried out thus far.

As a matter of fact, much content analysis evidence is lost in the absence of an international system of pooling, accumulating, and comparing data from innumerable national case studies that typically focus on a limited topic or time period. Taken together, such research evidence provides a great potential "to appraise and report annually upon the performance of the press" (as the Hutchins Commission put it). Indeed, a global overview of media performance based on content analysis evidence would help students and scholars in the field to better place their particular problems in an overall perspective. One might also self-critically observe that few fields of science have been as sterile in terms of assessing social and global responsibilities as has been the case with communication research. Where natural scientists are raising their voices regarding environmental problems, and medical scientists continuously assess problems of human health, communication scientists should have a natural role in taking stock of media performance—not only in isolated cases, but as a global issue.

One might ask why so much attention is paid to content, especially in this time of media concentration and globalization. Is not content just a reflection of structures of production and distribution, ultimately ownership?

The rationale explained here by no means suggests to undermine structural factors behind and beyond media content. It admits that there is a need for similar, indeed parallel, monitoring of media concentration, consumption, and so on. But the rationale is based on a firm belief that mass-mediated content constitutes a strategic part of broader reasoning about the media—their freedom and accountability, and ultimately their role in democracy.

Consequently, the idea is not particularly new or radical. Rather, at issue is a classic question of journalism paradoxically neglected in the prevailing tradition of media theory and practice.

The Implementation

Today it is encouraging to note that many studies and even institutions have emerged with similar objectives. For example, in the United States, "Project Censored" is already more than twenty years old (Jensen, 1997). Sometimes, such monitoring efforts link up with movements for citizen participation or community media production, as in the Cultural Environment Movement (CEM) in the United States, or the Media Foundation and its Adbuster programs in Canada.

In the United States, organizations interested in revealing the political biases of news reporting have sprung up across the political spectrum, from Fairness and Accuracy in Reporting (FAIR) on the left, to Accuracy in Media (AIM) on the right. Organizations such as the Center for Media and Public Affairs in Washington, DC, work to maintain a non-partisan image and claim to provide objective scientific analyses of news and media content.

"As the media watch the world, we watch the media" is the motto of *MediaChannel.org*, a New York-based public interest Web site dedicated to global media issues. While its mission follows the rationale and initiatives presented above, its scope goes far beyond simply monitoring media content (see *http://www.mediachannel.org/*). A more content-related agency is Media Tenor—founded in Germany by journalists—to monitor media content trends. Joined by social scientists from Europe and North America, they created a network of nearly two hundred researchers working in five countries with more than ten languages "to provide objective, in-depth, up-to-date media content information to help ensure and protect balanced journalism" (see *http://www.mediatenor.com/*). Buchinger, et al. use Media Tenor material in their chapter's analysis of African media's coverage of the 2003 Iraq War.

Another impressive indication of the timeliness of the monitoring idea comes from those circles concerned about the representation and portrayal of women in news media. January 18, 1995, was chosen as an "ordinary" news day on which activists in seventy countries were to record the main outlets of newspaper, radio, and television news and codify the stories and people in them, using over twenty common variables (see Margaret Gallagher's chapter in *IMM*). Although this media monitoring was limited to a single day, the number of participating countries makes it still perhaps the largest exercise of comparative content monitoring ever carried out. Participation in this effort was voluntary, which demonstrates how spontaneous interest can be mobilized around a good cause and with the help of an informal network. The exercise was repealed in 2000 with the same partners and enthusiasm, to be followed by another round in 2005—10 years after the first one (see http://www.wacc.org.uk).

A genuinely international media monitoring project is shaping up in the European Union around the topic of racism and xenophobia with the establishment in 1998 of the European Monitoring Center on Racism and Xenophobia, based in Vienna, Austria. Its task is to provide the "Community and its Member States with objective, reliable and comparable data at the European level on the phenomena of racism, xenophobia and anti-Semitism."

The monitoring at issue here is understood quite broadly to cover education and socialization in general, as well as the areas of social and legal policy, but media are also part of its mandate. Therefore it is expected to launch, in collaboration with national institutions (governmental and academic), a permanent system of media performance monitoring in an area so consequential to both the political and economic prospects of Europe. (For an example of this, see www.multicultural.net/edmm/index.htm).

The global women's monitoring and the European project on race and (in)tolerance show how the idea proposed may materialize thematically instead of as an overall survey, embracing various global issues at one time. Both topics have also been promoted through EU-sponsored reviews of relevant research literature (see *Images of women in the media,* 1999; *Racism and cultural diversity in the mass media,* 2002).

While official initiatives such as the European Monitoring Center take shape, the academic community of media scholars could establish its own global media monitoring system by simply pooling the thousands of case studies being carried out around the world by students and faculty alike. Existing studies already provide a vast potential of evidence regarding specific themes as well as the overall performance of media in society. They need only to be brought together for collective and comparative review.

Obviously, the monitoring of media performance is an idea whose time has come. It does not need any UN or UNESCO resolutions for implementation; it is evolving quite independently of governmental and intergovernmental structures. Nevertheless, the idea is also being promoted by governmental concerns such as those currently prevailing in Europe in relation to racism and xenophobia.

As a matter of fact, media coverage of race, ethnic minorities, and symptoms of intolerance such as xenophobia has become recognized as a social problem by politicians and professionals alike. It is logical, then, that the International Federation of Journalists (IFJ) proceeded in 1994 to establish, with the support of the Council of Europe and the European Union, a working group against racism and xenophobia—something that would have been unthinkable earlier.

The IFJ monitoring project pursued first and foremost in Europe, with highlights such as an international journalism prize for combating racism and xenophobia (sponsored by the European Union). It is supported by a parallel academic project that has grown out of the IAMCR working group on ethnicity, racism, and the media coordinated by Charles Husband, as well as the action program proposed by Teun van Dijk (see their chapters in *IMM*).

Thus, the idea is moving ahead along two tracks: professional and academic. Significantly, there is little or no friction between the two. They seem to support each other, unlike many previous cooperative efforts. Yet there is a recognition that the two should remain distinct to prevent professional journalists from withdrawing their active involvement and turning defensive under the well-known pretext that freedom was being suppressed by outside forces—including the critical intellectual challenge by academics.

A Proposal

It is encouraging to see how various actors are already implementing the monitoring idea, and organizations such as Media Channel and Media Tenor have impressively employed the Internet as a tool to make it happen. Nevertheless, a true materialization of the idea needs something more.

It needs a *worldwide network of collaborating scholarly activists.* It needs an *annual review summarizing tendencies within media coverage across the world*, prepared by scholars and eventually elaborated by an authoritative commission that would issue high-profile annual reports. Such a report could, ideally, win the status of the annual reports on media freedom and its violation, issued traditionally by organizations such as the International Press Institute, Article 19, and Reporters Sans Frontiers. In fact, we need a solid and globally representative report on the media content environment, which could be compared with the *State of the World* report on the physical environment, prepared by Worldwatch Institute.

In practice, what is to be done is, first, to set up a network of scholars from all major geopolitical and linguistic regions of the world. Elements of this already exist in the initiatives reviewed above, but they need to be pulled together into a loose project organization. Although it would mainly operate as a virtual organization through Internet, it also needs physical meetings—at least one for the process to take off. And this will cost money, even if meetings could be organized in connection with other relevant platforms such as academic conventions. Also, material resources are needed for recruiting at least ten core scholars and their eventual stringers, however committed they may be.[1]

Second, once the scholarly network collects the first harvest, an editorial team would prepare a draft report. This can be done in four to six months by three or four colleagues, requiring the resources for about two senior person years.[2]

Third, as an additional vehicle, a high-profile commission could be convened to discuss and issue the report. Such a "guru gallery" would demand a lot of mobilizing and connections, but could be relatively easy to achieve, given the magic (love/hate) appeal that political and business leaders as well as intellectuals hold towards the media.[3]

This scenario suggests a two-year pilot project, which could be launched at any time. All that is needed is a core group of committed operators and the necessary material means (less than $1 million U.S. dollars in total).

This book is a perfect case to demonstrate the usefulness of a truly global media monitoring project. Why not take this as a decisive push and establish the system, based on this and other studies on media coverage of recent wars, moving on from there to the role of media in dealing with other global problems.

Endnotes

1. The cost of all this would be at the level of $500,000 U.S.
2. This would cost about $200,000 U.S.
3. This could be achieved with about $200,000 U.S.

References

Deutsch, K.W. (1957). Mass communications and the loss of freedom in national decision-making: A possible research approach to inter-state conflicts. *Journal of Conflict Resolution, 1* (2), 200-211.

Eldridge, J. (Ed.). (1995). *Glasgow Media Group Reader: Vol. I: News content, language and visuals.* New York: Routledge.

Hackett, R.H., & Zhao, Y.(1998). *Sustaining democracy? Journalism and the politics of objectivity.* Toronto: Garamond Press.

Hamelink, C.J. 1997. Media, ethnic conflict and culpability. In J. Servaes & R. Lee (Eds.) *Media and politics in transition: Cultural identity in the age of globalization,* 29-38. Leuven: Acco.

Hancock, A., & Hamelink, C.J. (1999). Many more voices, another world: Looking back at the MacBride recommendations. In R. Vincent, K. Nordenstreng & M. Traber (Eds.) *Towards equity in global communication: MacBride update,* 269-305. Cresskill, NJ: Hampton Press.

Hardt, H. (1979). *Social theories of the press: Early German and American Perspectives.* Beverly Hills and London: Sage Publications.

Herman, E.S., &. Chomsky, N. (1988). *Manufacturing consent: The political economy of the mass media.* New York: Pantheon Books.

Herman, E.S., & McChesney, R. (1997). *The global media: The new missionaries of corporate capitalism.* London: Cassell.

Images of women in the media: Report on existing research in the European Union (1999). Brussels: European Commission (Unit V/D.5).

Jensen, C. (1997). *Twenty years of censored news.* New York: Seven Stories Press.

Kempf, W. & Luostarinen, H. (Eds.). (2002). *Journalism and the news world order, Vol. 2: Studying war and the media.* Göteborg: Nordicom.

Lippmann, W. (1995, [1920]). *Liberty and the news* (with a new introduction by Paul Roazen). New Brunswick, NJ: Transaction Publishers. [New York: Harcourt, Brace & Howe, Inc., reproducing essays published in 1919 in The Atlantic].

Many voices, one world: Towards a new, more just and more efficient world information and communication order. (1980). (Report by the International Commission for the Study of Communication Problems. Paris: UNESCO.

McQuail, D. (1992). *Media performance: Mass communication and the public interest.* London: Sage.

Nohrstedt, S. & Ottosen, R. (Eds.). (2000). *Journalism and the new world order, Vol. 1: Gulf War, national news discourses and globalization.* Göteborg: Nordicom.

Nordenstreng, K. & Griffin, M. (Eds.). (1999). *International media monitoring.* Cresskill, NJ: Hampton Press.

Nordenstreng, K. (2000a.) Media and democracy: What is really needed? In J. van Cuilenburg & R. van der Wurff (Eds.) *Media and open societies: Cultural, economic and policy foundations for media openness and diversity in East and West,* 29-47. Amsterdam: Het Spinhuis.

Nordenstreng, K. (2000b). The structural context of media ethics: How media are regulated in democratic society. In B. Pattyn (Ed.) *Media ethics: Opening social dialogue,* 69-86. Leuven: Peeters.

Parenti, M. (1993). *Inventing reality: The politics of news media* (2nd ed.). New York: St. Martin's Press.

Philo, G. (Ed.). (1995). *Glasgow Media Group Reader: Vol. II: Industry, economy, war and politics.* New York: Routledge.

Philo, G. (Ed.). (1999). *Message received: Glasgow Media Group research,* 1993-1998. London: Longman.

Racism and cultural diversity in the mass media: An overview of research and examples of good practice in the EU member states, 1995-2000. (2002). Vienna: European Research Center on Migration and Ethnic Relations.

APPENDIX A

Journalists Killed in the 2003 Iraq War

Compiled by Ralph D. Berenger

Terry Lloyd, British ITV News; disappeared near Al-Zubayr, then declared dead March 22, 2003.

Paul Moran, freelance Australian; killed March 22, 2003, at a checkpoint when a car bomb went off near Gerdigo.

Gaby Rado, correspondent for Britain's Channel 4 TV; fell to his death March 30, 2003, from the roof of his hotel in Sulaymania in northern Iraq.

Kaveh Golestan, embedded freelance cameraman for BBC; killed April 2, 2003, after stepping on land mine near Kifri in northern Iraq.

Michael Kelly, *Atlantic Monthly* and *The Washington Post;* killed April 3, 2003, while traveling with an infantry division outside of Baghdad

David Bloom, NBC correspondent; died April 6, 2003, due to illness.

Kamaran Abd al-Razaq Muhammad, translator working for BBC; killed in a "friendly fire" missile attack April 6, 2003, in northern Iraq.

Christian Liebig, reporter for German magazine *Focus;* killed in a missile attack April 7, 2003, outside Baghdad, while traveling with the U.S. military.

Julio Anguita Parrado, *El Mundo* correspondent; killed April 7, 2003, outside Baghdad, while traveling with the U.S. military.

Tareq Ayyoub, Al-Jazeera correspondent; killed April 8, 2003, during an attack on Al-Jazeera's office in Baghdad.

José Couso, cameraman for Spain's Telecinco; killed April 8, 2003, when the U.S. military shelled the Palestine Hotel in Baghdad.

Taras Protsyuk, Reuters cameraman; killed April 8, 2003, when the U.S. military shelled the Palestine Hotel in Baghdad.

Mario Podesta, correspondent for Argentina's America TV*;* died April 15, 2003 in a car crash while traveling to Baghdad from the Jordanian border.

Veronica Cabrera, freelance camerawoman for Argentina's America TV; died April 15, 2003, in a car crash while traveling to Baghdad from the Jordanian border.

Elizabeth Neuffer, foreign correspondent for *The Boston Globe*; died May 9, 2003, in a car accident in Iraq.

Walid Khalifa Hassan Al-Dulami, translator accompanying the foreign correspondent for *The Boston Globe*; died May 9, 2003, in a car accident in Iraq.

Richard Wild, British freelance cameraman; killed July 5, 2003, in central Baghdad.

Jeremy Little, Austrian journalist with NBC News; died of post-operative complications July 6, 2003, days after a grenade attack in Fallujah.

Mazen Dana, Palestinian cameraman with Reuters; killed August 18, 2003, while filming outside Baghdad's Abu Gharaib prison.

Mark Fineman, *Los Angeles Times* correspondent in Baghdad; died September 23, 2003, of an apparent heart attack while waiting for an interview in the office of the Iraqi Governing Council (IGC).

Ahmed Shawkat, editor of weekly *Bilah Ittijah* (Without Direction); killed by gunmen October 28, 2003, in Mosul

Duraid Isa Muhammad, producer and translator for CNN; killed January 27, 2004,in an ambush outside of Baghdad.

Ali Abdul Aziz, cameraman for Dubai-based al-Arabiya TV channel; killed by U.S. troops March 18, 2004,in central Baghdad.

Ali al-Khatib, journalist for Dubai-based al-Arabiya TV channel; killed by U.S. troops March 18, 2004,in central Baghdad.

Burhan Mohammed al-Luhaybi, Iraqi cameraman working for ABC News; possibly shot and killed by U.S. forces in Fallujah, March 26, 2004.

Omar Hashim Kamal, translator who worked with *Time's* Baghdad operation; died March 26, 2004,from wounds he received from unknown assailant as he was driving to an assignment on March 24, 2004.

Waldemar Milewicz, Poland's TVP television's best known war reporter, was killed when the vehicle in which he was riding was sprayed with bullets by a drive-by shooter near Mahmoudiyah on the road to Najaf, 20 miles south of Baghdad, May 6, 2004.

Mounir Bouamrane, a Polish-Algerian national working as a producer for Poland's TVP television, was killed when the vehicle in which he was riding was sprayed with bullets by a drive-by shooter near Mahmoudiyah on the road to Najaf, 20 miles south of Baghdad, May 6, 2004.

Hamid Rashid Wali, an Iraqi technician with Al Jazeera, was shot and killed by sniper fire early in the morning of May 21, 2004, just after a report was transmitted from the roof of a hotel in Karbala.

APPENDIX B

Timeline: Countdown to War On Iraq

Compiled by Ralph D. Berenger

From multiple international news sources

2001

Sept. 11—Terrorists skyjack four airplanes, crashing two into New York's World Trade Center's Twin Towers, and one into the Pentagon. A fourth hijacking is diverted by passengers but the plane crashes into a field in Pennsylvania, killing all on board. Altogether 2,976 persons—passengers, rescue workers and occupants of offices—and the 19 hijackers were killed. President George W. Bush and Prime Minister Tony Blair announce a war on terrorism and immediately blame Osama bin Laden's terrorist network, al-Qaeda.

Sept. 12—While expressing sympathy, Arabic newspapers reject allegations that Arabs could have been involved. Some suggest the United States deserved what it got because of its Middle East policies. Conspiracy theories blame Israel and even the United States itself; NATO for first time in its history invokes Article 5, which says that an attack on one NATO country involves all 19 NATO members; the U.S. stock market plummets, raising fears of recession as some companies never fully recover lost values, and some, like Enron, find their weak accounting practices exposed.

Sept. 14—Labor MP George Galloway issues an impassioned warning against all-out assault on Afghanistan, warning that such action could create "10,000 Osama bin Ladens," a refrain that would be echoed by anti-war elements during the coming Afghanistan and Iraq wars; less than 72 hours after terrorists attack the United States, several European countries and Russia begin to question the U.S.-UK war on terrorism

Sept. 15—Blaming bin Laden, Bush tells the nation to prepare for war. In a warning to other nations Bush avers, "you're either with us or against us."

Sept. 16—Blair declares war on terrorism.

Sept. 19—"Operation Infinite Justice" begins; warships and troops are dispatched to various bases in the Middle East.

Sept. 23—Taliban militiamen fire the first shots of the war; an unmanned surveillance drone is shot down; Saudi Arabia rejects U.S. request to base troops.

Sept. 25—Saudi Arabia severs ties with Taliban after bin Laden message to Pakistan urges all Muslims to resist "new Jewish and Christian crusader campaign that is led by the Chief Crusader Bush under the banner of the cross" drawing references to the 10th Century Crusades of Europeans to the Holy Land.

Oct. 1—Jordan's King Abdullah says Bush had promised not to militarily attack Iraq in retaliation for the terrorist attacks; Iran threatens to shoot down any allied airplane violating its airspace en route to bomb Afghanistan.

Oct. 3—Former UK Prime Minister Margaret Thatcher criticizes world Muslim leaders for failing to speak out against 9/11 attacks, sparking immediate outrage in the Arab world, which is unclear who was actually responsible for the attacks.

Oct. 4—Taliban confirm that British journalist Yvonne Ridley, arrested after illegally entering Afghanistan, is to face trial for espionage.

Oct. 6—Bush warns Taliban that attacks could begin any time.

Oct. 7—Air strikes begin on Afghanistan; Al-Jazeera broadcasts tapes of bin Laden's threats of retaliation for the attacks but doesn't blame al-Qaeda for 9/11.

Oct. 8—First Afghan casualties reported; Yvonne Ridley released after being held for 10 days; Palestinian leader Yassir Arafat turns guns on his own people in Gaza City to stamp out support for bin Laden; Tom Ridge becomes director of U.S. Homeland Security office.

Oct. 9—Al-Jazeera carries taped interview with bin Laden whose group now claims responsibility for 9/11 suicide attacks and promises more of them in his call for a holy war.

Oct. 10—Bush issues a "most wanted list" of 22 Taliban al-Qaeda leaders in Afghanistan; trouble brews between Blair and the BBC when PM's itinerary in Middle East is revealed, putting Blair at risk.

Oct. 15—Al-Jazeera broadcasts al-Qaeda warnings that Muslims in Europe and America should stay out of skyscrapers and off of airplanes.

Oct. 19—European Union governments pledge to support U.S. war on terrorism and work with the UN for a "stable, legitimate and representative" regime to replace the Taliban; anthrax outbreak in the United States targets politicians, journalists and broadcasters.

Oct. 21—Bush orders CIA to destroy bin Laden's al-Qaeda network and conduct "the most sweeping and lethal covert action" since the agency was founded in 1947.

Oct. 26—Taliban admits killing Northern Alliance opposition commander, Abdul Haq, in a shoot-out, thus eliminating one possible leader of post-Taliban Afghanistan.

Oct. 28—Blair administration anger over growing media pressure about the pace and direction of the campaign against terrorism reaches boiling point: It accuses the press and TV of constantly demanding fresh news, while increasingly neglecting the causes of the conflict.

Oct. 30—Blair goes on "emotional offensive" to re-sell the war on terror in Britain after poll shows support for him had dropped 12 points to 62% in just two weeks. In the U.S. a national opinion poll shows that 85-89% of Americans support Bush's anti-terrorism efforts.

Nov. 3—British officials label a "desperate fantasy" bin Laden's accusation over

Al-Jazeera that the coalition was exterminating Afghans. U.S. broadcasters warned that airing bin Laden tapes might be passing along hidden messages to supporters in the United States and United Kingdom. By year's end, nine journalists had lost their lives in Afghanistan.

2002

Jan. 29—In his state of the union speech, Bush declares Iraq along with Iran and North Korea as an "axis of evil." He vows that the United States "will not permit the world's most dangerous regimes to threaten us with the world's most destructive weapons."

May 14—The UN Security Council revamps the 11-year-old sanctions against Iraq, replacing them with "smart sanctions" meant to allow more civilian goods to enter the country while at the same time more effectively restricting military and dual-use equipment (military and civilian).

June 2—President Bush publicly introduces the new defense doctrine of preemption in a speech at West Point. In some instances, the president asserts, the United States must strike first against another state to prevent a potential threat from growing into an actual one: "Our security will require all Americans ... [to] be ready for preemptive action when necessary to defend our liberty and to defend our lives."

Sept. 12—President Bush addresses the UN, challenging the organization to swiftly enforce its own resolutions against Iraq. If not, Bush contends, the United States will have no choice but to act on its own against Iraq.

Oct. 11—U.S. Congress authorizes an attack on Iraq.

Nov. 8—The UN Security Council unanimously approves resolution 1441 imposing tough new arms inspections on Iraq and precise, unambiguous definitions of what constitutes a "material breach" of the resolution. Should Iraq violate the resolution, it faces "serious consequences," which the Security Council would then determine.

Nov. 18—UN weapons inspectors return to Iraq, for the first time in almost four years.

Dec. 7—Iraq submits a 12,000-page declaration on its chemical, biological and nuclear activities, claiming it has no banned weapons.

Dec. 21—President Bush approves the deployment of U.S. troops to the Middle East/Gulf region. By March an estimated 200,000 troops will be stationed there. British and Australian troops will join them over the coming months.

2003

Jan. 16—UN inspectors discover 11 undeclared empty chemical warheads in Iraq.

Jan. 21—BBC news crews are banned by U.S. military at Guantanamo Bay in Cuba after detainees from the Afghanistan war tried to talk to the reporters.

Jan. 27—The UN's formal report on Iraqi inspections is highly critical, though not damning, with chief UN weapons inspector Hans Blix stating that "Iraq appears not to have come to a genuine acceptance, not even today, of the disarmament that was demanded of it."

Jan. 28—In his state of the union address, President Bush announces that he is ready to attack Iraq even without a UN mandate.

Feb. 14—In a February UN report, chief UN inspector Hans Blix indicates that slight progress has been made in Iraq's cooperation. Both pro- and anti-war nations felt the report supported their point of view.

Feb. 15—Massive peace demonstrations take place around the world.

Feb. 21—*Wall Street Journal* officials confirm the execution of their reporter, Daniel Pearl, 38, in Pakistan. Pearl was seeking information on al-Qaeda when he was kidnaped Jan. 28 and his murder was graphically videotaped.

Feb. 22—Blix orders Iraq to destroy its Al Samoud 2 missiles by March 1. UN inspectors say the missiles have an illegal range limit. Iraq can have missiles that reach neighboring countries, but not ones capable of reaching Israel.

Feb. 24—The United States, Britain and Spain propose a resolution to the UN Security Council which states that "Iraq has failed to take the final opportunity afforded to it in Resolution 1441," and that it is now time to authorize use of military force against the country. Russia, France and Germany submit an informal counter-resolution to the UN Security Council urging that inspections should be intensified and extended to ensure that there is "a real chance to the peaceful settlement of this crisis," and that "the military option should only be a last resort."

Feb. 24–March 14—The United States and Britain's intense lobbying efforts among the other UN Security Council members yield only four supporters (in addition to the United States and Britain, Spain and Bulgaria); nine votes (and no vetoes from the five permanent members) out of 15 are required for the resolution's passage. The United States decides not to call for a vote on the resolution.

March 1—Iraq begins to destroy its Al Samoud missiles. In an unpleasant surprise for the Bush administration, Turkish parliament narrowly rejects a plan to deploy 62,000 U.S. troops in the country to form a northern front in the event of war. Earlier Turkey's government agreed to stage troops in exchange for a billion-dollar aid package.

March 3—Iraq claims that six civilians were killed and 15 wounded in allied raid on the port city of Basra. Meanwhile, on BBC radio, Russia hints that it might use its UN veto to block a resolution authorizing war.

March 5—The foreign ministers of France, Russia and Germany release a joint declaration stating that they will "not allow" a resolution authorizing military action to pass the UN security council. The hardening stance from the anti-war bloc increases the pressure on the United States and Britain to compromise on their draft UN resolution.

March 7—Blix gives another ambivalent report to the UN security council on Iraqi compliance, followed by a tense debate deepened the council's divide. Jack Straw proposes the UN issue an ultimatum that Iraq will be invaded unless the country demonstrates "full, unconditional, immediate and active cooperation" by March 17. France threatens to veto such a resolution.

March 10—Britain announces "six key tests" for Iraq to comply to if it is to avoid war, including President Saddam Hussein making a TV address admitting Iraq has weapons of mass destruction. The idea galvanizes some diplomatic support, but not enough to suggest the US/UK could win a second UN resolution, effectively authorizing an attack.

March 14—French President Jacques Chirac removes any lingering doubts about France's intentions on Iraq, confirming to Blair in a brief phone call that France was willing to seek a compromise on disarming Saddam Hussein but would not accept any UN resolution that set an ultimatum.

March 16—Speaking at a hastily-arranged summit in the Azores, Bush and Blair give the UN a 24-hour ultimatum to enforce its own demands for immediate Iraqi disarmament, or face an American- and British-led coalition that will go to war.

March 18—In a televised address at 1 a.m. GMT, Bush gives Saddam Hussein 48 hours to leave Iraq or face invasion. British government ministers John Denham and Lord Hunt resign in protest, along with four government aides. Parliament endorses an attack, 412-149, although the number of rebel Labor MPs voting for an anti-war amendment rises to 139, up from 122 three weeks ago.

March 20—The war against Iraq begins when the United States launches Operation Iraqi Freedom. Called a "decapitation attack," the initial air strike of the war attempts to target Saddam Hussein and other Iraqi leaders in Baghdad. Bush says the United States has begun attacks against "targets of military opportunity." Saddam Hussein gives a televised address to the Iraqi people at around 5:30 a.m. GMT, calling the attack a "shameful crime" and vowing to win the war. China, France and Russia denounce the U.S.-led action. At 6:05 p.m. GMT, U.S. planes begin a heavy bombardment of military targets in central Baghdad. Later on, British marines invade the Faw peninsula in the south of the country.

March 21—Parts of the port town of Umm Qasr, south of Basra, are seized by U.S. military. To the west of Basra, British troops help U.S. soldiers secure oil fields from possible sabotage. Some 15 oil fields are reportedly set afire by Iraq. Coalition forces suffer their first casualties when eight British and four American servicemen die in a helicopter accident over Kuwait. A U.S. marine dies during the battle for Umm Qasr, where sporadic fighting is continuing. Bombs and missiles begin to strike Baghdad for a third successive night, in a massive scaling-up of air strikes that are designed, say the U.S. military, to "shock and awe" Iraq into submission.

March 25—U.S. planes heavily bomb Republican Guard south of Baghdad to soften up the city's defenses, amid fears that Saddam Hussein may unleash chemical weapons as coalition troops invade the city. Farther south in Najaf, a fierce battle between U.S. and Iraqi forces may have killed as many as 700 Iraqi soldiers.

British forces bombard the southern city of Basra amid reports of a popular uprising and an increasingly critical humanitarian situation. British marines secure Umm Qasr, fueling hopes that humanitarian aid supply lines will soon be established. The UK's first combat fatalities of the war are confirmed to have been killed in action in the south, bringing the British death toll to 18. An opinion poll shows a majority (54%) of the British public supports the war.

March 26—Iraq claims U.S. missile struck a busy Baghdad market, killing "many"civilians. Overnight strikes aimed at Baghdad's national TV station fail to take the state channel off the air. Britain and the United States say aid is on its way to Iraq, as the HMS Sir Galahad supply ship sets sail for the now "secure" port of Umm Qasr.

About 1,000 paratroopers land in Kurdish-controlled Iraq to open a northern front.

March 30—U.S. Marines and Army troops launch first attack on Iraq's Republican Guard, about 65 miles outside Baghdad. Rumsfeld deflects criticism that the United States has not deployed enough Army ground troops in Iraq. Most embedded journalists now with U.S. and UK units in Iraq.

March 31—U.S. military officials say Fox News Channel correspondent Geraldo

Rivera will be expelled from Iraq after violating a war reporting rule by giving away crucial details of future military operations during a live broadcast. Rivera drew in the desert sand a crude map showing his location and the military plan as videotape rolled.

April 2—U.S. soldiers rescue badly injured American prisoner of war Pfc. Jessica Lynch, 19, of Palestine, West Virginia, who was captured March 23 in Nasiriya, becoming the first American heroine of the war; military videotaped the dramatic rescue. U.S. forces "surround and secure" the southern holy city of Kerbala; the United States claims Iraqis firing on troops from inside the Ali mosque in Najaf, an important Shia'a Muslim shrine, but American soldiers are not returning fire; farther north, U.S. troops continue their advance on Baghdad. CentComm claims coalitions forces are only 19 miles from the capital and inside the "red line," raising fears that Saddam's regime might use chemical weapons on troops. A Republican Guard division to the south-east of the city has been "destroyed" and a key bridge over the Tigris river has been secured, the U.S. military says.

April 3—U.S. troops from the 3rd Infantry Division reach and rename Saddam International Airport, 10 miles from Baghdad's city center, after heavy overnight bombardment; about 320 Iraqi soldiers are killed in the advance by some 1,000 U.S. troops, U.S. military sources say. Iraqi Minister of Information Mohammed Saeed Al-Sahhaf says Americans have been repulsed at the airport. The airport attack came hours after power blackout in Baghdad. Al-Jazeera says it would no longer cover the war inside government-controlled Iraq in protest at the ban imposed on two of its reporters.

April 5—U.S. tanks roll into the Iraqi capital and engage in firefights with Iraqi troops. Resistance weaker than anticipated. Heavy Iraqi casualties. In middle of media conference by Al-Sahhaf, who denies coalition forces have entered the city, reporters point to U.S. tanks across the street.

April 6—Forces loyal to Saddam Hussein appear to lose control of much of Basra after columns of British troops pour into Iraq's second city, destroying its Ba'ath party headquarters. Three British soldiers were killed in action. U.S. forces isolate Baghdad and claim to have closed off the major roads into the city, which is hit by air strikes and artillery shells; city is braced for a looming battle.

BBC reporter John Simpson witnesses a "friendly fire" attack in Northern Iraq in which his translator and up to 17 Americans and Kurds are killed. U.S. troops battle alongside more than 1,000 Kurdish peshmerga fighters to flush Iraqi soldiers out of the northern Iraqi town of Ain Sifni.

April 7—U.S. forces make their most far-reaching move into Baghdad, capturing two palaces, including Saddam Hussein's new presidential palace, which is on the west of the city by the Tigris river. Marines are pictured relaxing in its opulence. Resistance is moderate and U.S. commanders later confirm that the forces will not pull back. British forces take control of Basra, Iraq's second-largest city.

April 9—U.S. marines help crowds, apparently brought in for the occasion, to topple a giant statue of Saddam Hussein in the heart of Baghdad. Widespread looting breaks out unhindered in the Iraqi capital.

April 11—The entire Iraqi army's 5th Corps surrenders as U.S. special forces and Kurdish fighters enter Mosul. Kirkuk falls to Kurdish fighters but U.S. paratroopers arrive so Kurdish forces can withdraw. The U.S. military publishes a pack of 55 playing cards identifying its most wanted Iraqis. The cards immediately sold over the Internet.

April 13—U.S. marines enter the outskirts of Tikrit, Saddam Hussein's home town, encountering some resistance. TV crews report heavy damage to Iraqi army positions. Seven U.S. troops listed as missing are found alive on the road to the city from Baghdad and the United States confirms that Saddam's half-brother, Watban al-Tikriti, is captured apparently trying to reach Syria.

April 15—Gen. Jay Garner, appointed by the United States to run post-war Iraq until a new government is put in place, meets various Iraqi leaders to begin planning the new Iraqi federal government.

April 19—U.S. central command says that Iraqi police in Baghdad arrested the former finance minister, Hikmat Mizban Ibrahim al-Azzawi, who also served as a deputy prime minister.

April 25—Tariq Aziz, the former Iraqi deputy prime minister, surrenders to U.S. forces in Baghdad.

April 26—U.S. forces capture former Iraqi spy chief Farouk Hijazi near the Syrian border. Hijazi, who most recently served as Iraq's ambassador to Tunisia, was once a senior official in the Mukhabarat, Saddam's feared intelligence service. U.S. officials claim he met Osama bin Laden in 1998.

April 28—U.S. troops fire on a group of Iraqi demonstrators near Baghdad, killing at least 13 people and wounding 75 others.

May 1—President Bush declares an end to major combat operations, which is interpreted as the end of the Iraq war. Hundreds of Americans would die in the coming months.

May 2—U.S. troops arrest Saddam Hussein's minister of military industrialization, Abdul Tawab Mullah Hwaish, who is suspected of playing a central role in developing Iraq's weapons of mass destruction. One of Saddam's vice-presidents, Taha Mohieddin Ma'rouf, is also arrested, the 17th out of 55 deck of card members being sought.

May 5—The Pentagon announces that Huda Ammash, "Mrs Anthrax" for her alleged role in clandestine Iraqi biological weapons programs, is in U.S. custody.

May 7—The U.S. military says it has found a vehicle which appears to be a mobile bio-arms lab; Bush names Paul Bremer, a former ambassador and head of America's counter-terrorism office, as Iraq's new civil administrator.

May 9—The United States and Britain lay out their blueprint for postwar Iraq in a draft resolution to the UN security council, naming themselves as "occupying powers" and giving them control of the country's oil revenues.

May 12—A new civil administrator takes over in Iraq. Paul Bremer, a diplomat and former head of the counter-terrorism department at the State Department, replaces Jay Garner, who was seen as ineffective in stemming the continuing lawlessness and violence taking place throughout Iraq.

May 22—The UN Security Council approves a resolution lifting the economic sanctions against Iraq and supporting the U.S.-led administration in Iraq.

May 30—In separate speeches, Powell and Blair deny that intelligence about Iraq's weapons of mass destruction was distorted or exaggerated to justify an attack on Iraq. Both administrations face mounting questions because no weapons of mass destruction (WMD) have been found. Each had claimed that Iraq's WMD were an imminent threat to world security.

June 4—Blair rejects calls for an independent judicial inquiry into the case for the Iraq war.

June 15—Operation Desert Scorpion launched, a military campaign meant to defeat organized Iraqi resistance against American troops. U.S. and British troops face continued attacks; about one American soldier has been killed each day since the end of combat was declared May 1.

June 28—BBC's Andrew Gilligan says he will sue the Blair government unless it apologizes for calling him a liar over a report claiming the administration "sexed up" its WMD charges against Iraq to win public approval for going to war. Gillian heavily cited an unidentified source, later believed to be weapons expert Dr. David Kelly. The BBC also complained of intimidation by the Blair government.

July 1—A huge explosion destroys a mosque in central Iraq, killing at least five Iraqis and injuring four others, according to witnesses and officials. Some clerics blame US for the explosion.

July 6—After two weeks of apparent BBC bashing by the Blair administration, the corporation's governing body delivered an unexpectedly robust defense of the story by reporter Andrew Gillian at the center of the dispute.

July 7—Bush administration concedes that evidence that Iraq was pursuing a nuclear weapons program by seeking to buy uranium from Africa, cited in January State of the Union address and elsewhere, was unsubstantiated and should not have been included in speech. Blair's communications director, Alastair Campbell, is cleared by parliament of exerting "improper influence" on the drafting of the government's intelligence-led dossier on Iraq, but the Commons foreign affairs committee attacks the Blair government over its handling of the affair.

July 13—Iraq's interim governing council, composed of 25 Iraqis appointed by American and British officials, is inaugurated. The council has power to name ministers and will help draw up a new constitution for the country. American administrator Paul Bremer retains ultimate authority.

July 16—Gen. John Abizaid, commander of allied forces in Iraq who replaced retiring general Tommy Franks on July 7, calls continued attacks on coalition troops a "guerrilla-type campaign" and says soldiers who will replace current troops may be deployed for year-long tours.

July 17—U.S. combat deaths in Iraq reach 147, the same number of soldiers who died from hostile fire in the first Gulf War; 32 of those deaths occurred after May 1, the officially declared end of combat.

July 18—The body of Dr. David Kelly, the weapons expert at the center of the BBC-government Iraq dossier row, is found at a scenic spot close to his home in Oxfordshire, England. The controversial coroner's finding is suicide.

July 22—Uday and Qusay, Saddam Hussein's sons and his most feared lieutenants, are killed in a gun battle at their hideout in the northern Iraqi town of Mosul.

July 29—A tape recording of Saddam Hussein declares that his two sons died as martyrs for Iraq, and pledges that the U.S. will be defeated.

Aug. 7—At least 11 people are killed in a car bomb explosion outside the Jordanian embassy in Baghdad, sparking fears that guerrilla fighters may be turning their attention towards so-called soft targets.

Aug. 8—Six Iraqis, including a father and three of his children, are killed in Baghdad by U.S. troops who open fire on them as they hurry home to beat the curfew.

Aug. 9—U.S. combat and non-combat casualties reach 255 at 100-day mark after declared end of combat on May 1; 43 British have died.

Aug. 15—Saboteurs blow up a crude oil export pipeline in northern Iraq, starting a huge oil fire, halting all oil exports to Turkey and starving an economy in chaos of much-needed income to rebuild.

Aug. 17—Th United States attempts to restore Iraq's shaky infrastructure suffer a serious setback when guerrillas blow up a vital oil pipeline in the north for the second time. A hole is also blown in a water main in Baghdad.

Aug. 19—Suicide bombing destroys UN headquarters in Baghdad, killing 24, including top envoy Sergio Vieira de Mello, and wounding more than 100.

Aug. 29—A bomb kills one of Iraq's most important Shia'a leaders, Ayatollah Muhammad Bakr al-Hakim, as well as about 80 others, and wounds 125.

Sept. 1—Two Arabic television channels broadcast recorded message from Saddam Hussein, denying responsibility for last week's devastating car bomb in Najaf.

Sept. 2—Tens of thousands of mourners turn the funeral service for the murdered Iraqi cleric Ayatollah Mohammed Baqir al-Hakim into a show of defiance against the U.S.-led occupation.

Sept. 7—Continued violence and slow progress in Iraq lead to Bush's announcement that $87 billion is needed to cover additional military and reconstruction costs.

Sept. 10—A suicide car bomber attacks the U.S. intelligence base in the northern Iraqi city of Irbil, killing three people and injuring 41.

Sept. 14—Colin Powell meets Iraqi politicians in Baghdad as an American soldier is killed and three wounded in an attack near Falluja, where Iraqi police died in a "friendly fire" incident.

Sept. 25—Aqila al-Hashmi, the most prominent of three women on Iraq's governing council, dies of wounds sustained in an ambush. A planted bomb damages a hotel housing the offices of NBC News, killing a Somali guard.

Oct. 2—According to an interim report by David Kay, the lead investigator searching for weapons of mass destruction in Iraq, no WMDs have been found.

Oct. 5—White House reorganizes its reconstruction efforts in Iraq, placing National Security Adviser Condoleezza Rice in charge and diminishing the Pentagon's role.

Oct. 16—UN Security Council unanimously approves the U.S. and UK resolution on Iraq's reconstruction, which supports an international force in the country under U.S. authority. Several countries originally opposed the resolution unless Washington agreed to a faster timetable for transferring power to the Iraqis, but in the end voted for the resolution without requiring changes.

Oct. 23–24—The Madrid Conference, an international donors' conference of 80 nations to raise funds for the reconstruction of Iraq, yielded $13 billion in addition to the $20 billion already pledged by the US. This amount fell short of the overall target of $56 billion, the figure the World Bank and the UN estimated that Iraq needs over the next four years.

Oct. 27—Four coordinated suicide attacks in Baghdad kill 43 and wounded more than 200. Targets included the headquarters of the Red Crescent (Islamic Red Cross) and three police stations, in bloodiest day since the fall of Saddam.

Nov. 2—In the single deadliest strike since the Iraq war began, guerrillas shoot down an American helicopter, killing 16 U.S. soldiers and injuring 21 others. Other attacks over the course of the month make it the bloodiest since the war began: at least 75 U.S. soldiers die.

Nov. 4—Bush wins Senate approval for $87.5 billion to continue the U.S.-led occupation of Iraq.

Nov. 14—The Bush Administration reverses policy and in a deal with the Iraqi Governing Council, agrees to transfer power to an interim government in early 2004.

Nov. 29—U.S. troops return fire on insurgents in the central Iraqi city of Samarra after an ambush on a convoy. Seven Spanish intelligence agents, two Japanese diplomats, two U.S. soldiers and a Colombian oil worker are also killed.

Nov. 30—American soldiers kill 46 Iraqis and capture eight in three repelled ambushes on U.S. convoys in the central Iraqi city of Samarra, according to a military spokesman.

Dec. 1—Iraqi officials in Samarra challenge U.S. military accounts of a bloody battle, accusing American soldiers of spraying fire at random on the city streets, killing several civilians.

Dec. 9—Forty-one U.S. troops and six Iraqi civilians are wounded in a suicide car bombing outside a barracks near the northern Iraqi city of Mosul. A directive issued by Paul D. Wolfowitz, deputy defense secretary, bars France, Germany, Canada, Mexico, China, and Russia from bidding on lucrative contracts for rebuilding Iraq, creating a diplomatic furor.

Dec. 10—Pentagon excludes countries opposed the Iraq invasion from bidding for reconstruction contracts.

Dec. 13—Saddam Hussein is captured by American troops. The former dictator was is found hiding in a hole near his hometown of Tikrit and surrendered without a fight. He was the Ace of Spades in the Most Wanted deck of cards.

Dec. 16—Germany and France agree to a U.S. request to write off part of Iraq's $120 billion debt.

Dec. 27—Attacks on government buildings and foreign troops' bases in the southern city of Kerbala using suicide car bombers, machine guns and mortars kill 19 and wound about 120.

Dec. 28—BBC further angers Blair government when an email to reporter bans reference to recently captured Saddam Hussein as "former Iraqi dictator" in favor of "deposed former president."

2004

Jan. 11—The Grand Ayatollah Ali al-Sistani, the most influential Shia'a cleric in Iraq, says members of the country's interim government must be selected by direct vote. He opposes the U.S. plan to hold regional caucuses. While caucuses are less democratic than direct elections, the United States has argued that it would be impossible to ensure free and safe elections on such a tight timetable—the U.S. plans to hand control of the government to Iraqis on June 30.

Jan. 13—Army Spc. Joseph M. Darby, an MP with the 800th at Abu Ghraib, first reports cases of abuse at the prison.

Jan. 17—The number of U.S. soldiers killed in Iraq since the start of the war reaches 500. Of those, 346 soldiers died in combat and 154 died from accidents.

Jan. 18—A suicide bomber detonates a pick-up truck laden with 1,100 pounds of explosives at the main gate of the U.S. headquarters in Iraq, killing at least 20 people and injuring more than 100.

Jan. 19—The United States asks the UN to intercede in the dispute over the elections process in Iraq. Shia'a leader Ayatollah al-Sistani refused to meet with U.S. officials. The UN weighs sending election experts to determine whether there is enough time to prepare for direct elections. About 100,000 Shia'as march in Baghdad and other cities in support of Ayatollah al-Sistani's demand for direct elections. It is the largest protest since the occupation of Iraq.

Jan. 28—The Hutton Commission Report, released in London concerning the death of Dr. David Kelly, criticizes BBC and reporter Andrew Gilligan's coverage government's knowledge of Iraq's weapons program. David Kay, former U.S. weapons inspection team leader, informs a senate committee that no WMD have been found in Iraq and that prewar intelligence was "almost all wrong" about Saddam Hussein's arsenal. His report sets off a firestorm of allegations: Did the United States receive bad intelligence, or did the Bush administration manipulate the intelligence to build the case for war, or both?

Jan. 29—BBC director general Greg Dyke resigns in wake of report castigating BBC's journalistic practices in reporting intelligence about weapons of mass destruction in Iraq; hundreds of BBC employees walk off their jobs in spontaneous protest; resignation follows by one day departure of Gavyn Davies, BBC board chairman, the first time BBC news executives had ever resigned over a news story. Acting BBC Chairman Lord Richard Ryder and acting general director, Mark Byford, both apologize for their organization's behavior in reporting the Iraq WMD issue.

Jan. 30—Condoleezza Rice, one of Bush's most trusted lieutenants, admits that the intelligence that said Iraq had WMDs may have been wrong. "What we have is evidence that there are differences between what we knew going in and what we found on the ground," she tells CBS News. In London, journalist Andrew Gilligan admits making "some mistakes" in reporting and resigns from BBC.

Feb. 1—About 109 Iraqis are killed by suicide bombings in Erbil.

Feb. 2—Under pressure from both sides of the political aisle, President Bush calls for an independent commission to study the country's intelligence failures.

Feb. 10—About 54 Iraqis are killed in a car bombing while applying for jobs at a police station. The next day an attack kills about 47 outside an army recruiting center.

Feb. 12—UN envoy Lakhdar Brahimi, on fact-finding mission to Iraq to assess the feasibility of direct elections, meets with Ayatollah al-Sistani.

Feb. 19—U.N. Secretary-General Kofi announces the results of its report about Iraqi elections, concluding that "elections cannot be held before the end of June, that the June 30 date for the handover of sovereignty must be respected, and that we need to find a mechanism to create the caretaker government and then prepare the elections sometime later in the future."

Feb. 23—UN envoy Brahimi issues a report to the Security Council concluding that the earliest that credible, direct elections could be held in Iraq would be late 2004 or early 2005. He outlined several possible options for structuring an interim government that would rule the country after the June 30 hand over and until the results of elections in 2004 or 2005. He recommends that Iraqis themselves draw up a plan for this provisional government.

March 2—Suicide attacks in Karbala on Shia'a Islam's most holy feast day kills more than 85 and wounds 233 in an attempt to foment unrest between Shia'as and Sunnis.

March 5—An Iraqi translator for the Voice of America, and two members of his family, were shot and killed in Baghdad by unknown assailants. The translator, Selwan Abdelghani Medhi al-Niemi, was attacked in Baghdad as he was returning home in his car. His mother and daughter, who were travelling in with him, were also killed.

March 8—The Iraqi Governing Council signs interim constitution, which includes a bill of rights, a system of checks and balances, and a military subordinate to civilian rule. The signing was delayed by several days when Shia'as objected that Kurds, a minority, were given too much power in the interim constitution.

March 17—At least 27 people are killed and 41 wounded in the car bombing of the Mount Lebanon hotel in Baghdad just two days before the first anniversary of the coalition attack on Baghdad.

March 18—Jay Garner, the U.S. general dismissed as Iraq's first occupation administrator after a month in the job, says he fell out with the Bush circle because he wanted free elections.

March 19—Arab journalists walk out of a Baghdad press conference given by the Secretary of State Powell in protest at the shooting dead of two of their colleagues by U.S. soldiers.

March 22—Fourteen British soldiers are injured, three of them seriously, in Basra when hundreds of Iraqis throw stones and petrol bombs during protests about job shortages.

March 23—Nine Iraqi police officers and trainees die when gunmen spray bullets into their van south of Baghdad near the town of Mussayab.

March 24—Amec of the UK is one of few British firms to win a big contract ($1 billion) to rebuild Iraq.

March 28—Al-Hawza, a newspaper representing the cleric Moqtada Sadr, is closed down by the coalition for allegedly inciting violence against U.S. troops.

March 31—Four U.S. contractors are attacked in Falluja and their bodies burned, dragged by cars and strung up from a bridge by a mob. Five U.S. soldiers are killed by a roadside bomb outside Falluja to end the bloodiest month for coalition forces. During March, 115 U.S. soldiers were killed and 426 wounded.

April 1—One year after she was rescued in Iraq, Jessica Lynch says in a nationwide TV interview that she was no hero, but her squad members—11 of whom were killed March 23, 2003—and her rescuers were. The 20-year-old "country girl" has formed the Jessica Lynch Foundation to educate children of military veterans from the $1 million publisher advance for her biography she is writing with journalist Rick Bragg.

April 2—Pinewood Studios boss Michael Grade is named BBC's new chairman, succeeding Gavyn Davies who quit in January over the contents of the Hutton Report into the death of Dr. David Kelly. Earlier this week acting BBC chairman Lord Ryder announced his decision to retire from the corporation in June.

April 3—Mustapha Yacoubi, an aide of the cleric Moqtada Sadr, is arrested on suspicion of complicity in a murder. The cleric's group deny he is involved and he is later released.

April 4—Demonstrations by Sadr supporters descend into riots in the Sadr city area of Baghdad, as well as in Najaf, Nasiriyia and Amara. Nine coalition troops and more than

50 Iraqis are killed in the clashes, the worst unrest since Saddam Hussein fell.

April 5—Apache gunships strike against Shia'a supporters of the hardline cleric Moqtada al-Sadr, who attack a U.S. patrol in the Shuala district of Baghdad. Insurgency by Shia'a is reported in other towns including Basra, where gunmen loyal to Sadr occupied the governor's offices. Paul Bremer, the U.S. administrator in Iraq, calls Sadr an outlaw and vows to put down the revolt. Falluja is surrounded by U.S. forces at the start of an operation to pacify insurgents.

April 6—Coalition forces fight Shia'a gunmen and Sunni insurgents on several fronts, with British, Italian and U.S. troops involved in battles that kill dozens of Iraqis and at least 15 coalition soldiers.

April 9—Nine U.S. civilians are killed in a convoy near Falluja while further south the Shia'a militias fight on. Up to 200,000 Iraqi Muslims, many of them Shia'as, crowd into the precinct of Baghdad's largest Sunni mosque in the largest show of joint support against the US.

April 7—The coalition loses control of several areas as the Sunni and Shia'a uprisings spread from Kirkuk, in the north, to Kut, in the south. Dozens die near a mosque in Falluja.

April 8—Widespread fighting leaves 460 Iraqis and 36 Americans dead in Falluja. Meanwhile, local militias take control of the cities of Najaf and Kut amid the Shia'a insurgency, and three Japanese civilians are taken hostage.

April 12—U.S. military vows to "kill or capture" the radical Shia'a cleric Moqtada al-Sadr, who has led an uprising against the occupation authorities. A British civilian is released after a week-long ordeal.

April 13—The United States gives up on its demand for the handover of the people who killed four U.S. security guards and mutilated their bodies in Falluja, according to senior Iraqis. President Bush agrees to send more troops to Iraq.

April 14—An Italian security guard becomes the first hostage to be murdered. Three Japanese hostages held for a week are released. Russia will evacuate 800 civilian contractors amid security fears. Arab journalists accuse the U.S. military of threatening the media covering the conflict in Iraq and pressuring journalists into presenting a one-sided picture of events after a U.S. general accused both Al-Jazeera and Al-Arabiya of taking an "anti-coalition" stance in their reporting.

April 15—U.S. government urges CBS TV not to show sensational pictures of Iraqi prisoner abuse in Iraq until military has chance to investigate. Television network agrees to hold report for two weeks.

April 16—Five foreign hostages are freed but two more are seized, and the insurgency claims about another 30 lives as U.S. officials struggle to conclude negotiations to halt the violence.

April 19—Talks between the U.S. and leaders from the city of Falluja progress. John Negroponte, the senior U.S. envoy at the UN, is named ambassador to Iraq, and will replace the chief administrator, Paul Bremer, once the transfer of power is complete on June 30.

April 20—The U.S. military nears a deal with the radical Shia'a cleric Moqtada al-Sadr, after two days of secret negotiations. Meanwhile, 22 prisoners die in a mortar attack on a Baghdad jail.

April 21—At least 68 people, including Iraqi police recruits and children on a school bus, are killed in a series of bomb attacks in the British-controlled city of Basra. A kidnapped Danish businessman is found dead, and fighting flares again around Falluja. Maytag Aircraft, a U.S. military contractor fired Tami Silicio, a Kuwait-based cargo worker whose photograph of over 20 flag-draped coffins of fallen U.S. soldiers was published in April 18 edition of *The Seattle Times*, for violating company regulations.

April 22—NFL Football player Pat Tillman, 27, who turned down a multimillion-dollar contract with the Arizona Cardinals to join the Army, is killed in combat in Afghanistan. Tillman joined the Army Rangers shortly after 9/11.

April 23—United States begins hiring former Ba'athist regime members as insurrections to the invasion grows in populated centers such as Najaf and Falluja.

April 24—Two U.S. sailors die trying to board explosive-laden wooden boats near oil facilities in the Persian Gulf. Attackers detonated the explosives killing themselves and the sailors.

April 27—For the first time since the war started, most Americans disapprove of Bush's handing of the war, 52% to 41%. Support among Republicans remains strong at 77%, but only 15% of Democrats and 37% of Independents support the president on Iraq. Just over a year earlier the president's support was at 75%. Americans were divided on whether America did the right thing by invading Iraq, 47-46%. Fearing assassinations, contractors working on Iraq's power grid leave the country.

April 28—Warplanes pound Falluja with half-ton laser-guided bombs while Marines battle with insurgents on the ground. Commanders in Baghdad, however, insist a cease fire is holding. In a Gallup poll conducted in Iraq earlier in the month, 61% of Iraqis said Saddam Hussein's removal was good, but 57% want the U.S. to leave immediately. The figure is higher in Sunni and Shia'a areas, whereas 96% of Kurds interviewed want the U.S. to stay a while longer. Seventy-one percent of Iraqis, except Kurds, see Americans as occupiers, only 28% see them as "liberators." CBS airs photos allegedly showing U.S. soldiers abusing Iraqis in Abu Ghraib Prison, setting off international outcry. Bush first learns about these photos from the television report, his aides say.

April 29—U.S. forces announce an end to their siege of Falluja, allowing former Ba'athist officers to head newly created Iraqi security forces in the city. Al Arabiya and Al Jazeera air photos of Americans allegedly abusing Iraqi prisoners. According to a Gallup poll conducted in Iraq this month, 93% of Iraqis have television and overwhelmingly watch Arab news stations: Al Iraqiya, Al Arabiya and Al Jazeera get high ratings for credibility by Iraqis. Lowest credibility: BBC and CNN.

April 30—Prime Minister Blair says he's appalled by pictures of Iraqi prisoners allegedly being tortured by American and British soldiers; Arab world expresses outrage. The Associated Press reports that 1,361 Iraqis were killed in April—10 times the figure of U.S. dead.

May 1—On first anniversary of "end of major combat operations," 743 U.S. soldiers, 59 U.K. soldiers and 47 soldiers from other nations—a total of 849—died in the war to date, an average of two per day. About four times as many soldiers are wounded.

May 6—Bush apologizes to the Arab world for alleged abuse of Iraqi prisoners, says Rumsfeld will stay in his Cabinet despite calls from Democrats for his resignation.

May 7—Rumsfeld apologizes for prison abuse before being grilled by the U.S. Senate on the maltreatment of Iraqi detainees. He hints more sensational pictures might be forthcoming. A new recording attributed to Osama bin Laden offers rewards in gold for killing senior American and United Nations officials or citizens of any country that has troops in Iraq.

May 11—Arab language Web sites carry short video of the decapitation of businessman Nicholas Berg, 26, by armed Iraqi militants. Berg, a resident of West Chester, Pa., was a telecommunications field man in Baghdad who went missing late in April. His videotaped death was reminiscent of reporter Danny Pearle, who was killed in Pakistan in 2002. Like Pearle, Berg was Jewish.

May 12—U.S. Senators see more images of abuses at Abu Ghraib, including photographs of Iraqi women forced to expose their breasts and of guard dogs snarling at cowering prisoners.

May 13—According to the Web site Iraqibodycount.org, between 9,148 and 11,005 Iraqi civilians have been killed since the war began in March 2003. The Web site blames U.S. for any Iraqi death because it was the invading force. Another Web site (http://lunaville.org/warcasualties/ Summary.aspx) reports that in the 420 days of the war, 788 Americans, 59 British and 51 from Coalition countries had died in the war.

May 14—The *Daily Mirror* newspaper in London apologized for publishing faked photographs of alleged abuse of Iraqi prisoners by British forces, forcing the resignation of editor Piers Morgan, a critic of the Iraqi war who had maintained the photo's authenticity. *The Guardian* reports that ministers and Labor backbenchers have urged Blair "to recalibrate his approach to foreign affairs and publicly detach himself from the Bush administration."

May 15—Polls show President Bush's public support for war at lowest point yet, and for the first time over half now disapprove of the job the commander in chief is doing concerning Iraq. The same *Newsweek* poll shows Sen. John Kerry has taken a slim lead over the incumbent president. Most other polls agree.

May 17—*The New Yorker* magazine claims Donald Rumsfeld personally authorized the expansion of a special program that ultimately led to the abuses in Abu Ghraib prison, according to Pulitzer Prize winning journalist Seymour Hirsch. The head of the Iraqi Governing Council is killed in a suicide car bombing while waiting in his vehicle at a U.S. checkpoint.

****

June 30, 2004—Planned Iraqi takeover from the U.S.-led coalition.

Jan. 31, 2005—Expected deadline for elections to National Assembly to oversee drafting of permanent constitution, help appoint council ministers, prime minister and executive Presidency Council.

Aug. 15, 2005—Deadline for National Assembly to unveil permanent constitution draft.

Oct. 15, 2005—Deadline for national referendum to adopt permanent constitution. If referendum fails, National Assembly dissolved, new elections held by Dec. 15, new transitional government assumes office by Dec. 31.

Name Index

A

B

C

D

E

N

O

P

Q-R

S

T

W

Y-Z

Subject Index

B

C

D

E

F

G

H

I

J

K

L

M

N

O

P

Q-R

S

T

U

V

W

X-Z